Dr. Martin Luther 1483 –1546

This book was originally printed in German in 1883 by the George Brumder Publishing House of Milwaukee, WI, with the title, *Dr. Martin Luther*. The translation into English is with the title as shown on the front cover and stated at the top of this page. The book was offered to readers by its original author, August L. Graebner, while he was serving as Professor of Theology within what is now known as the Wisconsin Evangelical Lutheran Synod (or, WELS). His following words still apply:

"Biography of the Reformer Designated
for Partners in faith."

2020 Upgraded Translation By Pastor W. O. Loescher

Edited by Pastor R. P. Kujawski
With input by Pastors S. C. Melso and B. R.Golisch
Sincere thanks to family helpers as well as all other helpers.

Dr. Martin Luther 1483 –1546 © 2015. Short quotations of this publication, not to exceed 200 words, may be reproduced or transmitted in reviews, theological writings, sermons, or other settings without permission. For longer sections permission needs to be obtained from the copyright owner, currently Waldemar Loescher, 4712 Vista Rd. Manitowoc, WI 54220; (1-920-901-2735)

Library of Congress
Lutheran News, Inc.
684 Luther Lane
New Haven, MO 63068
Published 2020
Printed in the United States of America
IngramSpark, TN
ISBN 978-0-359-07936-0

Martin Luther (according to Cranach by G. Koenig)

Table of Contents

Foreword by the original author i
Brief comments about the original author iii
The Main Purpose of this Translated Book: iv

Chapters

1 In His Father's House 1
2 In Boys' School 8
3 At the University 13
4 In the Monastery at Erfurt 19
5 Beginnings at Wittenberg 30
6 The Journey to Rome 33
7 The Doctor Hat 36
8 Work and Growth until 1517 39
9 The 95 Theses 49
10 Consequences of the 95 Theses 65
11 Luther at Heidelberg 70
12 Attacks and Defense 72
13 Summons to Rome 78
14 Cajetan 83
15 Miltitz 97
16 The Debate at Leipzig 103
17 Consequences and New Battles 114
18 Rome before the People's Court 123
19 Luther and the German Nobility 132
20 The Papal Banning Bull 148
21 Before Caesar and the Empire 165
22 Patmos 182
23 The Wittenberg Disruptions 192
24 The Smothering of the Disruptions 203
25 Planting and Watering 211
26 Counsel for the High and the Low 217

27 The Allstedt Spirit 224
28 The Peasant War 230
29 Luther's Marriage 235
30 Erasmus of Rotterdam 240
31 The Spreading of the Reformation 247
32 In the Home of the Reformer 251
33 Congregation's Participation in Worship 256
34 Church Visitation in Saxony 259
35 Luther's Catechisms 262
36 Persecution of the Church in the Empire 266
37 The Protéstants 273
38 The Swarming Sacramentarians 276
39 The Marburg Colloquy 286
40 Coburg and Augsburg 294
41 The Turk, God's Peace Corps for the Reformation 313
42 A Free Christian Council (?) 322
43 The Wittenberg Concord 323
44 At Smalcald - The Smalcals Articles 331
45 Harvest Days During Stormy Weather 337
46 Later Life Labors 343
47 In the Luther Home at Wittenberg 363
48 Going Home 371
Short Interpretation of Revelation 14:6-7 379
Transference of the Footnotes in the Book 380

Illustrations

Luther, L. Cranach, by G. Koenig v
Martin's father by Cranach, 1527 3
Martin's mother by Cranach, 1527 5
Luther's Cell in the monastery at Erfurt 20
Wittenberg, a copper plate of 1546 31
Pope Leo X according to Raphael 51
John Tetzel 52
Exhibition of an Indulgence Market 54
The Castle Church in Wittenberg 62
Philip Melanchthon, by Albrecht Dürer 81
Caesar Maximillian, by Albrecht Dürer 86
Bilibald Pirkheimer by Albrecht Dürer 91
Dr. John Eck, an old woodcut 109
Ulrich von Hutten, an old woodcut 134
Addressing the Christian Nobility, title page 138
Luther, a copper plate by Cranach 1520 150
Luther's "Freedom of a Christian", title page 157
Self-Painting by Lucas Cranach 170
Luther as Squire George, a woodcut by Cranach 185
Franz von Sickingen, an old copper plate 221
Thomas Muenzer, an old woodcut 233
Elector Frederick the Wise, by Cranach 234
Martin Luther, by Cranach, 1525 237
Katharina Luther, by Cranach, 1525 238
Luther's Ring, Showing the Crucified, and Martyr Tools ... 239
Luther's Double Ring 240
The Luther House Augustinian Monastery 252
The Luther Family Room 253
Bugenhagen by Cranach 1543 254
Sketch of Luther, by Cranach, 1528 254
Sketch of Luther's Wife, by Cranach, 1528 255
Philip von Hessia, woodcut by Brosamer 272
Huldric Zwingli, an old copper plate 280

The Signatures under the Marburg Articles 293
Elector John the Steadfast, by Cranach 310
Seal for Letters written by Luther's 312
Luther's coat of arms, an old printing 312
Caesar Carl V, copper plate by Behams, 1531 317
Martin Būcer, an original woodcut by Reusner 326
Elector John Frederick the Magnanimus by Cranach 336
Count George of Saxony, an old woodcut 339
Luther, by Cranach, from his Genealogy in Berlin 344
Agricola, miniature portrait by Cranach, 1531 354
Justus Jonas, by Cranach 1543 358
Amsdorf, an old woodcut 360
Magdalene Luther, by Cranach 368
Luther in 1546, a woodcut by Cranach 376
Luther in the casket 377

Foreword

"I judge that no one who knows Luther could hate him. His books show his spirit. But if you had seen him face to face, if you had heard him speak about godly things in the apostolic spirit, you would say that the personal contact surpasses his reputation. Luther is just too great to allow any master jackanapes to render judgment about him. I know well of what I speak. I also have written books and issued writings, but by way of comparison with Luther I am a mere student. This verdict does not flow forth from love, but rather love from this verdict. I despise no one, and personally would rather be despised than praised; but on the other hand I will not tolerate it when Luther is despised as a chosen tool of the Holy Spirit. This I know: He will remain theologian for the whole world. I say this, because I now know him better than I did prior to having seen and heard him personally."

This is how the educated and highly gifted theologian Urbanus Regius wrote to Duke Ernst of Lueneburg about bringing home with him the experience of having met Luther, an invaluable treasure of the Duke's whole realm. The day that Regius, on his journey from Augsburg to his new sphere of activity, stopped to visit Luther at the Coburg, while Luther was at prayer and at work, he later described as the best day of his life. Reminded of that visit he wrote to a friend, "Luther is such a great theologian that all the centuries (*since the time of the Apostles*) have not been able to bring anyone forth even similar. ... To me Luther always was great, but now he is the greatest of all among teachers of God under Christ and His called Prophets and Apostles."

Without doubt, Luther is also special for all my readers. I know from personal experience that this powerful man of God does appear ever greater to us, who are of later birth, as we become better acquainted with him. If I should succeed to contribute with my inferior work that one or another of my brothers be led to make the words of the God-blessed Urbanus Regius his own and say, "Luther was always great for me, but now he is the greatest of all, for I now know him better than before," then I would truly have reached a much desired result.

I further know from personal experience that as Regius could call that day at the Coburg the most precious day of his life, so (*spending a little time*) in company with Luther, the God-trained and God-called witness of the evangelical truth and reformer of the Church during these latter days, can bring you inner delight and inner blessing. And if the projected picture of the great teacher as portrayed in following pages of this book, though projected by a far inferior student, should present to its viewers a few cheerful and blessed hours during this anniversary year (*the book was issued in 1883*) and perhaps even during following years, I would regard that as another undeserved but very pleasant result.

But as little as the viewing of the drawn life-picture (or biography) of our Luther can compensate us late-coming viewers, who have been denied personal company with him, which many of his partners of that time were allowed to enjoy, all the more important must it be for us what Regius expressed with the words, "His books show his spirit." If I have thus let Luther himself speak through my somewhat expanded forms of speech and explanation, I hope that you will not hold me accountable.

I do not want to leave it at that. In discussing the writings of Luther I have referred repeatedly to a selection of his writings under the title "Luther's People's Library". These references under the letter "LV" (*which in German stands for* Luther Volksbibliothek) are often cited in footnotes." These volumes of LV are available in fifteen handy double-ribbon bindings from the Lutheran Concordia Publishing House of St. Louis, Missouri, for a very reasonable price, either in their entirety or as individual books. I hoped that many a person who does not own one of the larger editions of Luther's works and does not have the means to buy one, that he would regard himself prompted to get this collection of books into his possession, either in its entirety or by individual volumes, in order to get to know ever more thoroughly and to love ever more dearly that magnificent man and his precious teaching.

> A.L. Graebner
> Professor of Theology
> Milwaukee, WI
> Seminary of the Synod of Wisconsin
> March 1883

Brief Comments about the Author:

August Lawrence Graebner (1849-1904) was born in Frankentrost, MI. After graduating from Concordia Seminary in Fort Wayne and Concordia Seminary in St. Louis, he served as a teacher at a Lutheran High School of St. Louis, beginning in 1872. In 1875 he accepted a call to teach at Northwestern College in Watertown, WI. In 1878 he accepted a call to teach at the re-located Wisconsin Synod seminary in Milwaukee. (See *Jars of Clay,* by John M Brenner and Peter M. Prange, copyright: Wisconsin Lutheran Seminary Press, 2013, pp. 80-81, 86-87). In 1887 he accepted the call to teach Church History at Concordia Seminary of St. Louis, MO. During his years of teaching in Wisconsin Synod schools he wrote this biography of Dr. Martin Luther, which was published, as noted in his foreword, in March of 1883, marking the 400th anniversary of Dr. Martin Luther's year of birth.

The Main Purpose of This Translated Book:

As we are observing the 500th anniversary of the 16th Century Historic Reformation, the 95 Theses of 1517 stand at its beginning. The Augsburg Confession in 1530 provides significant expanded insight. The Smalcald Articles of 1537 give yet more in-depth information.

However, faithful translation of God's infallible Word from Hebrew and Greek into common German at that time, and many other translations into different languages since that time, needs to be recognized as the central purpose of the same God provided Reformation. This is what the life of Dr. Martin Luther as servant of God was really about. The late professor August L. Graebner puts this central truth before us as it is entwined within the whole life story of Dr. Martin Luther. As you further reflect on this central meaning of the 500th Reformation Anniversary, may you also appreciate Martin Luther's continuously growing love for God's Word during his life time. The central teaching of God's Word is this: God justified the whole world through Christ's work of redemption. Along with this truth realize anew that forgiveness of all your sins is God's gift to you through God-given faith in Christ Jesus, your crucified and risen Savior, and this by God's grace alone.

About 30 original footnotes could be woven into this translation wherever they occurred. Many of the rest of the footnotes in the original book are listed in an eight-page section at the end of the book (page 380 ff.), and may be further pursued in the American Edition of Luther's Works, copyright of which belongs to CPH, St. Louis, MO. A short interpretation in reference to Revelation 14:6-13, especially vs. 6-7, is on page 379.

Chapter 1
In His Father's Home

At noon, on the 10th of November 1483, husband and wife, Hans and Margaret Luther, were blessed with the birth of their first child, a son. The next day he was given the name Martin at his baptism in St. Peter's Church of their town. This was in honor of St. Martin, on whose festival day the baptism occurred. The name of the town was Eisleben, which was located in the County (*Grafschaft in German*) of Mansfeld. The married couple had just recently become a part of this community.

It is important for us to learn what kind of parents these people were, to whom God entrusted the first care and rearing of this little boy, since this child, when he would have grown into manhood, would be the Lord's instrument for a very high purpose.

Hans Luther, his father, was the son of Heinz, or Henry, Luther of Moehra (also called More or Moere in older records). His father was a farmer whose land lay between Salzungen and Eisenach, a not so very fertile portion of the vast wooded area of Thueringen (*from here on called "Thueringia"*). The farmers of Moehra were hard working and determined. They had to be because it was such a difficult struggle to grow meager crops. These character traits were shared by the ancestors of Luther. Their hands were firm and hard. They knew how to use those hands not only for hard work but also as fists to fight for the preservation of their hard earned crops. They would often have to forfeit a portion of those crops as a penalty for damages caused by those fists. To this day there are three Luther families dwelling in this region who are still making their living off the land. These families still exhibit some of the facial features of the great doctor. Hence, Luther did not spring from nobility, but from simple farm folks. As Luther himself said, "I am a farmer's son; my father, my grandfather and homesteader, were farmers."

At the time of Luther's birth, a time when the written word and proper grammar were not taken very seriously, the name was also spelled Ludher, Luider, Lueder, or Leuder. Our Martin, when he was enrolled as a student in Erfurt, was registered as Ludher. The first letter that we have found written in his own hand was signed "Lutherus." His relatives in later days wrote their name, "Luther".

We don't know how many siblings Hans Luther had, although we have heard of two brothers, Veit and Heinz. The ancient custom of the local farmers of that area was for a father to will his possessions to only one son. According to a remark made later by Martin, as a rule it was willed not to the oldest, but to the youngest. Hans was not the youngest in the family;

Heinz was, and as the records show, he was a farm owner.

The fact, that the soil conditions of the region of Moera as mentioned before paid off meagerly in crops, easily explains why many people preferred to work in the more profitable field of mining, particularly in the pursuit of copper. To this day large piles of dross, cinders and ruts, refortified by slate, are still visible.

So, Hans Luther might very well have sought to establish himself in such a position in order to obtain better wages in his home village. However, even these ore-containing stones proved, like the crops, to be less profitable here than elsewhere. As a result, when Hans was ready to begin his own family, he decided to make that beginning elsewhere. After all, he had not married the daughter of a noble family and he had no prospect of starting his own farm. Most likely for this reason he looked for a place where he and his wife could work together to support themselves and in time build their own home. But where might they move?

The answer to this question was not that difficult. At that time a considerably successful mining operation was located in the Mansfeld area. The town of Eisleben in particular was attractive to anxious miners. This town, which at that time was the most important among the local towns in the County of Mansfeld, is bordered by two elevated areas of flatland; one north of the Mansfeld boundary, and one south in Thueringia. Both of these areas around Eisleben were rich with copper and silver. These two elevated flatlands had been regarded as profitable for mining operations as early as the 12th century.

It was here, where it was possible to get ahead in the world in a relatively short period of time, where a young ambitious man like Hans Luther might prosper. Since he was not afraid of honest work and with his young and brave helper at his side, Hans recognized and seized the opportunity. Hence, this is where the young son of a farmer decided to settle down with his wife, Maggie (*sometimes also called Greta, or Margareth*).

Now let's take a moment to consider Maggie's ancestry. There are two old versions of Maggie's (*Margaret Luther's*) origin. According to the testimony of Beerwald, superintendent in Zwickau, she is supposed to have come from the Lindemann family. Contradicting this account was Kyriakus Spangenberg, born in 1528 and later superintendent at Eisleben, who said: "It is certainly true and can be proven adequately with proper documentation that Hans Luder, or Luther, with the full knowledge and support of his father Heine Luther and his mother Margaret (nee Lindemann), who died at an old age in the valley of Mansfeld, had entered into holy matrimony with Margaret Zigurin." According to this declaration it was not Luther's mother but his grandmother who was a Lindemann. Hans Luther's wife was a "nee Zigur" or, as that name is also found, Ziegler. Like her husband, Margaret was small in size and had a ruddy complexion. She proved to be a diligent

Luther's father's picture in 1527
according to a painting by Cranach

and faithful wife with a cheerful spirit. Her son Martin, even later in life, carried with him his mother's special little rhyme: "You and I are both to blame when no one wants to hear our name." With that little verse she would comfort herself when facing hostility coming from different sources.

These two people, then, were the parents of the one who was being molded by God's hands to be the instrument through whom he would reform his Church. Martin's work would continue until he would end his life's labors in Eisleben, the place where he was born. His energetic eyes would be closed there, after he was to have lived a strong, courageous, and energetic life like his father. At the same time, he would also have lived a cheerfully brisk and lively life like his mother.

Martin was born in the home of Hans and Margaret Luther on November 10, 1483. (*It has been discovered through research since 1883 that this house was actually rebuilt. The rebuilt home stands in the same lot and has been turned into a museum.*) Visitors used to be led to a room in the basement of that dwelling and were informed that it was in this room, facing the street, where Martin was born. The former St. Peter's Lutheran Church which was renovated and given the name "Saints Peter and Paul Lutheran Church," still stands.

Whether Hans Luther, while living in Eisleben, thought that where too many persons want to share an equal life, each individual will not have enough, or whether life and activity there were not sufficiently acceptable - enough said - the firstborn son was barely six months old when Hans and his wife traveled to a somber area populated by miners, settling in Mansfeld. There Martin spent his childhood years. The area was dominated by the stately castle of Mansfeld's count, with its ramparts towering over the city.

Martin's parents continued to live in Mansfeld until first his father in 1530, and then his mother the year after, entered their eternal rest. If only there were some people, or some record of Mansfeld of those years, who had some recollection about that infant who arrived with his parents from Eisleben in 1484. If that were the case we might have a more complete picture of our reformer's childhood years. The same would be true if Luther had taken the time to tell the complete story of his youth to his later friends. Unfortunately, all we have are a few snapshots which can be found in Luther's own writings or scattered throughout the writings of his contemporaries. We must glean what we can from those sources.

You would think that Luther's father's home, which Martin in his later years would remember with heartfelt love and gratitude, could not have been an empty place void of love. Yet, one can find no notice of anything describing Luther's father's house as being outwardly prosperous or materially comfortable during Martin's stay. It seems as though his father, during his first years in Mansfeld, had begun to be visibly depressed over his inability to provide for his growing family. Perhaps this was because his children, eventually seven in all, needed increasingly more space while they were growing up.

Martin's mother, proving to be a true and faithful helper to her husband, was not only tending to her own duties at home but also worked with her hands outside of the home. Luther would later testify, "My father was a poor hacker (i.e. a miner with a pickaxe). Mother carried all her wood into the house on her back to raise us."

Mother and father found the work very tiring for themselves. As a result, it was assumed that the older children, especially during the nursing of the younger, would have to lend a helping hand. It seems as though Martin, as the firstborn, was very helpful in this regard. We are informed that he showed himself to be a model of a big brother in home behavior for his younger siblings. Since he had assumed this role, a loving relationship became apparent between his brothers, his sisters, and himself. We have learned that he and his brother Jacob were so close that neither could enjoy eating or playing without the other one being present.

The parents, however, did not mollycoddle their little flock, and Martin was no exception. To the contrary, he would later relate the firm discipline he received from both his father and mother. He recalled one particular time when his father so thoroughly thrashed him that Martin became angry with his father. His father had to work hard to reclaim his child's loving affection.

Picture of Luther's mother in 1522
according to a painting by Cranach

At times his mother would exert even further discipline over and above the times when his father was exceptionally stern. An example would be the story that Luther told, of how she once beat him so hard that he bled. All of this happened according to Luther, because he had merely taken a nut without permission. For that he was punished as though he had broken into the family's treasure box and had stolen money.

In his later years, even as he warned against too much chastening of naughty children, Luther also encouraged strict discipline all the way from the crib. According to Luther this could have the parents apply threats and spankings. Yet, bearing in mind his own upbringing, he offered the familiar advice regarding discipline, that the apple be paired with the rod, namely, that kindness be paired with strictness. As we bear in mind the harsh discipline he received, we can better understand that he was still carrying a goodly amount of fear and guilt as he was changing from youth into manhood.Nevertheless, Martin made it clear that his parents had intended everything for him from the goodness of their hearts. Nearly fifty years later with tears in his eyes Luther remembered how he had a sweet relationship with his father, a man who exhibited such a strict fatherly profile, yet also let his paternal love shine through.

Luther would later refer to pious souls as they would comfort themselves during the dark papal time and the wilderness of many false teachings. He commented that underneath it all they could find comfort for themselves with childlike faith in the merits of Jesus Christ. It is possible that he had his parents in mind.

We know that his father tried to lead uprightously. He enjoyed being in the company of priests. No doubt, he practiced prayer in his own home, often praying at the bedside of little Martin. But it also must have been true that the darkness of the papacy cast its shadow not only over Luther's parents' home but hovered over all Mansfeld as well.

Indeed, that shadow hovered over all of western Christendom. This is evidenced from the fact that St. George, in whose name the city church had been dedicated, was the patron saint of the city. The miners had St. Anne, the mother of Virgin Mary, as their patron saint. During the year in which Martin left his parents' home to attend school at Magdeburg two altars were being dedicated in the Mansfeld Church in honor of more saints. It was also proclaimed that sixty days of remission would be secured for all who would attend all of the masses that would be read on these occasions. Hans Luther would be among the first to take advantage of this offer.

Yet at the same time, as Martin later remembered, his father could proudly rejoice about the behavior of one of the counts of Mansfeld. As this count was nearing death he put his trust completely in Christ's blood and righteousness and thus commended his soul into his Savior's hands. Thus he was truly prepared to leave this world.

Later yet, Luther's ordination into the ministry was a major celebration for Hans Luther. He attended the event accompanied by twenty horses and many companions. At the same time he was capable of applying the Fourth Commandment to the manner in which the educated might consider a call as a spell of the devil. At one time when he believed he had an illness that might result in death he asked for a visit from the priest. When the priest encouraged him to give a larger portion of his will to the church, he dared to reply, "I have many children. I shall bequeath it to them. They have a greater need for it."

When all was said and done Martin Luther's enemies lay no blame on his father for his son's defection from the papacy. Yet at the same time there was a noticeable awareness in Hans Luther regarding true recognition and entrapment of false papal teaching, upright and outward piety, and vain good works of rigid legalism. It may have been the same with his mother. Despite an atmosphere of disguised idolatry every day, a spiritual spark remained buried within Luther. This might explain how our Luther had a certain sense of piety that expressed itself with diligence in his prayer life. Thus, with a heart that was filled with fear toward Christ and which longed for comfort from the saints, Martin was taken out of his father's home. He was taken into schools complete with all the same kind of spiritual confusion and distortions until a St. Anne drove him to a fear-spawned commitment of becoming a monk.

Of course, this was not Hans Luther's idea. He had not decided on a monastery for his son for such a so-called spiritual position. No, he had wanted him to become a jurist, a lawyer.

Chapter 2
In Boys' School

In the upper section of the small city of Mansfeld was a house, which was reached by a steep pathway. In this house unskilled schoolmasters sought to educate the young men of that city by pounding into their heads reading, writing, arithmetic, and the beginning lessons of Latin. Martin Luther's parents prayerfully turned the young lad over to these instructors for further discipline and instruction. Although he was well acquainted with his parents' strict ways, he would now experience much sterner treatment. Later in life he would describe this period as a time when the schoolmasters were tyrants and hangmen and the schools were prisons and hell. Children were treated like thieves. The days were spent in worthless pursuits. Instruction was turned into torture even though experiencing beatings, trembling, and quaking produced no positive learning. Luther later recalled how one particular morning he had been lashed fifteen times in that school. This happened not because he was in any way at fault, but because he was unable to recite a lesson that had never been taught to him.

Of all the lessons missing from that school were the sweet truths of Christ and his merits. Here as before, as he later complained, Christ remained to Luther a strict and angry Judge, even more to be feared than his father's or schoolmaster's switch. He said, "All of us were taught that we had to pay for all of our sins ourselves and that Christ on Judgment Day would demand an account of our payment with a number of good works we had done. And since we could never repent enough or do enough good works we remained terrified of his wrath. They taught us to look to the saints in heaven as the ones who would serve as mediators between us and Christ. They instructed us to pray to the dear mother of Christ and appeal to her breasts, on which she had nursed her Son. We were to ask that she would pull him aside from his wrath and by beseeching him as his mother find access to his grace that he might forgive us. And when that dear lady was not enough, we then went to the apostles and other saints. Finally, we appealed to some saints, who we didn't even know were saints. Indeed, most of them never were."

Yet, there were some lessons that those tyrants of the Mansfeld School taught him, for which he would become thankful, even though he learned them in misery and distress. This included the Ten Commandments, the children's faith (*"faith" is understood as referring to a simplified form of the Creed*), the Lord's Prayer, and good songs in Latin and German. Later in life Luther, who was so affectionately concerned with the instruction and Christian guidance for children, could also recall the difficult experiences he endured on the hard benches of Mansfeld's school.

Writing two years before his death, Luther recounted how from his earliest years, when his somewhat older friend Nicolaus Oemler often carried him to school, until his fourteenth year he continued to learn from what Mansfeld's school offered. But if his father's plan for him to become a lawyer was to be fulfilled, his education had to continue at an institution of higher learning. Luther, with the son of another Mansfeld citizen, would therefore travel. This boy was Hans Reinicke, the son of Peter Reinicke. Peter was foreman in mine-work, but he was also a good friend of Hans Luther. The two of them left Mansfeld in 1497 to continue their education at Magdeburg. Martin and his student companion remained friends many years into the future.

In 1488, a semi-monastic fellowship, the Brothers of the Common Life, had come into existence. They were also known as Lollbrueder, or Nollbrueder, who were found in a large number of locations throughout Germany. Martin Luther entered school with the Nollbrueder in Magdeburg. During the same time a student from Kolditz, Wenzeslaus Link, also enrolled. Though Luther departed after one year, Wenzeslaus Link remained at Magdeburg until 1501. Yet it may have been during that one year that a friendship began, which would later grow into a deeper bond as they would join together publicly in spiritual battle of God's reformation movement.

Luther's instructors at Magdeburg compared very favorably with the jail wardens, under whom he had languished at Mansfeld. A gentler more modern attitude held sway in their midst. Of special note was the northward movement of ideas of education values of older Greek and Roman cultures, which were welcomed in that general area of Germany. Yet there was no true new life to be found in the graves of ancient pagan skill and darkness. The ancient darkness of the heathen could not dispel the modern darkness of the papacy. The comfort of the gospel which was not offered to Luther at Mansfeld was also lacking from the teachers at Magdeburg. And when he was outside of the classroom he was surrounded with images of self-righteous holiness. He relayed the following in 1533 as a part of an article against Duke George of Saxony:

"When I was fourteen years old and attending school in Magdeburg I saw with my own eyes how the Count of Anhalt, a provost and later brother to Bishop Adolf of Merseburg, went about as a barefoot, hooded beggar. He would beg for bread and carry a sack on his back, bent over like a donkey. But his companion, a real donkey, walked alongside him unburdened. Thus the pious count could portray himself as the highest example in the world of grizzeled holiness. This count went so far as to labor in the monastery, working like any other brother. He fasted so severely, stayed awake so long, and kept beating himself until he looked like the image of death, only skin and bones. He died very early for he could not stand up under such a severe regimen. To be sure, anyone who looked at him was amazed at his devotion and was ashamed of his own worldly existence."

Our Luther also had a few experiences in Magdeburg with the gathering of "bread for God's sake". His father did not send his son out away from home with a full purse. Even though by this time Hans Luther was known as an honorable and dependable citizen of Mansfeld, known by 1491 as a business leader in town, still he did not possess the means and circumstances to be able to provide complete support for his son. Thus Martin, like so many other boarding students, relied in part on the generosity of strangers who welcomed the singing beggars into their homes. When Luther was lecturing his students on the book of Genesis during the last decade of his life, he told the following story as a part of his instruction about Joseph and his brothers:

"At first we don't understand this exhibition of God's grace and his good will. We compare his good will and grace, when it is placed before us, to our own fear and destruction. What happens to us is the same as happened to me and my friends many years ago when I was just a lad.

"Together we were gathering small gifts with which to satisfy our hunger during our studies. It was a time when the festival of Christ's birth was being celebrated in the church. We went through the villages from house to house and sang, in four voices, the usual songs about the child Jesus, born in Bethlehem. It so happened that we came to a farm which stood all alone at the edge of the village. When the farmer heard us singing, he came out and asked, in a rough farmer's voice, 'Where are you knaves?' But at the same time he brought out several small sausages that he wanted to give us. We were so frightened at his voice that we immediately scattered away from him and each other, even though there was no good reason for us to be scared.

"The farmer was offering us the sausages out of kind, good will. But our hearts were still afraid, so used to the threats and rigor we students had regularly received from the schoolmaster in those days. On account of this we were frightened by his rough voice.

"Then, as we were about to run away, the farmer called to us again. We mastered our fear and came to him. We took the small gifts, called 'Parteken', which he held out to us. In the same way we begin to quake and run away from God, when our conscience is guilty and we are afraid. We are thus also afraid of a bratwurst from those who are our friends and only desire good for us."

The student Luther was to find kind hearts in other areas of Magdeburg. One of those took place in the house of the Episcopal official, Dr. Mosshauer, who frequently welcomed him as a guest. From the account of Luther's stay in that city we have only one more account to relate. Once he had a fever. Years later, a friend, the medical doctor Ratzeberger, related, "Luther was very thirsty but was being kept from drinking during the heat of the fever. But one Friday, when everyone left the house after the meal to listen to a sermon, he was left alone in the house. Being unable to fend off the thirst any longer, he crawled on his hands and knees down to the kitchen. Gripping a container of fresh water, he drank it all with great relish. He then crawled again on hands and knees back to his bed. He crawled into bed just before the people arrived back from church. After drinking, he fell into a deep sleep and when he awoke, the fever was completely gone."

Luther would study at Magdeburg for only one year. He then returned to his father's home. While he was at home, the old Count Guenther of Mansfeld lay on his deathbed. Hans Luther was summoned to the castle to wait on the count, who respected Hans Luther highly for his good reputation and dependability. When the count passed away Luther boasted about his lord, now fallen asleep, who had left such a glorious testament of faith. When he was asked about this testament, Hans answered, "He said that he wanted to take leave of this world only by way of his Savior's merit and commended his soul to Jesus." As Martin listened to his father he did not understand his father's boasting. "For," he said, "if the count had dedicated something magnificent for the service of God, for the church, or for the monastery, that would have been a more impressive testimony than the one he gave." That was an example of Luther's understanding of Christianity that he brought home from the school at Magdeburg.

After a short stay under his father's roof it was time for Luther to go back to school. His parents favored the idea of sending him to Eisenach, where the city parish school at St. George was blossoming under the ambitious leadership of Johannes Trebonius. In addition to the school's reputation, other circumstances may have contributed to their decision. Eisenach was not far from the old home of the Luther family. The boy would have relatives nearby, both on his father's and on his mother's side. However, it seems as though these relatives didn't care all that much to help the boy. As a result, the singing for his bread was once again put into practice. Luther later said, "I too was such a 'Partekenhorse' (a beggar singing for small gifts of food) and I received bread in front of people's homes, especially in my dear city of Eisenach".

As is still true today the beggars knew very well which houses would not be visited in vain. The students at Eisenach were no different. One such house was that of the outstanding citizen, Konrad, or Kunz, Cotta, descended from a well to do Italian noble house. He was married to Ursula, a virtuous daughter of the Schalbe family from Eisenach. This noble woman's attention was drawn to this modest lad who appeared regularly before her door and sang his songs so seriously. One day, having been turned away from any number of other homes, Luther sang in an exceptionally moving manner. An idea that must have lain dormant for some time in this lady's mind came to life. With her husband's blessing she welcomed this boy into her home and to her table. This lady's relatives also held this protégé of the house of Cotta in high regard. They also bestowed special favors on the youth. It was through her that he would even gain admission to a Franciscan institution. This institution was called "Schalbe Collegium" due to the rich gifts contributed by the Schalbe family. Here, too, the young Luther enjoyed other gifts and education.

In his infinite wisdom the Lord of the Church led the boy who would become the reformer of his church into such an accommodating company of people. Although his crib, so to speak, lay in neither the home of the Cotta nor Schalbe families, nevertheless Luther spent these important days of his childhood among the sort of people who represented the higher class of the German nation. Thus, he learned to understand his fellow Germans. When he later stepped up as leader, he knew how to have himself understood among the people. No one since Luther himself has understood how to speak to and write for his people as did he. But he would also have to stand before noble lords and deal with them as well. This mingling of him with the noble families of Eisenach supplied him with an excellent additional education. At the same time his spirit was also being nourished in the midst of nobility. On the one hand he was being partially diverted from the atmosphere of the school, while on the other hand, he was relieved from worry about the persistent need for food and the feeling of inferiority that went with it.

What's more, the teaching in which Martin Luther could rejoice while studying at Eisenach, was also a good fit. Trebonius was a man with special gifts and understanding. As an especially gifted grammarian he was also of noble character. It is said of him that whenever he stepped into his classroom he would take off his cap. He would then put it on again when he sat in his teacher's chair. So would he honor his students. "For," as he said, "among these students may be sitting someone out of whom God might make a mayor, or another a chancellor, or another a highly learned doctor or a ruler." Included among his assistants, for whom Trebonius required respect from the students, was the man who would later become Pastor Wiegand. He had applied himself in a loving way to his position at Eisenach, for which Luther would gratefully remember him.

Luther lived four years in Eisenach. These years served as an important part for his spiritual growth and also for becoming ever more mature.

During this time Luther became proficient in speaking Latin properly, a skill which was actually necessary for the admission for continued studies at the university. At the same time he developed a growing desire and love for studying, as though he was walking along a flowery rather than a thorny path. But even here the most beautiful of the flowers remained hidden. Even here he was unable to find that one thing needful.

Chapter 3
At the University

A university existed in Erfurt since 1392. This university, although it was the fifth such institution established in Germany, had so surpassed all of her sisters, that by the beginning of the 16th century it happened that as Luther later said, all the other schools of higher learning were considered to be schools for beginners. This high reputation attracted young scholars from all over Germany. The advancement being achieved here was so great that a special proverb was coined stating, "There are as many masters at Erfurt as there are stepping stones in the street."

It was an amazing sight, when masters and doctors received their degrees during a ceremony accompanied by flags, lanterns, and all kinds of other pomp. Among the most brightly beaming scholastic stars of the day serving on the faculty of this renowned center of knowledge was Jodocus Truttvetter, called "the Erfurt Doctor." His name was well respected even by the proud lords of the University of Paris. In addition, there was Bartholomew Arnoldi of Usingen, who like the man previously mentioned, was becoming famous by way of his writing. So, it seems that Hans Luther had made a wise choice in selecting the school in which his son would progress toward his goal of being a lawyer. In addition, Erfurt was better for people living in Mansfeld, since it was closer. Thus "Martin Luther of Mansfeld" had his name entered in the rolls as a student at Erfurt during the summer of 1501.

His actual study of law would of course begin somewhat later. It was customary at the time for universities not to take up what we would call "major" courses right away. Instead it was believed best for a student to first become better versed with higher understanding through a general course of philosophy. In this way the students studied the rules of language and logic, gaining skill of transmitting thoughts into smooth and fitting sentences about nature, astrology, and other subjects. So, the students also became familiar with the writings of Roman and Greek authors of old.

According to both heathen philosophers and theological philosophers, (philosophical theologians of the papacy during the middle ages, the so-called "scholastics") philosophy concerned itself with questions about God, spiritual powers, and punishment. In this connection, the struggle to harmonize philosophy with the teachings of the Roman church by asking subtle questions was considered valid scholarship. What St. Paul or any of the other apostles said about such issues was of no concern to teacher and student alike.

Our Luther soon distinguished himself as one of the more gifted students in this educational pursuit at Erfurt. He devoted himself to these required courses with much enthusiasm and diligence. He listened, read, and debated at every opportunity. Among his fellow students he soon became known as "the educated philosopher." It was here that he would learn to recognize the tricky pathways of the labyrinth that his papal opponents would later present to him. He was thus able to accurately counter the weaponry and attacks they would use, as he would respond to them with the truth face to face. "I understand and have also studied your skill. I still know it very well. I can wield your dialectics and philosophies better than any of you. I was raised on such things and have since my youth studied your methods and fully understand the scope of your methodology."

But Erfurt was not only renowned for its famous faculty, Luther, and other zealous students in this discipline. The so called classic and humanist curriculum, revolving around the works of the ancient Roman and Greek masters, was also popular among faculty and students. The year that Luther enrolled at Erfurt, this city saw its first book printed in Greek.

Luther would also enthusiastically read the works of Cicero, Livius, Virgil, Ovid, Juvenal, Plautus, and Terence. It was undoubtedly at this time that he committed to memory the various references of these authors which would appear now and then in his later writings. Just as he had earlier gleaned proverbs and pictures from the daily lives of the German people, he did the same from those heathen authors. At this time, he limited himself to the works written in Latin. He did not yet understand the Greek language, nor would he acquire it while in Erfurt. That had to occur later, for the Greek professor who had been teaching at Erfurt moved to Wittenberg as early as 1502.

Luther later regretted that he did not spend more time and effort in these studies. He wished that he had read more of these authors and history instead of wasting his time and money on the works of the sophists. Still the benefits he had garnered through his familiarity with philosophy were stated earlier. On the other hand, his occupation with the Latin studies would stand him in good stead in that he could use that language with a high degree of skill. Although his ability was slightly less than some of his contemporaries, he was able to express himself with a great deal of refinement. He had become so skilled at this that a later opponent, who was a master of Latin, did not at first want to believe that Luther had edited the masterful work that had been directed against him.

So Luther rigorously proceeded on his way to academic honor. He attained the first step the year after his arrival in Erfurt, when he received the degree of Baccalaureus of Philosophy, having passed the exam on St. Michael's Day. To achieve the next step, for which this was a requirement, namely his master degree, would require diligence in study. Luther did not lack such diligence. If he was not spending his time at lectures or participating in open debate he loved to spend his time with books from the library.

One day Luther made a discovery which surprised him. He found a Latin Bible. That such a book called the Bible existed he knew, but he had not yet seen one. Until that moment, he had held the opinion that the gospels and epistles of the Sundays and other church holidays comprised practically the whole of Scripture. But now, to his amazement, he found that there was much more to be read in this book. The very first section he came upon was the account of Hannah and Samuel, at the beginning of the first book of Samuel. He derived such pleasure from reading this account that he began to wish that one day he would own such a book for himself. Yet because of the studying he had to do for philosophy, his time at Erfurt did not provide him with much of an opportunity to read the Bible he had discovered. The piety he had brought to Erfurt from his father's house and through Magdeburg and Eisenach was not diminished during his student days. Neither the heathen influence, to which so many of his friends committed with delight, nor the influence of the church dissuaded him. He had the habit of praying and hearing masses daily. If he were to become frightened or even feel threatened because of death, he would turn to the saints for refuge. On an Easter Tuesday, while heading home, he accidentally cut through an artery in his thigh with his student sword. While he was lying on his back he pressed down on the wound while a companion went to fetch a physician. Later that night the wound broke open again and feeling that he was in danger of bleeding to death he again called upon Mary for help. "At that moment," he said later, "I would have died placing all of my hope in Mary."

Luther was well aware that he did not have true holiness. Indeed, in his restless mind he was tortured by the fear that God, in his eternal counsel, must have decided that Luther would not become devout, but would be lost. The stern sermons of the city preacher Weinmann, well loved by the other students, could not take away his fear of Christ. As for a gospel sermon, well, there were none for him to hear! Later he wrote to the people of Erfurt, "For many years you have had a distinguished school in your city, a school where even I spent several years. But this I swear, that during my entire time not one true Christian lecture or sermon was delivered by anyone."

That Luther was a diligent student we have noted often enough already. Even his enemies were not able to claim that he led a loose life at Erfurt with drinking and unchaste living, even though they strove to find evidence for such. But that kind of outward holiness brought him no comfort. He often told his fellow students, "The longer we wash, the more unclean we become." "O, when will you become devout and do enough so that you may have a gracious God!" This was the cry that held sway in his fearful heart. Yet at the same time he could be a bright and cheerful companion. His lute playing, which he had learned during the time spent recovering from his thigh wound, earned him the additional nickname "Musicus" among his friends. Nor did he gradually withdraw from his studies. In 1505 he became Master of Philosophy. He passed the required exam with flying colors. He ranked second out of seventeen and attracted the attention of the entire university. (The mace on which the oath was administered to Luther for his degree currently belongs to the University of Berlin, according to Professor Graebner's footnote.)

From this moment on Luther pursued his studies in law. His father, who during this time had advanced his ranking somewhat in the community, would not let up supporting his son. He kept backing him as he had done throughout his son's university studies, regardless of how difficult it was for him to come up with the means to do so. In addition to other books he purchased for his son was the large and very expensive Corpus Jure, the main text for lawyers.

This father, who had hopefully envisioned an office, benefits, and a fortunate and rich marriage for his son, must have been devastated when he heard that his son had entered a monastery and had become a monk. It must have struck him like a bolt of lightning from the blue sky. That news came so unexpectedly right after Luther had paid a short summer visit home. Expecting to hear that his son had safely arrived back in Erfurt, he heard instead the news about the monastery and the new monk.

Chapter 4
In the Monastery at Erfurt

Fear caused by his father and mother's strict discipline; fear caused by the tyranny of his schoolmasters; fear caused by his perception of the burning wrath of the Judge seated on the throne in heaven; all these fears had been unleashed into Luther's mind and consciousness during his formative years. Now it would be fear that would drive him into the monastery. Remember that this was the Luther who as a youth was always aware of his sinfulness and kept asking himself, "When will you become devout enough in your behavior so that you may have a gracious God?" It seemed inevitable for him to take the step of becoming a monk. At that time the monastic life in general had the good reputation of providing a genuine kind of holiness. Through their rich endowments to monasteries sinful people of this world were also said to be able to gather small spiritual benefits.

However, other circumstances could also stand in the way of this learned young man to make this decision. On the one hand, life outside of the monastery promised greater success, namely, his circle of friends, the desires of his father, and an outwardly financially promising future. On the other hand, monastic life meant the burdens of monastery living and, first and foremost, the beggar's bag. However, the alluring future of secular life lost all of its attraction when facing death. This thought had confounded the young man during an illness and was compounded through the sudden end of a trustworthy friend. Hence, the terror of having to stand before the judgment seat of God was promptly reawakened and forced itself into the thinking of the young master.

Such were the various and foremost feelings and thoughts in the heart of the Erfurt master who was walking along the road on the 2nd of July. It was the holy day marked as the Celebration of the Visitation of Mary. Luther was on his way back from his parents' home in Erfurt. He was traveling without any friends. His only companions were his troubled thoughts. About to enter the village of Stotternheim he was close to the end of his journey, when a severe storm developed and the sky suddenly burst open with terrifying strength. A crackling bolt of lightning crashed near him. His terror overwhelmed him. It was as though God's burning wrath had sent this storm upon him, and the lightning bolt had been aimed at his head, which was weighed down with guilt. Trembling with fear he broke down. The saints would have to be his refuge in his great need! St. Anne was the first one to come to mind to this son of a miner. "Help, dear Saint Anne," he cried out, "I will become a monk!"

The tempest passed. The vow had been spoken. The time to fulfill his vow also came. Indeed, he would later regret his vow, but for now the commitment needed to be fulfilled.

He entertained his friends once more with the playing of his lute and cheered them with his songs on the evening of July 16th. Then those friends were allowed to accompany him, as he entered the monastery the next day. With tears in their eyes they saw the gate close behind him. (*Footnote: "It was the day of Alexius. From this a later legend ascribed the name 'Alexius' to Luther's friend, whose death had so touched him.") Martin Luther had broken with his past. He had taken some of his books back to the book stores. Only the works of Plautus and Virgil went with him into the monastery.

As he took this step Luther had no premonition of what plan God would be unfolding. Later, however, he recognized it as such and said, "It was God's will that I was to have personally learned about the scholarship of the universities and experienced the holiness of the monasteries. This means that I was supposed to have experienced those things by way of many sins and godless works. This was the reason why people could not attack me, their opponent later in time, as one who was uninformed and was condemning a situation that he had not experienced himself."

Before actually being received into the order of the monastic brotherhood the institution required the applicant to wait a year. During this year he would be free to change his mind. However, for Luther this time was shortened, enabling him to take his place within the order as early as the end of 1505. Until that time he was a novice. As a novice he already wore the clothing of the order in which he would ultimately serve. He had a white woolen shirt with a black cloth cowl over it, a leather belt, and finally a mantle which was to signify the yoke of Christ. This consisted of a strip of cloth with a hole in the center which he could slip over his head. The mantle would hang down to the earth in front and back. The chief of the novices, or the pedagogue, was an older monk who supervised the novices. Luther would later praise his pedagogue as a fine old man who remained a true Christian underneath his cowl.

Our novice remained patient, even though he was burdened with the lowest types of work assignments designed to produce or promote humility. This continued until the university, of which he had remained a member, intervened for him and applied some pressure that he be granted more acceptable treatment. His prayer life was constant, praying the prescribed Pater Noster and Ave Maria in due number of times, day and night. After all this was the part of being pious for which each monk was to strive and through which he was then taught to be earning God's favor.

Shortly after entering the monastery Luther received a gift from the monks for which he was truly grateful. They put a Latin Bible into his hands. Luther began to read this book often and attentively. At first this was out of obedience to the rules of the order as Staupitz, the deputy of the order, had prescribed. Although this new agenda of zealous Bible reading was for all, the rest of the monks gave little heed. Luther was the only true zealot for Bible reading in the monastery. In fact, even his teacher, Usingen, advised him to ease up on his Bible study and instead spend more time for studying the old church fathers. However, as long as Luther remained in Erfurt he continued favoring the reading of the Bible. He carried on not merely in obedience to monastic regulations or because of Staupitz's admonition, but because of his hunger to do so. He read his red bound Bible with such devotion that he later complained when he was not allowed to keep that precious book, which he had gotten to know quite well.

The trial period of a novice ended with a celebration marking the acceptance of the novice into the order. This took place with a focus on the dress code of the order and a threefold vow. "I, brother Martin, profess and promise in obedience to God the Almighty, and to the eternally sainted Virgin Mary, to you, brother prior of this institution, serving in lieu and in place of the head prior of this Order of the Hermit Brothers of St. Augustine, the bishop and his followers, to live in poverty, in chastity, and according to the rule of the same sainted Augustine, until death."

After Luther gave his vow, the prior and father confessor along with the other brothers extended congratulations. They rejoiced that now he was like a little child who had just been baptized and received a new name, in this case the monastic name of this order's saint, Augustine. Luther would later describe this as a vile despising of Christ and Holy Baptism, although his actual baptismal name, Martin, remained his most favorite.

He explained that he found not a single thread of comfort in his monastic baptism when he wrote, "When even confronted by a small moment of despair, I would collapse and not receive aid from either baptism or monkishness. Thus I had lost both Christ and his baptism for a long time. I was then the most miserable person on earth."

Yet his acceptance into the order marked the beginning of Luther's search for monastic piety. What would it have meant if Luther had derived some greater inner peace from the awareness of having made a complete denial of the world and of having dedicated himself to serve God? According to the belief of the day he would have had to admit to himself that the value of his new beginning was not in giving his vow, but in keeping his vow to its completion. Then he would not have been made pious through his profession, but the piety in such a profession would have been the cause of his zeal (to deny the world and dedicate himself to God). As a result, Luther strove with all his might to avail himself of the opportunity to perform so called holy works and exercises in abundance as the monastery would provide. A large portion of these exercises involved the prescribed prayers which had to be offered at predetermined intervals. With frightful care

Luther memorized them. With deep devotion he recited them, even though others were thoughtlessly babbling them like parakeets. Yet he did not dare to come before God with trust and confidence, like a child before his father. No, he still turned to the saints and appealed to them for help and intercession. After all, there was a huge flock of them, especially St. George and St. Anne, to whom he had turned as a child. But when the words, "I, the LORD your God am a mighty and jealous God," penetrated his soul, the artificial serenity granted by his calling on the saints completely disappeared.

The monastery also provided other opportunities to acquire holiness, namely: castigation of the body, nightly vigils, and fasting. Luther also had no equal peer in the pursuit of these. He would at times not eat or drink for three days. He far outpaced his brothers in the number of vigils he kept. Indeed, he so tortured himself that he kept losing weight in spite of his youthful healthy condition. This was also a cause for his later physical breakdowns.

A picture of Luther's cell in the monastery at Erfurt

(*This is the cell to which he had been assigned after he had taken the threefold vow. One could look into the monastery garden through its only window. This was still being displayed in the old monastery building before it was destroyed by a fire in 1872.)

"It is true," he later said, "I was a pious monk. I carried out my order's regulations so strictly that I may say that, if ever a monk got to heaven because of his monkishness, I would have reached that goal. All of my monastic companions will testify to this. For if it had continued much longer, I would have martyred myself to death with vigils, prayers, readings, and other works." His behavior and zeal was so exemplary, that even outside of his own monastery he was held up as a model monk. Yet, he spent so much effort not in order to shine before others but in order to win favor with God. In spite of all this he found himself lacking when weighing himself before God. He found evil thoughts in his heart, thoughts of impatience, and jealousy. Past sins which he could not undo stood naked before his soul. Trembling with despair, he was attacked again and again by the accusations of God's law in his conscience.

When undergoing such distress Luther turned to a third source of comfort, which was recommended to the brothers to be used frequently. This third source was confession. Here the solemn absolution of sins was delivered to the individual monk by the father confessor. But sadly, even this absolution had been robbed of its comfort under the disgraceful papacy. Indeed, it offered only new discomfort to the terrified conscience. First, the absolution was valid only for those sins which the confessor could remember, and then it would be valid only for such a sinner who had made himself worthy of forgiveness through a proper amount of sorrow. The sins would then be forgiven through the absolution, but true freedom from punishment could only be attained through the works of penance, which the father confessor would impose on the contrite sinner. One such dreadful form of absolution from that monastery read as follows, "The merits for suffering, the merits from the Virgin Mary and all the saints, the merits of the order, the humility of the confession, the contrition of the heart, the good works you have done and will do for the love of Christ will suffice for the forgiveness of your sins, for the increase of their merits and grace, and for the reward of eternal life."

Such a blasphemous declaration would no doubt make a carnal person secure and pharisaical, proud, and boastful. But it would never comfort and give rest to a heart terrified because of its sins and incompetence as was the case with Luther.

With painstaking care, he examined himself prior to his confession. Conscientiously, he would recite his sins and what he regarded as sin before his father confessor. With broken and contrite heart, he would plead for forgiveness. But what if he forgot some sins which had escaped his mind and which therefore remained unforgiven? Or what if his contrition and sorrow were not equal to the severity of the sin, thereby rendering the spoken absolution as invalid? Or what if the father confessor did not assign sufficient penance for him to do upon departure? Were these works, like castigation and the like, as strong as they needed to be to turn away God's punishment?

Questions like these could drive him to the edge of despair when he returned to his lonely cell after making confession.

To be sure there were also times when he believed himself to be exalted as an arrogant saint in his monastic devotion. But then he would descend again all the deeper into the torture and pain of disconsolate anguish, where he would search without success for some firm foundation to which he might cling. "If someone had told me, "he said later, "at what cost, however expensive, I could have bought peace with Christ, I would have fallen on my face and would have even given my life, praying only for the rescue of my conscience."

It is rather difficult for us to understand how a person, who was as earnestly concerned about his soul as Luther, would not quickly be led to the right answer through his continuous zealous reading of the Bible. He himself stated, "No other study gladdened me as much as that of Holy Scripture. I read it zealously and fixed it into my memory. From time to time a single passage I needed to comprehend would remain in my thoughts. The meaningful words of the prophet, which I well remember, I considered over and over, even though I was unable to grasp their meaning. For example, I read in Ezekiel, 'I take no pleasure in the death of the wicked.'" (Ez. 33:11 NIV)

One would have thought that this one passage would have brought comfort to his frightened heart, as he studied. But one has to understand that in addition to the blindness of the carnal heart, there was also the powerful force of deception to influence him constantly. In addition to Holy Scripture he also had to study the writings of the papal church leaders of the Middle Ages under his monastic teachers. There, for example, he learned a number of teachings about the grace of God, which were said to be necessary for salvation. This divine grace, according to the explanation of those teachers, was said to be a gift of God through which man is put into position to fulfill the highest demands of God's law and to do works which, by virtue of their value, would prompt God to grant him salvation. But this grace was supposed to make it possible for man to achieve it for himself, making himself worthy for it through the natural ability which was claimed to have remained in man after Adam's fall into sin. Those who had achieved this for themselves would have such grace poured into them by God's love and kindness.

These and other explanations like them hung like a blanket in front of the poor monk's eyes. They were like dark colored spectacles through which he would see all of the other passages about God's grace distorted. Thus, every passage was translated involuntarily into papist thought patterns.

For him it was the same with other Bible passages: "I am working with zeal and terror," he relates, "on how to understand the passage in Romans 1, where he tells us that the righteousness of God is revealed in the gospel. I searched for a long time, knocking on the door continuously. For that phrase, (*justitie dei*) the righteousness of God, was in my mind to be interpreted according to the common teaching: righteousness is a virtue of God, in which he is righteous for himself and condemns sinners. This is the way that all of the doctors, except Augustine, explained this passage. They said that the righteousness of God is the wrath of God. As often as I read that passage I wished that God had never revealed the gospel."

Indeed, there were times when his reading would suggest to him that some things were not the way the church fathers interpreted them. Then the question would arise, "Do you think you are the only one who is so wise?" Just like that, the evil tinted eyeglasses were in front of his eyes. They caused the merits of Christ and the grace of God to seem like something for which he had to make himself worthy, turning Christ into a terrible judge who in his great majesty was only to be feared by the sinner. "I assumed," he later said, "such a high regard for the pope that I believed that the one who does not agree with him on even the smallest issue, would have to be condemned and belong to the devil eternally." And again, "If someone at that time had taught me what I now believe and teach by God's grace, I would have torn him apart with my teeth." Such was the deception under which he was held captive and which kept Scripture hidden from him.

Out of this experience he would later write in his preface to Romans, "First of all we must become acquainted with and understand what Paul means through the words: law, sin, grace, faith, righteousness, flesh, spirit, and the like. Otherwise reading this letter will be of no use to us." And after explaining these words he concluded, "Without such an understanding of these words you will never understand Paul's letter or any other book of the Bible. Therefore, watch out for all teachers who use these words differently." Here we have, from Luther's own pen, the key to understanding Luther's mindset from those days.

In the opinion of the monks of his monastery and the other brothers of this order this learned and devoted monk, Martin Luther, was surely a wonderful and spiritually converted second Paul. He was a jewel of his monastery and his order. As a result, in order that such a light would also shine outside of the monastery's walls and bring it honor and gain, Martin's activity would have to be expanded. Indeed, during his second year the fathers of the monastery had taken the first step by accepting him into their number. He was ordained as one of the priests, who were called fathers in distinction from the common brothers of the order. Luther considered this promotion aimed at him as a sign of God's compassion. In this way he would be allowed to carry out even higher and more holy works.

The 2nd of May of that year was the day chosen for his ordination. That year it was the Cantate Sunday (*the 4th Sunday after Easter.*) This date was chosen out of consideration for the schedule of Luther's father, whom the son invited to attend this day of celebration. This would be the first time when father and son would see each other again, ever since that visit to Mansfeld, followed so quickly by his entrance into the monastery. The deep displeasure which the father had expressed at that news of his son, resulting in the withdrawal of some of his fatherly affection, had in the meantime mellowed and given way to acceptance. Two of Martin's brothers had died of the plague, and it had even been reported once that Martin himself had died.

The father arrived at the Augustinian monastery at the appropriate time with twenty horses, a number of his neighbors from among their Mansfeld friends, and a present of twenty guilders he had saved for the occasion. The farmers of his area also expressed their joy at Martin's ordination.

The least happy member of all of the participants was the guest of honor. Martin Luther stood before the altar in anguished fear after the dedicating bishop, Johannes von Lasphe, had bestowed on him the priestly sacrament. How he felt that day remained a vivid memory for him throughout his entire life. He still referred to it in his lectures on Genesis, "When I was to read these words in the mass for souls for the first time: 'We humbly pray of you, most gracious Father, etc.' or, in the same way, 'We sacrifice to you, the living, true, and eternal God, etc.', I was completely struck with fear." Indeed, if his monastic teacher had not held on to him, he may very well have fled.

Every error and every blunder against the rubrics of the observation of the ceremony of the mass, no matter how small, was regarded as a tremendous sin. Notice how differently he later assessed the consecration of a priest, "My consecrating bishop," he said, "as he made me a priest and put the chalice in my hand, said nothing except 'Accipe potestatem sacrificandi pro vivis et mortuis' (*Receive the power to sacrifice for the living and the dead.*) That in reply the earth did not swallow us up because of this wrong testifies greatly of God's patience and forbearance."

In referring to the sacrifice of the mass he wrote in his commentary on Galatians, "Here the priest of the mass, who as an apostate denies Christ and blasphemes the Holy Spirit, is allowed to stand before the altar and perform this work which should provide and serve as comfort and salvation, not only for himself but also for others, for the dead and the living, indeed for all of Christendom. ... Therefore, one can easily see, based on this one piece of evidence, the immeasurably enormous patience of our Lord God, in that he has not already, years ago, damned the papacy to hell, burning it with fire and brimstone like Sodom and Gomorrah."

As the attending guests from the university, the monastery officials, and those visitors from Mansfeld and Eisenach sat at the table after the consecration service, Luther's father brought the new priest back to reality, something which took no little effort. For when, in front of all of the guests, Luther in an amiable manner confronted his father and said, "Dear father, why were you so strongly opposed and even angry about me becoming a monk? Perhaps even now you fail to understand? Is it not a fine, peaceful, and godly life?" Father Hans hammered him back, "You who are so learned, did you not learn from Scripture that father and mother are to be honored? Contrary to this commandment you have abandoned your dear mother and me in our old age, a time when we should have finally received your comfort and aid, since I spent so much money on your education. Instead, you entered the monastery contrary to our wishes."

When it was protested that his son had been called to this vocation by an appearance out of heaven, he cut it off with these words, "If only it was God's will, and that it was not a demon from hell." In any event it was apparent that he was not wholeheartedly rejoicing in his son's decision. Those strong words of his father drove deep into the son's heart, although at the time he had hardened his heart in his own piety. As he later said, he felt as though God had spoken to him.

As a priest Luther pursued this piety zealously. He could not be at peace, he would later relate, unless he read a mass every single day, and in each mass call upon three of the twenty one saints he had chosen for himself. He also began to preach to the brothers of the monastery. By this (*his preaching*) he accomplished extraordinary success, as he had accomplished before with his vigils and fasting, and he could later truthfully say, "My life shone brightly before the people."

So, Luther achieved what he did not desire, namely honor among men. Yet he failed to achieve what he truly desired, namely peace for his stricken conscience. This was the case, even though the holiness of a monk's life was believed to be so rich and abundantly blessed that one could even share some of these blessings with those not so holy. Luther would later tell his students, "How it was my custom, when I was still a monk, to daily confess my sins, to pray, to hold sacrificial masses all solely in order that from these vigils, masses, and extra good works I could share with, or sell to, the lay members. The monks would take money, grain, and wine in payment. Even today there remain many official written records of this kind of buying and selling by monks and priests in which they offered their goods to the people as follows: "'We herewith want to share with you (name) our fasting, vigils, prayers, discipline, mass, etc. for a bushel of grain.' So, it was also our custom to write such letters and so did we sell our good works."

But while others may have found some peace of conscience in the good works of Father Martin, he found no comfort for himself. He approached the altar with doubts. He departed the altar with doubts. Neither confession nor the mass gave him comfort or serenity. When thinking of Christ upon seeing a cross and considering the sacrifice of the mass, he would be shaken to the core and in terror break out in a sweat. He wrote: "In those days we cried out to the papacy for eternal salvation and the kingdom of God. We even harmed ourselves physically. Yes, we nearly martyred our bodies to death. This was not done by sword or any other weapon, but with fasting and the castigation of our bodies. In this way we were seeking and knocking at the door, day and night. And as for me, if I had not been rescued by the comfort of the gospel, I would not have lived two more years. That is the way that I martyred myself and fled from the wrath of God. Neither did I lack in the shedding of tears and weeping. But through all of this we did not accomplish a thing."

As a result of his soul's anguish Luther once again slipped into the terrible conclusion that God, in his infinite wisdom, may have decided that Luther was unmistakably destined for eternal damnation. That explained the vanity of all of his striving and his works. Thus, his terror for God rose to its greatest height. When feeling this way, he said later, one finds himself tempted to blaspheme God, calling him unjust and cruel. Indeed, it would be better if there were no God at all.

Yet it was necessary that he, through whom God would lead his poor Christendom, enslaved under the papacy, out of captivity, learn for himself the brick-molding labors of Egypt and the chastising rod of the slave driver.

Even in the darkness under which Luther was living at this time and in the terror which surrounded him, God was holding his hand over him. God would allow the sun to rise for him in his own good time. Already in the monastery at Erfurt was he allowed to begin seeing the first glowing beams of the rising sun and slowly coming to life.

The Augustinian monasteries in Thueringia and Saxony had an excellent superior in the person of John Staupitz who had served since 1503. He was a gifted, educated, devout, and distinguished man. Descended from nobility he was also noble minded and managed those monasteries entrusted to him in true faithfulness. Among all of those monasteries he seemed to take special care in dealing with the one in Erfurt. Of all of the monks who lived there, it was brother Martinus who attracted the attention of his superior. Having been noticed because of his intelligence, his devotion to his studies, and his exercise of monkish piety, he responded to Staupitz with a fragile trust. This man, though he was quite distinguished, was not equal to the task which God had intended for Luther. Indeed, after the enormous work of the reformation was begun, he quietly withdrew into the background. Yet, God saw to it that he would serve as an important tool in preparing the reformer. Staupitz was the one, who had urged Luther toward a diligent study of Scripture and who then saw to it that he continued in that study. And it was Staupitz, who served as a St. Philip, leading this Bible reader to understand the central message of Scripture, even though his eyes had been kept sealed shut by the old papal teachers of the church.

As late as a year before his death Luther still spoke of Staupitz, "Of him I must declare, when I don't want to be a damned, unfaithful, papal ass, that he was my first father in introducing me to Christ. Because of him I am bound to serve everyone as he would demand it of me." For example, once the word "repentance" entered the discussion. Staupitz declared that there is no true repentance other than the kind that brings with it love for God's righteousness. "This statement," Luther wrote to Staupitz in 1518, "transfixed me like an arrow delivered by a master bowman. I began with those passages of Scripture that dealt with repentance to see for myself, and behold, what a sweet breath of fresh air! The words stood out in perfect harmony and everything fit together beautifully with this explanation."

Luther would also find a number of other comforting bits of advice. He sought these out both in person and in writing in order to soothe his conscience. The mere fact that Staupitz would not accept some of the things that Luther confessed as sin had a calming effect on this frightened monk. Staupitz explained that Luther tortured himself with bungler's work and puppet sins. But he also directed him to Christ, the Savior. Once, when Luther was in the depths of despair, Staupitz comforted him by saying, "You want to be a make-believe sinner and look to Jesus as a make-believe Savior. Accustom yourself to the fact that Christ is the true Savior and you are a real sinner. God is not playing a shadow game with us and he wasn't jesting when he sent his Son and gave him up." Staupitz managed to beautifully comfort him as he wrestled with his temptation regarding eternal election. Luther told his students, "Dr. Staupitz used to comfort me with these words: Dear friend, why are you torturing yourself with wild speculation and lofty ideas? Look at the miracles of Christ! Behold the blood he shed for you! The election shines forth from these!" Then he added, "The election is to be understood in the wounds of Christ and nowhere else. For it is written, 'Listen to him!' For all treasures lie hidden in Christ Jesus, but without Christ all of them (*all the treasures*) remain locked up. So, envision Christ well and correctly. And so, predestination is included in his work and you are already elected!"

The productive power of such comfort also showed itself in Luther's life. As late as 1542 he pointed to Staupitz as the instrument God used to save him from the depth of his woe. "If Dr. Staupitz, or more importantly God himself, had not lifted me out of that terrible depression I would long ago have drowned in it and would have gone to hell." Truly, throughout his entire life Luther had heartfelt gratitude for "his dear Dr. Staupitz," even though Staupitz's later timidity grieved him a great deal.

That gray haired monastic instructor was also God's instrument for bringing the first beams of healing to Luther's soul. On one occasion when Luther was tearfully recounting his dismay, that gray-haired man replied, "What are you doing, my son? Don't you know that our Lord God himself commanded us to hope?" This understanding was new to Luther and he later said, "That one word, 'commanded,' gave me such comfort! After that I knew that one must believe in the absolution and in the being set free from sin. I had often heard this before, but beset as I was by foolish thoughts, I believed that these words didn't apply to me or that I had to believe them."

It was also this hoary headed man who gently pointed Luther to childlike faith, as stated in the Third Article, "I believe in the forgiveness of sins." He expounded this idea, "It is not enough that one believes in a general way that there exists a forgiveness of sins. Even the devils believe that David and Peter have forgiveness. But God wants each person to believe for himself that his own sins are also forgiven. This was even confirmed by St. Bernhard, who in a sermon on the annunciation of Mary said, "In addition, also believe that through him your sins are forgiven to you. This is the testimony which the Holy Spirit gives in your heart: Your sins are forgiven to you. For the Apostle holds forth that man is justified, free of charge, through faith."

Luther would later admit, as Melanchthon reports, that these words not only lifted him up, but that he was also instructed in the meaning of Paul's words, where it says, "Justified by faith, we have peace with God through our Lord Jesus Christ." (Romans 5:1 KJV). Since he had studied many other interpretations of these words, he continued learning from that old brother. The comfort he received led him to conclude that all of the current interpretations were false. Through further study of the writings of the Prophets and the Apostles this doctrine kept becoming ever clearer, little by little.

Though it was during this third year of his life in the monastery, his last in Erfurt, that the light began to shine regarding the truths of Scripture, it would be a mistake to think that Luther had already fully understood how to properly evaluate the papacy. Such understanding would come much later and it would come gradually. That does not mean that there weren't many skirmishes. One occurred when he found a book in the library of the monastery. It was a book of sermons written by the Bohemian martyr, John Hus, whom the papists had burned at Costnitz a hundred years earlier. "In that book I found so much," Luther said, "that upset me. Why was such a man, who could apply Scripture in such a Christian and powerful manner, sent to the stake? But because at that time his name was so universally condemned I thought that the walls would turn black and the sun lose its light at the mere thought of the name "Hus." So, I closed the book and walked away with a wounded heart. But I comforted myself with the idea that perhaps he had written these sermons before he became a heretic."

Indeed, he later confessed about himself, "I regarded John Hus as such a damned heretic that I believed it was sinful and contrary to God's will to even think of him. I was so filled with enthusiasm for the pope that I longed to have been allowed to bring the wood, fire, and stones, with which Hus was killed. Thus, I would serve, if not with the actual deed, with good will and good intentions in my heart."

Even Luther's monastic way of life at times caused him to think. It seemed that the center of a truly Christian life, namely the practice of Christian love, was missing. We noted earlier how his father's serious comment about his ordination to priesthood caused him great concern. Still, for over a decade he clung to the monastic rule. And for a decade he devoutly read the papal masses, those same masses that he later would rightly abhor as blasphemous abominations. Even though he was a priest he was obligated to carry the beggar's sack through streets and towns in company with a monastery brother, and he did so willingly.

His studies continued to be based mainly on papal teachings. His ambitious learning was not limited to the scholastics but also included the writings of Thomas Aquinas, Duns Scotus, Wilhelm of Occam, Gabriel Biel, Peter of Alliaco, Peter d'Ailly, and Gerson. He committed large sections of these writings to memory and could soon pass as the most well versed expert on scholastic theology in the entire Augustinian order in Germany. The study of Holy Scripture still remained important to him. So, in the quiet of his monastic cell, he began to learn the Hebrew language in order to glean for himself the ability to study the Old Testament in its original form. He appears to have used a dictionary by Reuchlin for this purpose.

But again, it must be remembered that Brother Martin was not just a bookworm, studying only to gain extensive and thorough knowledge out of thick books, but to lack the ability to apply or even use such knowledge. On the contrary, we find him to have become a gifted man looking out for the best interests of his order. For this he was applying his acquired knowledge already in Erfurt. He even appeared on behalf of the order before Count Adolf von Anhalt, the provost of Magdeburg at that time. This appearance had to do with business concerns. The count would later talk about the zealous, pious, and respectful monk.

In truth Luther already stands before us as a man of high renown. We have followed his journey to this point and now we must leave Erfurt to travel with him to a new and more important phase of his life.

Chapter 5
Beginnings at Wittenberg

Elector Frederick the Wise of Saxony had established a university in his city of Wittenberg in the fall of 1502. This university was dedicated to God, to the Virgin Mary, and to St. Augustine. The university's theology school chose St. Paul as its patron saint. The school of law chose St. Ivo. The school of philosophy was under the protection of St. Katherine. And the school of medicine was under the protection of St. Kosmos and St. Damian.

This university was established with permission from the pope. However, it had also gained approval and support from Caesar (*The king of the Holy Roman Empire)*, and in that sense was not under spiritual rule like other institutions of higher learning. When Frederick the Wise founded and organized this institution he chose two specific persons in whom he placed his trust. One of these was his medical doctor, Dr. Pollich of Mellerichstadt, who had also accompanied the elector on a trip to Palestine. As an educated man he had an impressive reputation. He had distinguished himself magnificently as a professor in both the schools of doctor of medicine and of law in the city of Leipzig. He was established as the first chancellor of this new university. He also became a doctor of theology. Hence he was also qualified to lecture on that subject. The other counselor chosen by the elector was Dr. Staupitz, with whom we are already quite well acquainted. He was the first deacon of the theological department.

At first the financial support for running this new university came out of the founder's own coffers. But this initial investment was not enough to bring this institution to be equal to its sister schools. This shortage, along with the near poverty standard of living in the city of Wittenberg, was the reason why the enrollment for the first year was 416 but by the fourth year had shrunk to 127. To gain a better financial standing, the University of Wittenberg adopted a policy which had proven beneficial to other schools.

The wealthy castle church was established with papal approval as a foundation church with a chapter of several neighboring parishes added to it. This foundation was in close ties with the university. The professors were thus also to serve as foundation lords and so benefit from the foundation's income. In addition, Staupitz hoped to be able to add suitable men from his order as professors of the university. They would receive their room and board from Wittenberg's Augustinian monastery. In this way the funding for professorships was preserved and the number of professors could also be increased considerably. Having a large number of professors did not guarantee success. Those professors had to be proficient in their subjects in order to

Wittenberg on the Elbe River, Capital in the Electorate of Saxony, according to a copper plate of 1546

build up the university's reputation. At first Wittenberg lacked professors of that quality. Staupitz, because of his many journeys on behalf of his order's business, spent far too little time for his university lectures. Pollich, a man with a wide range of scholarship and high reputation, was able to win the hearts of his students through some bold ideas and kindness. Yet his achievements were hardly enough to distinguish him above an equal level with professors of other schools. Even when Luther's old teacher, Truttvetter, was brought from Erfurt to Wittenberg, whereby a trained and honored teacher was added to the faculty, they were merely adding another follower of the scholastic system. Two of the younger professors were Andreas Bodenstein of Carlstadt and Nicolaus from Amsdorf. The former had not yet ever seen a Bible, and the latter, though he was a bright, sincere, and zealous professor, had not yet attained a noticeable reputation outside of Wittenberg.

In 1508 Staupitz was again serving as deacon of his faculty. It seems as though shortly after stepping into office he found himself once again under pressure due to too many burdens. He rather swiftly reached the decision to call a man who would serve alongside himself. This man was one, whose zeal, gifts, and learning Staupitz had known for a long time. He was one, who Staupitz believed would work zealously and with success. This man was our Luther.

The move of Brother Martin from Erfurt to Wittenberg happened quickly. He did not even have time to say farewell to his friends. The move of this poor brother out of the monastery, who had very little to pack, was accomplished quite easily. He simply made the move by leaving one monastery for another, merely in obedience to his superior. He began his new position without any salary. However, this move did not completely please him because he had been called away from his study of Scripture. Here, as a master of philosophy, he would not be giving theological lectures. Instead he would be teaching Aristotle. But it was not Staupitz's intent in drawing him to this professorship to have him remain in the philosophy department. Soon after his arrival in Wittenberg we can see steps being taken to open the door for him to teach theology.

As early as March 9, 1509, Luther was given the degree of Bible baccalaureus and, along with it, the allowance of interpreting Holy Scripture for the students. This, according to the statutes of the university, was the first step toward a full professorship in theology. A person might think that this should have been the final step. But Holy Scripture was being despised to such an extent at that time that Bible interpretation position was assigned to beginners among faculty members. And even for those beginners it was not taken all that seriously, for it was required that a Baccalaureate had to teach Scriptural interpretation for merely one whole year (a half year if he belonged to an order), before he could take further steps toward a doctorate. Thus, it was possible to get one's doctorate without having seen the Bible, as had been the case with Carlstadt.

In regard to our Luther we cannot prove that he began his Bible instruction as soon as he was authorized to do so. It is apparent that for a baccalaureus Bible instructions were regarded more as a right, and less as a duty. Luther may even have taken the time to prepare for the next step in achieving full professorship, namely the step of becoming sententiarist. The sententiarist was required to conduct lectures on the sentences of the scholastic, Peter Lombardus, whose book was used in the schools as a textbook for theological study. This was so, even though as Luther later said, he spoke about the chief articles of the Christian faith way too shallow.

The twenty-six year old baccalaureate had already presented a disputation, a requirement for the next step toward being promoted. But shortly before attaining his goal, his work in Wittenberg was interrupted. For a reason unknown to us Luther was called to Erfurt. There he accomplished the promotion to Sententiarist, though with great difficulty due to the faculty's requirements. It was customary that the next two degrees, the licensure and the doctorate, were to be bestowed in quick succession, one after the other.

But before Luther would actually take his position as a professor of Holy Scripture, God wanted him to first experience something else. In regard to this he later remarked that he would not trade what he was now to see for any amount of money, because he would never have had the opportunity again. He, through whom the power of Rome would be overcome, was now given the assignment to travel to Rome.

Chapter 6
The Journey to Rome

A dispute arose among the German Augustinian monks, which cannot be easily explained. It appears that a rift developed between those who favored a stricter and those who favored a laxer rule. That seemed to lie at the root of the problem, and it was debated as to how the two sides could come together. Hence, input was to be obtained from Rome. This required appointing a person who was willing and able to present the situation accurately, and at the same time, was willing and able to determine what was best for the order. Staupitz was the leader of the faction seeking a stricter rule. He could think of a no more dependable man to be entrusted with this task than Brother Martin. After all, Brother Martin had already earlier proven himself in defense of the order and would also be able to adapt himself to worthily represent the order in Rome. Thus Luther, accompanied by another brother from the monastery as required, set out for Rome. He was heading to the city which he still believed to be the holy capital of Christendom. He still regarded that city as the place, where the greatest comfort for a heart yearning for salvation was to be found.

According to information from Luther's own writing, his stay in Erfurt began in the fall of 1509 and lasted one and one-half years. Since he reported finding ripe grapes and pomegranates in Italy he would have begun his journey around the middle of 1511. He very likely set out directly from Erfurt, although it is possible he made a short visit to Wittenberg.

The two monks traveled on foot toward their goal, most likely via the most direct route, through Bavaria. They received food and lodging in the monasteries that they passed. Some of these brothers distinguished themselves with warm welcomes which they extended toward their guests. This was especially true after entering Italy. But while the rich fertility of the Italian landscape filled them with amazement, the libertine ways of the rich and prosperous Italian monks filled them with dismay. On one occasion they became victims of an illness of head and body, as they were sleeping next to an open window with Italian humidity on both sides. When this happened the monks of that Italian monastery proved to be quite malicious, since they had been confronted because of their licentious way of living. In their malice they sought to kill our travelers. The kindness of the monastery's gate keeper saved them. He helped them by guiding them in their flight.

When Luther finally beheld Rome, he stretched out his arms toward it and cried out, "Greetings, holy Rome!" and he cast himself piously to the earth. The Roman papal throne was occupied at that time by Pope Julius II, a spur-clanking and fighting lord. For him the coat of mail fit much better than the cassock. Peter's sword agreed with him much more than the shepherd's staff. He was known to make use of the papal ban against military opponents when his other arrows did not yield the desired outcome. In other ways Julius presented himself as an improvement over his predecessor, Alexander VI, who had grown gray because of all of his abominable depravities. That unworthy pope finally died of poisoning, a poison he had intended for a wealthy cardinal. With his death the Roman people were unexpectedly joyful.

The new, war happy pope would have had little time for a Saxon monk and his problem, since his head and hands were fully occupied in a war with France. Yet, somehow the issue that had brought Luther to Rome seems to have found a satisfactory conclusion. However, the matter was not settled in one day. During the time when his issue was being examined Luther found quarters in the Augustinian monastery near the Porto del Popolo. He had enough time to explore the city and all of its famous sites. Seemingly with every step this simple, honest German found more and more to discourage him. He had expected to see and hear holy practice and respectful piety everywhere. Instead he found frivolity buzzing and fluttering around streets and palaces. He saw that, what he had seen and heard about the warrior politician Julius and his cardinals had implanted itself everywhere he looked. He was exposed to hideous unnatural abominations being practiced in shameless insolence, even by highly placed churchmen. As he would later say,"These abominations made Sodom seem like child's play." He even heard the most vilely infamous tales of the former pope, Alexander, and his children. Those tales were told openly and with certainty, being still fresh in the thoughts of the then current living citizens of Rome.

Malicious games were being played even in respect to the saints. "There a person sees," says Mathesius, "the holy father, the pope, and his gold covered religion, and the impious whores and court servants." These sights gave him great motivation later on when he was doing his important writing against the Roman abominations and idolatry. As he often stated at the table, he would not take a thousand guilders for the experience he had in seeing Rome. For in Rome he had wanted to rescue his friends from purgatory through his saying the sacrifice of the mass, as everyone believed at that time. So he conducted his mass very deliberately and devoutly. During the same time, a priest at an altar next to him said seven masses before Luther finished his one. The Roman conducting the mass said, "Passa, passa, passa! Away! Send this woman's son home again soon!" Luther himself reported, "In Rome I heard whores laughing and bragging in vile language how some were saying masses using these words over the bread and the wine, "Panis es et panis manebis; vinum es et vinum manebis. (Bread you are and bread you remain; wine you are and wine you remain.)"

In spite of this experience he would later relate about himself, "I was such a holy fanatic in Rome. I walked through all of the churches and catacombs. I believed everything that was deceitfully invented even though it stunk like a pestilence. Whether I held one mass or ten I was deeply sorry at that time that my father and mother were still alive. I would have liked to have saved them from purgatory through my masses, or better yet, with my other good works and prayers. There is a saying in Rome: Blessed is the mother whose son says a mass for her on Saturday at St. John. How dearly I would have liked to have sanctified my mother there. But it was too crowded and I could not get close enough. I ate a rustic herring instead."

Among all of the sacred deceptions, multitudes of which were taking place then and even today, was the so-called Pilate staircase. This staircase, which was standing in front of the Sancta Sanctorum Chapel, was said to have been transported in a miraculous way from Pilate's judgment hall in Jerusalem to Rome. For centuries it was promised that whoever would work his way up these steps on his knees, steps on which the feet of Jesus had touched, would receive nine years of indulgence for each of the 28 steps. Even our "holy fanatic" didn't want to miss out on this blessing and so piously climbed all of these steps on his knees.

But Luther could not find true solace in any of the laudable acts which he so devoutly performed in Rome. In fact, there was much less solace afterward. He first felt bitterly disappointed, even though he did not dare to admit it to himself or others. He felt he was going mad from his experience in regard to those things he had considered holy and precious.

Even then there was a beginning of the injection of a truth of Scripture. It would pierce his forsaken soul like a mighty, rushing wind that surrounded him. The Word of God came to him and surrounded him with wondrous persistence, echoing louder and louder, until its low register vibrated through his soul like loud thunder against his false work of reconciliation. This Word of God was, "The righteous will live by faith." God had given him this teaching to accompany him on his journey to Rome. It occupied his thoughts. It harassed him in his wild piety. It traveled with him from place to place. And though he could not find its basis, it held his soul captive. When he took leave of Rome after his four week stay he did not take back with him everything he had brought. But that word he did bring back. It was becoming for him the gateway to paradise.

Chapter 7
The Doctor Hat

Now if you might think that Luther returned to Germany as a son of thunder ready to rail against the apostasy of the pope, the separation from Babylon, and assume the mantle of the reformer, you would have to simply change your mind. This much is certain, Luther was maturing through various forms of testing. As he had earlier come to understand that not everything was right in the teachings of the highly distinguished papal leaders, now he had to experience his own personal disillusion. He had to admit that much in the papacy was downright corrupt, in fact much more corrupt than he had known or suspected up to this time.

At the same time, you could be sure that this man, who had learned so much through his awareness and experience, was still a long way removed from sounding the alarm, exposing the pope's disgrace, and preaching a holy war. Even less did he believe himself to be the spearhead of a reformation. He was not even at the front of the battle in the small circle of his own preaching influence. It seems that at the beginning of his renewed time at Wittenberg he withheld himself from all public teaching activity. Instead, he applied himself only to his monastery duties, duties which he now assumed in the position of subordinate prior.

A portion of those monastic duties, now as before, included preaching in the monastery chapel. Mykonius writes poetically about this little church. "The foundation for the church had been laid in the new Augustinian monastery in Wittenberg, but it had not grown beyond ground level. An old chapel was still standing in the midst of it. Made of wood and held together with clay, it stood about thirty feet long and twenty feet wide. It was dilapidated and needed to be propped up on each side. It included a small, old, and sooty nave in which twenty worshippers could stand, crowded together."

Along the southern wall could be found a preaching chair fashioned out of old, un-planed boards. It stood about one-and-a-half cubits tall. Truly, it had the appearance that artists give to the barn in Bethlehem in which Christ was born. In this poor and miserable chapel, God caused his holy gospel and the dear infant Jesus to be born anew, to be unveiled and shown to the entire world. It was neither a cathedral nor a huge central church which God had chosen for this purpose, though there were thousands from which to choose. But soon this church proved to be too small and Luther was commanded to take his preaching to the parish church. Thus, the baby Jesus would also be brought into the temple.

The scholarship and teaching skill of Luther was to prove valuable for the university (according to the direction of Staupitz), for the elector (who would also listen to Luther's sermons), and for the brothers of his order (who in part had been enrolled as students). As a result, Staupitz encouraged Luther to be given the title, Doctor of Theology. It wasn't Luther who requested the promotion. In fact, when Staupitz approached him, he tried to decline and pleaded to be spared. He said that he would soon collapse under the work. He also stated that he lacked the means to pay for what the doctorate would cost and brought up many other excuses.

Staupitz, however, destroyed all of his objections in a conversation that took place under the pear tree in the inner yard of the monastery. He raised a valid argument which he knew would convince this conscientious brother monk. He invoked the debt of obedience to the superior of the order. "It is apparent," he said, "that our God shall soon have much to be done in heaven and on earth. For this reason, he will need to have many young doctors doing the work through which he will carry out his plans. Whether you live or die, God needs you in his battle plan. Therefore, be obedient in respect to the duty your house is giving you according to the debt you owe. What you need for your expenses your gracious elector will supply. He will do this out of his devotion to our God, to promote this university and monastery, according to his grace."

In reality, it was the argument pertaining to his obedience to his superior and to his monastic vow which caused Luther to reconsider. As he later wrote, "I was called and forced to become a doctor against my desires, purely out of obedience. Thus, I had to accept the doctorate and swear upon my praised and most loved Holy Scripture to preach it faithfully and clearly." At the same time he invited the vicar and fathers of the order at the Erfurt monastery to remember their obedience and accept his invitation to the ceremony.

According to the rules a person had to become a licentiate before he could earn the degree of doctor. This happened on the 4th of October and was the occasion on which Luther swore to valiantly defend the evangelical truth against all error, the oath he referred to in the previous statement. His doctoral disputation was held on the afternoon of October 18th under the chairmanship of Carlstadt and was attended by gentlemen of the university and numerous guests. The next morning the usual ceremonies took place. These involved the swearing on the mace, the presentation of the doctor's hat, the doctor rings, etc. And so, Martin Luther was proclaimed and duly sworn in as doctor, promising not to present vexatious or foreign doctrines, or doctrines which were condemned by the church. He was not to present evil teachings to holy ears.

So, we have standing before us on the 19th of October, 1512, the Augustinian, Dr. Martin Luther. He was a man from among the people, of fearful conscientiousness, reared by his father and mother. He was a man of deep introspection acquired particularly in the quiet of his monastic cell. He was a man versed in the basic knowledge of his day, garnered through his studies at the various schools he attended, as well as his private study. At the same time, he was a man increasing in his understanding of the one thing needful which he was slowly beginning to acquire through his persistent searching of the Scriptures. In addition, in spite of all the insight he had gained concerning the enormous damage that was becoming evident in his church, he remained a zealous and faithful, submissive son of the Roman church. And now he was a doctor of theology, having taken his sacred oath in all sincerity.

Where else might one have found another man who would measure up to all these qualifications?

Chapter 8
Luther's Work and Growth to 1517

Martin Luther had stood alone in the study of Holy Scripture while in the monastery at Erfurt. He also stood alone in Wittenburg, even as he began the duties which came with his doctorate. None of the other university professors held the Holy Scriptures as the foundation of their theology and teaching as did Luther. This must have immediately become obvious to Luther's students and colleagues alike. This seems to have been especially true in the case of the elderly Dr. Pollich, who, in noting Luther's penetrating eyes, accurately predicted that this monk, having his position founded in the writings of the Prophets and Apostles and the words of Christ himself, would ultimately outshine all the other doctors and overturn the doctrine which was then holding sway in the universities.

It is now appropriate to take a closer look at those men who were at that time associates of Luther and in regular communication with him. We begin with Luther's old acquaintance and brother monk, Dr. Wenzeslous Link. Dr. Link had become a part of this group of teachers of theology at the same time as Luther. He had studied at Wittenberg as early as 1503. He had earned his own doctor's hat a year before Luther, and was now serving as the prior of the monastery where they both lived. He was the deacon of the faculty.

Then there was Andreas Bodenstein of Carlstadt. He had stepped into the professorship which had become vacant with Trutvetter's return to Erfurt. A part of this professorship included the archdeaconry of the church foundation and receipts from the parish of Orlamuende. While Link was a noble and devout man serving with Luther, Carlstadt proved to be much more of an impure spirit. His education and career revealed that he was at heart an average Thomist. (*A Thomist was a follower of Thomas Aquinas.*) In addition, he was a restless and ambitious man, who in order to present something dramatic would resort to the oddest methods. For example, he arrived at the notion that theology and jurisprudence actually belonged together. This resulted in a journey to Rome in 1515 to begin his study of jurisprudence. This study was against the expressed stipulation under which the university had granted its permission for the journey, a permission he had sought five years earlier. Carlstadt showed the same lack of responsibility when he failed to keep his promise of having a substitute for himself during his absence. Before he left for Italy he had roamed throughout the country to gather contributions for his pilgrimage. Throughout this time the university had no certain knowledge as to his whereabouts. After a time, they finally learned that he was indeed in Rome. He had been granted leave to be in Rome for four months, yet he remained for an entire year. When, in addition to this, he brazenly requested that his income be forwarded to him, the elector demanded his immediate return. Carlstadt did not comply. The result was that the count notified him on February 23, 1516, that if he did not return to Wittenburg by St. John the Baptist Day, his office would be declared vacant and filled by another. That helped.

A more respectable figure in Luther's circle was Georg Burkhard, originally known as Belt Spalatin. He and Luther were students together at Erfurt, where he was included among those who admired classic antiquities. This group was known as the "Poets." He became Magister after his first year as a student and he began to study law. He later also studied theology. He was the recipient of special honor by the elector, who put his trust in him. Two nephews of the count, who were studying at Wittenberg, were placed under his personal supervision. Spalatin was later made court chaplain. He also served as mediator between Count Frederick and his friend, Martin Luther.

John Lange was another member of the circle of "Poets" as well as a friend of Luther. He was also drafted to Wittenberg in 1515, where he achieved top honors in theology and was assigned with Luther as a teacher in the monastery. Because of his knowledge of Greek, in which he had demonstrated his proficiency as a student, he became a valuable fellow worker with Luther, as well as a close friend. Luther felt deeply indebted and grateful to him.

The old Dr. Pollich, whom Luther had met on his return to Wittenberg, was not allowed to work with Luther much longer. He was called out of this world as early as 1513. With his departure Luther lost the last of his old professor friends at Wittenberg.

But what Pollich had predicted for the young scholar was now coming to pass. For as Dr. Luther began his theological lectures he based them not on the sentences, but on the books of the Bible. He began with Psalms, those wonderful hymns. On the one hand, those songs clearly expressed the teachings of sin unto damnation and the fear and misery of a broken heart. On the other hand, they rejoiced in the childlike trust of God's children and in the compassion of God. While there is no clear record of Luther's lectures to the students, we do possess a copy of the Book of Psalms in which Luther noted his personal comments. It is reasonable to assume that these comments give us a sense of what his lectures were like. Already in these remarks the central teaching of Scripture, justification by grace through faith, was set forth with clarity and certainty. For example, in commenting on Psalm 32:1, Luther wrote: "In Romans 4, the Apostle speaks against all those who want their sins to be forgiven by God on account of their own works and merits, and demand to be declared righteous through their own works. Hence, Christ would have died in vain, since they wanted to become holy without his death, by their own works. This is false."

Concerning Psalm 61:7 he wrote: "According to the explanation of Augustine, God's mercy means that God does not look on our merits, but on his grace and goodness. This is the reason why he removes punishment and gives eternal life. The truth is that he actually fulfills and imparts what he promised. Both are the effects of his grace, namely that faith justifies us. This is mercy. This is what he had promised. This is truth."

Regarding Psalm 51:9, Luther wrote: "For Christ leads to salvation directly, by the shortest and the straightest path, while the law takes a detour. But Christ is exalted and has drawn everyone to himself. He is the Mediator of all. A person who has him has everything in his perimeter."

Indeed, Luther's theology continued to flow, just as we met it already in his interpretation of various Psalms. It still leads us on the short pathway of faith to salvation, and Christ is at its center. To be sure, there remains a lengthy portion in which he comments, "That we, as is our custom, have been diligent in allegory (i.e. the use of picture language) and were counseled through them. This worked quite well for me when I was young." But even there he makes use of every opportunity to bring in Christ, since everything refers to him. This book of Psalms further illustrates how Luther was learning, especially from Paul's letter to the Romans. This understanding was then communicated to his listeners through his lectures on the Psalms. But beginning in 1515 Luther also began holding lectures on Romans itself. And then in 1516 he progressed to Paul's letter to the Galatians. As he dedicated himself to the study of the Greek language under the guidance of his friend Lange, it became increasingly easier for him to understand and apply these important New Testament writings.

A further examination of his lectures on the Book of Psalms reveals that Luther also made use of the writings of the church father, Augustine, in his exegetical presentations. He now began to use the old Lyra to interpret the Psalms, although he later commented that when he began to study theology he had no use for it, because the Lyra zealously adhered to the text and was hostile to allegory. But at this time, he preferred Lyra. In Augustine he discovered that the inabilities of natural man were strongly asserted, just as Paul had so powerfully emphasized. He came to comprehend sin and grace better as he learned to differentiate between law and gospel. He presented the law in all its sharpness and the gospel in all its sweetness. Because of this he could better comprehend how his own experiences were leading him in the right direction. He had previously suffered under the weight of the law with its threats and condemnation, as has already been noted repeatedly. But now he acknowledged his own incompetence as a natural man in regard to spiritual matters. At the same time, he also was experiencing the sweet comfort of the Gospel with its wonderful quickening power in his heart.

The skill with which Luther could write and speak about the righteousness of faith can be best shown in a letter which he wrote on April 7, 1516, to his dear friend and brother of the order, Georg Spenlein of Memmingen.

In this letter we read: "I, more than anything else, desire to know the condition of your soul. Is it finally sick of its own righteousness, and has it learned to be restored in the righteousness of Christ and to put its trust in him? For in our time many are viciously attacked in arrogant madness, especially by those who want to be righteous and devout by their own ability. They do not know the righteousness of God which is imparted to us in Christ, which is given abundantly and free of charge. They seek to achieve their own righteousness until that day when they would joyfully stand before God, adorned with their good works and achievements, although such a thing is impossible.

When you were with us, you also got caught up in this error, even to a greater extent. I, too, was a part of this and even now must battle against it, having not completely conquered it.

Therefore, my dear brother, learn the truth of Christ crucified. Learn to sing to Him and despair of yourself, saying, "You, Lord Jesus, are my righteousness, but I am your sin. You took to yourself what you were not and have given me what I had not." Watch yourself that you don't seek to attain such a holiness which will cause you in your own eyes to neither want to look like a sinner, nor actually be a sinner.

Know that Christ lives only in sinners. For this reason, he came down to earth from heaven so that he would also live with sinners. Ponder the depth of his love. In it you will find sweet comfort. For if we should have to achieve rest of conscience by way of our own work and struggling, then for what purpose would he have died? Thus, only in Him, after having been convinced of the folly of saving yourself by your works, will you find peace. What's more, you will learn from Him that as he Himself has carried you and taken your sins upon Himself, so he has made his righteousness your own. If you joyfully believe this (*as you must, for the one who does not believe is cursed*), then reach out to your brothers who are still imprisoned in their error and bear with them patiently. For if you are a rose or lily of Christ, understand that you are to live among thorns. Watch out, lest through impatience, overly hasty decisions, and secret pride, you become a thorn yourself.

"Christ's kingdom is in the midst of his enemies, as the Psalm tells us (For example see Psalm 110:2). But what did you think? Did you think that he should be in the midst of his friends? So, whatever you need, be sure to kneel before your Lord Jesus in prayer. He will teach you everything Himself. Just always bear in mind what he did for you and for everyone. In this way you will learn what you must do to others. If he would have had to live only among the good and have had to give his life for friends, for whom in the world would he have died? Or with whom on earth would he ever have been able to live? So, carry on with your labor, dear brother, and pray for me. The Lord be with you."

Through these words we see with what a tender inner spirit he expressed himself along with the clear and deeper understanding of Christ's salvation! May this characteristic of that doctor, who went through such a hard struggle, strike a chord in each of us. Yet we know that, at the same time as this letter was written, Luther became better acquainted and influenced by a teacher from the Middle Ages, who expressed himself with the same sort of warmth and intimacy. When he at the same time contemplated this teacher's deep, devout theology, Luther called the learning of his own era an "iron-like" or "pottery-like" knowledge. This teacher was the Dominican monk, Johannes Tauler. His sermons were studied and loved by Luther. Tauler had died in the garden house of his sister at Strassburg in 1361. It was in his sermons, even though they contained all kinds of bad papal counsel and odd speculations, where Luther found the teaching of salvation in Christ Jesus presented so beautifully and richly. Luther often maintained that Tauler's sermons "led him in the spirit."

Since he had such a special deep desire to be rid of the empty human identity of this world and to find true rest and peace with God, Luther found great comfort in these sermons. At the same time, he learned to treasure the individual union with Christ, in which the believer says, "You are mine and I am yours." It was this truth which began to take an ever firmer hold on him. Later in life he would encourage others more strongly, but at this time Luther simply recommended the sermons of Tauler to his friends, including Lange and especially Spalatin. "Taste and see," he wrote to Spalatin, "how friendly the Lord is," and vowed that he would get the book for himself.

Luther discovered another enjoyable 14th century work that sang the same tune as Tauler's sermons. He passed portions of it on for printing in 1516. Two years later he saw to it that the complete work was published under the title, "Ein Deutsch Theologia, das ist ein edles Buechlein vom rechten Verstand, was Adam und Christus sei, u.s.w." (Translated: "A German Theology, That Is a Noble Booklet of Proper Understanding, What Adam and Christ Are, etc.). This is the title that it has retained ever since. By using this title Luther was showing what had attracted him both to Tauler and this other anonymous and untitled booklet. He had discovered a theological work written in German, since at that time little was produced in German while the lion's share of theological writing was in Latin. He even spoke highly of Tauler in front of Spalatin, praising the flow of his German phrasing. Having been so pleased to be able to find the truth printed in his native tongue (literally, "In German dress"), which was so dear to his heart, Luther applied himself even more diligently to have the counsel of God proclaimed to his fellow Germans in their mother tongue.

Through persistent preaching he demonstrated his commitment at every opportunity. The papacy preaching had diminished to such an extent that in some areas of Christendom sermons were absent for almost a year. The sacrifice of the mass for the living and the dead had nearly crowded every other element out of the divine service. Even where some preaching could still be found, it was not based on the Word of Christ. "Preach the gospel," Luther later said. Speaking of this era he continued, "Previously a preacher was ashamed and timid; indeed, it was regarded as unfitting, womanish, and a disgrace to proclaim the name of Christ from the preacher's chair.

The Prophets and the Apostles were never considered, nor were their writings quoted. Instead the rules for preaching styles for all preachers were as follows: First, choose your theme, quotation, and question from Scotus, or Aristotle, the heathen master. Secondly, divide the same. Thirdly, follow with the Distinctions and the Questions ("Distinctions" in the sense of basic philosophical statement and "Questions" in the sense of exploring and debating by way of reason in regard to spiritual entities. The two terms are derived from the 13th century teacher, Thomas Aquinas, who seemed to have intermingled ancient Aristotelian philosophy with Bible related thoughts. Thomas Aquinas is a revered teacher in Roman Catholicism.) In the same sense, the men who were considered to be the best did not dwell on the gospel and did not treat a single passage of Scripture; indeed, Holy Scripture was covered up, unknown, and buried."

Thus, Luther could write to people in Erfurt, that in his student days he had not heard a true Christian lecture or sermon from anyone. Many priests were incapable of preaching a sermon, with the result that the people were spending their lives in the depth of ignorance. In Wittenberg, of course, there were a number of educated people holding church office. But the pastor of the church at that time, Simon Heins, had his preaching hindered due to illness. Since the city was going to assign him an assistant, pressure began to be put on Luther to accept the position. After all, he had already earned a reputation as a fine preacher because of the sermons he had preached in the monastery chapel. The end result was that as Mykonius said, "The child Jesus who had been in the barn until now was also brought into the temple."

Luther applied himself to this new assignment with amazing zeal. Whereas prior to this time the poor ignorant people had only heard the priest mumbling the Latin as he presided over the mass accompanied by the choral works in Latin, now Luther was committed to see to it that the people would hear messages that would instruct and edify them.

In a letter to his friend Lange Luther reported that among his labors he had to preach daily in the parish church. In fact, during Lent in 1517, he preached twice a day. It even happened that one day he preached three times. What's more, his sermons were not mere philosophical treatises or the retelling of the legends of the saints. Instead he preached "the wisdom of the cross so that the people could learn to despair of themselves and hope in Christ."

As he did this he did not follow the example of Zwingli, who as soon as he had become the preacher in Zurich, pushed aside the pericope texts. Luther stayed true to the Sunday and festival gospels and epistles, the same pericope we are still preaching today. In addition, he preached a series on the Ten Commandments through the summer, and during Lent of 1517 he preached a series on the Lord's Prayer from the pulpit. (*Getting ever stronger in faith*)

In examining all of these themes, one notices a regular focus on the daily needs of spiritual life among his listeners. His presentation on the Commandments focused on the many varieties of conditions and occurrences of human life, but he always returned to the central point that every human must recognize himself as a lost sinner, even that "all saints are sinners". Comfort could be found only in Christ and in his fulfillment of the law. Our hope could only be grounded on God's mercy. As he comments on the First Commandment, our works produce only more and more despair. "Christ," he continued, "lived for us and is our merit, as we believe in him. However, those who believe in him do not henceforth live for themselves, seeking to heap up their own merits, but serve Christ."

Next to such gold, silver, and precious gems of wholesome truth these sermons also contain all sorts of wood, hay, and straw. But as Luther steadily grew in knowledge he dropped one after another of the latter, which becomes apparent when we compare these sermons on the Ten Commandments with another presentation on the same subject, which he presented the following year.

At this time Luther was not only concentrating on preaching in order to educate and instruct people in Christian truth. He also busied himself with other special written lessons for his people. During the spring of 1517 he issued a short and simple explanation of the seven penitential psalms, dedicating the foreword to "all the members of Christ who read this booklet." "Seven Penitential Psalms with German Commentary" is the title of this publication, which Luther produced personally. Since the interpretation of each psalm was intimately connected with the text of the psalm, he always presented the text before the commentary. Thus, we have in this work a beginning of the Lutheran Bible Translation. Note how the 130th Psalm is worded as translated into German: (*The following is an attempted reproduction into English by the translator.*)

1. "Oh, I have cried to you from the depth, O God hear my crying.
2. Oh, that your ears would give attention to the crying of my praying.
3. If you will pay attention to sin, Oh, my God, Oh, God who can stand.
4. Then there is forgiveness only with you, therefore you also are to be feared.
5. I have waited for God and my soul has waited and I have built on his Word.

6. My soul is waiting toward God from the morning watch again to the morning watch.
7. Israel, he waits toward God, for the mercy is with God and manifold is redemption with him.
8. And he will redeem Israel from all his sins."

As we compare this translation of the psalm with the one produced by Luther's later efforts in the German Bible, we recognize a certain clumsiness of language in this beginning work. Yet already in this early work we find the same powerful yet simple writing which would later in Luther's translation be advanced to a more flowing speech. But even in this earlier work we find Christian doctrine streaming from our doctor's pen, as he interpreted the psalm in a clear and fresh way.

Yet we fail to find any direct attacks by Luther, as he would incorporate in later writings, against errors that had at that time been adopted and were being publicly implemented. Rather, like the Israelites of past ages proceeded, with trowel in one hand and a sword in the other, so here Luther seemed to proceed similarly, remaining calm in regard to gross public contradiction. He, who would not be aware of subsequent history, would surely not conclude from this peaceful booklet that there was an anti-Christian pope and an indulgence scandal.

Nevertheless, Squire Tetzel was already in Saxony with his trunk, and Luther's dear superior, Staupitz, had already made several journeys to purchase more holy relics so as to gain from them more indulgence blessings for both his electorate's collection and the Wittenberg church foundation.

During Staupitz's journey and also after he returned, we find Luther actively tending to his duties. He was serving as district vicar of Meissen and Thueringia. The 1515 convention in Gotha had appointed him to this position. In addition to seeing to extensive and time-consuming correspondence, he personally visited the eleven monasteries which had been entrusted to him. He did so in a paternal way, assisting individual brothers in the order, practicing serious and loving discipline wherever necessary, and coming to the aid of the priors and their underlings with advice, admonition, and comfort. We find him in Grimma, then in Erfurt (where he installed his former prior, Lange, in his former monastery), in Gotha, in Langensalza, in Nordhausen, in Magdeburg, in his birth city of Eisleben, and again in Dresden, where he preached in the castle church. At that time, he wrote to his friend Lange, "I am monastery preacher, preacher at the table, am required to preach daily in the parish church, am guide for the monastic studies, am vicar (the equivalent of eleven priors), am curator of the Litzkauer fishpond, and am manager of the Herzbergers estate in Torgau. I present lecture readings about Paul in addition to the Psalms. I do all this, including my written correspondence, which as I have told you, consumes most of my time. Rarely do I find enough time to observe the horen (the hourly prescribed time of prayers for the monks). Add to these: I am personally tempted by the world, the flesh, and the devil. Ah, what a man of leisure.

During all of this activity Luther's influence kept growing. This influence extended through his teaching, as more and more students were crowding into his classroom. The same was taking place from the pulpit, where his sermons were being preached in growing numbers. And finally, there was his influence as a vicar, in which he was involved in the development of many valuable and multi-faceted activities outside of the walls of Wittenberg. This was how Carlstad found Luther right after he returned from Rome, and whom he soon engaged in controversy. This happened as follows.

That Luther issued sharp condemnation of sin from his pulpit, but also contrasted it with his proclamation, that forgiveness of sins and salvation depend on faith in Christ, not on one's own works, soon aroused opposition. The fact that as a theologian he had begun to base theology on Holy Scripture and that he sourced his lectures from the books of the Bible, in contrast to the traditionally accepted way of teaching, could be seen as conspicuously new. Indeed, the Roman Church recognized the Bible as the Word of God and Augustine, to whom Luther often referred, was admired as a true believer and teacher of the church. However, the scholastic teachers of the middle ages were also accepted as valid instructors in Roman Catholic theology and were regarded as standard models. The fact that Luther would set these aside and mark certain of their teachings as false could already be regarded as a deviation from sound and healthy doctrine. It also seemed that suspicions began to be voiced in regard to Luther's lectures.

One example of this type of suspicion came about when Luther's student, Bartholomaeus Bernhardi from Feldkirch, presented theses for a disputation over which he wished Luther to preside. In these theses he denied all spiritual power by the natural man. It was assumed from the beginning that he had prepared these theses under Luther's influence. While writing this disputation, the writing, "Concerning True and False Repentance" was used as reference. Even though this teaching had been ascribed to Augustine, nevertheless, it had been used as the main source for the errors of the Middle Ages. Luther boldly declared subsequent arguments deduced from this writing as false. With this declaration Luther, as he himself admitted, delivered a massive blow to everyone's thinking. This especially applied to Carlstadt, who was now Luther's firm opponent.

But Carlstadt would soon learn who had the upper hand. It was difficult among the Wittenberg students to find some who still wanted to listen to the ideas of the higher schools of learning that had previously held sway. Carlstadt had to apply himself to the study of Scripture and Augustine. As early as the next spring Luther rejoiced in the fact that on Misericordias Domini

Sunday (*2nd after Easter*), the festival of relics for the castle church, Carlstadt posted 152 theses for the customary disputation scheduled for that day. In regard to those theses Luther cheerfully commented, "These are no longer statements from Cicero, but those of our Carlstadt, indeed, even of the holy Augustine. ... Praise be to God who once again is letting light shine forth out of darkness." It is important to note the magnanimity in Luther's support for Carlstadt! While he rejoiced greatly in the work of his former opponent, he was well aware of his shortcomings.

Yet Carlstadt was now presenting his theses to the Elector with the intent of honoring him. If the count chose to respond by paying the 30 guilders for printing costs, Carlstadt would then issue these theses, dedicating them to the count and bringing honor to the university.

Luther rejoiced, as did the apostle Paul, in the fact that Christ was being proclaimed, even though some might have been motivated by jealousy. His joy was evident in his correspondence with Lange about the whole episode. He noted that the true theology of God's grace was gaining ground at the university, ever more squeezing out Aristotle and the scholastics. He continued to work vigorously in building up biblical theology and tearing down the papal theology handed down through the years. He allowed his student, Franz Guenther of Nordhausen, who became baccalaureate during the summer of 1517, to dispute regarding the natural inabilities of man.

Among the sentences of this dispute he defended the following: "It is true that man, after he had become a rotten tree, could desire or do nothing but evil." — "It is not true that free will can decide in both directions; moreover, it is not a free but a captured will." — "On man's part you can find nothing save inability. In fact, rebellion against grace is placed above grace." — "We are not masters of our actions, but slaves from beginning to end." — "We will not be justified by doing good works, but when we have been justified we do righteous works." — "It is not true to say that without Aristotle one cannot become a theologian." — "In fact, no one will become a theologian, who will not become one without Aristotle." As these assertions were being made Luther was unaware of any conflict with the teachings of the Roman Church, though he did recognize a deviation from the scholastics. Because of that recognition he was anxious to discover how Erfurt would react to these statements, since the scholastics still held sway there. He was willing to debate in Erfurt what he maintained in Wittenberg.

Yes, the fact that Luther had the role of spiritual leadership in a very short time was demonstrated by his blossoming influence in his university, where people from as far away as Sweden came to sit at his feet. Yet he still remained the tempered, humble, monastic brother he had been before. When in 1516 the plagues visited Wittenberg and caused much devastation, he replied to Lange's advice to leave the city: "This world, I hope, will not collapse when brother Martin falls."

Chapter 9
The 95 Theses

In May, 1518, Luther revised the 95 "Theses" and also renamed them "Resolutions". (See p. 72)

During the middle ages the Catholic Church administered indulgences. Indulgences were declarations of the remission of punishment for sins, or for the penance imposed by church authorities. As early as the 2nd century, during the time of Irenaeus, we read about strong penalties imposed on members of Christian congregations who had committed some serious offense. The intent was not for the people to have a better standing before God. Rather, it was intended to make the congregation better able to recognize true contrition and to warn others against committing similar sins. The time frame for carrying out such penance was often an extended one, but for the sinner who showed sincere penitence that time was shortened.

During the earlier days of persecution these penalties were imposed on those who denied the faith. So, if others interceded for the offender, testifying about the sincerity of that person's faith, the time of the penalty was reduced. The first general council of the church, held at Nicea, declared that when the penitent displayed numerous and clear proofs of his repentance, his bishop was allowed to reduce his sentence.

As centuries passed and the church was falling prey to more and more vices and apparent sins, the list of types of penance kept growing longer. Sins were divided into categories and types. This required lists of penitential regulations, which assisted the priests in determining sins and assigning works of contrition more consistently. These also made it possible for the sinner on whom a penalty had been imposed to exchange his particular penance for a different one. For example, if his penance was fasting, taking no food or water for a day, he could instead pray fifty psalms while kneeling in church. But there was an exchange that was of particular benefit for the wealthy. This also fed the greed of the priests as it allowed for considerable sums of money to be paid in view of the prescribed penance. Still, the right to arbitrarily assign monetary indulgence did not belong to a common priest or bishop. This authority belonged solely to the pope. These papal indulgences led to the complete destruction of all church discipline.

This self-assigned right of the popes was most widely exercised during the crusades. A full and complete indulgence was granted to all those who took part in those wars. In 1300, Pope Boniface VIII, expanded the use of indulgences even further when he issued the first great year of Jubilee indulgence. He ascribed not only complete, but most complete, indulgence to anyone who would visit the churches of the apostles Peter and Paul in Rome. If the person was a Roman, his time in the churches was to be thirty days; if an outsider, fifteen.

The success of this indulgence exceeded the pope's wildest expectations. The hundreds of thousands of pilgrims brought immeasurable wealth to the papal coffers. It is no surprise that succeeding popes found the one hundred year wait for the next Jubilee, as dictated by Boniface, was too long a period of time. Thus, the time span was reduced, first to 50 years, then to 33, and finally to 25 years. When the second Jubilee was held in 1350 under Clement VI, not only had the number of pilgrims greatly increased, but the money that was brought into Rome greatly surpassed the first collection. By the time the third Jubilee was held, Pope Boniface IX made another decision. He sent his ambassadors into the different countries. These agents had his full authority to offer the same full indulgence for the amount it would have cost the prospective pilgrim to travel to Rome. By using this method his success far surpassed that of his predecessors. In 1500, the disgraceful Alexander VI took the sale of indulgences one step further. He extended the benefit of indulgences to those in purgatory, so the benefits of the Jubilee offering could be applied to friends and relatives.

With this last distribution of indulgences, the century of the great councils came to an end. That meant that another Jubilee year could not be celebrated for some time. However, indulgences could still be sold. In fact, this type of sale occurred a number of times under Julius II. These sales took place by the pope's sending his agents into countries at large, where the indulgences would then be peddled. These agents had the full authority of a year of Jubilee. In Germany, there was one such agent who amassed large sums of money with the help of his aide, John Tetzel. This Dominican monk had been sentenced to drowning for the crime of adultery. A letter of indulgence exists from that time which granted complete indulgence not only to the two spouses who had forgiven him, but also to their parents and beloved benefactors who had already departed this world. They were to receive eternal benefits from all prayers, intercessions, alms, fasting, pilgrimages, and the like, which had taken place in the church militant. It was claimed that the money received from all indulgence sales would be used to build St. Peter's church in Rome.

At that time the papal throne was held by Leo X, who was from the famous House of Medici. This well-educated man, a patron of the arts, was considered no better than a heathen, due to the infamous reputation of his house. The cardinals to whom he owed his election were thoroughly disappointed in that house. He was not elected because the cardinals considered him more devout than he showed himself to be. No, their hope was that papal power would be reduced. Instead, this pope aimed to increase his power. It so happened that one of the most distinguished of the cardinals per-

Picture of Pope Leo X by Raphael

sonally approached this pope to assassinate him with a dagger concealed under his robe. After reconsideration, he decided to eliminate the pope by using poison. However, in the meantime the assassination plot was discovered. The reaction that followed was that Leo destroyed his enemies and by appointing 31 cardinals immediately secured the majority needed to be elected. Very quickly he received large sums of money by dispensing special favors. After all, the excellencies were expected to produce the clinking of many coins to show their appreciation for such favors.

But Leo also spent immeasurable sums of money. Not only did he have to pay back large sums to his relatives, but his political maneuvering devoured thousands of coins as well. As a result, he constantly had to find new sources of wealth. Indulgences were to prove themselves as one of those sources, with the ongoing building of St. Peter's church in Rome providing the excuse for a new distribution. Thus, three commissioners were entrusted with the management of this latest indulgence sale. One of these was the Archbishop Albrecht of Mainz and Magdeburg. He was selected by the monasteries within his territory, because of a promise he had made regarding the money to be paid to the pope for the pallium, the archbishop's white collar, blessed by the pope and adorned with crosses. He promised not to take the funds from the arch-episcopal foundation, but to raise the money himself. Accordingly, he borrowed 30,000 gold guilders from the rich House of Fugger in Augsburg. In order to pay this pressing debt and to be able to satisfy some other expenses, he now assumed the reins that allowed him to raise half of his payment from the sale of indulgences in his expanded territory. Soon the agents of these lords were traveling from city to city. These peddlers went from door to door, offering the sale of indulgences with lots of

Picture of John Tetzel,
Dominican Monk and Seller of Papal Indulgence

ceremony.

Among the door to door sellers was the very ardent and brazen John Tetzel, mentioned earlier. He had been hired by the Elector of Mainz. This salesman knew how to exploit both the superstitions and the carnal desires of the people. He knew how to camouflage his foul dealings with gaudy splendor. Before entering a city, he had someone announce his arrival. Soon the phrase could be heard, "He's coming!" The corpulent monk and his entourage were then met by a festive procession of priests, monks, teachers, students, town council representatives, men, and women. They would be waving banners, sounding trumpets, and carrying burning torches.

This whole train of humanity would then enter the city accompanied by the ringing of bells and shouts of joy. At the sound of the organ they would enter the church where the indulgence salesman took center stage, erecting his red cross surrounded by papal banners. In other churches the salesmen priests were required to proclaim the glories of indulgences according to prescribed instructions.

Tetzel understood better than any other how to glorify his wares. His natural glib tongue honed by years of experience, served him well. But there was also no one who would speak about indulgences with as much insolence and blasphemy. He called indulgences the highest and most glorious gift of God. He declared that the papal cross he erected offered just as much as the cross of Christ. He asserted that he had no desire to change places with St.

Peter in heaven, because, after all, he saved more souls than Peter. He claimed that the pope had higher authority than all the Apostles, angels, and saints. These all were under Christ; but the pope was equal to Christ. Since his ascension into heaven until the Day of Judgment Christ need not rule any more in the church. He has transferred his lordship to the pope as his steward.

So the rush to get to Tetzel's indulgence market was intense. The rich and the poor, the noble and the ignoble, even those who had to beg money for themselves, all bought indulgences. First, they bought for themselves and their relatives, but especially for those who had died and were believed to be in purgatory. And this purgatory was a place of torture as described with lurid terms by Tetzel and his aides. For a special price you could buy an indulgence not only for sins committed, but for intended future sins. It didn't bother him that from time to time someone would cheat him. He more than made up for it with the money he put aside for himself, giving him a gloriously joyful life. It is certain he would have set aside even more for himself if an agent from the House of Fugger had not kept a sharp watch on his trunks and bowls.

The financial harm which this salesman did to those people was serious. These poor souls had been visited by the failure of their harvests and the terror of the plague. Yet this harm was minimal compared to the harm done to their souls. After all, consider what they were promised in buying indulgences. First, anyone who would confess his sins with a contrite heart and buy an indulgence was assured of the grace of God and freedom from purgatory. Then, for an additional payment, a person could also obtain the following three extras:

1. Instead of going to his own father confessor he could choose a different confessor more to his liking. He could choose one who could absolve sins not yet forgiven and who could exchange difficult penances for easier ones.
2. He would receive a share from all prayers, fasting, pilgrimages, and other good works from the entire church militant.
3. He could accomplish the instantaneous release of those dead souls in purgatory.

These three extras were even accessible without prior contrition and penance and were to be granted as soon as the required payment had been received. In regard to the last extra gift of the indulgence (number 3) Tetzel had composed a little rhyme:

As soon as the money falls into the chest,
The soul jumps into its heavenly rest.

About Indulgence from Rome A person can become holy,
by way of reference to the divine Holy Scripture

On Aplas von Rom
kan man wolselig werden
durch anzaigung der göttlichen
hailigen geschryfft.

Illustration of an Indulgence Market Title page from a pamphlet
during the time of the beginning of the Reformation

(The above is the translator's attempt to phrase the original rhyme into a rhyme with the same basic meaning as was implied in the German rhyme):

**"Sobald das Geld im Kasten klingt,
Die Seele in den Himmel springt."**

Word was brought to Luther about the devastating effects these false teachings imposed on the consciences of the people. He was also informed of Tetzel's blasphemous teaching. So was our Wittenberg doctor forced upon the path which would take this story far beyond its first need for being corrected.

The first report of Tetzel's presence in Saxony reached Luther in the spring of 1516, as he, together with Staupitz and Link, was overseeing the Augustinian monastery at Grimma. When he would again be made aware of Tetzel's continued peddling of indulgences in the area around Wittenberg, he could not help but sound a warning to his parish children from his pulpit. In these sermons, one as early as 1516, and others in the spring of 1517, it is plainly evident that Luther feared the damage enacted on the spiritual condition of his flock through the influence of indulgences. In a sermon preached on the tenth Sunday after Trinity, in 1516, he still acknowledged the right and power of the pope to grant pardon for certain transgressions, for present time, and in purgatory, by way of intercession which had been applied. However, he lamented the fact that the indulgence preachers did not instruct the people properly and left them with the delusion that they are saved if they have an indulgence document. Therefore, he warned his listeners not to be led away from Christ and his cross by indulgences, and not to be led into carnal security and laziness.

We hear the same laments and admonitions in his sermon for the festival of St. Matthew in 1517 (Sept. 21st). As a result of one sermon on this subject preached in the castle church, he had fallen into disfavor with the count. As he later recounted, this was because there was a direct connection between the treasury of relics in that church and the treasury of indulgences gained for the church foundation through those relics.

But Tetzel was also informed about what was being said about indulgences in Wittenberg. We learn that in his anger he boldly denounced those who were demeaning indulgences. As a master over heresy he kindled a fire to illustrate the danger that came from attacking the pope's indulgence.

Meanwhile the fallout from Tetzel's misconduct became more apparent. In large numbers, people would travel to Jueterbock, Zerbst, and wherever else indulgences were available. They came back with their indulgences, full of praise for the high value Tetzel had assigned to them. Luther listened to the reports of this brazen monk's conduct with terror and shock. Luther watched with deep sorrow to what was happening to his parish children.

They were being deluded regarding the confession of sins! Many demonstrated a newfound frivolity. Others were even rebellious and insolent when the seriousness of their sins was pointed out. When they showed no contrition, their doctor refused to absolve them. They stubbornly pointed to their indulgence document, and even returned to Tetzel with their complaints.

Why should they struggle to improve their sinful lives as Luther admonished them? Why should they accept penance? They had made their purchase from the immeasurable treasury of the merits of the saints! If Luther did not want to absolve them, fine. They had bought the right to seek out a different father confessor, one who would not be so strict and would show more respect for the indulgences.

Where would all of this end? If this went on, wouldn't all church discipline become void? Wouldn't the people get to the point of wickedly and insolently despising God's holy law and the precious blood of Christ? There were others who had similar experiences and were harboring similar concerns. Luther had heard from others about the sale of indulgences, both in writing and face to face.

All Saints Day was coming, as was the date for the dedication of the castle church in Wittenberg. Many guests would stream into the city for the festivities and these guests would have the opportunity to buy indulgences. Luther may well have wrestled as to the best way to respond to this situation. He could not remain silent. That would have brought him just criticism. Even if he had wanted to remain silent, he would have been unable to avoid the opinions expressed at such an event attended by many other theologians. And so he decided to proceed as follows.

Since the church foundation was also closely connected to the university, academic activities were going to play a role in the festivities. The announcements of such academic activities were publicized by being posted on the church doors. This was where Carlstadt had posted his previously mentioned theses earlier in April. And so this is how Luther chose to inform the presiding leader of the church and university, Bishop Hieronymus Scultetus of Brandenburg, about his concerns in connection with the abuse of indulgences, and what he intended to do about it.

In the meantime, he had discovered that Archbishop Albrecht of Mainz was involved and that the instructions for selling indulgences were being issued in the archbishop's name. So Luther also wrote a letter to him. He pleaded with all humility and expressed his respect for the archbishop. But it was his expressed firm and decisive request that the archbishop would remove this offense, which endangered so many by damaging their souls. "What danger and fear must a bishop expect," he wrote, "who pompously allows indulgences and nothing else to be spread among the people.

Meanwhile the gospel is omitted and left silent. This bishop is much more concerned with indulgences than with the gospel. Will not Christ address you as the one, who filters out mosquitoes and swallow's camels? In addition, most honorable father under God, it is said the instructions have been issued under knowledge and intent of your highness.

"Those indulgences offer to bestow incredible grace by which man is said to be reconciled with God, and the fires of purgatory extinguished; even more, contrition is not required for those who buy indulgences. But what can I do, most highly Honored Bishop and most Highly Serene Elector, except to plead before you, highly Honored Archbishop that your Electoral Grace would keep an eye of fatherly care on this issue and completely do away with these instructions. May you also command the indulgence preachers, to proclaim indulgences in some other way, lest some person arises, who will refute both the indulgence preachers, and those instructions to the highest disgrace of your Most Highly Serene Highness."

In his letter Luther included a number of his theses with the added comment, "If it please you, highly honored father, examine these theses of mine concerning this dispute so that you might understand that the illusion these indulgences provide is a very uncertain promise, though they dream that the promise is a very sure thing."

Luther completed his letter to the archbishop containing the theses on October 31st. That afternoon, since it was the eve of All Saints Day, the dedication festival of the castle church began. Luther was to preach for the opening service. Before the divine service he posted the articles of dispute, or theses, 95 in all, on the door of the castle church. They were intended for learned debate and issued in Latin. The heading and announcement were also in Latin, rendered here in English:

"DISPUTATION OF THE THEOLOGIAN, DOCTOR MARTIN LUTHER, FOR EXPLANATION OF THE POWER OF INDULGENCES"

"To bring the truth to light out of love and diligence, debate will be held concerning the following statements under the presiding of the honored Father Martin Luther, by the free abilities, by the masters of holy theology, and by the regular instructors thereof. Those who are unable to speak with us in person due to their absence may do so in written form.

In the name of our Lord Jesus Christ. Amen."

We shall now consider some of these Theses *(footnote: A translation of the 95 Theses [into German], "Luther's Volksbibliotek," Vol. 17. 18 p. 247 ff. Vgl. Foreword p. 3)

The first was worded:

"Our Lord and Master Jesus Christ, in saying, "Repent" etc. wants the whole life of the believer to be repentance."

This first sentence already has tremendous significance. Positioned at the beginning, and thereby at the top of the entire document, is the name of him, in whom alone salvation is to be found for poor sinners. This is not the statement of a famous church father, but a word from the mouth of Christ. This is the word with which the Prophet who came from the right hand of the Father, also began his preaching. This has been laid down as the fundamental statement for the entire debate. At the same time this beginning statement sets forth the practical issue of the day which Luther was addressing with these Theses. The faith and the living by faith of every Christian were threatened by the entire use of indulgences, and were now to be protected. So was Luther entering the fray on behalf of Christ, the Word, and the believers.

In the following theses there is no doubt that Luther recognized the right of the pope to distribute indulgences. But he limited that right to church penance, which the pope himself would impose.

Thus the **5th thesis** states:

"The pope shall and can remit no punishments except those which he himself has imposed according to his own or the church's command."

Still, Luther wants such punishments to be applied knowingly only to the living. He makes this clear in the 8th, 9th, and 10th theses.

The **11th Thesis** reads:

"The weed seed that church punishment can be exchanged for pain in purgatory surely must have been sown while the bishops were sleeping."

In this way, without confronting purgatory itself, Luther confronted the corrupt practice which taught that any life of repentance could be postponed to purgatory, and even then, be completely removed from the dead through indulgences; customary indifference was supplied with every possible excuse. After explaining in the **20th** thesis that the pope understands that by rendering a complete indulgence for all punishments does not mean all, but only those which he himself imposed, Luther attacked the indulgence seller directly in the **21st Thesis** as he wrote,

"Hence, the indulgence commissioners, who state that a person is set free, separated from all sins, and saved through the pope's indulgence, are in error."

Thesis 27 also made the same point. It reads,
"Those who say that as soon as the money rings in the chest, the soul jumps out of purgatory, are preaching teachings of men."

Thesis 32
"Those who believe themselves to be sure of their salvation through indulgence documents will be eternally damned together with their masters."

But Luther attacked not only the promises of the sellers of indulgences. He also dared to attack the declarations of the before mentioned directions by the Archbishop of Mainz, as he wrote in

Thesis 33
"A person should diligently watch out for those who say that the pope's indulgence is the priceless gift of God through which man is reconciled with God."

Thesis 35
"Those who teach such, who want to buy souls and indulgence documents, are not proclaiming Christian teaching."

In the next two theses, he in contrast states that every true, upright, and penitent Christian has full forgiveness and shares all the blessings of Christ and the church, without an indulgence document. Then he returns to the issue of manner and style used by those selling indulgences for money. He attacks the ceaseless praising of the indulgences and the debasing of the works of compassionate love when compared with the sale of indulgences. So he stated:

Thesis 39
"It is a very difficult thing, even for well-trained theologians, to exalt the riches of pardon and the true substance of contrition for the people while this is going on."

Thesis 41
"The apostolic absolution should be preached carefully, lest the people understand it, as though the same (namely, purchase of indulgence) is preferred over other good works of love."

Thesis 42
"The Christians are to be taught that it is not the pope's intent for the purchase of an indulgence to be considered identical with works of compassion."

Thesis 43
"Christians should be taught that he who gives to the poor and lends to the needy is doing a better deed than buying an indulgence."

Thesis 45
"Christians are to be taught that someone who sees a starving person, and instead of helping him buys an indulgence, does not bring the pope's absolution but God's disgrace upon himself."

Thesis 47
"Christians are to be taught that while they are free to buy indulgences, they are not commanded to do so."

We have heard earlier of the pomp and ceremony with which people would approach the indulgence sellers, as well as how the sellers performed in the churches. Luther also took a stand against these practices. He wrote,

Thesis 53
"Enemies of Christ and of the pope are those people who permit God's Word to be completely silenced in churches by the preaching of indulgences."

Thesis 54
"Wrong is done to the Word of God when a sermon contains as much or even more teaching about indulgences than God's Word."

Thesis 55
"Only this can be the intent of the pope that the indulgence, which is the least, is celebrated with a single bell and simple ceremonial procession; but the gospel, which is the highest, is proclaimed with a hundred bells and hundredfold procession and ceremony."

Since it had been declared that the pope had the right to distribute indulgences from the assumed treasury of the merits of Christ and the saints, Luther opposed this, too. After he contradicted this concept in reference to the merits of Christ and the saints in thesis 58, he went on in,

Thesis 62
"The true treasure of the church is the most holy gospel of the glory and the grace of God."

Thesis 63
"This treasure is logically the most hated, because it makes the last the first."

Thesis 64
"The indulgence treasure, on the other hand, is logically the most pleasing, because it makes the first out of the last."

Indeed, with disdain he went on to state in the next thesis how in days gone by rich people were being fished for with the net of the gospel; now the indulgence treasure is the net with which the wealth of people is being fished, and in this context the indulgence grace is huge.

He admonished the bishops and parish lords in the next theses to accept the sellers of indulgences honorably, but to pay attention that they are proclaiming what the pope has declared and not their own dreams. But notice how far removed Luther remained from personally attacking the indulgences themselves. The fact that he only wanted to debate the misuse of indulgences is apparent from the next two statements.

Thesis 71
"May he, who speaks against the truth of the apostolic indulgence, be accursed and condemned."

Thesis 72
"But he who is concerned about the careless and frivolous words of the indulgence preachers is blessed."

Thus, he believed that he was speaking in complete harmony with the pope, as the next two theses show.

Thesis 73
"As the pope hurls his ban rightfully against those who scheme to do damage to the use of indulgences,"

Thesis 74
"So does the pope even more intend to hurl his ban against those who aim to use indulgences to disguise their fraudulent activity against holy love and truth."

Here it is apparent that Luther, as he would later admit, had not yet grasped a true understanding of indulgences or the pope. As he had done earlier, he continued to intercede for the pope in his theses. After he had denounced a number of the reckless claims of the indulgence peddlers, he charged bishops, pastors, and theologians that they would be held accountable for allowing such preaching among the people. He lamented indulgence preachers had made it difficult for even a learned teacher to defend the pope against pointed questions posed by the common man. Still his confidence in the pope shows itself again in the 91st thesis.

Thesis 91
"If indulgences would be preached according to the pope's understanding and intent, then all the questions about them could be easily resolved, indeed, they would not even exist."

Picture of the Castle Church of Wittenberg from the year 1509

In the last two theses he finally returned to the thought from which he had parted, and said,

Thesis 94
"Christians are to be admonished to occupy themselves in following Christ, their Head, through pain, death, and hell."

Thesis 95
"And so they should comfort themselves that they enter into heaven through many hardships, not through peaceful security."

Here he points us again to Christ, the Head, the salvation for all souls of Christians, and a Bible passage (Acts 14:22 NIV) as a foundation. This work expresses the same spirit at its conclusion as it did at its beginning.

The 95 Theses are a remarkable work in a number of ways. Luther was aiming his blows at a target that was remarkably narrow in range. He didn't want to challenge the pope, the teaching of purgatory, or indulgences themselves. On the contrary, we have seen how he purposely placed the pope and his indulgences under his protection while treating the indulgence sellers as enemies of both. Still, the writing and the publishing of these statements were truly an act of reform. It was a decidedly different attack launched by the Parisians and big councils of the previous century. What they had failed to do, Luther did. He let Christ be the Alpha and the Omega, the beginning and the end.

Once this happened the pope would inevitably be revealed as the antichrist, even though Luther did not recognize him as such at the time. He applied the Word of God as the yardstick. As this was being done, the papacy would eventually have to be revealed as a dungeon, which the prince of darkness had built, to rob Christians of the freedom, with which Christ had set them free. With these theses God had begun the work of exposing the evil one and whom he will finally destroy with the breath of his mouth (*II Thessalonians 2:8 NIV*). Therefore, we rightly celebrate October 31 as the anniversary of the Reformation.

There is a story that the Elector Frederick the Wise had a wonderful dream the night before the posting of the 95 Theses. It appeared to him as though he saw a monk, a son of the Apostle Paul, writing large letters on the door of the castle church in Wittenberg. The letters were so large that they could be read from the Electorals main residence in Schweinitz. He was writing with a rattling large quill which reached all the way to Rome. In Rome it went into the ear in the head of a lion and came out again through the other ear. It then stretched out even farther and struck the threefold crown of the pope with such force that it was tottering and the count struggled to hold on to it. All of the people in Rome and throughout the empire came running. They attempted to break the feather in two and rescue the pope. But it was in vain. They had to let the monk write on.

In regard to the accuracy of this story, we shall let it stand on its own. At the same time, it is true that every detail of this dream is reflected in the history of the 95 Theses and their consequences. Soon the lion in Rome began to roar. From all directions people rushed to his side to break the feather of the student of St. Paul, the feather which would quickly cause the papal crown to shake and totter. It wasn't difficult for the entire army gorging itself on the indulgence monetary trough to understand what could happen. If the fundamental truths set forth in the Theses were to gain ground, especially those which directed the people toward repentance and faith, the paper on which papal indulgence was written would become worthless. The result would be that the river of gold flowing into the sacks and chests of the prelates and popes would run dry. If Luther had attacked Christ and the gospel, Rome and Mainz would have forgiven him. But what he had done with the theses was a sin, a sin for which there would be no indulgence.

Chapter 10
Consequences of the 95 Theses

As claps of thunder and bolts of lightning alert us to the coming of life-giving rain, so did the powerful theses of the Wittenberg Monk echo throughout Europe. It continued until the first rumblings of the storm brewing in Germany were heard on the other side of the Alps in sunny Italy and Rome. The time was just right for the publication of Luther's 95 Theses and for their availability to the masses. It appears most likely that they were immediately copied from the manuscript posted on the church door. These copies were personally taken along by visitors in Wittenberg, as they were returning home. What happened was not what Luther had intended. Those theses, which had been meant for a small group of scholars, were soon distributed throughout the land. Now they were being read not only by scholars, but by the common people as well, after they had been translated into German. As borne by the wind or angels, they spread through all of Germany in two weeks, and they caused a sensation everywhere they went.

Luther himself, as well as his colleagues, reported on how these theses were received. "Many devout men spoke out publicly," a foreword of a later edition of the theses reported, "how pleased they were with the theses and how highly they were valued." His student Methusius related, "Devout monks, seeking their holiness in their monasteries and continuing to struggle with the suspicious nature of the Costnitz affair, received the theses with joy. This was the testimony of the devout Dr. Fleck, who had preached the dedication sermon for the University of Wittenberg, and had foretold that the entire world would gain wisdom from this white mount (the meaning of Wittenberg). "I tell you about a certain monk, who never held a mass in his entire life. He found the theses posted in his rectory at Steinlausig. As he began to read it he cried out with joy: 'Ho! Ho! He is coming, the one for whom we have waited for such a long time!'" Luther referred to that man's reaction later in a letter, "I like Fleck, for he was a comforting man. His words were very soothing. He wrote a wonderful letter to me right after I had issued my theses. I would pay ten guilders for that letter, if I could still recover it."

Others felt less induced to write letters of encouragement to Luther. It may have been that they considered what Luther was trying to do was hopeless. "You are speaking the truth, good brother, but you will accomplish nothing. Go back to your cell and pray for the Lord's mercy." This was the reaction of old Dr. Albert Krantz of Hamburg, when he read the theses shortly before his death. At Hexter in Westphalia, another had this to say, "My dear brother Martin, if you are able to address purgatory and the selling of indulgences and do away with them you are truly a great lord." (In the original this comment is recorded in Low German: "Min leewe Broder Marten, wenn du dat Fegefueer un de Papenmerketenderei stoermen un weg schludern kannst, bist du vorwahr en groter Herr.")

In Wittenberg Carlstadt once again disagreed with Luther. For him Luther had gone too far. The brothers of his order already envisioned the triumph of their enemies, the Dominicans. Now an Augustinian would have to burn, as Savonarola and others of their order had been burned. Luther's friend, Dr. Schurf, held the same opinion. "What are you doing? It will not be tolerated!" To which, of course, Luther responded, "What does it matter if one has to suffer?"

Luther, however, was not as confident at the time as it might appear from his response. He had been looking for a debate, but there was no one volunteering for such a debate as he proposed. What was developing before his eyes was something he had not been looking for. His theses were being spread not as an invitation to debate, but as an expression of his convictions. While they were generally accepted with approval, a public defense in support of them was not to be found. As had been the case with his monastic lectures on Scripture and again at his university lectures on the books of the Bible, he stood alone in his attacks on the misuse of indulgences. He refers to himself in uncertain terms as a frail, emaciated, monk, "more like a corpse than a man." But the die had been cast and his opposition would soon step up its counter attack against the theses. The ball was rolling.

It was expected that Tetzel, whose actions were the main target of these theses, would be the first to respond when he got back to his business. It made perfect sense. He had been attacked while serving under the authority of the Archbishop of Mainz, and so turned to him for support. But Albrecht seems to have been of the opinion: you cooked the stew; now you have to eat it. Although he was certainly not pleased with Luther's assertions, he was content "to let that complainer's chestnuts burn," because he himself did not want to get involved. As a result Tetzel was forced to take matters into his own hands. With the help of his old friend, Prof. Wimpina of Frankfurt, he posted two columns of theses which had been debated at Frankfurt on the Main (River), as a part of his attempt to receive the degree and title of doctor. In these theses he fearlessly defended the total authority and inerrancy of the pope in matters of faith, even in those cases where the pope's doctrinal decisions could not be supported by Scripture. Luther had no respect for these theses. What they presented was nothing new, and coming from Tetzel and his friends, they caused him little concern.

On the other hand, the heading of a document he received at the beginning of 1518 caused a completely different reaction. When he read it, Luther was startled. He had sincerely believed that the pope would declare himself in agreement with his theses. But this document was issued by one of the foremost of the pope's court officials. This was Silvester Mazolini of Prierio, the Roman censor of books, and the judge of matters of faith and doctrine. He attacked Luther in his response to the 95 Theses. His answer was dedicated to the pope. His reply was a proud, harsh repudiation of Luther's declaration of the papal understanding of indulgences. This document referred to several basic principles which had been unacceptable to Luther for quite some time already. This was in response to Luther's 91st thesis, "If that were the understanding of the pope, as you imply in your writing, then it would be a badly informed opinion and a meaning far from a true understanding of the pope." In the principles, with which he prefaced his individual responses, Silvester maintained the following. He stated that whoever does not accept that the pope is inerrant in matters of doctrine and the rule of faith, from which even Holy Scripture receives its authority and power, is a heretic.

What was Luther to do? It would have been a simple matter for him to counter the statements of Silvester. But how was it possible for such a respected member of the pope's inner council to have produced something so abominably wrong? Was it not much more probable that one of those anonymous mockingbirds, the scholastic opponents of the learned Reuchlin, the authors of the year-old "letters of the dark men," had done so out of hatred for the monks? Surely they must have pulled this dirty trick and had published this document under Silvester's name. If Luther were to respond seriously, surely he would become the laughing stock. And so Luther did as his friends advised. For the time being he remained silent in regard to this attack from the pope's representative of Prierio.

However, this does not mean that Luther stayed idle as a result. He had offered up the 95 Theses for debate. From the time of their posting he occupied himself with further explanation and clarification of his theses. And still no one stepped up to debate. Yet the very fact that the statements were going out into the world without debate resulted in the appearance that they may stand as written commentary. Luther was in the process of producing his written commentary for the scholars in Latin. But before he was even finished he also produced this writing in the language of the common people.

To be sure he had desired to do so right after his theses had been published. But at the request of the Bishop of Brandenburg he had put a stop to it, even though the printing process had already begun. But now, in the spring of 1518, he allowed it to be published under the title, "A Sermon about Indulgences and Grace." Once again he refrained from rejecting indulgences in plain language. But he did say, "Indulgence is permitted on account of the back-sliding and lazy Christians, who do not want to exercise themselves in good works. ... For this reason one should not speak against indulgence, but at the same time one should not also seek to persuade anyone by speaking in favor of it."

Furthermore, "Much better is the work done on behalf of a person in need, than on behalf of a building; it is also much better than to donate for indulgence. First, one should consider giving for the poor, then for the local church, then for the building of St. Peter, and indeed not for the cause of indulgence. For St. Paul says that the one who doesn't do good to those of his own house is not a Christian and worse than a heathen. You can depend on this, that whoever tells you differently is misleading you. He is looking for your soul in your wallet, and if he would find some pennies, they would be more precious to him than souls. Hence you say, 'Therefore, I will never buy another indulgence,' to which I reply, 'I have already told you that it is my goal, desire, plea, and advice that no one buy an indulgence. Let the lazy and sleepy Christians buy indulgences. You go your own way.'"

"Whether or not souls are pulled out of purgatory by way of indulgence I do not know, nor do I believe it to be true, though some new doctors are saying so. In regard to these points I have no doubt, since they are sufficiently supported by Scripture. Therefore you should also have no doubt and let the scholastic doctors be scholastics. All of their opinions gathered together would not be enough to strengthen one sermon. Some of them, to whom this truth is so damaging to their coffers, most likely will denounce me as a heretic. I do not mind their declarations. Their preaching is so disorderly, because they are dark brains who have never smelled a Bible, never read Christian doctrine, never understood their own teachers, but merely rot in their own pierced and torn thoughts. For if they had understood, they would also have known that they should fault no one without trial and conviction. May God give good sense to both them and us. Amen."

We are faced with two important thoughts in his written comments. First, there is Luther's powerful openness with which, while he doesn't clear the air with the Roman church, he nevertheless confronts the new doctors. Second, we note the source of his confidence. He knows that Scripture is on his side and that he has a fairly firm grasp of what it says.

Luther's warning against indulgence in this writing was against false Christians finding false comfort. At the same time, his sermons from this era directed his hearers to the Savior of sinners, the One in whom faith finds the comfort and peace which our works cannot give. He also edified others at this time with a lesson on Psalm 110, which taught the same lesson. He wrote it in response to Scheurlis' request that he write something for his friend, Hieronymus Ebner of Nuernberg. It was subsequently published by Spalatin.

In commenting on verse four, he remarked on the sworn assurance from God that is designed to serve "for unspeakably sweet comfort for us poor, sinful people, that we may believe and hope all the more confidently that Christ is a priest, for it is easier to believe that Christ is Lord over all things, which terrifies a man because of his enormous power. But that Christ is a priest is more difficult to believe, because our abnormal and sinful conscience, which despairs and is easily frightened by God's power, finds it hard to trust that our sins have been forgiven. This abject terror God confronts as he lifts us up and comforts us by crying out that Christ is a priest; that is, a Patron, Intercessor, Mediator, Atoner of all sin. He does so by swearing an oath, declaring even more vehemently his compassion instead of his power, in order to elevate human trust rather than fear.

Therefore this verse should be adorned with gold and precious jewels because it sounds so comforting and gracious."

Chapter 11
Luther at Heidelberg

In the second column of his Wimpina-flavored theses Tetzel had asserted that a convent of Dominicans had assembled 300 brothers of his order in Frankfurt, who had taken up his cause. On the other hand, he admitted that Luther's theses, as well as his sermon on indulgence and grace, had found eager readers far and wide, especially in the cells of Augustinians. And so it could be easily understood that there was a growing desire in many brothers of that order to see Martin, that bold monk, personally. Their desires could now be fulfilled. A general convention of German Augustinians was called to order at Heidelberg, in April of 1518. The residents of Heidelberg, and other cities, were happy to learn that Luther would be attending. The Elector was not pleased for his doctor to go on journeys which would keep him away from his university for any longer than necessary. And so he entrusted his superintendent, Staupitz, to make his desire for a quick return known to Luther.

Luther journeyed with his friend, Lange, whom he had met during his stay at Wuerzburg. On April 21st he entered Heidelberg, and was enthusiastically received by brothers of the order and students. The fact that a great number of those attending the convention supported Luther can be derived from the fact that his patron Staupitz was reelected as the order's vicar. In addition, his close friend Lange was elected as District Vicar. But the rightful level of celebrity that Luther enjoyed became evident when an open debate was scheduled to be held in the monastery's lecture hall upon the conclusion of the convention's business. For this debate Luther set forth a set of theses. Their basic spirit can best be demonstrated by two of them which are as follows:

Thesis 25
"Not he who does many works is justified, but he who firmly believes in Christ."

Thesis 26
"The law says, 'Do this,' and it never happens; grace says, 'Believe in him,' and everything is already done."

This debate drew large crowds. The entire university, teachers, students, brothers of the order, all attended. Secular lords, for whom Luther carried "a precious letter of confidence" from his Elector, were also present. The manner in which the professors participated in the debate brought joy to Luther's heart.

One of those who intently listened to the debate was of Tetzel's order. His name was Martin Būcer, and at the time he was a Dominican monk serving as baccalaureate and monastery magister. We have a direct report on the disputation from him in a letter he sent to his friend, Beatus Rhenanus of Basel, on the day on which Luther took his leave. He wrote about Luther in this way:

"During the convention of his order Luther functioned as chairman among the festive gymnasium of the learned. As such, he posed and defended a column of statements, which not only exceeded every expectation, but even seemed heretical to most of the theologians. ... As much as those main participants in the debate tried to unseat him through their pointed comments, they won nothing, not even a finger's width, from him. It is astonishing how he answered them so graciously and how he listened with incomparable patience. He takes hold of the knots of objections and solves them with truly Pauline rather than Duns Scotus-like depth. The result is that with replies taken purely from Scripture, through his concise and convincing words, he like a magnet attracts nearly everyone to himself."

This Dominican was well versed in ancient languages, including Hebrew. In addition, he had a Greek/Latin New Testament and a Hebrew book of Psalms in his possession. He seemed in a much better position to assess the debate than most of the other listeners. He had been fervently taking notes during the debate. He did the same the next day when he learned much from Luther during a long conversation. After reporting much of what he had experienced, he closed his letter to his friend with the following words,"This, my dear Beatus, is what I personally recorded in my notes and from the conversation I had with the author himself the next day. I gleaned this from his unbelievable teaching ability and his spirit- inspired elucidations. ... Finally, I beg of you, most dear friend, and swear to you under oath, that you do not share this writing with anyone other than a confidant, lest anything unpleasant happen to me as a result."

Just as it had been with Būcer, so did the debate make a lasting impression on others who attended. An example was the case of the nineteen-year-old John Brenz. This young man, who already enjoyed a considerable reputation as a highly learned magister, remained faithful to Luther's cause from this time on. The same could be said for Erhard Schnepf, who would also go on to become a learned theologian.

Luther arrived back in Wittenberg on the 15th of May. He had been gone for five weeks. The trip had invigorated him, and with renewed strength he was ready to face the new work that was awaiting him.

Chapter 12
Attacks and Defense

Shortly before Luther's journey to Heidelberg a document had appeared opposing the 95 controversial theses. It was entitled "Obilisken" (Obilisk being the name for a small wedge, or poniard shaped mark used to indicate a questionable passage in a book). Originating from the pen of Dr. Eck of Ingolstadt, it was copied by hand, and a copy was given to Luther. This was an attack that troubled him. This attack, considering its source, needed a rebuttal. Such was the opinion of Luther and his friends. However, the Heidelberg convention intervened and forced a delay in framing his reply. But before Luther returned from Heidelberg, his ambitious colleague, Carlstadt, went ahead, and without Luther's approval, responded with two columns, 402 theses in all, to Eck's attack. Such was his desire to measure himself against a worthy opponent.

But when Eck found out about the publication of his theses in Wittenberg, he attempted to fend off a confrontation. He asked Carlstadt, whose friendship he valued, to attack the Frankfurters, Tetzel and Wimpina, instead of openly confronting Eck himself. His obilisks, a hasty bit of writing, had not been intended for publication. But it was too late. Carlstadt would not have considered remaining silent anyway. He replied in a letter to Eck, that it was Eck, who had broken their new friendship. He, Carlstadt, would prefer to take on a lion, rather than a donkey like Tetzel or Wimpina.

Luther disapproved of Carlstadt's presumptive reply. He asked that Eck would delay a response to his colleague's statements. He wrote an amicable letter to Eck and sent it to Scheurl in Nuernberg for delivering it. Yet at the same time he drew up a personal reply to Eck's obilisks which went to the printer in August. Once again, upon his return from Heidelberg, Luther zealously applied himself to his previously mentioned explanations of his 95 Theses. Luther first sent a copy of this extensive work to his superior, the Bishop of Brandenburg, in a letter dated Exaudi Sunday (*6th Sunday after Easter*). It was entitled, "Resolutions for the Disputation concerning the Power of Indulgence" on the first printed sheets. Luther had also approached the bishop concerning indulgences prior to posting his theses.

Luther began his letter by explaining how he was compelled to write his disputation due to the unheard-of presentations by the indulgence peddlers. He also had to respond to the many questions posed to him regarding such preaching. This was his intent in writing his theses, not to declare any final assertions. As a result, he was not pleased that his theses had been so widely distributed and was willing to submit to the church and its verdict in regard to everything. He concluded by testifying again that he was not setting forth assertions but that he only desired debate. He did so fearfully, though not with fear for bulls and threats from those who demanded fearlessly that everything they imagined was to be accepted as the gospel.

Another person, who was to receive a copy of his "Resolutions" prior to their being printed, was none less than the pope himself. In fact, Luther had even dedicated his writing to him. He sent it addressed to Leo along with an accompanying letter. He sent this package to his old friend Staupitz to forward to the pope. In the letter he wrote to Staupitz, he pointed out how he had arrived at the understanding which lay at the foundation of his theses. He reminded him that it had been Staupitz himself, who first led him to the idea that true repentance begins at the point where others thought it had ended. When the new indulgence preachers began bringing out their false, godless claims, he decided to debate. The result was that he incurred the wrath of those money-preachers. When they were unable to discredit any of his teaching, they set up a straw man argument that these debates were undermining the power of the pope. And so, Luther, who would happily have stayed in his corner and quietly watch the battle, was now forced into the open. He therefore begged that his writings be forwarded to "the best Pope Leo X" as quickly as possible that his writings could speak there as quickly as possible in his defense against his enemies.

Still, feeling that matters might develop to his disadvantage, he absolved Staupitz of any responsibility. He comforted himself with Reuchlin's proverbial saying, "a poor man fears nothing since he can lose nothing." He continued, "I have no possessions, nor do I desire them. If I ever held a position of fame and honor, let whoever so wishes take it. Hence, nothing is left for me other than my weak, constantly deprived, tired out body. Should they take that away from me by force or cunning, they will perhaps shorten my life of service to God by one or two hours. My sweet Redeemer and Reconciler, my Lord Jesus Christ, is enough for me. I shall sing to him as long as I live. And if no one wants to sing along with me, what does it matter? He shall weep, if he cares to, for himself alone." So Luther trusted that Christ would accept his teaching and would lead the pope's voice and the hearts of kings to the right decision.

The letter sent along to the pope was a remarkable piece of writing. In it Luther explained how the actions of the indulgence preachers had flayed the flesh off the bones of the poor, even as they fattened themselves with their incredible greed. As a result, he was driven to do something and so issued the theses on paper for discussion and invited the learned to debate with him. In this context he declared that such was his right as a doctor of theology, a right which perhaps his enemies did not want him to have. Still he regretted that his theses were being so obscured from their original purpose, that now they were hard for anyone to understand. Then he wrote, "What should I do now? I cannot take it back, even though I see that the steps I have taken have resulted in such hatred for me. Uneducated and immature person that I am, having yet to grow into full bloom, I do not enjoy this open debate. But it is necessary, requiring me to cackle like a goose among the swans."

His desire was that his explanation of his theses be issued under the protection of the name of the pope that it may be recognized how faithfully he had submitted to the holy father. "Therefore," he concluded, "most holy father, I lay myself at the feet of your holiness with all that I am and have. I shall recognize your voice as the voice of Christ, who rules and speaks in you. If I am deserving death, I shall not refrain from dying. "The earth is the Lord's and everything in it." (Ps. 24:1 - NIV) May he be praised eternally. Amen. On the day of the Holy Trinity, 1518."

What a remarkable letter! On the one hand, we read of Luther's humble submission, his willingness to acknowledge the voice of Christ in the voice of the pope; yet, on the other hand, the declaration, "I cannot take it back." Both statements are surely intended seriously and honestly. Luther submits to the pope, trusting that he will do what is best for him as far as possible, even though he declares both to Staupitz and the pope the possibility that he would see himself condemned and punished in his body and his life. All this harsh self-criticism was submitted for the sake of the doctrine, which he "cannot take back", and, which is divine truth.

Though as the monk he was very respectful in his letter, as the doctor he maintained control in the "Resolutions". One after another he took up, clarified, and explained his theses. He set forth the doctrine of righteousness by grace through faith in a clear and decisive way. The faith depends on God's Word, spoken in the absolution by the administrator in God's place. Only the believer will be a partaker of the grace found in the Word and Sacraments. Furthermore, faith is required to receive divine grace. For the one who has Christ through faith has everything: righteousness, life, and blessedness. Therefore, Christians are to be instructed so that they do not seek comfort and peace by way of their own achievements, nor from their contrition, nor in the numbering of their sins during confession, but only through faith in the divine word of forgiveness. And so, faith is also necessary in the use of the Sacraments, for it is faith that enables the possession of the salvation which they offer. Therefore, a person does not share in the merits of Christ through indulgences but only through faith. As for the merits of the saints, which they had supposedly earned in excess, they do not even exist. For no saint has fulfilled God's Commandments at all, let alone achieved extra. This point was so ingrained in Luther that he was ready to face death by fire and considered those who taught otherwise to be heretics.

The only thing the pope could grant was earthly authority. He had no lordship over souls. Truly, according to Romans 13:1-2 (NIV), honor was to be paid to the pope as to every earthly authority. This held true even when wrong was being done, as when the church was at that time placing endless burdens on the people. But his authority was not based on the phrase: "What you shall bind on earth," etc. (Matthew 18:18 [NIV]) – Translated from an older Martin Luther translation, published about 100 years ago by CPH) as the pope has declared some to be bound by the church, who in fact are not bound before God - but rather on the basis of the word, "Settle matters quickly with your enemy ..." (Matthew 5:25 [NIV]), and, "If someone strikes you on the right cheek, turn the other to him also..." (Matthew 5:39 [NIV]), and Romans 12:19, "Do not take revenge..." (NIV) The pope cannot make new articles of faith, but can only make judgments based on those that already exist. If it were otherwise, the church would be in constant danger, since the pope can err in matters of faith just as in earthly matters. He was unimpressed with papal decisions. The pope is a man as any other man, and many popes had made horrible decisions. However, he alleged that in the person of Leo X they had an honorable pope. But he wondered what even this honorable man could accomplish in the midst of the present confusion. After all he lived in Rome, the true Babylon, where even the best of popes have been mocked.

Truly the church was in need of a reformation. However, that time for that reformation was known only to the One, who had created time. The present time was so terrible that even highly educated and holy men could not help the church. But rather than have the truth be completely silenced it was better to be spoken by children and fools. Perhaps then the educated and the wise would become bolder, as they would learn that even an immature person like himself felt the need to raise his voice according to the Word of God. "If they keep quiet, the stones will cry out." (Luke19:40 [NIV])

Yet, Luther did not want to separate from the Roman church. That is why he rejected the Bohemian brothers who had separated from the church, calling them heretics and unholy people, who rejoiced in the disgrace of Rome, as the Pharisee looked down on the tax collector. He wrote: "Oh, we know our failings and lament them; but we do not flee like the heretics; we do not pass by those who are half dead. ... The more pitiable the church is, the more faithfully we stand at her side. We come to her aid with weeping, praying, admonishing, and pleading. This is what love compels us to do, namely to carry one another's burden."

These closing words provide us with a key to understanding Luther's actions at this time. Even though we know that he would later mean something different when he said, "knowledge is but piece-work," he really believed that it was his duty to take the stand he did and to give his testimony. But the time was not far off when he would praise Bohemia and bless them, along with all the others who had stepped away from the Babylon of Rome. Then he would declare that he no longer had any desire to side with the Roman church.

While the printing process of the Resolutions was still going on, Luther's restless pen produced two more publications in swift succession. For Tetzel had issued a refutation of "Sermon about Indulgence and Grace," concerning which Luther could not remain silent as he did with the Frankfurter theses. He responded under the title, "Freedom of the Sermon about Indulgence and Grace." In it he reproached Tetzel about the manner in which he used Scripture. He wrote, "It is a tremendous cause for lamentation that one has to endure the rending of Scripture by such an arrogant blasphemer. Would that he treat me in such an evil way, calling me a heretic, an apostate, a speaker of evil, and a victim of his evil desires. I would accept it and never attack him; indeed, I would gladly pray for him. But the fact that he does not handle Scripture properly cannot be tolerated. He treats Holy Scripture, our comfort, the way a sow treats a sack of oats." He then proceeded to address the individual points. Consider what Tetzel wrote, "He who buys an indulgence is doing a better thing than giving alms to any poor man who is not yet on his deathbed."

In response Luther wrote: "Beware, and may God have mercy on you! This is a so-called teacher of the Christian people. From now on it is not so terrible to hear how the Turks dishonor our church and cross. We have in our midst hundreds of worse Turks, who in their blasphemy take away from us our most sacred possession, the Word of God. The holy Apostle John says, "Anyone who sees his brother starving or in need and hardens his heart against him, how can the love of God abide in him?" (I John 3:17 – Luther applied his own transliteration) The blasphemer approaches this text and hurls it a thousand miles away with the comment that the one starving or in need must be understood as being on his deathbed. With this I have no patience because this comment comes from an evil spirit."

He followed through a little later, "The fact that such false teachers do not know Scripture, don't understand Latin or German, and above all, blasphemously berate us makes me feel as though an uncouth donkey is braying at me. Certainly, I am glad and not sorry at all that such people fervently revile me in my Christianity." Tetzel, even though his loose and cavalier style of life was well-known, had boasted that he was prepared to endure water and fire for the sake of his teaching. So, Luther concluded with the words, "For him I offer this free advice. He should ask for vine-branch-water (wine) and for the fire that steams from the roasted geese he enjoys so much."

Though Tetzel had pointed out in a veiled manner that people like Luther should have to face prison or burning, another Dominican, Jacob von Hoogstraten of Koeln, went much farther. He declared statements of Luther to be heretical and urged the pope to make short work of Luther, to attack him with fire and sword. The idea that the truth would be suppressed with bloody violence affected Luther very strongly. In a devastating pamphlet, he sent that jail keeper fleeing. What follows is the conclusion of that work, which was published in German.

"So be gone, you evil, bloody murderer, thirsting only for your brother's blood! Spend your time looking for fleas in horse dung until you learn what true sin, error, heresy, and what else belongs to this kind of knowledge actually is. For I have yet to see a more stupid ass than you, especially one who brags about the many years he spent in the study of dialectics. It is no surprise that you condemn the best statements of the best of men as heretical. You still have no idea what is contrary to Scripture and, as a result, don't know what is to be condemned or heretical.

"It gladdens my heart that you have condemned me, you whose brain is so foggy. I beg and plead with you to never call me a Christian or a believer in Christ, lest others think you are lying or speaking out of ignorance. Please continue to denounce me as a heretic. For then there will be those who will defend me and say that Hoogstraten judges in the same way as a blind man distinguishes colors. So now you are warned, man of blood and enemy of the truth. Should your madness drive you to attack me again take care to act thoughtfully and take your time in the attempt. I am giving you this warning in advance. God knows what I shall do, if I am alive. I have every confidence that I would show the whole world that for the last 400 years no more destructive heretic has ever lived than Jacob Hoogstraten. Be kind to yourself, dear reader. July 13, 1518."

Chapter 13
Summons to Rome

By writing "Freedom of the Sermon about Indulgence and Grace," Luther again challenged his opponents to debate. "Here I am," he wrote, "in Wittenberg. Dr. Martinus Luther, Augustinian. I am exposing myself to a jail keeper who believes himself able to devour iron and rip apart mountain-sized boulders. I am informing him that he can have protection, free admission, free lodging, and expenses covered from the gracious allowance of the honorable and Christian Duke Frederick, Elector of Saxony. From now on may those who have printed blasphemy understand that this count was in no way supporting heresy, as they delighted to slander and defame him in their last drunken ramblings, accusing him of protecting me as heretic, contrary to the truth."

The idea, of separating the bold monk from the peaceful protection of his count, originated in Rome. Leo X does not easily allow himself to be separated from his regal life style, his hunting, his bawdy plays, amusements, and card games. He had originally regarded what was happening in Germany as trivial. The theses had been written by a drunken German who needed sobering to change his mind. However, it didn't take long for the situation to become uncomfortable for him. Perhaps it was that the flow of wealth from indulgences dried up. Maybe other discouraging news arrived. In any event we take note that already in early 1518 the first attempt to extinguish the Wittenberg flame, with the bucket of water that Silvester Prierias had poured on that Wittenberg fire, failed to calm Rome.

Now Rome resolved to adopt other options. As early as April, a letter was sent to the Elector instructing him to submit to the pope's desires. More than that, he attached an official complaint against Luther. The papal legate, Mario Perusco, raised the accusation to heresy. The pope appointed judges for the case, one of whom was Silvester Prierias, who had volunteered to be the first challenger out of the papal camp against Luther. It was as early as August 7th, that the accused received the summons to appear in Rome within 60 days.

So, this is the answer that Luther received to his letter, in which he had addressed the pope, and from which he expected to receive some kindly direction. Later he reflected, "While I was expecting blessing, lightning and thunder crashed down on me." Now there was no longer any doubt as to the pope's position on this issue. What would he do now?

He first responded in a way that he would have done anyway. He sent the printed reply he had written to Eck's "Obilisks" under the title of "Asterisks." (Asterisks are the little stars which point toward remarks made at

78

the bottom of the page explaining the context.) In a response such as this he was in no way indebted to his opponent. He attacked the lamentable weakness of his Obelisks, in which Eck argued neither from Scripture nor from the church fathers, but purely from the scholastics.

The argument was so light that it could be blown away like a house of cards. "If the author of the Obelisks only were as fine a theologian as he is a sophist" (almost calling him a philosopher), he writes, "and I request that, if you will write to me again some other time, you will be content to only mention your argument three or four times in the one piece of work, rather than how you have foolishly made your point in every sentence, which is laughable. For your information, I don't want to hear about any scholastic theology unless it is based on church theology. Was this what you wanted, that I do nothing else than laugh at you? You offered nothing for me to read that I didn't question and against which I now debate."

Luther had to respond to an especially malicious attack which compared him to the Bohemian (John Hus) poison. He stated that he followed Christ's example, saying, "I do not have a devil." He served at an excellent university, in an acknowledged order, under a highly renowned Duke of Saxony, and in a sizeable bishopric, where everything was catholic. He attempted to force Eck to substantiate his lies and his blasphemous tongue. He formulated his conclusion by saying, "I am ashamed of such extended foolish talk. Eck is a theologian. He tries very hard to ignore the fact that a Christian's freedom comes from his peace of conscience which no indulgence can provide. It comes only from the forgiveness of sins by grace alone ...but finally this should be enough to silence the talk of such a thoughtless, uninformed, inexperienced, that is to say, scholastic theologian. Finis! August 10, 1518."

But Luther was not content with that response. Even though he had remained silent concerning the attack of Prierias up to this point, now the question of how Rome stood toward him was answered with the summons to Rome. Prierias had composed his letter in three days. In this regard also did Luther outdo him by giving a considerably longer "Answer to the Dialog of Silvester Prierias" in two days. At the same time, he reproached his opponent, informing him that he failed to understand Scripture, either having failed to apply it at all, or having applied it incorrectly. Instead he garnered his weapons of defense from the scholastics. They had often erred, since no human being, pope, or council is infallible. Because Prierias had maintained the convoluted idea that the word of an indulgence is God's Word, Luther argued that it was the word of man and refers only to human opinion. He stated that God's Word speaks differently, namely, "Faith justifies," (In reference to Romans 3:28 [NIV]) and "The gospel is the power of God for the salvation of all who believe." (Romans 1:16 [NIV] But the indulgence declaration does not justify, nor does it produce anything except that it promotes laziness in regard to doing good works.

He responded to the threats of his opponents, "Just stop your threats. Christ lives. Indeed, he not only lives but he also reigns. He reigns not only on earth, but also in Rome, no matter how much Rome may rage. If it condemns for the sake of the truth, I will praise the Lord. The censure of the church shall not separate me from the Church, as long as the truth binds me to the Church. I would rather be condemned and banned by you, if you and your kind continue in such manner, than to be blessed with you. I've got nothing to lose. I belong to the Lord. If I die, I die to the Lord, which means I live. If you want to frighten someone with your actions, look for someone else."

In conclusion he wrote, "Note, honorable father, it has taken me only two days to respond to you because what you have said against me carries so little weight. Therefore, I could answer you with little preparation, as the words came out of my mouth. But if you choose to continue this debate then see to it that your Thomas enters the field of battle better prepared. You don't want to suffer more than you already have in this confrontation. I have been holding back, not wanting to repay evil with evil. May you farewell."

Proof that this work struck a nerve with his opponents can be found in the fact that this, like Luther's other works, was being widely read. But the copies of this one were all purchased throughout Germany by the brothers of the order of Prierias' in order to keep it quiet. The publisher had nothing to complain about regarding this quick sell out. When it sold out in September, he simply printed a new one.

Phrases we read from this work like, "The censure of the church will not separate me from the church, when the truth binds me to the church," Luther had used before. He had detailed them in his congregational sermons even before this publication. He referred to the fact that a real ban declares that the banned individual has been shut out of the spiritual fellowship of the Church. But it is so decreed, because such an individual had previously separated himself from Christ. In contrast, a so-called ban, which has been declared against a person who espoused a just cause, is truly not a ban, but an honor. A person may bear that joyfully. The one who is unjustly banned because of the truth must therefore not deny the truth in spite of the ban.

Using phrases like this, Luther provided comfort and serenity to many a Christian heart. He earned the sincere gratitude of those who had been threatened with a ban by the preachers of indulgences, a ban just because they followed Dr. Martinus and his teachings.

To his enemies this last sermon especially proved to be like fat in the fire. Since much of what Luther said was taken out of context, the preacher felt compelled to recall that sermon from memory and print it after the fact. He did this, as he said in his introduction, to prove that there was nothing to regret in this sermon, either by the one who preached it or the devout member who heard it.

What Luther was at that precise time teaching the people about the ban was important. This referred especially to the unjustifiable ban, decreed against the proclaimer of the truth. It was important because he could expect that due to the way things stood with Rome, Rome would come after him with a ban, if other plans did not work out. A correct understanding of this subject would negate the intended effect on the people, once the ban would be delivered.

At that time Luther expressed such a thought to Staupitz in a letter he wrote shortly after his summons to Rome, "Have no doubt, my honorable father, that I shall keep my freedom in the future by searching and holding on to the divine Word." He remarked further to Staupitz, "Should I be put under the ban, I fear only one thing, namely that this might serve as a stumbling block for you, because I am sure that God has led you to a right understanding in the matter." He also added a copy of his "Sermon regarding the Ban" to this letter.

Luther received a warmly written reply from Staupitz, who at that time was staying in quiet retreat with the Archbishop of Salzburg. His letter closed with the encouragement that Luther leave Wittenberg for a while, since he was being rejected for Christ's sake, even as Christ himself was rejected. He ought to come to Salzburg. But Luther could not accept this well-intentioned heartfelt advice. His responsibilities were in Wittenberg, and he intended to carry them out until God would tell him to go. The university stood in beautiful support of Luther. This included the whole theology fac-

Philip Melanchthon according to Albrecht Dürer

ulty, except for a single licentiate in the study of law. The students were encouraged to diligently continue their study of Scripture. How those students regarded Luther can be shown from the following story. Tetzel's theses were brought into Wittenberg in March of that year. The students took 800 copies, some purchased and some taken by force. They solemnly burned them in the marketplace. For this action Luther seriously reproved them from the pulpit.

In the days that followed his receiving of the summons to Rome, the new professor of Greek, Phillip Melanchthon, arrived in Wittenberg.

Philip Blackearth was born on the 16th of February, 1497, in Bretten, in the Lower Palatinate. His father, a famous weapon smith and honest man, died while the boy was still wearing the shoes of childhood. The careful upbringing of the boy, begun by his father, was carried on by his grandfather. Later, after his death, his grandmother, a sister of the highly educated Reuchlin, took up the task. In fact, it was Reuchlin who gave the name of his young and very promising relative its Greek form, Melanchthon. Philip was not yet thirteen years old when he entered the University of Heidelberg, where he became baccalaureate with honor at the age of fifteen. From there he moved to the University of Tuebingen. He diligently applied himself to the study of philosophy and became Magister in 1514 at the age of seventeen. He became familiar with most subjects, even with medicine. Then he turned to theology. Regrettably this was scholastic theology that was being studied in the schools. And though he was already familiar with the New Testament, having read it in the original text, he did not grasp a true understanding during his time at Tuebingen.

So, this was the Magister Philippus who arrived in Wittenberg on August 25, 1518. He had previously declined calls to Ingolstadt and to Leipzig. Despite his plain outward appearance, he soon was held in high regard by colleagues and students alike. In fact, as early as four days later Luther would write to Spalatin and tell him that Melanchthon's lecture hall was packed full. Luther joyfully recognized that his new co-worker would stand alongside Luther not only as an aide in language instruction, but also in studying Scripture. He recognized this when Magister Philippus gave a lecture on Homer, and immediately announced one on the letter to Titus.

Luther would have had to be a Staupitz to leave Wittenberg voluntarily under such circumstances. However, he also did not dare to attempt such a move without considering the Elector. He could not leave his post without his command or permission. At that time the Elector was staying with his court preacher Spalatin at Augsburg, where an important imperial diet was being held. In spite of the many types of business that occupied his time he did not forget about his doctor in Wittenberg.

Chapter 14
Cajetan

The man Frederick the Wise was dealing with, while in Augsburg, was the papal legate. His name was Cardinal Thomas Vio von Gaeta, called by his city's name, Cajetan.

This highly placed Dominican had been named a cardinal the previous year, and now the pope entrusted him with directing papal concerns at the imperial diet. Being of the opinion that a papal legate held a higher position than a king, he presented himself accordingly. His specially chosen garments were so outlandish that the master of ceremonies responsible for the attire burst out laughing. His white horse was bridled with crimson red velvet, and his room was decorated with carpets of the same color. With a proud and pompous display, he carried out his duties at the ceremonies of August 1st. He placed a cardinal's hat on the Archbishop of Mainz, and handed the sword and hat, consecrated by the pope, to Caesar.

So, Frederick began to deal with this red eminence on Luther's behalf. By the good reputation which Frederick the Wise had in the council of the counts and professionals it must have appeared advisable even to Cajetan to treat the Elector quite respectfully. After all, the pope had made big plans in context with this Imperial Diet. His plan was to thoroughly fleece the Germans again, a plan for which the royal participants had no stomach. When Caesar and the legate requested money for the war against the Turks, they answered with a decisive "NO" on the 27th of August. They then approached the papal chair with a number of long lists of complaints. These complaints had been gathered in respect to the simony hunters (most likely in reference to Acts 8:9-24) and seekers of German gold, who were unbearably oppressive to the German people. As a result, things were not looking good for the pope, and it would have been worse than foolhardy to aim a blow at the head of a man like Elector Frederick.

Even Caesar needed to show respect to the elector, for not only were complaints being directed at Maximillian by the accusers, but Maximillian had his own agenda. He was planning to offer Caesar's crown to his nephew Karl, the king of Spain. Thus, Frederick had the advantage of wielding his influence. (Note: When a "Caesar", the title of the head of the Holy Roman Empire, died or was removed from office for some other reason, it was the duty of seven out of the many counts to decide who would serve as the next Caesar, or head of government of the Holy Roman Empire. These seven were the only counts who had "electoral" rank. Only six of these seemed to have functioned in the 16th century, namely: Mainz, Trier, Cologne, Pfalz (West of Bavaria), Saxony, and Brandenburg. The King of Bohemia, the 7th, was excluded from the 7 during the 16th century. Caesar Maximilian died in 1520, and was succeeded by Charles V of Spain as Caesar.) This was another reason why the pope and his legate needed to win Elector Frederick to their side. For the pope was doing all he could to prevent such a concentration of political power to be given to a man already wearing many crowns. For this purpose the pope needed the Electors. The manner in which the pope and the cardinal regarded Elector Frederick can thus be easily understood.

A papal letter to Frederick arrived on August 23rd. In it the pope alleged that a certain Martin Luther, "a child of evil" and "blasphemer of God," was boasting that he stood under the protection of the Elector, and therefore feared no other human authority or punishment. Thus, the Elector must take care in this matter, lest he come under suspicion of aiding Martin Luther, and according to the legate, Luther was to be delivered over for trial before the holy seat. Then, soon after, another message arrived from Rome. This one stated that the pope was of a mind to bestow on him the Golden Rose, as a sign of his personal favor.

Yet, before any of this transpired, the Elector had personally confronted the legate with the wish that Luther be given a hearing on German soil. The Cardinal very willingly agreed and reported back to Rome. On the 23rd of August, the legate had received his instructions regarding Luther. He was to use every possible means to arrest Martin Luther, whom the papal auditor had declared an impenitent heretic under his power. He was to do this with the help of the secular authority and then to hold him securely until receiving further instructions to bring him before the holy seat. The cardinal was also given full power to welcome Martin Luther back into the fellowship of the church, if he would recant willingly and penitently. The harshest punishment of the church would come down on everyone, who would oppose this decision, or give protection, assistance, lodging, etc. to this heretic. All cities and countries where he remained would be placed under the interdict. (An interdict was a punishment in which all functions of the church, with few exceptions, would be suspended until the pope had been obeyed.) Either due to the new instructions he had received from Rome, or acting under his own general authority, Cajetan made the offer to the Elector for Luther to be granted a hearing in Augsburg. Frederick found this offer agreeable with his demand and directed Luther to appear in Augsburg.

And so, Luther set out for Augsburg as his Elector requested. He was accompanied by one of his students, and a brother from the monastery, Leonhard Beier. He traveled through Weimar, where the Elector was residing, to Nuernberg. If anyone saw him traveling on foot, so poorly dressed, he would never have suspected that this was the man with whom the pope, the cardinals, and the counts, had begun to deal. The meager amount of money he needed for his journey did not belong to him. He had received it from the Elector. Once at Nuernberg, he borrowed a better monk's habit from his friend Link in order to appear more acceptable before the cardinal. However, under that monk's robe beat a heart that was timid, yet at the same time cheerful. "My thought while traveling was," he would later say, "Now I have to die. And I often said, 'Oh, what a disgrace I will be for my parents!'"

He also journeyed in confidence, trusting in his God, and fully aware that his cause was really God's cause. "Even in Augsburg," he wrote, "even in the midst of his enemies, Jesus Christ reigns. Christ lives. Martinus dies." When Kestner, the prior of the Weimar monastery, expressed his fear that the Italians might burn the dear doctor, he replied, "With nettles this will all pass, but with fire it would get too hot. Dear friend, pray a Pater Noster to our dear Lord God in heaven and to his dear Child, Christ, to whom belongs my cause, that he will be gracious to me. If he will preserve the cause for me, then it is already preserved. But if he does not wish to preserve it, then I will also not be able to preserve it and must bear the disgrace."

On October 7th, Luther, who had traveled the last three miles in a wagon due to an illness, left the Augustinian monastery in Augsburg to take up quarters in the Carmelite monastery. He wanted to avoid all confusion that he was coming to represent his order. While at the Carmelite monastery he received excellent hospitality under the care of his friend Johann Frosch, a Wittenberg attorney. Upon his arrival he immediately informed the legate through Link, who had come along to Augsburg. It wasn't as though the legate hadn't already heard. The entire city was talking about the bold monk.

So, the cardinal immediately summoned Luther to come before him. But Luther had been advised from all directions not to become available immediately for a hearing. It was considered strongly by the cardinal that this stormy German be kept in a peaceful state of mind. For this reason, a close Italian friend of Cajetan, Urbanus of Serralonga, had informed him that he would be summoned for discussion two days after his arrival. So, Luther was allowed to postpone his appearance before the cardinal until then. In reality Urbanus made it clear to him that this appearance revolved around only six letters, "r-e-v-o-c-o" (I take it back!). He would need to speak these letters and the whole matter would be settled. It amused him to hear from the German that the need for speaking these letters could only arise from a previous conviction. How anyone could object to the business of the indulgence preachers, which brought in such nice profit, was a mystery to the Italian. But when he saw that Luther was serious he turned serious as well. He pointed out that the use of force was a possibility and asked Luther whether he thought that the Elector would resort to weapons, putting lands and people at risk on this behalf. When Luther explained that he desired no such thing Urbanus asked, "Where do you wish to stay?" "Under the sky," Luther fired back. Instead of such treatment causing him to waver, Luther gained much confidence for the approaching dealings with the cardinal. All this was due to this pitiable mediation by Urbanus, whom he recognized as the Cardinal's tool.

The German friends for Luther's cause, whom the Elector had recommended, were on the other side. They advised strongly against an immediate appearance before the legate. Though the papal instructions given to Cajetan were not known at that time, these men did not trust Cajetan. They stopped Luther from appearing before Cajetan without receiving an official document from Caesar. The obtaining of such a letter involved a time-consuming process, especially since Caesar had left the city on September 18th, just a few days before Luther's arrival. Maximillian had ridden out filled with dark foreboding, ill, and depressed. Yet as he departed he called out in farewell, "God bless you, dear Augsburg, and all devout citizens in you! From time to time we truly enjoyed some good days. Now we shall never see you again." Yet, before he left, he spoke with the legate and urged him to be gentle in his handling of the Wittenberg Doctor.

Since Caesar still had to provide the letter, Luther's friends insisted on waiting for its arrival. Not until the letter arrived, October 11th, did Luther proceed to the cardinal's residence. He was accompanied by Link, another brother of his order, prior Frosch and two Carmelites. At the Cardinal's residence they met Urbanus of Serralonga, a papal nuntio, along with a number of other Italians. When the news spread that the bad monk had arrived, other foreigners came from their rooms out of curiosity. In order to avoid any complaints about failure to show proper respect toward the cardinal, Luther

Caesar Maximillian according to Albrecht Dürer

had allowed himself to be taught regarding the etiquette for proper behavior before such a high spiritual official. He threw himself facedown to the ground before him. Then, when the cardinal bade him rise, he rose as far as to his knees. Only after more bidding did he finally stand on his feet. Since the cardinal seemed to be waiting for him to speak, Luther did so. He explained that he had appeared in obedience to the papal order and his count's command. He said that he was prepared to be instructed concerning the statements for debate, which he had made public. Since this struck the legate as being a very short speech, he made it his goal to have an easy dismissal of the whole matter.

Luther had presented himself as an obedient son of the church. Thus, the cardinal got straight to the point of reproving that dear son by referring to the holy father in his reply. That holy father demanded three things from Luther. First, Luther was to retract. Second, he was to refrain from making any further comments of the sort. Third, he would do away with anything and everything which could disrupt the peace of the church. Luther then asked for specific references to the material which he was to retract. The Cardinal chose one statement from the disputations and one from the resolutions. The first was what was alleged in the 58th thesis, that the treasure from which the pope provided the indulgence was not the merit of Christ. Luther had made this statement in opposition to the Constitutio "Unigenitus" issued by Pope Clemens VI in 1343. The claim was made in it that Christ had earned a treasure for his church, a treasure to be managed by Peter and his successors. This treasure could never run empty due to the unending merit of Christ, and the excessive virtue of the righteous. The papal legate sought to excuse Luther for what he had written by expressing the opinion that perhaps Luther had never read the papal declaration.

But he was wrong. Luther explained that he had, indeed, read the Bull of Clemens and also the one of Pope Sixtus IV (1471-1484), which was worded the same way. But he did not consider them to be binding over against Scripture, as the pope twisted the meaning. This was too much for the legate who stated that a person has to submit to a papal declaration. Luther had pointed out that the Parisian theologians had appealed this point to the pope for a council. The legate responded that they would have to take their punishment.

The statement out of the resolution, which Luther was asked to retract, was the one in which he alleged that in order to be a worthy recipient of Holy Communion, the receiver must have faith. Luther's refusal to retract this statement prompted the Italians who were present to start to laugh upon hearing a teaching, so contrary to their own opinions. To this the cardinal declared, "Whether you want to or not you must retract today. If you do not I shall reject and condemn all of your teachings because of what you have said."

Luther could actually have retracted in Wittenberg. It would have been far easier and less stressful. As a result, he was genuinely surprised to hear the cardinal's opinion and his refusal to conduct a real in depth debate about the issues that had been raised. When he saw how things stood, he ended the audience by requesting a recess of one day to think things over.

The legate's right-hand man, who had already been reproached by the cardinal for sticking his nose into the discussion, ran after Luther and accused him of sophistry. Luther unceremoniously brushed him off saying he had enough and so withdrew.

Luther found his old mentor, Staupitz, in his quarters. He had arrived in Augsburg on that day to make good his promise to stand at Luther's side. They discussed what should be done. The next day the cardinal might have been surprised by what he saw. For in Luther's company he saw the Caesar's counselor, Dr. Konrad Peutinger, along with two other imperial counselors, the Electoral Counselor Philip of Feilitzsch, Staupitz, and a notary. All of these appeared before him. Luther proceeded to read a protest which was clear in every sense. In it he explained that he could not retract without having been convinced of his error. He then offered to debate his statements publicly in Augsburg or anywhere else, or to defend himself in private. He was also ready to answer the legate in writing for anything that could be brought against him. He was furthermore open to a verdict by the four universities of Basel, Freiburg, Loewen, and Paris, as to where he may have erred.

In regard to this proposal, which appeared to give the Cardinal a wide variety of options, the Cardinal only smiled and commanded Luther once again to retract. In doing so, he warned him that it would prove difficult for him to kick against the goads. (See Acts 9:5 KJV for intended meaning.) Luther's request to be allowed to respond about the statements in writing, the statements which had been selected by the cardinal, was initially abruptly denied. Yet, he did allow it after Staupitz lent his support.

Luther had his response ready the very next day. The truth of the first statement under attack was presented with crystal clarity, in spite of Pope Clemens' bull cited by Cajetan. He then put forth anew his allegation that every Christian has the right to compare any doctrine, even the pope's, with what Holy Scripture says. In this regard, he used Peter as an example. Peter had to be corrected when he had strayed from the truth of the gospel (Mt. 16:22,23; Mt. 26:69-75; Gal. 2:11-21 [The NIV may be consulted for all three of these indicated Bible passages]). So also, without hesitation, did he defend himself against the legate's objection to the statement in Luther's Resolutions. He proved from Scripture that only faith in Christ's Word can produce a living, worthy, and properly prepared guest at the Lord's Supper, and that everything else leads only to insolence or despair. Since this is the teaching of Holy Scripture, he could not depart from it. He must obey God rather than man.

Cajetan's failure to accept anything that was offered was no surprise. However, the legate acted as though the written statement no longer applied to him and promised to send it to Rome. Once again, he commanded Luther to retract. The very next day Luther reported to Spalatin how the discussion ended.

"I started to speak several times, but he kept thundering, growling, trying to rule and lord it over me. Finally, I also began to raise my voice, saying, 'If it can be proven from that before mentioned Extravagentus (the bull Unigenitus of Clemens VI) that the treasures of the indulgence are the merits of Christ, I shall retract in agreement with the will and pleasure of your highness'." In response Cajetan became very unruly, burst out laughing, and picked up the book in his hands. He eagerly read the Extravagentus as fast as he could until he came to the place where it is written that the Lord Christ arrived at (in the sense of "accomplished"; the German word "erlangt" which could also be translated, "gained", or "earned".) the treasure through his suffering, etc. Then I said, 'Highly-Honored-Father, Your Highness may wish to consider the word (referring to the word "erlangt") and zealously apply it. Since Christ has earned (or, accomplished) a treasure through (or, by way of) his wages (earning), it is not the wages which are the treasure, but rather this (is the treasure), namely, what the wages have supplied (or, provided), the keys of the church (These are the treasure.) As a result, my assertion is true."

"So the legate was put to shame. Yet not wanting to appear ashamed, he forcefully changed the subject and immediately forgot about my proof. I replied calmly and with the proper respect, 'Very Highly Honored Father, Your Highness should no longer be of the opinion that we Germans don't possess or understand grammar. It is one thing to be a treasure; it is another thing to earn a treasure.' (The treasure being "forgiveness of sins")

"Since the legate had lost his confidence, he roared once more that I should retract, saying, 'Go away and don't come back unless you are willing to retract.' That is how I took my leave from the legate."

Whether or not the cardinal truly wanted to break off the meeting with Luther, Luther took him at his word. Luther was firm in his resolve not to retract. That very day he wrote to Carlstadt, "I have no wish to become a heretic by retracting the very truth whereby I became a Christian. I would sooner die, be burned, be driven out, be cursed." (Footnote reference: LV, Vol. 7, p 7ff.) Hence, he sought nothing more from the legate after those last words. In the same way the Cardinal had lost all desire to deal with the German monk who had debated with him so energetically and had backed him into a corner with such heavy armaments. "I do not want to speak with that beast any more, for he has deep eyes and amazing ideas in his head," he said in discouraged manner to Staupitz and Link. He had been speaking with

Luther's two friends that afternoon, advising them to try to get Luther to retract.

These friends also concluded that any further discussion was at an end. This was so, even though at another meeting with Link, Cajetan claimed that Luther had no better friend than himself. In fact, he would first await further instruction from Rome, where he had sent Luther's written defense. He would do this instead of using the full power at his disposal of immediately placing Luther under the ban.

Luther's two friends didn't trust this offer of peace and on Saturday proceeded to return from Augsburg to Nuernberg on different roads. Prior to that time, Staupitz, acting as his superior, released Luther from the order's rule. As a result, he would be free to move without being hindered by his vow of obedience or any other rules of the order.

But Luther, even though he had little hope in regard to the cardinal, did not believe himself free to leave the city as long as there was the slightest chance of being summoned once more, since he had been summoned by his count's command. He had written a letter to Carlstadt, "He is perhaps a Thomist by name, but a hazy, hidden, ignorant theologian, or Christian. For this reason, in sitting in judgment on this case, understanding or deciding this issue, he is as skilled as a donkey is skilled to play the harp. As a result, my case is in so much more danger, since it has judges, who are not only enemies, who are angry with me, but are also incapable of recognizing or understanding the issue."

Luther desired to take at least a few steps toward satisfying the cardinal's desires, as he had been encouraged by Link and Staupitz. So, he decided to do whatever he could still do with a good conscience. He wrote a humble message to the cardinal the day after his two friends departed. In it, he admitted that he may have written too brashly. He also declared himself ready to let the entire indulgence controversy rest on this condition that those sellers of indulgences, who had driven him into action, would have their activities restricted with set boundaries and goals. When he received no reply from the cardinal, he followed with another message the next day. In it he proposed to the legate, that since he had been forbidden to show his face to the cardinal without retracting and since he was short of food and did not want to be a burden to the Carmelites, it was useless for him to stay in Augsburg. After all, he was now appealing to the pope, begging that he would look upon him with favor.

The appeal to which he referred he had already submitted on Saturday, in the presence of a notary and witness, as "an appeal from a badly instructed subject to the pope who is able to better instruct him." This appeal also contained a request for retraction of the citation to come to Rome and appear before the court, from which he could not expect a just decision about his concern.

When the legate maintained his utter silence after the second message, Luther's friends became very uneasy. In the middle of the night between October 20th and 21st, a small gate in the city wall was secretly opened and two men rode off toward the north. The one was an elderly man who knew all of the paths and roads. The other, dressed as a monk, was sitting on a hard-gaite nag without saddle, boots, or stirrups. He was called Martinus Luther. Brother Leonhard had stayed behind in the city in order to deliver the letter of appeal to the Cardinal in the presence of a notary and a witness.

The riders arrived in Monheim in the evening, where Luther was unable to stand after dismounting, and instantly fell into the straw. In Nuernberg, his friends strove to succor Doctor Luther as best they could after the troubles and dangers he had endured. The learned patrician, Billibald Pirkheimer, provided both food and shelter. We shall hear later about what this cost this Nuernberg humanitarian.

On the first anniversary of the posting of the 95 Theses, Martin Luther read a mass in Kemberg near Wittenberg. Later that day he arrived in Wit-

Picture of Billibald Pirkheimer according to Albrecht Dürer

tenberg, well rested and full of joy and peace. It takes little wisdom to conclude that the cardinal and his commander, the pope, would not stay satisfied with what had taken place.

The actual instructions of the pope, to which the Cardinal had referred as a threat at their last meeting, were first brought to Luther's attention in Nuernberg. Luther could not believe that the same instructions were genuine, that the pope had condemned him as a heretic before the time, which had been allowed for his citation, had expired. Even when Luther shortly thereafter put a sharp rebuke into print in the form of a short report, he still regarded the pope's instructions to the Cardinal as forgery.

As early as October 23rd the Cardinal had sent a letter to the Elector, agreeing with the papal brief. In it he bitterly complained that Luther had appeared before him with royal escort, had remained disobediently impenitent to his fatherly admonition, and had put the reasons for justifying his actions into writing. The final straw was that, without letting him know, both Staupitz and Luther had traveled away, and so had betrayed him. For this the legate asked the count to either send Luther to Rome or into exile. The Elector passed this letter on to Luther. Luther in turn tore apart the legate's arguments in his response to the count, which completely satisfied him.

It must have been especially reassuring to the count that Luther constantly showed himself striving, in whatever way possible, to keep the trouble away from him as the head of government. He even wrote a letter saying that he was ready to leave the country and head into misery. "For this reason," he wrote, "that nothing evil may happen to your Electoral Grace on my account. In God's name I am willing to leave the land of your Electoral Grace and go wherever the eternal and merciful God wants me to be." In this way he showed that he had been serious when he had declared to Urbanus in Augsburg that he would "remain under the sky."

Still he did not want his count to turn into a Pilate toward him, delivering him who had not been convicted of any wrong to a sure death in Rome. In truth, the Elector for some time entertained the thought, that should the ban be imposed very soon, Luther might leave the country. His idea was for Luther to go to France where it was hoped he would fit in with the Parisian doctors. The count would not hear of surrendering him to Rome. Instead he wrote to Degenhard Pfeffinger, his ambassador to Caesar, to try to convince Caesar to set up a non-partisan hearing for Luther in Germany.

He then wrote a letter to the legate. In it he declared his open astonishment with the demands made of Luther and himself: of Luther, that he was ordered to retract without having been convicted; of himself, that he deliver Luther to Rome without more ado or send him into exile. He requested that an orderly debate with Luther be held, or that his alleged errors be proved in writing. If that would happen he would know how to respond. Up to this point no one had been able to show him that Luther's teaching was godless, though some, who had seen a decrease of income for their money chests, had attempted to do just that. He included in the letter a copy of Luther's critique of the letter of complaint sent to the Count by the Cardinal.

When Luther got to read that letter, he was so delighted he read it over and over. That was the first time he learned with some degree of certainty what his ruler thought about his (*Luther's*) position and how he stood in regard to the pope. He was well satisfied with it.

While all this was going on, Luther remained active. First, he published a report in Latin about what had taken place in Augsburg. This included his written arguments of October 14th, with which he defended the two points, which the legate demanded to be retracted. In reading his epilogue one finds opposition to papal authority unheard of up to this time. He not only provides proof that Scripture was violated and misused by papal decrees, but he chose for such proof a case in which the misuse of Scripture was intentionally used to produce a (*falsfied*) source for proof by which the pope claims spiritual supremacy.

Luther first disproved the papal interpretation of the passage and then the issue which the passage was intended to support. He rejected as foolishness the view of those who believe that someone who does not live under the pope cannot be a Christian. He pointed out that at the time of Gregory the Great he did not have the title of universal bishop, and more to the point, Gregory rejected it. He added that there have been large groups of Christians who were never under papal authority, and that in ancient days the other bishops addressed the Bishop of Rome simply as brother. He did not wish to deny the sovereignty of the pope. He suggests that the papacy allow itself to have its authority proven from Scripture. If so, perhaps only from Romans 13:1 (NIV), "There is no authority except that which God has established. The authorities that exist have been established by God." He was fighting against those who, in place of Christendom, were erecting a Babylon with the operation of the Roman Church.

So we see how Luther, on account of the attacks of his opponents, was driven ever more into the entrenchment of God's Word, from which he was induced to catapult ever heavier cannon balls against the papal bulwark. Luther combined his growing understanding with the axioms he had developed as he now asked for a free Christian council. This was in addition to the appeal he had sent to the instructing pope.

With this request, which he again presented in the correct form before witnesses, he attacked the proposed ban head on. He did so by arguing that the validity of such a ban depended on the decision of a council. He added this to his sermon on the power of the ban, in which he proclaimed that a ban for the sake of truth was an honor for the one under the ban. Even as he was informing his friend Link about the appeal, the printer, contrary to Luther's wishes, was making it a public matter. His publication included this remarkable statement, "My pen is already working on more important matters. I don't know where these thoughts come from. I am thinking that the real struggle has not even begun, even though the great lords in Rome may hope that the matter has already ended. I am sending you my ideas. I do this that you might consider whether my supposition is correct, that the real Antichrist of whom Paul speaks rules in the Roman court. I think that I will be able to prove that he is worse than the Turk."

In the midst of all these battles, this remarkable man also took great pleasure in pursuing peaceful works. He reworked an explanation of the Lord's Prayer, which had been distributed by his "good friends" after his sermons of 1517. He allowed it to be issued in its new form under the title, "A German Explanation of the Lord's Prayer, by Doctori Martini Lutheri, Intended for the Common Man, not for the Learned." In it, Luther instructs the people in what one has to know in order to be saved, and he does so simply and powerfully. "He is justified before God," he writes among other things, "who humbly confesses his disobedience and sin, including the judgment he deserves. He offers a heartfelt plea for grace and has no doubt that it will be given to him. So the Apostle teaches that a justified person may stand before God with nothing except his faith and trust in God. Hence his comfort and refuge comes not from his works, but from the bare mercy of God."

"Instruction and knowledge of Christ occurs when you understand what the Apostle says in I Corinthians, chapter 1 that Christ has been given to us by God for our wisdom, righteousness, holiness, and redemption. You comprehend this when you admit that all of your wisdom is damning folly, your righteousness is damning unrighteousness, and your redemption is miserable condemnation. You grasp that before God you are merely a foolish, unclean, and condemned man. You demonstrate this not only with your words, but with your whole heart and with your works. You acknowledge that you have no comfort and salvation except that God has given Christ to you, in whom you are to joyfully believe. Only his righteousness will keep you." - "This letter, which was sealed with Christ's wounds and confirmed by his death, has almost faded and rotted away because of the tempests of Roman indulgences."

There was a huge audience waiting for anything Luther wrote. The printers throughout Germany reaped great profits from the vast number of German publications from Luther's pen. In the fall of that year, 1518, the first Latin collection of nearly all of Luther's writings was produced by the famous and well-respected printing firm of Johann Froben in Basel. The actual printer was not named. Capito, the Basel court preacher of that time, wrote the foreword, but also withheld his name. Among the statements included in that foreword we read the following, "Here you have the theological writings of the honorable Father Martin Luther, who, as most people believe, has been sent by Christ, who has finally looked upon us with compassion. He is a second Daniel, sent to expose the abuses which have arisen in the church, while other theologians are neglecting the gospel and Pauline theology. ... Therefore, my brothers, it is time that we arise from our slumber."

Froben sent Luther a copy of this edition to his honor, as a gift. A letter accompanied. And Capito wrote that copies of this entire large edition had been shipped to Italy, France, Spain, and England in one and one-half months. He related that even many of the Parisian doctors were pleased with his writings.

While Luther's writings made his voice heard in ever wider circles, Luther remained busy at home, in the pulpit and at the lectern. Nevertheless, he always stood ready to leave city and country at a moment's notice. He would tell his congregation, "Fare well," in case he would suddenly have to flee and not return. It is said that Luther had a farewell dinner with his friends, at which they advised him to flee. He is said to have cried out, "Father and mother may forsake me, but the Lord will receive me." Luther would soon find a place of refuge. The following year Capito wrote to him, "When Cardinal von Sitten, the Count von Geroldseck, an honorable learned bishop, and a number of others among us learned that you were floating in dangerous waters, they immediately offered to help you escape. Not only were they ready and willing to provide you with funds, but also to provide you with a safe refuge where you could live openly or clandestinely, however you would choose. So, you see that when it was made known that you might have to enter a miserable existence, many offered to help you with generous support."

In the meantime, Rome was having difficulty getting accustomed to the fact that times could have changed so much. Unlike earlier conflicts, accusations which were raised against the actions and teaching of the Roman court, could no longer be swept away with the power of papal declarations. Even so, a papal bull relating to indulgences appeared on November 9th. It had crossed the Alps with full intention of its enforcement. It declared that the errors recently proclaimed by certain monks stood solemnly condemned. These errors pertained to teaching which Luther also had been attacking. This teaching pertained to the distribution of the treasure of indulgences. This treasure was being described as official doctrine of the Roman church. Everyone who dared to teach differently was threatened with the ban.

This very bull, which did not accuse Luther by name, gives us more evidence that a change of direction in church matters was in full motion. For no one respected this bull, even though it was endorsed by Cajetan. This became clear when a German bishop wanted to stop debates on the topic of indulgences because of this bull, as he maintained that the matter had been settled. Even though this occurred in a German university city with strong papal ties, the local authorities dared to tear down the bull that demanded the halting of debate as the bishop had posted. In fact, the one whom the bishop had directed to post the bull took it down and put it in his pocket.

Luther soon realized that they were again dealing with him by way of proclamations. But in the face of them he remained calm and cheerful. He shared his thoughts with Spalatin when he said, "The more they rage and plan how to use their power, the less it frightens me. I will only realize freedom from those Roman snakes all the more. I am ready for anything and everything, and trust for guidance which comes by God's Word." ("Ich habe mich auf alles gefasst gemacht und harre auf Gottes Rat.")

Chapter 15
Miltitz

Urbanus von Serralonga did not journey to Augsburg without good reason. He had come to encourage Luther to visit the cardinal's residence at once without waiting for Caesar's escort. Nor did Cajetan afterward complain without reason that he was not being trusted. For by first securing Caesar's escort, as a Catholic historian admits, the legate's "whole plan was debunked." It had been the plan to put the uncomforting monk under arrest and have him deported to Rome, which he surely would not have left again. Rome and its legate, who under normal circumstances would have struck terror into the hearts of kings and counts, had been defeated by this poor monk, and they knew it. In fact, the cardinal didn't seem to have been able to shake off the impression, which Luther with his Bible theology had made on him. At any rate from this time on he zealously undertook the study of Scripture, even going so far, as an old man, as to learn the original language of the New Testament.

The pope, however, wrote a new tune when the song didn't play out as he liked. Luther remained where he had been, in Wittenberg, diligently applying himself to his work under the Elector's permission. It is reported that the legate, who had instructed him to exile that little monk, was told to cool off. But while Luther and his friends were spending their days in Wittenberg awaiting the papacy's next move, a new series of maneuvers appeared in Wittenberg even before a response had been heard regarding the Augsburg negotiations. It is possible, that these originated as a result of the support Luther had received in Augsburg and the reception of the imperial letter.

While Cajetan was trying to ingratiate himself with Caesar in Austria, a new messenger of the pope appeared in Germany. He was the Chamberlain Karl von Miltitz, and he carried with him a number of papal decrees, dated October 24th. Miltitz was a multi-talented man descended from noble Saxon blood, a wise and skilled courtier with a glib tongue. Back in 1515, the Elector had told him of his desire for the Rose. This was the Rose which was consecrated by the pope every year on Laetare Sunday (the 4th Sunday in Lent). It was then delivered with great ceremony as a sign of special favor from the pope to a noble individual the church considered worthy of recognition. This honor was now designated to the elector, and Miltitz had been chosen as the bearer of this "highly valuable and personal gift." This flower, whose scent was said to grant the highest joy connected with the redemption of humanity and the precious body of the Redeemer being represented by it, was connected with a plan. It was designed to direct the heart of Frederick, that beloved son of the church, to become willing and inclined to follow the papal instructions as outlined by Miltitz. His response was to be that he would cull that diseased sheep, Martin Luther, from the clean sheep of the Elector's flock and leave that son of corruption to the judgment of the papal nuntio.

The intent to arrest Luther became even more apparent, when a request came to the municipal council of Wittenberg to grant special license to Miltitz for his actions. And all of this was directed at Luther, who was said to have been pricked by the devil. If it happened that Miltitz would actually get Luther under his control, he had been supplied similar dispensations for other German cities, which would allow him to freely journey through their territory with his prisoner. Thus, Luther was correct when he at the time wrote that the papal nuntio was coming to arrest him and deliver him to Rome.

In addition to those instructions it seems as though Miltitz was going to have to face other opposition to his task, both in Wittenberg and during his travels. The nuntio could expect two things during his journey to Saxony, if he had not already been made aware of them. One was that the pope's credit in Germany had plunged; and the other was that Luther had many friends. John Tetzel, the one responsible for Luther's attack and whose greed and loose tongue further diminished the pope's indulgence in the eyes of the people, was well aware of that situation. For when Miltitz summoned him to give account of himself, he wrote a deplorable letter from his monastery in Leipzig, claiming that he couldn't appear in public for fear of his life. When Miltitz later went to Leipzig and reproached him, Tetzel fell apart. He died in that monastery the following year on the 4th of July, even while Luther had been trying to comfort him with a letter.

On top of all of the problems that Miltitz presented to the Elector, even greater difficulties arose to bring all sorts of consternation to his mind. While the negotiations with Caesar were proceeding, the vague concerns that Caesar had expressed at his departure from Augsburg arrived. Before he could even return to his imperial headquarters, his physical condition had deteriorated. He had tried to improve it by way of diversion and exertion of the hunt and with various home remedies. But it was all to no avail, so much so, that even the doctors, who swiftly left Vienna to meet him, could give him little hope. He drew up his last testament on December 20th, and as the new year began, Maximillian's end was very near. If Caesar were to die now, the empire's regency of Germany would become the responsibility of Luther's Elector and would remain so until a new Caesar was chosen. The word of the Elector would carry heavy weight in that election. In fact, if the Elector had put himself forward, it was possible that the name of the next Caesar could well have been Caesar Frederick V.

All of these factors shed some light on everything that Miltitz did. The nuntio arrived at the Elector's residence in Altenburg December 27th. He had not yet brought along the consecrated Rose. That had been consigned to the Fugger House in Augsburg for safe keeping. Most likely this was because he wanted to be careful not to give it to the Elector in haste, and instead allow its scent to have its maximum effect. The discussion with the Elector quickly led to a temporary solution. It was agreed that Luther and Miltitz would meet at Altenburg. Luther obeyed his count, and by the first week of the new year stood face to face with the papal nuntio. He conversed with him, dined at his table, and was dismissed with a parting kiss.

This certainly sounds different from the description of Luther's departure from Cajetan! While Cajetan had received Luther in a cold and aloof manner, Miltitz welcomed him with open warmth. "Dear Martine," he addressed him, "I thought that you were some old, worn out theologian, who sat behind his stove and debated with himself. But I see that you are still a strong young man. If I had an army of 25,000 with me, I would not try to take you out of Germany. For while I traveled, wherever I went I tried to find out what people are thinking, and what they think of you. What I found was that for everyone who was on the pope's side there would be three on your side against the pope." Miltitz also admitted that for the past hundred years nothing had proven to be as much of a headache to the lords in Rome, as his case. He added that, if the issue could be resolved by paying 1000 ducats, it would be worth the price.

He allowed Luther to speak freely, even admitting that Tetzel had caused great offense with the way he acted. Even the demand for a retraction, which he had originally brought up, he did not pursue. He offered the opinion that the issue be transferred to a German bishop for examination, suggesting either the Bishop of Salzburg or the Bishop of Trier. Once more Luther was prepared to let the whole matter die and to maintain his silence, if it was agreed that both sides would do the same. If one side was forbidden to preach and to write about the matter, then the other side was to agree to the same prohibition. Miltitz was to report to the pope about where matters stood and urge him to accept the agreed upon stipulations. In addition, Luther was also to do his part. He was to write to the pope and to produce a pamphlet in which he would encourage the German people to honor and be faithful to the Roman church. Luther himself wrote a letter to his Elector about their agreement. (*LV, Vol. 7.8, p. 11ff.) He did, however, end his letter with the short, decisive statement, "The retraction will not happen."

If one looks only at the way this resolution was worded, one might get the impression that the talented Miltitz had achieved notable success. But when a person examines it more closely, one realizes that Miltitz had drawn a number of zeroes with no number in front of them. Of course, neither of the main players Luther and Miltitz, nor Luther's attending friends, Spalatin and the counselor Fabian von Freilitzsch were fully aware of it. Luther on his part faithfully kept his side of the agreement. He issued a pamphlet to the people entitled, "Doctor Martin Luther's Instruction in Response to Several Articles That Have Been Imposed and Assigned against Him by His Grudging Opponents." This "Letter" is important for us for a number of reasons. On the one hand, we recognize that in regard to certain sections of Christian doctrine, Luther himself was still held captive under some of the papal errors. These are parts of doctrine which today, thanks be to God, are understood correctly in line with Holy Scripture by every properly instructed Lutheran catechuman, thousands of whom have been liberated through Luther. Luther, however, had not yet shaken off all Roman false teachings at that time. His words in this letter therefore seem surprising, "It is to be firmly believed concerning purgatory, and I know it to be true, that those poor souls in it suffer wretched pains. A person owes it to them to pray, fast, give alms, or whatever else one can do. But what sort of pain this is, and whether its purpose is only to atone or to improve, I don't know. Indeed, I don't think anyone does."

On the other hand, we can clearly see that carrying through with the promise he had made at Augsburg, he did not surrender one iota of the truth as he understood it at that time. We also see how he confessed those parts of the truth openly and freely. Those were the truths he had come to know very well and were a thorn in his enemies' eyes. He wrote this about indulgences. "If someone fails to give to a poor person, or does not help his neighbor, and still intends to buy an indulgence, he is doing nothing less than despising God and himself. He does not do what God has bidden him to do, and does that which no one has bidden." Concerning the dictates of the church he wrote, "The command of God is to be honored over the commands of the church as gold and precious gems are to be esteemed more than wood and straw." "Concerning good works," he wrote, "I have said and still maintain that no one can be holy and do right, unless the grace of God has first made him holy. No one will become holy by doing good works, but good works can only occur through him who is holy. ... God wants us to despair of ourselves, our entire lives, and our works, to teach us that we cannot by ourselves be acceptable to God with the very best of our works. He wants us to take comfort only in his boundless grace and compassion."

His promise to urge Christians to be faithful to the Roman church he was implementing in a way that would not be satisfactory to the Romans. Among other things he wrote, "The current situation in Rome could certainly be better. Yet, the problems that exist are not so large, nor can they be, that a person should tear himself away or separate himself from the church." That he would think differently after further study we have mentioned before and will speak of again. In this current writing Luther added, "We should not oppose papal rules for our physical lives."

However, he was not submitting to the pope in spiritual matters with these words. He simply desired that the pope would be honored and esteemed like any earthly power. He wrote in this same section, "But in regard to the power and authority of the Roman throne and the extent of that power, let the learned men settle this. For the blessedness of the soul does not depend on them. Christ did not build his Church on outward appearing power and authority, nor on any temporal matter. These things are left to the world and the worldly. Therefore whether the power is great or small, over all things or some things, we should be pleased to be satisfied in how God distributes it, just as we should be satisfied with how God distributes other temporal goods, honor, wealth, favor, skill, etc." But that was not what the pope wanted. It was his belief that the church was built on the papal throne, and acknowledging himself as the church's ultimate authority would result in the blessedness of souls.

Luther also carried out his promise to write directly to the pope. On March 3, 1519, he sent a letter to Leo, by which he showed himself extremely humble, yet also serious and frank. He described himself as human excrement, the dust of the earth, and a bleating lamb of the blessed father. He went on to state that what he had done to honorably rescue the Roman church had been misinterpreted as disrespect.

As before he decisively dismissed the idea of retraction, going on to explain that such an action would not help the matter. What he had written had already been dispersed more widely than he had ever hoped and had been taken strongly to heart by so many, that it could not be retracted. Because of the high spiritual atmosphere in Germany, retracting would only bring disgrace on the Roman church and expose her to attacks from the nations.

He asserted that he had never had any desire to question the Roman church, or the power of the pope. In fact, he stated that the power of the church stands higher than anything else, with the exception of Christ. Yet in making this exception, he retained the right to judge the teaching and the regulations of the Roman church on the basis of the Word of Christ. He declared himself ready to submit to silence about indulgences as per his agreement with Miltitz, if his opponents would also remain silent. He added that he would agree to address the people as he had in his pamphlet and perhaps expand on its contents.

Miltitz, too, continued to strive along the path set forth at Altenburg. It was important to him that Luther's issue would be brought before an arbitrator as soon as possible. Although he had received no permission at all from Rome, before Rome could make a decision, he urged the Archbishop Richard of Trier to serve as arbitrator, and set a time frame for the hearing.

However, on the same day that Miltitz sent along the recommendation to choose Archbishop of Trier, Caesar Maximilian died. This meant that the Archbishop of Trier, who was also an elector, would have his hands full during the following days. There would have to be an election for a new Caesar, a matter which would occupy most of his time. Since prolonged correspondence was cause for even more delays, Miltitz traveled to the Trier territory in person in an attempt to attain his objective more quickly and securely. He met Cajetan in Koblenz and was allowed to inform Luther that the archbishop was willing to undertake the hearing. The legate had forgotten everything, so Luther should just come. The archbishop himself responded in similar fashion.

In Altenburg, Luther had shown himself to be very agreeable. But if those lords thought that Luther would grab his hat and come without further ado, they were much mistaken. Instead, Luther replied that he would have to be a fool to make the long journey to Koblenz from where he was living quietly and safely in Wittenberg. In addition, he lacked funds to travel, nor had he received a summons from pope or archbishop to come to the archbishop's hearing.

Nevertheless, the archbishop had indeed sent a written summons to Luther. But he had sent it to the Elector to give to Luther. The Elector, however, was holding the letter in his files because it didn't seem right to him. He left for the Diet at Frankfurt where he wanted to discuss the matter further with the archbishop. It is understandable that the two counts had little time for Miltitz in those days and regarded his concern as a secondary issue. But after the election of a new Caesar, the situation would be considerably different.

Despite the glowing reports of huge success which Miltitz had to have sent to Rome, nothing had changed at the core of the issue. The conflict actually existed between Luther and the pope, and this conflict remained the same as before. We have ample evidence of this in regard to Luther. Though he had sincerely promised to let the matter rest, he had made no concessions in regard to the actual disagreement. Yet it was this disagreement which remained a thorn in the pope's flesh. For his part the pope remained the same and he likewise conceded nothing. This is apparent from a writing that would later surface, directed to Miltitz in response to his report on Luther. In it the pope addressed Luther as his son, yet repeated his demand that this "dear son" should come to Rome immediately and retract.

Others, too, had not changed. These were the ones, who needed to remain silent, once Luther agreed to be silent. They were worthless to Miltitz's wise plans. These persons would let those plans turn into water, even vinegar.

Chapter 16
The Debate at Leipzig

We recall that during Luther's absence at Heidelberg the Ingolstadt doctor had published his "Obelisks." Luther's colleague, Carlstadt, had responded with several hundred statements. Eck had answered him in mid-summer of 1518, speaking about the doctrines of repentance, sin, and the freedom of the human will. Carlstadt sharpened his pen again in defense against Eck. He offered to submit himself to the judgment of the Roman throne, the universities of Rome, Paris, and Cologne, indeed to anyone who had studied the church fathers. Yet, he maintained that Holy Scripture is the final authority. Toward the end of the year Carlstadt followed up with a small, half satirical work on the whole subject. The result of these polemics was that the stage was set for personal public debate between these two opponents. Eck had suggested the debate and a mutually agreeable university, and Carlstadt responded with his acceptance, provided that costs and security were guaranteed and that the speeches and counter speeches would be recorded by notaries.

During those important days he spent at Augsburg, Luther and Eck, who was also present, had a friendly discussion about the situation. Luther had invited Eck to Wittenberg, but Eck declined, suggesting Cologne, Paris, even Rome for a debate. Luther, in return, did not agree and finally offered Leipzig and Erfurt as suggested sites. Eck, who had the privilege of choice from Carlstadt, chose the University of Leipzig. He made this choice because Leipzig was much closer to Eck's views of spiritual matters than Erfurt. In addition, their envy of the Wittenberg faculty meant that Eck would have an advantage.

The theologians of Leipzig were not happy with the decision to have the face-off dragged to their university, and did not give their consent to the agreement. Meanwhile Eck, without waiting for comment from the Leipzig contingent, even before leaving Augsburg in December 1518, had already published twelve theses for the debate. In it he announced the debate and indicated that Leipzig would be its location. He had also sent these theses to Luther. Responding with a letter of January 7th, Luther informed Eck that the Leipzig group had declined to host. Until this point there had been no discussion of Luther participating in the debate, and the acceptance of Leipzig was still being sought for the debate between Eck and Carlstadt.

This is where matters stood, with Luther remaining silent as agreed at Altenburg, provided that his opponents would remain silent as well. When he returned from Altenburg and saw Eck's theses he was stunned. In reality those theses were not against Carlstadt, but against Luther. The first eleven were directed against the very point that Luther had made in a number of his writings. It was only later that another item was added to the seventh which pointed directly at Carlstadt. Eck supposedly maintained that he had forgotten it in his hurry to get them out. But now to top things off, it was made the final thesis. The point made in that thesis was one with which Carlstadt agreed at the time. It was Luther who had maintained deviations in regard to the point, both in his resolutions and in the epilogue of his report about his dealings with Cajetan. This is what the thesis said, "We do not agree with the idea that before the time of Silvester the Roman church had not stood above other churches; rather, we have always regarded the one who sat upon Peter's throne as the successor of Peter and as steward of Christ." Contradicting this view Luther had pointed out in his resolutions that prior to the 7th century large areas of the Church had not recognized Rome's supremacy. And in his Augsburg statements he had maintained that the eastern and also the African Christians, who had never acknowledged the pope, dare not be cast out of the church and that even Gregory the Great (590 A.D.) (Gregory the Great 540-604 as dated from a recent almanac) had repeatedly rejected the title of universal bishop.

The fact that Eck had planned to attack Luther from the beginning became much clearer in a letter sent to Luther on February 19th. In it he without apology told Luther that he must have noticed that he, Eck, had directed his theses more against Luther than Carlstadt.

It is also understandable why Eck was more eager to do battle with Luther than Carlstadt. The polemicist of Ingolstadt had often faced off against opponents like Carlstadt, but never against someone like Luther. Luther's name had already gained wide renown, and in stepping forth as Rome's defender, Eck expected great reward from Rome. And so he sought and anticipated his victory over the man who had proven to be too strong for a cardinal.

It was soon apparent to Luther what he would have to do. In February 1519, he sent a letter to Carlstadt in which he declared his intention to participate in the debate. Moreover, he wrote to his Elector on March 13th:

"Most Serene Highness,

"I had received a number of encouragements through Your Electoral Grace's chaplain, Mr. Magister Spalatin, reminding me of what the honorable Carolus von Miltitz and Your Electoral Grace desired of me, namely, that from now on I would remain silent and start nothing new, as we had agreed at Altenburg. Now, God knows that such was my sincere intention, and I was happy that the whole game would be ended as far as I was concerned. I even remained resolute to adhere to that agreement in dismissing Mr. Silvester Prierias Replicam, although I had ample justification to respond. * (Footnote: Prierias had published a response to some of Luther's writings). And even though I despised the mocking arrogance of my adversaries, I remained silent, contrary to the advice of my friends. Thus our resolution still stood, as Mr. Carolus well knows, that I desired to remain silent, if my opponents also remained silent. But now Eck has attacked me

without warning. Many people think that in doing so, he seeks to bring disgrace and dishonor not to me, but to Your Electoral Grace and the University of Wittenberg. Thus it did not seem right for me to ignore such windblown, treacherous tricks, nor to allow the truth to be mired in such blasphemy. For if I were to sew my mouth shut and allow everyone else's to remain open, Your Electoral Grace can well expect that the one who would otherwise not wish to look at me would fall upon me as well. It is still my heartfelt desire to obediently follow Your Electoral Grace's advice and remain silent in every way, if only they would remain silent as well. For truly I have many other things to do and take no pleasure in this matter. But if I do not remain silent, I beg of Your Electoral Grace in all submission that you will not hold it against me, for I do not know how to allow my conscience to abandon the truth."

The Elector then gave Luther permission to participate in the debate. But this did not resolve the issue. Though the chancellor of the Leipzig University, Bishop Adolf of Merseburg, had agreed with the stance of the Leipzig University faculty to oppose the debate to be held in Leipzig, the same faculty finally consented to let Eck and Carlstadt meet in Leipzig. In this, the Leipzig University faculty was obeying the wishes of Duke George, who had become strongly and personally involved. But when they read Luther's public response to Carlstadt that Luther also wanted to debate, they wrote to him immediately. They expressed their surprise at his desire to participate in the debate, since neither the Duke nor the University had invited him to do so. When Luther then appealed to the Duke, the Duke referred him to Eck and left Luther's admission up to Eck's discretion. And Eck, who delighted in embarrassing Luther, let Luther wait in vain for his decision, though Eck had received a letter from Count George in which Eck was fully informed about his, the Duke's, answer to Luther.

Yet on March 14th Eck did issue a public response to Luther's public letter that he wished to debate with Luther. He stated that earlier, on the recommendation of a mutual friend, Scheurl, he had been friends with Luther. However, he could not remain so, not since he [Martin Luther] had revived heresies that had been dealt with long ago and had kindled a pile of ashes into a new flame. With those words he wished to imply what he would later say openly - that he regarded Luther guilty of the heresy of John Hus.

Luther did not hesitate to answer the malicious letter that Eck had attached to his theses, which now numbered thirteen. He wrote that from now on no one could expect him to be patient any longer. His mild behavior would come to an end, and from now on he would aggressively bite and devour the Cajetans and the Ecks. The accusation that he was guilty of Hus' heresy he dismissed as a guess. He was not intimidated, for he sent Eck an equal number in answer to Eck's thirteen. In the last one, he maintained that the teaching that the Roman church has superior status, was based on the papal decrees of only the previous four centuries, and that this teaching stands in opposition to the witness of eleven centuries of history, Holy Scripture, and the Council of Nicea.

This one sentence was enough to command the papacy to get down from the position it had usurped, from which height she had lorded over the emperors and kings of the nations, and had imposed untold burdens not only on treasuries, but also on consciences. Luther was well aware that the way the question with which Eck was pressing him was handled would be of importance in a wider range. "This debate," he wrote to Staupitz" will, if Christ so wills, deliver a terrible blow against Roman rights and origins, the crutches on which Eck leans." He diligently prepared himself for battle. "I am now reading," he wrote, "a great deal for my debate. As I read the decretals of the popes, I whisper in your ear, I am now uncertain whether the pope is the Antichrist himself, or is his apostle. That is the truth, since Christ is so miserably crucified by him in those decrees."

Luther's studies led him to understand with increasing clarity what the church is, and how the pope had enslaved her. His indignation grew along with his understanding. Even before the debate he brought the detailed resolution of his final thesis into view. In it he identified the true Christian Church, referred to in the Apostles' Creed, as true Christians everywhere, where the Word and Sacraments are used, also outside of the papal church. He now began to denounce even the commands of the bishops when they attempted to usurp the God-ordained authority of other congregational shepherds and teachers.

This brave man's friends were concerned for him, as though he were standing under a stone archway that was starting to crumble. Luther on his part, kept appealing to Duke George for permission to take part in the debate. But the Duke, as mentioned before, had deferred the final decision to Eck. Since Eck gave no direct response to Luther's request but merely provoked Luther with his published writings, the Duke chose to permit Luther's presence in an indirect fashion. Since he cherished the idea of seeing Luther's defeat at his university, he stated in a letter to Carlstadt that he would welcome all those "whom he would bring along." As a result, Luther could appear in Leipzig, or choose to stay away. He did the former, placing himself under Carlstadt's wings, until the latter exercised his right to petition the Duke to permit Luther's admission. In response, the Duke then personally granted Luther's admission to the debate.

As the date which the Duke had set for the debate drew near, extensive security measures were employed in Leipzig under Caesar Pflug, the Duke's Counselor, who served as the chief guardian in the name of the Count. Throngs of guests, of all professions, arrived to attend the debate. Since the university had no audience hall large enough to accommodate so many, the

Duke allowed a large room in his castle, the Pleissenburg, to be equipped and prepared for the debate. So, it would take place as Luther had originally suggested but Eck had decisively rejected. The debate would be held in a secular location. Quarters for the guests were provided by the city council, and the residents took over the security.

Eck was the first of the participants to show his presence for the battle for which Leipzig had prepared. He arrived accompanied by only one servant, and for Corpus Christi Day he walked along with the procession dressed for the mass. But he also conducted an in-depth examination in regard to the goodness of Sachsen beer comparing it with Bavarian beer, and at the same time made acquaintance with the sinful women of the city. This can be gleaned from his own letters.

On the 24th of June the contingent from Wittenberg arrived. It included Carlstadt, Luther, Melanchthon, Luther's friend Lange, Nikolaus Amsdorf, three doctors of law, and an additional two hundred magisters and students. They entered through the Grimmisch City Gate, their students accompanying their lords as they ran alongside the wagons with spears and halberds. Dr. Carlstadt rode in the first wagon, followed by Dr. Martinus and Philip in a similar trundle. None of the wagons were curtained or covered. The word that the Wittenbergers were arriving drew a large crowd of people. Carlstadt met with an accident when his wagon broke down and he fell into the filthy street in full view of everyone, while Luther's wagon wheeled past him. This caused the people to immediately predict Luther's victory and Carlstadt's defeat.

With all of the attention focused on the Wittenbergers, an agent of the Bishop of Merseburg made the most of the confusion by posting a decree on the church doors. The decree forbade the debate alongside a copy of the bull regarding indulgences recently issued by the pope (which no one cared very much about). But even under such circumstances, the documents were not permitted to shine very long on the church doors. They were torn down, and the one who had posted them was imprisoned.

Leipzig had not seen such excitement for a long time. Everyone on the streets and in the homes, was talking about the upcoming debate. Heated arguments and counter arguments could be heard in the inns. Arguments between the students of Leipzig and Wittenberg nearly turned into fist fights. A former colleague of Tetzel, magister Baumgaertner, became so angry at one of these quarrels that he (*actually*) died of rage. The Leipzig students were especially stirred up by Hieronymus Emser. He, who had been traveling around with an indulgence preacher, the cardinal's legate Raimond, had come to Leipzig for the express purpose of agitating for Eck.

As the anticipation was reaching its highest level, something happened that made it seem as though all the security precautions were for naught. Those who had longed to see the battle waged before their eyes, feared that the cannons rolled up into position, would be rolled away without firing a shot. Eck had previously agreed to the suggestion of the Wittenbergers that the arguments and counterarguments of the debate would be recorded by scribes. But now he, whose style of fencing involved confusing the issue with a flood of references from the ancient church fathers in a blustery and thundering manner, had changed his mind. In response to Eck's negative behavior, the Leipzig doctors and directors of the festival took Carlstadt aside, the Sunday before the debate. They attempted to talk him out of the requests he had made in matters of protocol. Although Carlstadt would not yield on the issue of the debate being recorded, they at least got him to make the concession that the notes were not to be published until they had been approved by the judges.

But when they approached Luther on the Monday after the opening of the debate, he told them that he did not want to hear anything about those conditions.

He stated that if they would not allow the debates to be conducted freely, he would refrain from participating in them. Perhaps Eck did not mind this turn of events at that time. He may have later regretted that he had taken on such a dangerous opponent in this battle, but at the time it must have seemed as though all of the preconditions of the debate were shaping up in a way, which would thoroughly disgust Luther or have him submit to disgrace at the hands of hostile minded judges. How could Luther possibly expect a just verdict in regard to the debate? Even his friends thoughtfully shook their heads at his demands.

But it was Carlstadt who had accepted the conditions and the debate would proceed between him and Eck. The debate was begun with a welcome speech by the Leipzig Professor of Ethics, Simon Pistoris, given in the large university lecture hall on the morning of June 27th. From there the festive group proceeded to the St. Thomas Church for mass. The Leipzigers and Wittenbergers had lined up in pairs.

The cantor and printer, George Rau, lent beauty to the service with a new twelve-voice choral work. From there the procession, accompanied by a large crowd, traveled to the castle. A group of citizens equipped with weapons stood guard there. Then the gifted young scholar, Peter Schade, so named from the area Mosellanus where he was born, gave a two-hour Latin lecture about the proper way to debate. The whole assembly fell to their knees in respectful silence and listened to the triple presentation of the hymn, "Come, Holy Ghost, Creator God". After 2:00 PM they reassembled in the well decorated large chamber. In this chamber, there were two lecterns facing each other, many seats for the audience, and tables for the scribes who were to record the debates. Eck stepped to the lectern decorated with a picture of St. George. The other one was occupied by Carlstadt. His was adorned with an image of St. Martin, another military saint. The actual debate had begun.

We shall not go into detailed reporting of the exchanges between Eck and Carlstadt. For the first two days Carlstadt presented volumes of material to occupy his opponent. Eck understood that the only way to avoid impending serious setback on Tuesday afternoon was by yielding a portion of his response time. That afternoon he figured out a way to take advantage of the situation. He had a much better mind for memory and at the same time did not care whether the church fathers had actually said what he quoted them to have said. Carlstadt's memory was lacking and he had to have books and notes at hand. Eck also knew whom the judges of the debates favored – after all, he had chosen Leipzig for a reason – and before the end of the second day, he demanded that the judges deny the use of books and notes.

The debate from the lecterns was recessed for the next two days, since they were church holidays. But it was noteworthy that a new voice appeared in the pulpit. At the request of the principal of the University of Wittenberg who was in attendance, namely, Duke Barnim of Pomerania, Luther was to preach at the castle. Since the report of this decision attracted a large audience, Luther had to preach in the spacious debate hall instead of the castle chapel. In keeping with the festival pericope, he preached on Matthew 16:13-19. His subjects were the two main points of the debate, the grace of God and the inability of man in spiritual matters, and the primacy of Peter and the pope. His first part showed that flesh and blood are totally incapable

Dr. Johannes Eck according to an old woodcut

in spiritual matters and that Christ would not acknowledge or accept anyone, in whom the Father has not produced such action, as he did in Peter's case. His second part showed that the Keys were not given to Peter as a person, but were lent to the church in Peter. They were given to comfort the poor troubled consciences, which would cling to the words of the absolution with strong faith and not dispute all that much about the power of the pope.

This sermon so raised the displeasure of the doctors of Leipzig that they asked Eck to preach against Luther four times in various churches throughout the city. At the same time, in spite of the desires of many in attendance, they arrogantly denied the use of a church to offer a contrary position. The counselor Caesar Pflug made his opposition clear when he said, "I wish that Luther would have saved his sermon for Wittenberg."

The debate between Carlstadt and Eck was resumed on July 1st. Though Carlstadt launched a sharply worded attack against his opponent in the morning, by the afternoon he had been driven into a corner and could only help himself by denying what he had previously said. After the celebration of St. Mary's Visitation had been observed on Saturday, the debate continued on Sunday, when Eck extended the thrust, with his so-called rapier, which he had inflicted during the first few days. While this was going on, Luther's refusal to submit to the conditions set up for the debate and his decision not to participate, was foully interpreted, as though he was afraid to debate. Since his friends were pressing him to submit to the conditions, he finally gave in to the rules, insofar as he understood the referral of the protocol to a deciding panel of judges. He signed his agreement, in which he expressly excluded Rome from the judge's bench, and reserved for himself the right of appeal. This took place on July 4th, the day John Tetzel died in a nearby monastery.

Luther stepped up to the lectern on the designated date with a bouquet in hand. Those who saw the two opponents may have anticipated a lopsided battle. On the one side was the large, squarely built, long striding, well fed, screamer Eck, who paced back and forth during the debate. On the other side was the smaller, emaciated from worry and work, Augustinian monk of Wittenberg in opposition. But as the battle was waged, it soon became apparent that the deeper scholarship especially in the depth of Scriptural understanding, the greater strength and courage in spirit, and the better ability to debate were on the side of the man from Wittenberg.

With a pleasant and clear voice Luther's first words explained that he would have avoided this confrontation out of respect for the pope and the Roman Church. He would have done so except that his opponent had forced him into it. After Eck contradicted him, the actual debate resumed at the point of contention, namely the theses of Eck and Luther in regard to the power of the pope, as had been previously introduced. Luther did not attack the general authority of the pope. He only attacked the divine right of supreme papal power within the Church. As Peter had occupied first place among the other apostles, so the pope was granted first place in comparison with all the other bishops. However, this was not in spiritual authority but in honor.

Later Luther expressed amazement as to the amount of respect he conceded to the pope at Leipzig. He wrote, "Now look and learn, Christian reader, from my example, how hard it is to disengage or save oneself from such errors, errors which the whole world confirmed with her example and through time-worn habit. They have ingrained themselves into the very nature of living in this world. I had diligently read and taught Holy Scripture for seven years at home so that by this time I already had committed everything to memory. In addition to all this, I had the first fruits of knowledge and faith in my Lord Christ. I knew that we are made righteous and saved through faith in the Lord Christ. Yes, I also defended my public declaration that the pope was not the head of the church by divine right. At the same time, I could not yet see the logical progression, namely, that of necessity and certainty the pope had to be from the devil."

Even so, what Luther did say on that 4th of July, was enough to have him seem to stand in contradiction to the Roman doctrine of the papacy. Whereas, for example, Eck maintained straight out that he who does not obey the pope cannot be saved, Luther disagreed. He maintained that the true church existed also among those who in form had separated themselves from the Roman church. Many of those who were not members of the Roman Church, like those in the Greek Church, were a part of the Communion of Saints. This Church needs no earthly supreme head, since Christ is the only head of this Church and has promised that he will be with her to the end of days.

Here in Leipzig was not the first time that these declarations, as Luther set forth, resulted in arousing opposition. But they had been condemned by a church council earlier in Costnitz, where they had been presented by John Hus. Eck knew how to use this to his best advantage and presented it to Luther the next day with venomous words.

However, to the amazement of those present, Luther not only held fast to his assertions, but fearlessly and directly explained that it didn't matter to him whether Hus or anyone else had made the statements. In any event they were true, and there were a number of declarations among those of the Hussites and Bohemians which were downright Christian and evangelical, which dare not be rejected.

In the view of those assembled, something monstrous had occurred. This was a university that had been established in opposition to the Hussite movement. It was located not far from the Bohemian border. It had experienced the terror of the Hussite War. Yet in the presence of high counts and lords, whose ancestors had shed their blood in bygone battles against Bohemians, Luther had dared to praise statements of John Hus as Christian and evangelical statements of a man who had been burned as a heretic and who had been rejected and condemned by a large, esteemed synod of the east. Duke George reacted with indignation. He got up, with hands set into his sides and elbows extended, shook his head, and aired his feelings. With a loud voice that could be heard throughout the hall he blasted forth this curse, "This is the way of the plague!" (or, "the rule of contagious disease" from "Das walt' die Sucht!")

Eck succeeded in what he had attempted. He had forced Luther to confess openly that he had things in common with Hus, which made Luther appear very dangerous. As soon as he had the floor again, he drew such conclusions from Luther's words that Luther had to interrupt and accuse Eck of speaking downright lies. But Luther stuck with what he had said.

In the following days he always returned to his assertion that even councils can err and Holy Scripture alone is infallible. Whatever Scripture does not demand to be believed, no one has the right to impose on Christians as articles of faith. Yes, even later when issues like purgatory, indulgences, and repentance were being debated, Luther held firm to this point. As a result, Eck realized he was being challenged, when Luther argued that purgatory cannot be proved from Scripture.

Eck wanted to support his position with a proof passage from the second book of Maccabees. But Luther contradicted him, stating that this reference does not apply since it was taken from a non-canonical book. He added that even if the Roman church would recognize its validity, it did not compel him, for the church does not have the right to assign greater authority to a book than it possesses within itself. And in regard to the three previously mentioned doctrines, he would not allow any council resolutions to bind him either.

The fact that Eck was unable to properly apply the Scriptures was a final farewell word in Luther's last speech on July 14th. He ended with these words, "I am saddened that the doctor delves into the Scriptures as deep as a water spider enters into water. Indeed, it appears to flee from its own reflection as the devil flees from the cross. In place of this I judge the authority of Scripture as supreme, without any disrespect to the fathers. I offer this as food for thought to my future judges."

That is the way the debate between the two German farm boys came to an end at 8 a.m. on July 14th. While Eck immediately confronted Carlstadt again, exchanging low-scoring punches with him for the next two days, Luther left Leipzig immediately. After all, what was there to keep him in that hostile city? The Wittenbergers, and especially Luther, had been treated with contempt to the extent that even common hospitality had been denied them. Yet Eck had been celebrated in every way and was covered with honors. While the Duke had often invited the Wittenbergers to dine, he always treated Luther in a hateful manner because of what he had written. He had even expressed the opinion that if anyone were to pray the Lord's Prayer as Luther advised he could hardly finish it in four days.

Only a few of the Leipzig doctors had deigned to share company with Luther, and even then timidly and secretly. "Summa Summarum," Luther wrote, "I have experienced jealousy and hatred, but never more insolent and more blatant jealousy."

In view of all of this it is clear enough how the debate was viewed in Leipzig. It was an event at which Eck glimmered as the pope's polemicist. What's more, many of the doctors and magisters, unable to be interested in the whole event, had slept through the debate, allowing themselves to be awakened when it was time to eat. But Amsdorf wrote to Spalatin about those who paid attention to the debate, "Simply put, everything that Eck wanted was right and soon granted, but whatever we asked and sought was rejected as unreasonable and unseemly. As such we were in a most inconvenient and dangerous place, among worst kinds of enemies."

That is how it was. Eck was permitted to slander Luther as a heretic and patron of heretics, a heathen and a tax collector, without being reprimanded for being out of order. The Wittenbergers, on the other hand, were often directed to the rules which had been dictated by Eck. Eck always wanted to have the last word and was allowed to proceed boisterously, while the Wittenbergers were always held strictly to the clock. When the rules of protocol were being established by the judges, they rejected Luther's proposal to use the universities of Freiburg and Basel, and Paris and Erfurt were chosen instead. This resulted in the exclusion of the Augustinian monasteries of Erfurt, which prompted Luther to insist on the exclusion of the Franciscans and Dominicans as well. The Duke also denied another of Luther's requests. He, who had the right to make the decision, chose to deny the request that the entire faculties, not only the theologians, would render the verdict. He did so in order to please Eck. All of these decisions proved to be of no consequence since none of the universities agreed to take up the requested assignment.

The debate was closed abruptly on July 15th, with a speech by Professor Lange of Leipzig. The castle needed to be readied for the reception of a nobler guest, the Elector of Brandenburg.

Chapter 17
Consequences of the Debate at Leipzig and New Battles

So what fruits were to be gleaned from the battle which had been fought at the Pleissenburg in Leipzig? The doctors of Erfurt and Paris, who had been originally appointed to render a verdict, were not allowed to do so. That Eck appropriated this honor to himself is understandable for anyone who knows Eck. In a letter to the papal court he sang his own praises regarding his conquest of Carlstadt and Luther.

As soon as the debate was ended, and before the Wittenbergers could report to the elector, Eck wrote to the elector about what Luther had done, rubbing it in his face. He reported that Luther did not acknowledge the validity of the authority of the church fathers. In addition, he presented himself as one who espoused the error of Hus, the heretic. This contradicted the decision of the Council of Costnitz; and he denied that Christ established the primacy of Peter. In fact, he admonished the Elector to consign to the pyre what Luther had written about the primacy of Peter.

Carlstadt responded with a writing, which the count shared with the Wittenbergers. He replied that Eck's outburst originated in the proven fact that he had falsely quoted the church fathers, resulting in his disgrace. He stated that he had no desire for further debate with such a boastful screamer.

The fact that his own Wittenberg colleagues did not grade Carlstadt's efforts highly can be gleaned from a letter written by Melanchthon. In it he wrote that in observing Carlstadt and Eck he learned firsthand what it means to actively engage in sophistry. But Luther also reported to the Elector that Eck had to openly concur with the central issue of Carlstadt's theses, abandoning his former position.

For Luther himself, however, the debate at Leipzig had very important consequences, his low opinion of the event not withstanding. First of all, the fact that he stepped forward earned the respect, if not the approval, of many who previously despised him or had not known him. This was worrisome not only to Eck, but also to Carlstadt. Carlstadt was plagued with jealousy and allowed himself to be estranged from Luther because his colleague received the higher praises from both friend and foe. It bothered Carlstadt to such an extent that he would accept no help from Luther during the ensuing war of words between Eck and Carlstadt, much to Luther's dismay.

But there was a much more important consequence beyond the fame Luther gained for the work he had begun in God's name. A few years before his death he put it this way, "We don't realize how good it is for us to have opponents and that heretics attack us with all their might, ... for when I began to write against indulgences, and the pope and Dr. Eck threw their weight against me, they woke me up. I wished with all my heart that he would have repented and thought straight, I would have given my fist (perhaps a slang expression for "yield" - "ich wollte die Faust drum Geben") for him to repent. But if he insisted on remaining as he was, then I wished him to become pope, for he had earned it. He forced me to begin to think in opposition to the pope, bringing me to a point I would never have reached otherwise."

That is how it was. Already at Leipzig Luther, being pressed by Eck, fought with increasing clarity and decisiveness for the majesty of the Word of God over and against all human teaching. Since he was not able to outline his arguments against the polemical barriers as thoroughly as he wished, upon his return to Wittenberg he issued explanations of his theses. In these he clarified a number of points. He conceded nothing he had said, but maintained all the more decisively and strongly that Holy Scripture was the only authority in matters of faith.

Eck, too, did not remain idle following the debate. What he had achieved and what he had failed to achieve in Leipzig drove him to further attacks against Luther. Even before the debate at Leipzig, a Franciscan convent at Jueterbock attacked Luther and filed a complaint against him with the Bishop of Brandenburg. In response, Luther threatened that if they did not retract their accusation he would take them down in disgrace. They found a patron in Eck who intervened on their behalf. He submitted a number of statements in distorted form to the bishop along with venomous explanations as basis for the accusation against Luther. When the bishop issued these without hesitation, Luther responded at once with a powerful exposition against them. It was to be expected that he would not spare Eck or the Franciscans in his reply. The prior, who desired to preserve his order's reputation, considered it important enough to ask Luther to hold off with his reply. Luther was willing to do so, if they would pay for the publisher's expense. However, it was too late. His response was already published.

Eck reacted with a "Cleansing Publication", full of slander against Luther, in answer to Luther's exposition of his Leipzig theses, the addendum of which had been addressed to Spalatin. Luther had there made comments regarding Eck's conduct at the debate and after it. Luther fired back as he was reacting to that so called "Cleansing Publication". He bade Eck a formal farewell, a farewell to a man who was full of lies and with whom he had been involved far too long already. He would now leave it to others to take on this insolent "Bramarbas" (from Spanish word for "screamer"), and there were those who would do so in ways that would affect Eck in the most sensitive way.

Eck produced still another attack against Luther. He alleged in an addendum that Luther's addition consisted of thoughts which merely came from a few uneducated foundation lords. An anonymous author responded with a work entitled, "The Answer of the Uneducated Highly Learned Foundation Lords." * (Footnote: The preacher of the main church of Augsburg at that time, Johann Oekolampad, later admitted being this author.) Accompanying the work was a lampoon with the title, "The Planed-Down Eck" (German, "Der abgehobelte Eck"). It had as its main printer, Bilibald Pirkheimer, whom we have already met, and it was produced in the same way as "The Letters of the Dark Men". This so plainly laid bare the "Planed-Down One" that he became a laughingstock. Even Luther expressed his displeasure with it. Eck seethed with anger and plotted his revenge. Only Reuchlin's intervention prevented him from beginning the New Year with a ritual burning of Luther's works in Ingolstadt. Then his anger together with his greed drove him to Rome.

Oekolampad had lowered his lance in the previously mentioned attack against Eck. Now Eck swiftly acquired his own spear-man to assist him, a soldier who outdid him in vileness. We met this person earlier when he agitated the Leipzig students to revolt. His name was Hieronymus Emser. He had played a cunning trick against Luther after the debate at Leipzig. He had written an open letter to the administrator of Prague, Johannes Zack. In it he seemed to defend Luther, lest the Bohemian heretics should believe that in the learned Luther they had found a patron. Luther had angrily rejected any connection with the Bohemians at Leipzig, and had decisively condemned their separation from the Roman church. He stated that he would, without a doubt, abandon a stance that would give the appearance that he agreed with the Hussites.

Emser had laid a clever double trap for Luther. If Luther agreed, it would seem as though Luther had conceded his teaching. On the other hand, if he renounced the praise, which Emser had here ascribed to Luther, he would rightly seem to be someone who confessed himself to be bound together with the famously hated Bohemians.

Thus, it was right for Luther, in the sharp response he fired at Emser, to compare Emser's letter with the deed of Joab against Abner, and with a Judas' kiss. But throughout he uprightly adhered to his theses and explained once again that he would not retract them, just because the Bohemians were pleased with them. Indeed, he rejoiced that they were pleased and only wished that they would please the Jews and the Turks, and yes, even Eck and Emser. In reference to Emser's coat of arms which was printed on his work and featured a mountain ram (Mountain Ram" in German "Steinbock"), he titled his writing, "Answer to the Emser Ram." In it he compared himself to a hunter who has loosed his hounds after the ram. But the vehemence with which he lashed out against Emser reflected the deep dislike Luther had for any and all deceitfulness. Emser responded to this putdown with a venomous response in which he called Luther a dog theologian. He further posited that

Luther's hatred of the pope stemmed from jealousy toward the indulgence preachers and their financial gains.

Partnering with such a writer for opposing Luther, Eck responded with the above-mentioned publication titled, "Against Luther's Irrational Hunt". This work is also noted as the first in which Luther's followers are named "Lutherans".

New Battles

Another attack aimed at Luther's connection with the heresy of Hus came from a different direction. This was mounted under the clever calculations of Eck, and the scheming malice of Emser. It involved a work that was published at the end of 1519, under the title, "A Sermon on the Highly Valued Sacrament of the Holy True Body of Christ." Among other subjects in this work, Luther had asserted that it would be suitable and permissible for a council to resolve that in that holy evening meal instituted by the words of Christ, both elements would be distributed not only to the priests but to all communicants. True, in this writing he had not yet gone as far as he later would, recognizing and explaining that depriving lay members of the cup according to the Roman custom was actually a sinful mutilation of the Sacrament. He could certainly have written more in his recommendation that both kinds be distributed, but not "for the simple reason that one kind would not suffice."

Once again, such a statement immediately aroused new opposition. Duke George had scarcely held the pamphlet in his hand, when he directed a letter be sent to the Elector, warning him of this dangerous sort of writing. He pointed to the double danger that its content appeared to be the same as Prague held, and that it was given to the people in German. In explaining his concern, he cited how it had come to his attention that because of this sermon the number of people in Bohemia "under both kinds" had increased by six thousand. The two monsters with which the printer had decorated the sermon were providing proof for Luther's leanings toward the Bohemian heretics.

In the Elector's reply he avoided the issue. He would not attempt to make a judgment about the pamphlet. However, he was hearing "that until this time the teachings of the same Martinus were honored and held to be Christian by many learned and understanding men." But Luther recognized that his writing had led to much bitterness. He had even heard that it was being said that it would not be a sin to kill him. And so, it was declared: Luther was a Hus heretic, and Luther's point of view was incompatible with that of a true Saxon. A story was being spread in all seriousness that Luther had been born in Prague and was raised by Hussites. It was claimed that his own father had confessed it to be true.

In response, Luther felt compelled to give an answer to these attacks with a short work entitled, "An Explanation of Several Articles of Dr. Martin Luther in His Sermon of the Highly Valued Sacrament of the Holy and True Body of Christ." Concerning the distribution of the cup to the laity, he went no further here than in his previous writing. "Therefore," he wrote, "I find fault with the Bohemians for not going along with the majority and obeying the ruling authority. Let one kind be enough for them." Since Luther himself had not yet come to a proper understanding of this doctrine he explained further, "To regard the appreciation of both kinds as a heresy is a disgrace to Christ and is blasphemy against the holy gospel and this Sacrament. For Christ instituted it in two kinds, and it cannot be denied that the entire church throughout the world used both kinds for hundreds of years." But he proved that the Roman church had no reason to reproach Luther as he wrote, "But the fact that the Bohemians took both kinds in the sacrament is not the reason why they are reviled as heretics. For the Roman church never considered it to be heretical and was happy to hear someone offer a differing opinion, though he were educated as deeply and highly, as long and wide, as he might want to be. For the church permitted the Bohemian behavior long ago, as it is well known. What may be understood is that such usage never has been and never will be heresy, unless someone wanted to blame the Roman church for blasphemy, as though she commanded and permitted heretical teaching."

With great dexterity, he led the blasphemers to the ignorance in their own theology when he said, "I also have noticed that the accusation of heresy comes from a number of ignorant individuals who were too weak in their knowledge of Scripture to debate with the Bohemians. Instead they resorted to avenge themselves with harsh accusations."

Luther demonstrated a very clever mind in the manner in which he used this work to address the accusation that he had been born a Bohemian. He wrote, "My friends seek such an accurate picture of me! They shout that I was born in Bohemia, raised at Prague, instructed in Wycliffe's * doctrines. (Footnote: John Wycliffe was a 14th century English theologian, who translated the Bible into English, and was a forerunner of the reformation as he fought against papal falsehoods and abuses. Hus was very grateful for his works.) They even claim that my father has confessed to all of it. And so as not to omit anything they have interpreted my name, Luther, in Bohemian. Plus, they explained in a manipulative way, those two monsters published on my sermon pamphlet, as though I had given them as a sign to the Bohemians, that they should retain the use of both kinds. On top of all that they show themselves to be so sharp-sighted that they have seen two geese in one monster, all because John Hus means John Goose in Bohemian." "Where might I find two better looking carnival masks than these high-minded and depth seeing prophets claim? But because they are acting with such nobility and dedicated to the truth among the powerful, I had to have mercy on them and tell them about my birth:

"Dr. Martin Luther, born at Eisleben in the County of Mansfeld."

"There is a noble, famous County located in the bishopric of Halberstadt, and the principality of Saxony. Its name is Mansfeld. Nearly all of my gracious lords know my father and me personally. They include Count Guenther, Ernst, Hoyer, Gebhard, and Albrecht. So, I was born in Eisleben, raised at Mansfeld, taught at Magdeburg and Eisenach, became a magister and an Augustinian at Erfurt, and am now a doctor in Wittenberg. I have not been in Bohemian territory near Dresden my entire life. Since I am in such a good mood, I could not withhold such information from my dear prophets, monster hunters, and goose gagglers."

"Since these two monsters have been printed as they have, I plead with those who are high-minded to be gracious to me. For I truly have not the time to pay attention to what kind of picture, letters, ink, and paper my printer uses. It has never happened before, nor have I ever expected that such things would be required of me." "They also wrote that the Bohemians visited me and wrote to me. But I truly and heartily regret that the Bohemians have not come bravely to see me and have not written. I would happily and freely welcome them. In fact, I would do the same for everyone, Jews, Turks, the heathen, and yes, even you, my enemies. I hope that I would be acting properly and would not allow your poisonous breath to disturb a single hair."

At almost the same time as this defense of the sermon under attack was being offered, a new attack came against that same sermon. This was an attack of a much more serious nature, in that it was the first official denunciation of Luther by a German bishop. It was prepared for publication in every way, and it was officially posted. This was a declaration from the Bishop of Meissen, drawn up at the bishop's residence at Stolpen and discharged under the official seal of the spiritual court. In it Luther's pamphlet on the distribution of the Sacrament in both kinds was declared to be in opposition to the resolutions of the latest church decrees, and this pamphlet was to be seized.

How should Luther respond to this latest attack? Should he proceed to oppose the bishop, thereby placing his forehead under his name against the whipping post? Or should he leave the bishop completely out of the matter and only attack the content? He chose the latter and issued a small pamphlet in German under the title, "Dr. Martin's Reply to the Slips of Paper Which Were Issued under the Official Seal of Stolpen." In it he chopped down on the decree so hard, that chips were flying. He explained that if he were a Bohemian and someone presented him with such a rotten and clumsily distorted face, he would not be able to refrain from thinking, "The Germans are drunk!" He also ventured the opinion that such a paper would be viewed, especially in Rome and before all reasonable men, as more clumsy than stupid (German: "mehr toelpisch denn stoelpisch").

"First," he continues, "the highly educated author of these slips of paper must admit that I did not teach that both kinds should be extended, although it seems good to me. For I set forth my opinion as a rule or doctrine for no one. I have expressly stated my preference for a common Christian council to deliberate this so that both elements could be distributed in obedience to the council's decrees. Since this paper-slip master has no basis for his position on this matter, I would gladly be instructed from his baseless wisdom why his council decision is better, while my council regulation is more scandalous. ... In addition, this is not a small thing he has undertaken, but a huge rupture of Roman authority and power regarding the Bohemian schism. The author of the poor, bare, naked slips of paper offers nothing as a basis for his position other than the latest Roman council. This council is not yet ten years old, and is regarded as nothing in Rome itself and has achieved little respect in Germany and other countries. ... Then he draws in the Bible passage that obedience is better than sacrifice. That is exactly the same passage the Bohemians quote against us, and apply it more strongly. For they scold us as being disobedient to the gospel, in which both elements were ordained by Christ. But I notice that this master wants to teach us how to fence in this way, namely, that we give the Bohemians a sword in their hand and then strike blows against them with our bare head. I did write against the Bohemians and am still willing to write further, but the nice paper slip author crashes in on my work and paper slips me into confusion."

For the remainder of his response he ventured his opinion that in the end it takes no skill to knock down his writings and burn them. But refuting them takes brains, and there seems to be a shortage of them in the slip master. "Hence, burn away," he closed, "since you are surely the most alert and highly educated doctor and have solved everything with such little effort. With this move along, dear grudger, and remember that no matter how much you purr or growl, there are some who don't give a hoot."

Luther also issued a Latin response to the earlier German one that tore the decree into pieces. And to throw a new scare into his enemies, he declared that since the decree had already made his desire a crime, he tossed out the idea that a person might have a desire for a council to allow pastors once again to marry, the same permission that is granted to Greek pastors.

Luther's friends were terribly frightened as they watched that brave man aim his cannon and fire against an official decree of a high church court. When Spalatin seriously called to Luther's attention the danger he was throwing himself into, Luther answered that his enemies were in greater danger than he. He held that God's Word is a sword. It would not allow itself to be turned into a downy feather. He was not seeking anything, but there was One who was seeking something. Whether Luther himself stands or falls, he gains or loses nothing. It was not his cause, but the gospel's cause, he was pursuing.

What else the Meissner bishop might have done in reaction to Luther's response, history will never know. For it happened that when Luther's answer to his slip of paper reached him he was sitting with Miltitz following the evening meal, "relaxing with a drink." Miltitz personally reported how he laughed lustily at the situation, while the Bishop was cursing away. The next day, the bishop asked Miltitz to carry the pamphlet to Duke George. When he handed it to the Duke, the Duke read all of it and laughed "excessively" over it. This may have so halted the bishop that he stopped any further action against the pamphlet. The matter may have turned out differently if Eck had been present. He would have blown on the fire and added straw on top of it. Instead, it was Miltitz who quickly poured water on the flames.

But Luther would get no rest because of it. A few weeks later he received the official condemning decisions from two universities, the one in Cologne, and the one in Louvain. They had published and issued those judgments which required Luther's writings to be burned, and Luther himself to be forced to recant. Printed along with them was an approval of those verdicts from the hand of Cardinal Hadrian of Tortosa. But Luther soon paid the debt of a response. In his reply he exposed the pitiful behavior of his hasty and uncalled-for judges, and said he would prove to them that he would take care of what they had left out. He stated that they had only condemned, but not proven anything. He added that if he behaved as they had, there would be a fight. But it would be a fight such as (*some*) women might have where one says, "No!" "It's true!" "It's not true!" "It is true!" In conclusion he wrote, "It was not necessary for you to state openly that you did not like my concerns and that my concerns were in error. That I already knew and for that reason I let them be exposed. Nor did I have to search much deeper into the matter, since you kept referring me to your authors as though they were unknown to me. But you must convince me from Scripture and powerful proof passages that what you are saying is true and what I am saying is not."

Luther had barely finished with the donkeys of Luvain and Cologne when he had to reach for defensive weapons anew. In May, a publication from his old enemy, Silvester Prierias, was brought to him. In it, Prierias was harping his song about the majesty of the pope on the same string, but in a higher scale. This was really a portion of a writing he intended to be longer, but the rest never saw the light of day. Luther took this new publication to the whipping post with a new pamphlet of his own. This new pamphlet was complete with foreword, epilogue, and marginal notes.

He had never before spoken of Rome as he did with these reactions to Silvester's writings. "If it is being held and taught," he wrote, "in these terms with the full knowledge of popes and cardinals - which I hope is not the case - then I state and testify freely with this publication that the true antichrist is sitting in the temple of God, Babel is ruling in it in gaudy reds and pinks, and the Roman court is Satan's synagogue."

"But should I offer even a small response to the apparent crazy insanity of these blaspheming devils? The best refutation is this that I merely allow his pamphlet to be published and disseminated as he has written it. It contains in itself a stronger refutation than any I could have desired.

"Hence read, dear reader, and weep that the glory of the Roman church has fallen to such depths. She not only conceives and consumes such heretical, blasphemous, Satanic, and hellish poison, but she is also spreading it throughout the entire world. Let whoever wishes, go and boast that the Roman church has never been stained with heresy. This individual Silvester produces more than Arius, the Manichaeans, Pelagius, and all other heretics.

"If that is the faith of Rome, then blessed is Greece, blessed is Bohemia, blessed are all who have separated themselves from her and have left this Babylon. But all those who are in fellowship with her are damned. And I also personally declare that if the pope and the cardinals do not pluck out this blasphemous mouth of Satan and force him to recant, you may note that I will not remain in the Roman church but will decry it together with the pope and the cardinals as the abomination that causes desolation, standing in the holy place." (Matthew24:15)

"Go on then, unblessed, damned, and blasphemous Rome. The wrath of God has finally come upon you as you have deserved. While so many prayers have been offered on your behalf, from day to day, you have striven to become more evil. We wanted to heal Babel, but she refused our help. May she then go on to be a house for the dragons, the unclean spirits, the goblins and monsters. May she be, as she is called, a place of eternal confusion, filled to the brim with idols of greed, perjurers, apostates, Sodomites, sex-fiends ("Priapisten"), roving and prowling thieves, Simonists, and countless other prodigies, a new pantheon of godlessness. Take good care of yourself, dear reader. Apply some balm to my pain, and don't neglect your compassion."

He ended the epilog with the following words: "I am exonerated and speak according to the words of Christ and Peter: If the count, the bishop, and every believing Christian do not admonish, punish, accuse, and correct the pope when he errs as a heathen, then they are all blasphemers of the way of the truth and deniers of Christ. They deserve to be eternally condemned along with the pope. I am finished."

Chapter 18
Rome before the Court of the Christian Laity

Dr. Eck had especially pressed Luther on the question of where the real church exists and what connection there is with the power of the pope. Luther had to have first sifted that question before the scholars. The conclusion of the previous chapter shows us how far the debate had taken him.

The Christian community needed to be instructed on what Luther had requested in his epilog to Prierius, namely that "every believing Christian" was to admonish and punish the pope and, wherever he did not improve, "hold him to be a heathen." Luther saw to it that this instruction took place, and again the enemy drove him to do so.

A new opponent came riding into battle on his high horse with much clattering and "seven swords." A Franciscan, Augustin von Alveld of Leipzig, burst onto the battlefield with Luther via a Latin work "from the apostolic seat." At first, Luther did not deem it worth his while to make the effort to confront him. Instead, he chose to hand the work over to one of his students to take him down a peg. But when that "Alved Ass" (in the sense of "donkey") translated his work into German, Luther himself wrote against him in German under the title, "From Popedom in Rome, against the Very Famous Roman in Leipzig." And so, Luther now also brought before the people the matter, which von Alveld had dealt with in his work.

"Once again," he wrote in his foreword, "something new has shown up on the battle plain. After all it has rained well this year, and many things have lately begun to sprout. Many have attacked me with disgraceful words and glorious lies and have not quite succeeded. Now at the head of those attackers entering into the field are those brave heroes of Leipzig. Not only do they wish to be considered honorable, but they wish to conquer every challenger. They are quite well equipped. The likes of them have not attacked me before. With their helmets on their feet, their swords on top of their heads, their shields, and breastplates on their backs, and their spears in their scabbards, their whole armor fits them quite well. It would be fair to think that a person would be afraid of them so that their efforts and intentions would not be in vain. If Leipzig produces such giants the soil must be rich indeed."

"But so that you understand my meaning, listen now: Silvester, Cajetan, Eck, Emser, and now, Cologne, and Lyon, earning honor and fame, have carried out their knightly quests against me. They would have been better advised to have tried to protect the pope and his indulgence from me in a different manner. As a last resort, some have decided that their best strategy would be for them to attack me like the Pharisees attacked Christ. They would throw a single attacker against me. If he wins, we all win. If he loses, he alone has lost. That highly educated grudger thinks I won't catch on! Well then, in order that they don't fail in everything, I will pretend that I don't understand the game at all. In that way perhaps, they will fail to notice that if I beat on the sack, I had wanted to have the donkey as my target."

He then went on to plead that they might understand that he scoffs at this Romanist and those behind him in holy sincerity, and that he will confront such blasphemers, only as they deserve.

Then he gets to the point, "For what is at stake is this," he wrote, "whether the papacy in Rome with its fraudulent power over all Christendom, has as they claim, arrived at this stage by divine order or by human order. And if that is so, whether one might truthfully say that all other Christians in the world are heretics and apostates, even though they profess a unity of spirit with us regarding the same baptism, sacrament, gospel, and all articles of faith. They differ only in that they do not allow their priests and bishops to be confirmed by Rome, or as so often happens now, to buy the office with money, as the Germans have allowed themselves to be aped and fooled - I have contended and still contend that those people are not heretics and apostates, but perhaps better Christians than we."

He then informs his Germans about what they have allowed the pope to do to them. "The Bishop of Mainz has purchased nearly eight bishop mantels from Rome, each one costing about 30,000 guilders, not to mention the countless bishoprics, prelacies, and fiefs. This is how they blow their noses at us German fools. Then they tell us according to divine command no one may have a bishop without the authority of Rome. I am amazed that Germany, although only one half is spiritual, would give one penny to those unspeakable, unaccountable, and unfaithful Roman thieves, bullies, and robbers. The pope does not defend us from this blasphemous villainy, as anyone can see through his fingers. Still they regard such a worldly villain higher than the gospel of God, and imply that we are damned fools. After all, it is according to divine command that the pope has his hand in the entire brew and does what he wants with everyone, as though he were a god on this earth."

Then he delves a little deeper into Alveld's work. "I recognize three basic points," he wrote, "with which that prolific noble pamphlet of the Leipzig Romanist is attacking me. The first and strongest is that he defames me. He calls me heretical, insane, a blind fool, possessed, a snake, a poisoned worm, and many other such names. He does so not once, but throughout the entire pamphlet, on nearly every page. ... Since this Romanist asserts that the Jews conquered Christ on the cross with such defamation, I, too, must submit to being captured. I must further admit that so much defamation, condemnation, abuse, and blasphemy is valid. The Romanist doctor has overcome Luther, and I must allow this fundamental statement to stand."

"The second basic attack", he continued, "the Romanist derives from natural reason. He maintains that every community on earth must have a head and so Christianity must likewise have a head. Next, he shows how foolish it would be to try to prove from reason that something exists by divine order. Then he destructively proves that his opponent's reasoning cannot stand, even by the use of reason. He shows how the Romanist makes the big mistake; when, he concludes that the visible community is the church. I can well see," he kept writing, "that this poor dreamer would hold to his opinion that a Christian congregation is like any other worldly organization. Thus, he makes it clear that he has never learned what Christianity or the Christian Church means. ... Therefore, I must first explain to this uncouth brain and to the others who are misled by him, what Christianity and the Head of Christianity truly are."

Thereafter Luther follows through with the concept that Christianity is a spiritual Church, the Communion of saints, which is united through faith. As Christ himself said, his kingdom is not of this world, and it does not come outwardly but is found inside of his people. "Therefore, whoever says that an outward assembly or union constitutes Christianity, he is forcefully speaking his own opinion. And if anyone were to draw this teaching from Scripture, he would be leading divine truth to his lies and making God into a false witness. That is what this miserable Romanist is doing, when he submits everything that has been written about Christianity to the outward splendor of the Roman authority. Still, he cannot deny the fact that the greater section of this mass of leaders, especially Rome itself, are not in spiritual unity, that is in true Christianity, because of their unbelief and evil way of life. ... From this it follows, as indeed it must, that just as being united with Rome does not make one a Christian, so being outside of Rome does not make one a heretic or unchristian. ... Therefore, it must also be wrong to say that to be under the Roman church is a divine command."

After he explained what Christianity is, Luther also showed who her head is. He wrote that Christianity is a spiritual Church; therefore, it cannot have a worldly head. Much more importantly, the head of the church is Christ, and only Christ. The Apostle said this clearly (Ephesians 4:15, 16 [NIV]). But should one ask, who the prelates and the bishops are, even a lay member can answer and say with the Apostle: They are messengers and servants. Even here no one stands above another, just as Christ sent out all of the apostles with equal authority. "The fact that the pope subjects all of those messengers under himself is the same as if a count's messenger were to stop all the other messengers, and send them out according to his own will, while he himself would go nowhere. Would that please the count? He would surely find out about it."

What Luther said he also proved from the Apostles' Creed. He wrote, "All this is confirmed through the Article: I believe in the Holy Spirit, a holy Christian Church, a Communion of saints. No one speaks as follows: I believe in the Holy Spirit, a holy Roman church, a communion of the Romans. Thus, it is clear that the holy church is not bound to Rome, but is as wide as the world. It is gathered together in one faith, spiritually, not physically. For what a person believes is neither physical nor visible. The outward signs by which one can recognize where that church exists in this world are baptism, the sacraments, and the gospel, not Rome or this or that place. For where there is baptism, the sacraments, and that gospel, saints will be present without a doubt, even if they were only a lot of children in their cribs. Therefore, I advise this Romanist to go to school for another year and learn what Christendom and the head of Christianity are, before he tries to expel poor heretics with such deep, wide, and long dissertations."

The third point which the Leipzig "Alphabet" set forth was this, that the Old Testament was a preview of the New Testament. Since the Old Testament is said to have had a physical high priest, therefore the New Testament also has to have one, since Christ says that, "Not the least stroke of a pen will be unfulfilled." (Luther's transliteration of Matthew 5:18) Luther took him to task on this as well. He showed, that if the physical models of the Old Testament have to be filled physically down to the last detail, if the models of the Old Testament high priest is to be completely fulfilled, then the pope should also take a virgin for his wife, not allow his hair to be cut, own no land, obey the king, and let himself be circumcised, all things that the high priest did. Instead the pope despises and forbids marriage, has a bald head, has stolen land, cities, and estates, and wants to be the king of all kings. Where do you find any fulfillment in this?

Luther again took advantage of this opportunity to demonstrate how these matters had to be fulfilled spiritually and not outwardly or physically. He again made the point that Scripture had to be the source of understanding rather than reason. In addition, Scripture provides further information unknown to the Romanist. The Old Testament high priest was not a pre-figure for the pope, but a pre-figure for Christ, the true, spiritual, heavenly High Priest."So, what do you say to that, you highly educated Romanist?" he asked him. "Paul said that Christ was the extension of the high priest; you say St. Peter. Paul says that Christ did not enter a temporal tabernacle; you say he is in a temporal building in Rome. Paul says that Christ entered it once, and had achieved eternal salvation. Thus, he fulfills the image completely, spiritually, and heavenly, which you still present as earthly and physical. What do you want to do now?"

"I'll give you a bit of advice: Take your fist and smash it into his mouth and tell him that he has lied, is a heretic, and poisonous, as you are doing to me. But if you claim that Peter was also foretold in Aaron along with Christ,

I say why stop there? Why not go on to say that the Turk was foretold in Aaron? Who can stop you, since you enjoy such useless prattle? But you have promised to fence on the basis of Scripture. Do so, and leave your dreams at home."

But that papists based their practice on the passage, Matthew 16:19 (NIV), in which the Lord tells Peter, "I will give you the keys to the kingdom of heaven; whatever you bind on earth," etc., Luther rebuts by pointing out that the Lord gave this power to all the apostles in Matthew 18:18 (NIV). Indeed, he had given it to the entire Communion of Saints. In addition, he did the same in John 20:23 (NIV), giving the power to all the disciples, and that the power to forgive and not to forgive sins on earth, is lent to the entire Communion. In light of these other passages, one must then interpret that just as Peter as speaker for all of the disciples made his confession in answer to the question: "Who do you say I am?" so Jesus spoke his words to all. Truly he proves extensively that this passage, including the previous passage, Matthew 16:18, "You are Peter, and on this rock, will I build my church" etc., as well as the passage of John 20:23, which the popes had also used to make their claims, "are stronger against the papacy than any other."

What stand should a Christian take over against the papacy? Let us hear what Luther had to say at that time.

"My opinion of the papacy is as follows: We see that the pope occupies the position of power over all of the bishops. He could not be in that position without the counsel of God, (though I do not believe he received it from the gracious counsel of God, but rather out of his wrathful counsel, the counsel that in addition to the world's plague God also permits people to oppress others). Since I do not want anyone to oppose divine counsel, but to fear it, therefore, honor that position and bear it with patience in the same way, as if we were under the Turk. In that way you will do it no damage. But I would like to write about two points:

"The first: I will not tolerate it, that people establish new articles of faith and scold all other Christians throughout the world, blaspheme, and condemn them as heretics, apostates, or unbelievers, just because they are not under the pope. It is not required that for his (the pope's) sake, God and his saints on earth be blasphemed.

"The other: Everything else which the pope establishes, constructs, or does, I will receive as follows: I shall first judge it on the basis of Scripture. As far as I am concerned he must submit to Christ and allow himself to be judged through Holy Scriptures.

"...When these two things are permitted to me I shall leave the pope alone, yes, even help, that he be held in as high of honor as is always desirable. Where these two things are not permitted to me, I shall want him neither as my pope nor as Christ. He who does not allow these things is making an idol; but I will not worship him.

"But I will allow as follows, that kings, counts, and other nobles agree that all appointments from the bully in Rome be denied, and that bishops' cloaks and fiefs stay outside of the secular rule. It is a pity that kings and counts have such poor devotion to Christ, and that his honor moves them so little, that they allow this disgraceful ascendancy in Christendom to maintain the upper hand; at the same time that they see that those in Rome are not mindful except to evermore increase insanity and multiply misery on earth, so that there is no hope, except by way of worldly power. If this Romanist comes again, I will have more to say. This is enough for now. God help us that we just once open our eyes. Amen."

From these statements we recognize three things: first, that Luther wanted consciences set free from papal authority, and that in matters of faith and doctrine, the pope has no authority at his disposal; second, that he wanted the people to respect the external order of things as they existed in church management, at that time. He personally respected the papacy as a cross that had come upon the Western church and had to be borne, since God was allowing it, and the worldly governments were not stopping it; but third, that he considered it the duty of existing governments to put an end to this misbehavior instead of supporting it, as they had up to that time.

This was not some idea that he tossed out on the spur of the moment. At the end of the quotation is an indication that he had more in mind concerning this subject. That is how it was. He had wielded his pen to impress on the people the importance of the message of Scripture. He applied himself to that subject extensively in order to light several candles "in regard to the papacy at Rome." But as he wrote to Spalatin, he was ordering his thoughts for a letter to the entire German nobility, who were still clanking about with their spurs in the dark.

So now we see Luther turning his attention to the "laity," the common people, and the nobles. The failed attempts at reform from the previous century offered sufficient proof that there was no hope for a reformation led by clerics, the popes, and bishops. What Luther had personally experienced up to this point was further proof. As long as the clergy kept enslaving poor consciences, the shackles which had been welded onto Christianity would not fall. Luther had recently experienced how little the high spiritual powers were ready or inclined to listen to the Spirit of God, who was allowing himself to be proclaimed through the blasts from Luther's trumpet. He had also seen how they viewed the common man with fear and concern. After following Spalatin's advice, he had turned to the Bishops of Mainz and Merseburg, and received polite answers from them. But from those letters he learned that those high lords had little time to pay attention to Luther's writings. They only feared that the people might read them and become unruly because of them. The Archbishop Albrecht of Mainz and Magdeburg, the highest ranking church official in Germany, was occupied more with his debts which were exceeding his income. He was more dedicated to the pursuit of pleasure than to deal with the questions of Luther. They may have kept Luther busy day and night, but the high lord described them in his letter as being trivial.

From this it can be easily understood why Luther was turning away from "the spiritual powers," which had become "very inattentive," to the "lay powers," hoping God might help his church through them.

But when one takes a look at these "lay people" one has to again admit that as they then existed, they in no way gave the impression that they were the people through whom a new and happy reformation would take place. The huge mass of people, existing in horrible ignorance, raw understanding, and spiritual ruin, first had to learn the language of Canaan, so to speak. If at this time a reformer had spoken to them as a nonsense spouting enthusiast, calling the people to action, to throw off the disgraceful yoke of Roman slavery, he would only have produced bloody confusion. The result would have been a pitiable spiritual generation of homeless children, who either would have been miserably destroyed or at last happy to be again under papal rule. We shall get to know some such ill-favored reformers.

Here Luther proceeded differently. We have already noticed how he, with amazing energy, worked hard to build his congregation up spiritually from his pulpit in Wittenberg. He expanded that work during the time we are describing. In both Sunday and weekly sermons, he proclaimed to the old and young alike those important truths of salvation. He did so in simple and thorough manner. He preached both Sunday and holiday texts from the established pericope. In addition, he preached about entire books of the Bible, from both the Old and the New Testament. He also specially used the Ten Commandments and the Lord's Prayer to instruct the young.

Smoothly, and with simple yet powerful words, Luther gave his numerous hearers the Word of life, which sets consciences free and builds the hearts on the one foundation already laid, namely, Jesus Christ. So, he began to draw them away from that useless religion of salvation by good works, which they had received under the papacy. He did all this work, which in itself would have been enough to keep a person fully occupied, along with all of his other duties. He did it all without pay, only now and then, receiving little gifts from his magistrate, in recognition of his work.

Desiring that people grow spiritually, Luther also stayed busy working in other wider circles. He accomplished this by producing more and more printed pamphlets for the common people, as they kept flowing from his continuously active pen. In these works, he wrote in a simple style about the "Ten Commandments", "The Articles of Faith", "The Lord's Prayer," "Repentance," "The Confession of Sins," "Holy Baptism," "Holy Communion," "Good Works," and "The Proper Way to Prepare for Death." It didn't bother him, as many of his German pamphlets were being criticized as being too simple. That he was capable of producing works of scholarship, even better than those who criticized him were producing, he had already proved and would continue to prove.

His enemies, on the other hand, were incapable of producing simple pamphlets to counter those produced by Luther. Many copies of his small pamphlets, at least 100 of them in 1520 alone, were being dispersed in part by itinerant sellers. These sellers offered no other books that might turn out to be divisive for common folk readers. Some formed reading circles, which purchased copies jointly, and circulated them. Then there were also pamphlet circles which obtained new editions. The itinerant sellers would spread them here and there throughout the country. The illiterate would have others read these pamphlets for them. Traveling students were especially useful for the purpose of serving as itinerant sellers. They would enter the very homes of citizens and farmers to supply these pamphlets. As people's enjoyment of these pamphlets grew, so their taste and hunger also kept increasing. Luther, who said he would have been satisfied if he had been able to help only one individual improve, had become a leader for thousands, as he brought them the knowledge of salvation and guided them to the life that comes from God, the God whom the papists had allowed to wither away and die for such a long time. So, it happened that this Wittenberg doctor, who had risen from the ranks of the common people, was showing warmth of heart toward them, by writing the wonderful pamphlets for them in their own language. He, in turn, became well-known and dear to them, and was respected by them.

Just as St. Paul had once drawn Timothy, Titus, and others to his side to help in the work entrusted to him, so Luther also had begun to equip others for bringing the Gospel out of the thousand-year dust, back into bright daylight for the people. He did this, by way of his professorship, at the university. He was instructing about 400 students who had flocked to his classroom at that time. He taught them Holy Scripture and drew from this well of the water of life, the powerful theology of the gospel of the cross for them. Since 1516, he had been interpreting the letter to the Galatians to his students. He next resumed lectures on the Book of Psalms. In order to become better qualified to interpret Scripture he applied more effort to his own study of the original languages, especially the Greek language, since Melanchthon, his colleague, was able to provide him with excellent tutoring. As he placed high value to the study of languages, he also directed his students to do so as well. So that there would be no shortage of books for use in the university, Luther saw to it that a capable printer, the son of a Leipzig printer, Lotter, settled in Wittenberg and that he equip his shop with German, Latin, and Greek letters.

For those scholars who were not able to attend his classes he issued a Latin commentary of Paul's Letter to the Galatians, and a treatment of a number of the Psalms, in 1519. These works found wide distribution. The commentary on Galatians was immediately translated in far away Spain, into the Spanish language.

Luther's work was also receiving validation at other universities. For example, the younger generation of "the poets" at Erfurt began to read and study the New Testament. Luther was now no longer standing alone in the department of theology for the cause of the Reformation. Melanchthon especially rendered valuable assistance. Luther rated him higher than anyone else. In addition to teaching Greek, Melanchthon had also begun to serve as teacher of theology. Through Luther's prompting, he lectured on Paul's letter to the Romans, for the first time in 1519. From these lectures grew the first comprehensive teaching manual for the Lutheran church. This textbook of the Christian faith was Melanchthon's "Loci." Almost against his will, Magister Philippus was awarded the theological rank of Biblical Baccalaureus, a rank that satisfied him for the rest of his life. He also assisted Luther in producing some small works in Latin. Luther boasted of him as the most powerful enemy of Satan and the scholastics, and that he was accomplishing as much as many Martins together. He even boasted that "the little Greek" surpassed him in theology.

Luther did not only have his Timothy at his side in Wittenberg, but by this time, here and there, preachers began to present gospel truth from their given pulpits. Their parish children were amazed, as they received gospel truths they had never heard before. Thus, the new planting of gospel teaching in Germany had a happy beginning, and care was being taken that this sowing would continue to be carried on by the hands of an increasing number of sowers, as the planted seeds took root and grew toward maturity. So did the reformation keep progressing.

The German nobility was an important component of the German Laity. Luther was now bringing proud Rome before their court. With an eye on the conditions of that time, he also made special efforts in their direction. In fact, Luther directed a special reformation work to them. In it, he more than ever before, laid bare the harm that had been done by the papal church and gave instructions about what was needed to forward reformation.

Chapter 19
Luther Addresses the German Nobility

The flower of German knighthood had been watching the activity of the Roman clergy with resentment for a long time. As they lived in their castles located on the heights behind thick walls and wide moats, they were often in isolation. They observed how the greed of the church was impoverishing the old noble families, while the high and low tonsured were growing wealthy off the fat of the land. The church claimed one piece of land after another, and annexed one vineyard after another. That foreign snake looped its coils ever tighter and narrower. Secular authorities of the kingdom had repeatedly brought charges against Rome, but always in vain.

Then Luther raised his voice, not from the spires of a castle built on the rocky crags along the Rhine River, but from the fortress of God's Word. God's Word meant little to the knights. As a result, it took some time for them to realize that Luther's uprising had a far deeper meaning than merely a monkish quarrel. Rome had thought the same at first. But the writing of the Wittenberg doctor, which had influenced the citizens and the farmers, would also influence the sturdy castles of the knights. After the Leipzig debate, it appeared as though Luther would no longer be able to remain in Wittenberg. The leading nobles of German knighthood offered him a place of refuge in his mighty castle. From there, Luther would be able to continue scoffing at his enemies. And he was not the only one to have considered it an honor to have Luther under his protection.

However, it turned out that there was no pressing need for Luther to escape at that time. Although attempts were made by Rome to estrange the Elector and his Doctor Martinus from one another by way of bribes and threats, the same attempts accomplished nothing. They failed because of the good opinion the Elector had in his inner thoughts, and because of the care the wise Frederick was taking to not do anything against the truth. In addition, he must have known that Luther's teaching had already sunk deeper roots into the hearts of the people. And if he hadn't noticed, men like Spalatin would have told him.

That is the way he responded to Valentin Teutleben, who had warned him from Rome, that Luther's actions could become a problem for him. The Elector wrote that Luther's teaching had already sunk deep root into the hearts of the German people, and a person should be on guard, lest he attack Luther with power instead of good reason. If he did, the issue wouldn't be settled in Germany without unrest and rebellion. Indeed, the Elector did not want to take responsibility for Luther's teachings. He repeatedly explained that he would not dare to render a verdict in such matters. However, he wanted Luther to have the opportunity to defend his teachings before competent judges, without personally endangering himself. So, when he attended an election of the Caesar at a Diet in Frankfurt, he met with the Archbishop of Trier, whom Miltitz had chosen as Luther's judge. In that meeting, he agreed that he would bring Luther along to the next diet, where he would receive a hearing.

Miltitz had not stopped his plotting. He attempted to endear himself to the elector by now formally presenting him with the Consecrated Rose. The Elector, however, did not let himself be bribed and accepted the gift in a casual manner. He did not permit any sort of ceremony, but instead directed that the rose be handed over to his counselors. However, when Miltitz again sought a meeting with Luther (which later took place at Liebwerda), he consented and bade Luther to present himself, readily and willingly, for the meeting at which he would appear before the Archbishop of Trier. Luther would do so. But when Miltitz later alleged that Luther had promised to travel to Trier with him to carry out the Elector's desires for this journey and insisted upon it, he was told that it wasn't going to happen that way. Luther would not be permitted out of Germany without sufficient assurances of his safety. Instead Miltitz should have prevented Eck and others from attacking Luther and forcing him to continue the battle. So, Luther left it up to the decision which the Archbishop and the Elector had reached at Frankfurt, even though he would have been willing to take the risk of a journey to Trier, had his Elector so commanded.

Of course, the count urged Luther to keep himself under restraint, communicating this through Spalatin. Luther submitted to the Elector's desires as much as possible. That is why Luther, at the prompting of the Elector, sent his letters to the Archbishop of Mainz and Magdeburg, and to the Bishop of Merseburg. But Luther was confident enough toward the Elector to let him know that his restraint had boundaries, boundaries which he would cross only if absolutely necessary. That was the reply he gave to the Elector when he was presented with the letters of admonition from Rome. Since he was already charged with sin, he would not make himself further guilty by failing to carry out his office or denying the truth to the detriment of many thousands of souls by giving in at this time. He sought neither money nor honor, and if he were to be forbidden to speak, then let them take away his office, and allow him to live and die in some secluded corner. But if he were to stay in office, then he must also be allowed freedom to exercise that office. Therefore, he publicly recognized what the Elector had done and thanked him for it, both privately and publicly. This he did, holding his Elector in highest esteem, even though the Elector could have intervened for the sake of the truth more strongly, had he so desired.

When he was working on his interpretation of the Psalms in 1519, he dedicated the work to the Count. He included the following under this dedication: "Your highness has garnered so many concerns, conditions, expenses, and dangers because of this monster, which was given birth through me because of this indulgence affair! The whole country knows that the count has shown more concern for me than I have shown for myself. In my boldness, I have rolled the dice, prepared to go all out and fully expected the worst. I had hoped, if worse came to worst, to be excused from my task of instructing others. I could then find a corner and get away from this notoriety that I detest. But then your highness stepped in. While I was ready to endure whatever they chose to throw at me, your highness would not let them."

Earlier, on Trinity Festival of 1518, as he wrote to the pope, Luther had referred to the Elector with these words, "If I were really the person that they are trying to describe me to be, ... it would have been impossible for the highly eminent count Frederick, Duke of Saxony, Elector of the empire, etc, to allow such a plague in his university. He is the most zealous lover of catholic and apostolic truth."

Woodcut of Ulrich von Hutten

At this time Luther did not have sufficient cause to accept any of the invitations extended to him. In addition, he was surely wise to remain safely at his post in Wittenberg. Nevertheless, the invitations he received from such men proved very dear to him. One individual, whom we earlier referred to as the flower of German chivalry, was Franz von Sickingen.

This heroic knight first saw the light of this world at Ebernburg castle. He was a veteran who had led the way in many daring battles. The beat of his recruiting drum was answered by thousands, both lance-bearing knights, and men of arms. As they fought under his coat of arms, he acquired the highest reputation for bravery, as well as the respect of the most noble in the kingdom. His voice carried great weight in the leader's counsel. At the same time he kept an open mind when it came to the study of knowledge. He had recently demonstrated his ability to Luther's most vocal enemies, the Dominican monks. During the straining heresy trial of Reuchlin, the great uncle of Melanchthon, he took them down a peg. The trial was an expensive one for the accused, and the knight granted him 111 gold guilders for his defense.

At this time, he was joined by another German knight, Ulrich von Hutten. A descendant of an ancient noble line, he came into the world in 1488, in the Steckelberg Castle, on the Main River. At the age of eleven he was placed in the monastery at Fulda. But with the help of a friend, he made a clandestine escape from those hated monastic walls in 1504. He had studied in Cologne, and then later in Frankfurt on the Oder River where he became Magister. After a number of cruises back and forth to Rostock, he next worked as a teacher of ancient languages. He had come to Wittenberg in 1510, and from there traveled on until surfacing in Pavia. When this city was conquered, his residence was plundered, although he had only a few possessions. Then, after a short stay in Bologna, he became a soldier of Caesar because he faced such bitter poverty. After a short stay in his fatherland, he traveled to Rome in order to study law. He returned to Germany in 1517, and was crowned as the Caesar's poet. Caesar crowned him in person before his court using the laurel wreath which had been woven by the Caesar's beautiful daughter.

Finally, the next year he entered into service at the court of the wealthy Archbishop Albrecht of Mainz. He even traveled with him to the Diet of Augsburg where Luther was to have his hearing before Cajetan. But if you were to conclude from his history that this man must have been an obedient, faithful, and submissive servant of the Roman court, you would be mistaken.

Even prior to his acceptance in the court of Mainz, Hutten had distinguished himself in a way that brought no honor to the papal clerics. In addition to some biting satires he reissued a work by the scholar, Laurentius Valla, who had died about a half century earlier. It was dealing with the fabricated, "Donation of Constantine."

This seven-hundred-year-old document contained an important truth regarding the papacy. It declared that long ago, Caesar Constantine, the Great, had ceded his old western capital, Rome, to Pope Silvester. After a friend had sent this to Luther in February of 1520, Luther at first regarded it as a lie. "Good God," Luther then wrote to Spalatin after reading it, "How dark and worthless are the degenerated Romans! They have not only claimed, but they have ruled under this for centuries already. One has to wonder about the judgment of God. ... I am so deeply troubled, that I hardly doubt any longer that the pope is truly the antichrist, for whom the world is waiting. His whole life, his actions, his speeches, and his judgments fit the description so closely."

Hutten had, in addition to this document, followed up with a number of his own pamphlets filled with biting sarcasm. He even continued his writing while serving at the court of Mainz. But soon complaints arrived from Rome. The court had to bid the unbridled and restless knight farewell. That is when Hutten found protection and lodging with Franz von Sickingen. As ever blacker storm clouds were filling the southern sky, Luther was anticipating being put under the papal ban. Hutten von Sickingen was given the task of sending an invitation to Luther. At the beginning, Hutten did not write to Luther directly. Instead he wrote to Melanchthon, informing him that the noble Sickingen was inviting Luther to accept his protection in case he was no longer safe in Wittenberg. Then a letter from Hutten was sent directly to Luther. In it, the knight expressed his joy to the doctor that both of them had God on their side. He warned Luther to carefully keep his eyes open, lest their good cause would lose him, their vigorous vanguard officer. He assured Luther that if his enemies came with force, his friends were ready and able to meet them with greater force.

At the same time, Luther received similar offers and promises from the French knight, Silvester von Schauenburg, whose son was attending the University of Wittenberg. In his message he told Luther that he would find a welcome refuge with him if his own ruler withdrew his protecting hand. He also wrote that he intended, with the help of God, to gather 100 nobles who would protect Luther from his enemies, until his cause had been decided by a reliable judge or Christian council.

And Luther? What did those promises, coming from castles built on rocky heights and issued by steel-clad heads of the knighthood of the German nobility, accomplish with this German farmer- and miner-son of Wittenberg? Do you think he left his cell, his lectern, and his pulpit to take a place in the Ebernburg castle? No! Perhaps he declined the knightly offer in a spirit of pettiness? Again - No! On the contrary, he well knew how to understand the mindset which prompted their offers; and it is easy to see how he could appreciate the effect such offers had on his enemies. He immediately forwarded those letters to Spalatin with the encouragement that those Roman-like lords who were warning the Elector to take action against Luther, ought to reconsider. After all, if they should succeed in their plan to get Luther out of Wittenberg, their position would not improve but worsen. There were men in central Germany who were prepared to take him under their powerful protection. The result would be that he could attack Rome more productively than at the present, when he had to be more circumspect because of the Elector and university. He wrote obstinately, "Those gainsayers should know that they dare not take credit for what I have failed to do to them. I have spared them, and their tyranny, and their reputations, not because of them, but out of respect for the count's reputation and his connection with the university. So far as it concerns me, the die has been cast. I despise Rome's rage and its favor. I will not be reconciled with them, nor will I have fellowship with them. They may condemn and burn my writings. I, on the other hand, as long as I don't run out of fire, will condemn and publicly burn the entire papal administration, that nest of vipers, and there will be an end to the meekness I have shown up to this point. The enemies of the gospel will no longer be puffed up due to my lowliness."

However, it was not the German knights who made Luther so confident and courageous. Rather, he wrote to Spalatin, "Though I do not despise their aid, I will rely on nothing but Christ's protection. He is the One who most likely gave such a spirit to Schauenberg." (*Perhaps in this context we realize why Luther called Psalm 118 his favored prayer.*) He did not want to hide under the wings of the nobility; no, he wanted to be the one who would elevate the German nobility. He wanted those nobles, who in their ignorance did not grasp what he was attempting, to soar high into the brilliant blue sky with the powerful wing-stroke of his eagle-like spirit, more rather, by the Spirit of God. For it was the Spirit of God who would lift him so that they together might be seen plummeting down upon the devastators of the garden of the German church and nation. And so he quickly dipped his pen and wrote another strong work to that other part of the German laity, "To the Christian Nobility of the German Nation for the Improvement of Their Christian (Existing) Condition." "The time of staying silent has passed," that is what he wrote in the added writing to his friend and colleague, Nikolaus of Amsdorf, dated June 23rd. "The time for speaking has come," as we read in Ecclesiastes (Eccl. 3:7. Luther translation, translated into English) In keeping with our struggle, I have gathered together several pieces which apply to the improvement of the Christian state. I bring them to the attention of the Christian nobles of the German nation to see whether God would help his church through those laymen, since the spiritual leaders who ought to be responsible have failed completely. I am sending all of this to you, so that you will use your abilities to judge the work, and wherever necessary improve it. I am well aware that I am not above reproach. I do not consider myself as being so lofty, that I, a commoner of little regard, may be the only one to address important matters of such high and grand import. It is not as though there is no one else in the world besides Luther who can address the Christian state and give advice to such important people.

"I owe one more folly. Let anyone who wishes reprimand me.

Perhaps I still owe one foolish act to my God and to the world. This goal I have set for myself, should I succeed, to pay a debt verbally and at the

Title page of the original second main edition of Luther's Address
"To the Christian Nobility of the German Nation about
Improvement for (*Existing*) Christian Condition

same time become a court jester. If I do not succeed, I still have one thing going for me: No one shall buy a cap for me, or shear my head ...

"Also, because I am not only a court jester, but also a doctor who has vowed to uphold Holy Scripture, I am glad for the opportunity I have been given to fulfill my vow in the same foolish courtly manner. I ask that you would excuse me among those who are of self-controlled learned rank; for I do not know how to earn the favor and grace of those who are very learned. I so often sought their favor and grace with much effort, but now no longer want or give heed to it. God help us so that we seek not our own honor, but his honor alone. Amen."

Luther turns to the "Most illustrious, highly powered majesty of Caesar and Christian Nobles of the German Nation" with his work. He explains that it was not indiscretion but the huge need of his misery-laden nation, which forced him to cry out. He desires, with the help of God, to illustrate the trickery and malice of those who are responsible for this misery. He adds, "God has given us a young and noble leader, so that many hearts may be awakened toward a good and growing hope. Along with this gift, it is proper for us to add our efforts to make the best possible use of our time of grace."

For the "best possible use of our time of grace" Luther does not envision the plan that might be countered with might. And so, he expands on what has just been quoted. "The first thing we need to do is that we begin in all sincerity, taking care not to put our trust in great power or logic, as though all the authority in the world belongs to us. For it is not God's will that we begin a good work by trusting in our own power and reason, nor will he allow for that. ... The matter has to be approached with a despairing of our personal strength, a humbly trusting in God, and with sincere prayer for seeking God's help. We need to envision nothing else except the laments and needs of Christendom in its misery, without a thought of what evil men deserve. If this is not the case, then the entire game would start with a big show, but once started, the evil spirits would cause such a calamity that the whole world would float in blood, and nothing would be accomplished. Therefore, let us handle the matter at hand with the fear of God and act wisely. The greater the power, the greater the misfortune, when matters are not handled with fear of God and in humility. Until now, the popes and Romans with the help of the devil have caused confusion among the kings. They may well continue to do so, if we try to do battle with our own power and skill, without the help of God.

"He follows by getting to the heart of the matter with which he is concerned and begins to "illuminate" the treachery and malice of the degenerate Romans. He writes: "The Romanists have erected three walls around themselves in a skillful and clever manner. Those walls have so well protected them up to this day that no one wanted to reform them. The result was that Christendom has experienced a horrible fall.

"The first wall which they erected protected them when being pressured by the secular powers. They declared that secular power has no authority over them, rather, the spiritual is above the secular.

"The second wall they erected, when they were being taken to task by Holy Scripture. They declared that no one except the pope is allowed to interpret Holy Scripture.

"The third wall they invented, when they were threatened with a Council. They asserted that no one could summon a council except the pope.

"May God now help us, by giving us one of the trumpets which caused the walls of Jericho to tumble, that we may also blow down these straw and paper walls."

We now turn to some excerpts from those writings in which Luther advised the majesty of Caesar and the Christian nobles of the German nation. He writes, "It has been learned that pope, bishops, priests, and monastic residents are to be called the spiritual state. Counts, lords, common professionals, and plowmen are the worldly state, which is a pretty fair assessment, and worth noting. But no one should be intimidated by this for this reason: the spiritual state actually consists of all Christians. There is no difference among them except as to their office, ... for only these three, baptism, the gospel, and faith, determine what is spiritual and a part of Christendom. ... If a small group of upright Christian lay people were to be captured and carried into a desert without a priest, consecrated by a bishop, the following would be possible. Considering their situation, they could meet together and choose one of their number, married or not, and commit to him the office of baptizing, holding mass, absolving, and preaching. That man would truly be as much of a priest as though all the bishops and popes had consecrated him.

"From this it is derived that in the case of an emergency anyone can baptize or grant absolution. Such a thing would not be possible if we were not all priests, ... though not everyone may be fit to hold such an office. For though we are all priests, no one is to put himself forward or establish himself without our approving and choosing him to be a priest. We all have equal power in this process. For no one may take for himself such a public position without the desires and direction of the congregation.

What's more, if someone were elected to such an office only to be removed from that office because of his abuse of his position, he would be the same as he had been before. Therefore, a priest in his position should be no different than any other office in Christendom. While he is in office, he is above others; but when he has been removed, he is a farmer or citizen like everyone else.

"Hence, it follows that lay member, priest, count, bishop, as they are called, are not basically different from one another either in the spiritual or secular realm, except in regard to their office or work, but not on account of their status, for all of them are of an equal spiritual rank. Similarly, those who are called "spiritual", i.e., priests, bishops, or popes, are not to be set apart from other Christians into an elite group. They are not worthier, except in their duty to handle the Word and the Sacraments. That is their work and office. Thus, the secular authority has the sword and the rod in his hand, to punish the evil ones and to protect the upright. Therefore, the secular Christian authority should carry out his office unhindered, regardless whether or not it pertains to pope, bishop, or priest. He who is guilty has to suffer. Whatever spiritual right is claimed to the contrary, is a lot of Roman dreamt up abuse.

"Thus, in my opinion, the first paper wall has come down. If we were to allow some human decision to put down divine command and truth, something which we had vowed in baptism to uphold with body and life, we would be held accountable for all the souls who would be abandoned and misled by it. The following declaration had to have been set up by the chief devil in person: It stands written in spiritual law that if the pope were so damagingly evil that he would lead a whole mass of souls to the devil, he could still not be deposed. In Rome they continue to build on this damned foundation of the devil and think that the whole world should be allowed to go to the devil rather than to take a stand against their bullying.

"The other wall is even weaker and more unfit, namely, that they alone want to be the master of Scripture. Even though throughout their entire lives they have learned nothing that it contains, they dare to assume that authority for themselves, dangling before us the vile claim that the pope cannot err in matters of faith, whether he is evil or holy ... and that they would make the decision as to what in Holy Scripture is needed or useful. Let us then burn the Scriptures and be satisfied with the ignorant lords of Rome. They have invented a fable in their malice. They cannot produce one letter whereby they can prove that the pope alone has the right to interpret Scripture or to confirm its interpretation. They have claimed this authority for themselves. On top of all of this, we are all priests, as was said before. We all have one faith, one gospel, one kind of sacrament. How should we not also have the power to test and judge what in our faith is right and what is false? Therefore, it behooves every Christian to study his faith, to understand it, to defend it, and to condemn all false teaching.

"The third wall collapses by itself when the first two have fallen. For where the pope is acting contrary to Scripture, we owe it to Scripture to stand by the Bible, to punish the pope, and take steps against him according to the Word of God - Matthew 18. Therefore, where the need demands it and the pope offends Christendom, anyone who is able should, as a faithful member of the entire body, begin to work toward a truly free Council. However, there is no mention in Scripture (in German "geredt") of the fact of which they boast to have the power, namely that it is wrong to debate against them.

There is no one in Christendom who has the power to do damage, or to forbid defending against damage. There is no power in the church except the power to improve. Therefore, let us hold on to this: Christian might cannot be used against Christ, as Paul says, "We cannot do anything against the truth, but only for the truth." (2 Cor. 13:8 - NIV). But if Mother Church takes action against Christ, then it is the Antichrist's or the devil's might, even if she should send downpours and hail in form of miracles and plagues.

"Herewith I hope that the false and fearful lies of the Romans are dismantled. They have been used by the Romans for a long time, and have made consciences timid and weak. Those Romans are under the sword just as we are. They do not have the authority to interpret Scripture by their force and skill. They do not have the authority to prevent a council, or in connection with their recklessness to tax or bind one's conscience, or to take away freedom. When they do, they are truly the antichrist and the devil's synagogue and have nothing that is from Christ except the name.

"Now let us look at those issues which, if they love Christ and his Church, should receive just hearings in the councils and which should occupy popes, cardinals, bishops, and scholar's day and night, if they love the Church. But if they will not do so, then may the entire Church and the secular sword step in, despite their excommunicating and thundering.

"First, it is an abomination and frightening to watch how the holder of the highest office in Christendom boasts that he is Christ's vicar, and St. Peter's successor. He lives in such a majestic fashion by the worldly standards that no king or Caesar can equal him. The fact that he allows himself to be called the most holy and the most spiritual, shows that he is worldlier than the world itself. He wears a threefold crown, while even the highest kings wear only one crown. If this is comparable to the poverty of Christ and St. Peter, then it stands as a new standard.

"They claim that he is a lord of the world. That is a lie. After all, Christ, for whom he boasts to be the vicar and keeper of his office, said before Pilate, 'My kingdom is not of this world.' (John 18:36 NIV)

"Secondly, of what use are those people called cardinals in Christendom? I want you to know that Switzerland, including a section of France, and Germany had many rich monasteries, foundations, fiefs, and parishes. What is not known is that they could not simply be annexed to Rome. Cardinals were created and were given the bishoprics, monasteries, and prelates as their property and in this way trod divine service under foot. That is why one can now see that Switzerland is nearly empty. No Turk would have been able to ruin Switzerland that much and to stop the divine service. Now that Switzerland has been sucked dry, they have begun to come into the German nations, albeit gently; but watch and see how Germany will soon be like Switzerland. We already have several cardinals. The drunken Germans are not supposed to grasp what the Romans are looking for, until they no longer have a bishopric, monastery, parish, fief, dollar, or penny. As it is being declared, the antichrist must raise his treasures from the earth. How have we come to the point where we Germans must endure such theft and extortion of our possessions by the pope? ...

"Thirdly, if you were to take away 99 percent of the papal court, and leave only one percent, it would still be large enough. I believe that Germany is currently giving far more to the pope in Rome, than was in the past given to Caesar. Indeed, some believe that every year 300,000 guilders leave Germany for Rome, purely without return, free and clear. We receive nothing in return except mockery and shame. Yet we are amazed that our counts, nobles, cities, foundations, land, and people are becoming poor. We should be amazed that we still have food to eat.

"Some time ago the German Caesars and counts agreed to collect the first fruits of all fiefs for the pope. That amounted to one half of the tax of every fief for the first year. This agreement was reached as follows: with such large sums, the pope was to gather a treasury with which to do battle against the Turk and unbelievers. In order that it would not be too difficult for the nobles to fight to protect Christendom on their own, the priesthood would also be contributing to the fight. So now they send out the message to gather money to fight against the Turk. Often indulgences are peddled with the same scheme, to fight against the Turk. Thus the stupid Germans should continue to stay dead stock fools, to keep our agreement of giving, which agreement they have no intention of keeping so much as one hair's width. And this even though we can plainly see that, whether from the first fruits or the indulgence money, or from any other income, not one dollar is used against the Turk. Instead it always goes into their bottomless sack. Afterwards it is claimed that the holy name of Christ and of St. Peter accomplished all of this. In this regard, the German nation, bishops and counts should also conduct themselves as Christians, and protect the people against such ravenous wolves - the people whom they are to rule in regard to their temporal and spiritual possessions."

After this he pointed out individual instances of various ways the pope uses to rob the nations. He continues, "Insofar as I am too limited in my knowledge to offer suggestions to improve such a dreadful state of existence, I yet want to sing out my fool's song. I will state, as far as my understanding allows, what is desired to happen and what should happen either through earthly might, or common Council." Then he identifies 26 spiritual improprieties and recommends how to shut them down. A few examples might show how he proceeded. He writes:

"After this we come to the huge pile of those who promise much, but adopt little. Don't become angry, noble lords, I mean it well. It is a bittersweet truth that the building of beggar monasteries should no longer be allowed. God help us! There are already far too many of them. Would to God that all of them could be gathered together from far and near to two or three locations! They do not do any good, and will never do any good. Therefore, my advice is that ten of them, or however many are necessary, be combined into one location. If it receives sufficient support they would not need to go begging. ... They are to be exempted from preaching and hearing confessions, unless so called and desired by bishops, parishes, congregations, or the government. In this way the various types of orders should be discontinued and that there would be the distinction of only one.

"According to my way of thinking it would be necessary to order, especially during our dangerous times, that all foundations and monasteries would be set up this way and that all of them would be free to remain there as long as they desired ...

"14th: We also see how the priesthood has fallen. Many a poor parson, overloaded with woman and child, burdens his conscience as no one pitches in to help him. I do not know whether such a situation can still be helped or not. The bishops and pope let such things happen, whenever it happens, and let spoil whatever spoils. So, I shall clear my conscience and raise my voice, may it grieve pope, bishop, or whomever, and speak as follows:

"In accordance with the institution of Christ and the apostles each city should have one pastor or bishop. Paul clearly writes in Titus 1 that a pastor may have a wife, and not be forced to live without one. Should you complain that this is offensive, and that the pope must first make dispensation, I say that whatever offense there is in this, the fault belongs to the Roman throne that established such a law without any right and against God. It is not offensive to God and Holy Scripture."

"16th: Let New Year's Day, festivals, and masses for souls be discontinued, or at least reduced. This is due to the fact that we can see with our own eyes that there is nothing left in them except mockery. Thus, God is greatly angered with everything aimed only at money and excessive eating and drinking."

"17th: A number of penitential works, or penalties by way of spiritual law, would have to be discontinued. This especially applies to the interdict. The ban is not to be used in any way except the manner in which Scripture directs it to be used. It is to be used against those who do not believe correctly, or who openly live in sin, not for acquiring temporal possessions.

"What also applies here is that fasting be left as a free choice for everyone, and that all sorts of food be declared free as the gospel allows. The Romans themselves scoff about fasting. They let us, who are outside of Rome, consume types of oil, with which they would not even grease their shoes, and then sell us spiritual freedom to eat butter and all kinds of food, though the Apostle (Paul) says that we already had such freedom under the gospel. (See I Timothy 4:3-5 [NIV]).

"In this vein you should either discontinue, or leave out, or make common for all the churches those things the pope sells on his carrion counter, including freedom and bulls. That is what I advise. But if such foolish operations are not discontinued, then let every Christian open his eyes. Let him not allow himself to be confused with Roman bull, seal, and hypocrisy. Let him stay at home in his own church, and let baptism, the gospel, faith, and God, who is the same in every location, be what is best for him. Let the pope remain a blind leader for the blind. Neither angel nor pope can give you as much as God gives you in your parish. Truly, the pope misleads you in respect to divine gifts, insisting that you buy from him those things that are free of charge. Thus he gives you lead for gold, skin for meat, rope for the purse, wax for honey, promises for possessions, and letters for the spirit. You see it in front of your eyes and still don't want to notice. If you plan on traveling to heaven on his parchment and wax, your wagon will soon break down and you will be heading for hell, but not by God's name."

"23rd: Continuing along the same line in regard to brotherhoods: drown and destroy all letters of indulgence, butter letters, mass letters, dispensations, and the like; these are no good at all ... next, all papal messengers and their entourages should be chased out of Germany. Their selling of their high-priced wares amounts to bullying. They are only there to take our money, and they validate unjust possessions as good, dissolve vows, commitments, and promises. ... This information would be proof enough for anyone to confirm, if there were no other treacheries to be found, that the pope is truly the antichrist. O Christ, my Lord, look down! Let your day of judgment break forth and destroy the devil's nest in Rome! Here sits the man of whom Paul said that he would exalt himself above you and sit in your church, proclaiming himself to be God. He is the lawless one, the man doomed to destruction."

"25th: The universities are also in need of a good, strong reformation. I have to say it, no matter what grief it causes. No one may make me feel guilty for talking too much or rejecting what I know nothing about. Dear friend, I know very well what I am talking about. It would sit very well with me to keep Aristotle's books about logic, rhetoric, and poetry. Perhaps they could be prepared in a condensed form to make them easier to read, and enable the young people to practice proper speaking and preaching. In addition, I would desire that there be the languages; Latin, Greek, and Hebrew, plus the mathematical disciplines. I recommend that the histories would be made easier to understand. All this would happen on its own if a reformation were seriously desired.

"Truly much depends on this. For here our Christian youth and the nobility of Christendom should be taught and prepared. Concerning physicians, I leave their reformation to their faculties. Lawyers and theologians, I'll take. ... My dear theologians have excluded themselves from hard work, ignore the Bible, and read Sententias. This is what I mean: Young theologians begin the Sententiae. The Bibles are reserved for the doctors. This way, as it is now, is the completely turned-around procedure. Instead, the Bible is to be first and continue to the Baccalaureus. The Sententiae are to be last. These should forever stay in the doctorate section. How can we be blessed, if we so wrongly proceed with our practice of putting the Bible, the Holy Word, as last.

"The number of books would also have to be reduced, and the best ones picked out. It is not the number of books, nor the amount of reading, that leads to wisdom. Instead, read good books and read them often; for however small they may be, they make a person knowledgeable in Scripture and upright in behavior. Whether in higher or lower schools, it is most important that the most preferred and common lessons should be from Holy Scripture. For young boys, it would be the gospel. And, God willing, every city should also have a school for girls, where girls could hear the gospel daily, may it be in German or Latin.

"We should refrain from sending everyone to schools which are most concerned with large numbers. This is what everyone is interested in now, and everyone wants to be a doctor. We should send students to those higher schools which are diligent for studying Scriptures. That is where the most gifted, who had been well trained in smaller schools, are to be sent. But I advise no one to send his child to a place where Scripture does not rule. Everything that does not relentlessly pursue God's Word must face destruction.

In conclusion he writes, "I am aware that I have sung at a high pitch, have suggested many things which will be regarded as impossible, and have attacked many things too sharply. But how should I act? I am indebted to speak. If I could do it differently, I would. But I prefer that the world rather than God be angry with me. As far as I am concerned, the most that anyone can do is take my life. Up until this time, I have offered peace to my enemies. But as I see it now, through them God has forced me to open my mouth ever wider. He has allowed me to bark at them, holler at them, and write enough to them, because they are too lazy to write. Oh yes, I know another song about Rome and them. If their ears are itching, I'll sing that one as well and set the notes at the highest pitch. Understand well, Rome, what I mean.

"Many times, I have offered my writings to be studied and heard, but none of that helped. If my stance is correct, I understand very well that it will be condemned on earth, and will only be justified in heaven before Christ. May God give Christian understanding to us all, and may he especially give a true spiritual courage to the Christian nobles of the German nation, that they will do what is best for the church. Amen.

Wittenberg, the year 1520."

What Luther did in this writing, explaining the individual points so thoroughly, and at the same time gathering everything into a single framework, he had not previously done. Before he had witnessed the disorder which the papacy had brought to the nation of Germany, under which the Germans suffered. The high notes he sounded here rang out once again into the ears of his friends. They rang so loudly, that in Erfurt, Lange and Spalatin sent him a letter pleading that he would not send out this writing. But it was too late. Four thousand copies had already been printed, and after a few days, another edition had to be published which appeared in greater numbers. A letter from a frightened Melanchthon and a letter from Wildbrett, which at that time arrived from the Elector's court, contained no objection to this penetrating work. Nor was there an objection in the news that this book was "not entirely displeasing" at the Elector's court.

That bombs had exploded in Rome can be seen for what happened there. Already in the autumn a writing by Thomas Rhadinus appeared. He released it under the title, "Words to the Counts and People of Germany against the Heretic M. Luther, a Disgrace to the Honor of the Nation." This immediately went to press a second time in Leipzig. Emser also directed a work against the book, "To the German Nobility." While Luther left it up to Melanchthon to write a response to Rhadinus' work, all those polemical writings had now opened another door for more polemics. Luther, after receiving the first sheets from Emser, responded with a piece entitled, "To the Buck at Leipzig." To which Emser immediately returned, "In Regard to Raging Reply by the Steer at Wittenberg." Luther countered with "To the Reply of the Buck at Leipzig." And when Emser's book against "To the German Nobility" appeared in full, Luther wrote his "Answer to the Excessively Christian, Excessively Spiritual, (and) Excessively Artful God of the Buck Emser at Leipzig in which Murner, his Companion, is also Given Consideration." The Franciscan monk, Thomas Murner, ("Murnur" also meant "Tomcat") had also attacked Luther's book. Hence, he was being butchered together with the Emser "Buck". When Emser later replied once again, Luther bid him farewell with his, "An Opposing Statement by Doctor Luther in regard to His Error, Forced Out by the Most Highly Intellectual Priest of God, Mr. H. Emser."

While Luther had been producing his book to the Nobility, the pens down in Rome had also been busy in another direction. As the book to the Nobility made its way through the lands of Germany, it met on the way a papal bull with a ban, newly penned.

Chapter 20
The Papal Banning Bull

Filled with rage because of the beating he had taken in Germany, Eck was heading for Rome to quench his thirst for revenge. To avoid coming empty handed he had put together a book on the primacy of the pope. In it, he elevated the pope over all Kings and Caesars as his own subjects. Incorrigible papist that he was, he supported his "facts" with the forged decretals and other types of falsified documents. It was also said that the Fugger financiers, who had also taken their lumps in Luther's writing to the Nobility, had urged Eck to journey to Rome in haste, lest they completely lose the profit they were making from the sale of indulgences. The result was that Eck's book was shining a bright light on the danger that threatened the threefold crown in Germany. A commission was immediately established which began to produce a banning bull at once.

A draft of that document against the monk on the other side of the mountains was completed as early as May. Cardinal Accolti had drawn up the draft. Yet the papists had learned to be somewhat cautious. Detail after detail was examined and filed in four ecclesiastical courts. The issue was so important that Cardinal de Vio, even though he was ill, had himself carried to the sessions. A smaller committee, attended by Eck and the pope himself, put the final touches on the document. The task was finally completed by June 16, 1520.

The bull began with a prayer to God to rise up, judge, and save the situation. It also called upon St. Peter and St. Paul to defend the honor of the Roman church. Then it called upon all of the saints to bring peace to the church by interceding before God. Luther's 41 statements were condemned as heretical. Those statements included these: The pope was denied to be Christ's steward on earth over all of the churches of the world; It was not the will of the Holy Spirit to burn heretics; Purgatory could not be proven from the canonical books of Scripture. The pope condemned these statements and forbade all Christians, under the penalty of the ban, against standing with Luther, or reading his writings. He then commanded Luther to submit all of his writings to the bishops to be burned. He admonished Luther, whom he reminded of how gently he had been dealt with, to refrain from his errors, to stop preaching immediately, to retract his errors within sixty days, and within an additional sixty days allow credible proof of his retraction to reach Rome, or to bring that proof to Rome in person. However, if he should refuse, the pope declared that he was banned and commanded all spiritual and secular authorities to overpower him and his followers, and send them to Rome. He also threatened anyone who would object to the publication of the bull with the ban, and all with whom Luther might find protection with an interdict. The papal nuntio Aleander and Doctor Eck were entrusted with the enforcement of the bull. Aleander was a baptized Jew. Dr. Eck appeared in Germany and energetically applied himself to his new task under his new title of Papal Protonotarius and Nuntio. At the same time, Eck was given full authority to place the names of those he judged to be followers of Luther, under the verdict of the bull.

Eck took advantage of this authority by including a number of names of those whom he didn't care for. Among these were Carlstadt and Feldkirchen of Wittenberg. Pirkheimer and Spengler of Nuernberg were also on this list in spite of the intercession which was voiced by the city residents, by Bishop of Barnberg, and by Duke William of Bavaria. Finally, he added the name of his monastic brother, Adelmann, for the two had gotten into a huge argument at a dinner which had almost led to fisticuffs. They had argued about different doctrines. Adelmann would now have to clear himself of suspicion that he was supporting Luther's heresy. He would have had to confirm it with an oath. Pirkheimer and Spengler also succumbed to the bull and sent their submissive explanations to Rome. Yet Spengler, who would attend the Diet of Worms as a delegate, personally testified to the truth as the city scribe. Carlstadt and Feldkirchen stood firm against the attacks leveled at them by Eck.

Eck's posting of the bull met with mixed results elsewhere as well. The bull was accepted in the Bishoprics of Meissen and Merseburg, as well as in Eichstadt and Augsburg. In Ingolstadt, Luther's books were sequestered and sealed. In Lyon and Cologne, they were burned. In Mainz, the spiritual capital of the kingdom, there was a growing resistance. The executor, after Luther's books had been piled up and were about to be set on fire, stepped onto the scaffold and asked whether the one whose books were to be burned had been legally and rightly condemned. The whole assembly shouted, "No!" Responding to this, the executor, declaring that he would destroy nothing in this world which had not been correctly judged according to the law, jumped down off the scaffold. The mass of people were jubilant. Aleander, who was personally present, had to depart rather quickly due to the shouts of: "Jew! Traitor! Bully!," lest he be pelted with excrement off the street.

Nevertheless, he accomplished the burning of a few books during the following days. This was done by a grave digger with only the market women to watch. Meanwhile, a mocking song about him was posted in all of the alleys and even on the door of his residence. It said that he had not burned Luther's books, but those of Eck and Silvester Prierias.

In other areas it was especially the students and the commoners who gave Eck pause. In Erfurt the professors refused to publish the bull. When Eck arrived in person and had a bookstore dealer distribute the bull, the stu-

Picture of Dr. Martin Luther
On an engraved copper plate by Cranach in 15

dents took all of the copies they could lay their hands on, either by purchase or by force. They threw them into the water while scoffing, "Bulla est, in aqua natet." (It's a bubble, let it swim in water")! The academia took no action against them.

Church authorities in other parts of Germany were also harboring doubts and said so. Duke William of Bavaria even went so far as to attempt to have the bull rescinded. German lawyers also spoke out against the serving of the bull, and Caesar's counsel, Hieronymus von Enndorf, offered his honest assessment to Caesar, that he should not allow such an intrusion of the church authority into his secular rule. However, in Leipzig Eck succeeded in spreading the bull through city riders. Nevertheless, he personally met such danger in the city streets that he was forced to seek refuge in the Pauline monastery, and soon tried to travel by night. Starting something in Wittenberg was futile. When Eck personally sent the bull to the rector of the university, it was brought up for discussion. Luther and Carlstadt were present, and it was tabled. The few priests, who left Wittenberg as a result, were easily replaced with the great influx of daily arriving new students. Whenever Luther was preaching, the churches were filled like never before.

Most anxiously awaited was the reaction of Luther's Elector. He had journeyed to Aachen for the crowning of Caesar. On the 4th of November he had arrived in Cologne on his journey home, and was attending mass. There the papal delegates, Aleander and Caraccioli, approached him and handed him the pope's command to execute the bull. This upset the Elector deeply. After all, the pope had issued his verdict in Rome. This was done in spite of the Elector's request that Luther be given a hearing in Germany, and in spite of the agreement that had been reached with the Archbishop of Trier. All further negotiations were cut off as the venomous personal enemy of the unjustly condemned Luther had brought the bull into Germany during the Duke's absence from his territory.

At the same time this posed a considerable threat to his university. At first, he would give absolutely no answer to the legate. Then, after fourteen days, he allowed a response to be given through his counselors in the presence of two bishops. He replied that he remained unconvinced that Luther's teachings, writings, and sermons were so dangerous that they were to be burned. He continued that while he had no involvement with Luther's cause, he nevertheless insisted that Doctor Martin be given a hearing before unbiased judges, with guards for security, and in a suitable and safe location. He asked the legates to try to arrange such a meeting and stop the procedures which had burst upon Germany. The legates clenched their fists inside their pockets and retreated to a place where they believed they would find like-minded people. They did so while uttering threats. But the Elector was determined not to give in and gave the legates no more of his time.

So, what was Luther's personal reaction to the bull? Luther actually had been expecting it. For quite some time he had surmised that something like this was in the works. Von Hutten had received a harsh letter through the Archbishop of Mainz in which he was forbidden to publish Luther's books. Von Hutten responded by printing the bull, and accompanied the same with scathing commentary. Soon thereafter Luther learned that Eck had arrived with the bull.

But while Hutton tried to stomp armies out of the earth and raged like a boar, who had been struck by a bullet, Luther remained calm. Even when the bull was presented to him on October 11th, he calmly informed Spalatin about it as the business of the university, and opined that the Elector would do well to ignore it. Indeed, immediately after reporting to Spalatin he once again held out his hand in peace. Miltitz was clinging to that hand with fierce tenacity, even though Eck had personally handed him a copy in Leipzig.

Miltitz remained a serious contender. The reason for this was that he recognized that he had been called to an important task; or, perhaps he wanted to earn some great reward from the Elector by accomplishing what the Elector desired; or, perhaps he wanted to do away with all of Eck's work. In any event, he hung on to his role as mediator, though he had been too late with trying to prevent the publishing of Luther's "To the Nobility."

Then, through a convention of Augustinians at Eisleben, Miltitz together with Staupitz, Link, and some others, appealed to Luther, asking him to respond to the pope in writing. He was to assure the pope that he had never intended to attack him personally. Luther listened to the advice of his old fatherly friend, Staupitz, who after resigning his position as Vicar of the order at Eisleben, had been replaced by Link. Staupitz had then retreated from the battlefield and had withdrawn completely into retirement at Salzburg. Luther had not declined this petition of Staupitz. Luther could also honestly have written such a letter without yielding anything regarding the main cause for which he had been fighting. Though he was ready to write the suggested letter to the pope, Luther was not about to yield anything in regard to the main issue of the conflict. What Luther actually thought about carrying out the advised action, we can glean from the writings that continued to flow from of his pen.

Back in the early days of distributing the Book to the Nobility, Luther had written to the common laity, simply yet thoroughly, to go after the chief abomination of the papacy, the sacrifice of the mass. "Sermon of the New Testament, i.e., about Holy Mass," was the title he had given this pamphlet. In a very loving manner he instructed those Christians as to what the Holy Supper is and how a person is to properly prepare himself for receiving it worthily and with appreciation. He went on to describe what blessing is derived from this Sacrament, and how this healing Sacrament is so abominably treated by the papacy in the sacrifice for the living and the dead. In this connection he also addressed the universal priesthood of all Christians, thereby shattering the assumed priestly power of the Roman priests by which they enslaved consciences and filled their pockets with offerings.

At the end of his book to the nobility, Luther had announced that he still had another short song to sing to the papists. Well, he struck up its prelude in the book, "Prelude of the Babylonian Captivity of the Church." He did not allow the news of the impending bull to rattle him, as he sang. Instead, at the beginning, he testified to his opponents, Prierias, Eck, and Emser, that through them he was becoming more and more educated, whether that had been their intent or not. Two years earlier, he had written about indulgences. At that time, still a captive of Roman idolatry, he believed that indulgences need not be completely rejected. But now, thanks to Silvester and his brothers, he had learned that indulgences are nothing less than a fraud perpetrated by the Romans. He wished that everyone, who had read his earlier writings would burn them, and in their place, adopt the motto: Indulgences are a disgrace of the self-flattering Romans.

Later Eck, Emser, and their co-conspirators, continued their instruction of Luther, when they began to teach him about the primacy of the pope. Luther again learned much from them. Earlier he had accepted the premise that the papacy exists by human right. But now he knew for certain that the papacy is the kingdom of Babylon, and has the power of Nimrod, that mighty hunter. Until now he had foolishly been of the opinion that it would have been good if a council had resolved that the Sacrament be offered to the laity in both kinds. But now he had concluded from the clear passages of Scripture that it is ungodly and tyrannical to deny one of the elements, namely the cup, to the laity. No angel could forbid the cup, not to mention a pope or a council. The fact that the pope did so anyway was described by Luther as the first captivity of this Sacrament.

For Luther the second captivity was the Roman doctrine of transubstantiation, in which it was said that the bread and wine turn into the body and blood of Christ in the Sacrament. They didn't teach that the body and blood of Christ were received in, with, and under the bread and the wine, but that bread and wine were no longer present at all.

As the third and most ungodly, all-inclusive captivity of this Sacrament, he names the manner in which the body and blood of Christ are presented as a sacrifice. From this teaching had flowed countless other errors. Then he set forth the true doctrine of Holy Communion from Scripture, the appreciation of it, and the huge benefit to be derived from it.

He praised God that when it came to Baptism, that Sacrament at least remained preserved and not mutilated. But he lamented that its power and fruit, which affects the entire life of a Christian, had been depleted so much. This took place especially because of the high value that had been placed on the vows connected with the rite, which he stated should properly all be stopped.

He still allowed confession to stand as a sacrament. This was because the bestowal of grace rested on the application of the promise of God through the words of absolution. He allowed this, even though in the actual practice of confession the earthly element is lacking, meaning that its identity as a sacrament does not apply. But he laments again that because of the papacy, the main part of confession, namely the comforting promise of the forgiveness of sins received through faith, was allowed to fall away. Instead, all value in confession depended upon the sinner being crushed, especially with the imposition of penitential works with the result that consciences were enslaved, and the pouches filled with money.

Luther did not consider the other four sacraments of the papacy to be sacraments at all. Confirmation was not instituted by God. Marriage does not have a promise of salvation and a place in heaven. The ordination into the priesthood was not instituted by God. The same could be said about extreme unction. The apostle James didn't intend his words as an anointing of the dying, rather as a means for physical healing.

Luther understood very well that what he was saying would be displeasing to those who adopted their doctrine about the number and use of the sacraments from the Roman throne rather than from Scripture. In his conclusion he wrote: "I'm hearing again that papal bulls and curses have been readied for me, which are supposed to force me to recant or be called a heretic. If that is true, then I would like this booklet to be a part of my future recanting, so they would not complain that they had boasted about their tyranny in vain. If Christ grants me his grace, I shall present the rest in such a form as the Roman throne has neither seen nor heard until now, and shall in this way richly bear witness to my obedience.

In the name of our Lord Jesus Christ. Amen.

> *What scares you, hostile Herod, thus*
> *That Christ, the Lord, is born to us?*
> *He seeks no mortal kingdom Why?*
> *He brings his kingdom from on high!"*

This work had left the press a few days before the bull arrived in Wittenberg and Luther announced it to Spalatin as a "trumpet call to battle." In spite of this, at this very time Miltitz dared to remind him of the promise he had made to the brothers of his order. So, in the midst of all of the ongoing with the bull, Luther traveled to Lichtenberg, accompanied by Melanchthon. There he met with Miltitz in the monastery of Anthony, the place to which Miltitz had invited him. Even at this point in time Luther was actually of a mind to keep his promise. So that his latest writing would not appear to have been prompted by the bull, it was dated retroactively to September 6. It was to appear in German and Latin. In addition, Luther wanted to give Miltitz a brief doctrinal writing to take along. "If it works," he said, "good. If it does not work, also good; yet this is the way that is pleasing to God."

This is how he wrote to Pope Leo. He had been pressed by a number of godless flatterers of the pope to the point that he request a special council. But as far as he knew, he had said nothing disrespectful against Leo as a person. Rather, he sought to protect him against Silvester. It is true that he attacked the Roman throne again, but the pope himself had to admit that the Roman court was now worse than Sodom, Gomorrah, or Babylon ever were. The pope must have noticed that it could no longer be counseled or helped out of its evil. For a long time, the only thing that had come out of Rome was harm for both body and soul. The Roman church had become a den of thieves and a kingdom of sin. "In the meantime," he continued, "you, holy father, are sitting as a sheep among wolves, as Daniel among the lions, as Ezekiel among scorpions. What can you accomplish on your own against so many wild animals?

"Surely it is intended that you and the cardinals would work to defend against this wretchedness. But the disease scoffs at the medicine, (that is, the intented reforms) and horse and wagon no longer care about the driver (meaning, the pope). That is the reason why I felt sorry through all of this that you, upright Leo, had to become the pope at this time, when you are worthy to be the pope during better times. The Roman throne is not worthy of you and others like you, but an evil spirit should be the pope, since he rules in Babylon more than you. Would to God that you would be set free from that honor, as they, destructive enemies, call it, and could support yourself from your prebend and your father's inheritance! (Dictionary definition of prebend [German: "Pfruende"]: 1. The part of the revenues of a cathedral or collegiate church paid as a clergyman's salary; 2. The property or tax yielding such revenues; 3. A prebendary or his benefice.) Hence, Holy Father Leo, I am coming now to lie at your feet and beg you, if possible, to lay your hand to the task of bridling those self-flatterers. They make believe that they want to achieve peace, but they are enemies of peace.

"But my recanting of our teaching will not happen, nor should anyone try to force me to do so, unless he desires to turn the entire matter into even greater confusion. I, being an enemy to quarrels, do not want to arouse or provoke anyone on my part. But I also do not wish to be provoked. If I am provoked, I will neither be speechless nor will my pen be stilled. May Your Holiness take on all of this quarreling yourself and exterminate it, with simple and short words. In place of it bid silence and peace, which is what I have always wanted. Therefore, my holy father, may you not listen to those sweet voices, who croon into your ears that you are not a mere human being, but rather a mixture with God, who is in command over all things. It will not happen that way. Even you will accomplish nothing. You are a servant to all of the servants of God and are in a more dangerous and more miserable profession than anyone else on earth. Do not let yourself be betrayed by those, who lie to you and in their hypocrisy tell you that you are the lord of the world. They will not allow anyone to be a Christian, unless he is put under your rule.

"In conclusion, I do not come before Your Holiness empty handed, but I am bringing along a pamphlet. This pamphlet has gone out under your name, and for a good wish and beginning of peace and good hope, from which Your Holiness may derive a taste with what procedure I greatly desire and also productively occupy myself, if that should be possible for me to do in the presence of your unchristian flatterers. It is only a small pamphlet, if one is only looking at the value of its paper. Yet it sums up the entire life of a Christian, if one understands its sense. I am poor. I do not have anything else with which I might express my service to you. And you may no longer be edified with anything else besides spiritual gifts. With this I commend myself to Your Holiness. May Jesus Christ preserve you eternally. Amen."

(published November 20, 1520)

The work which Luther sent along to the pope with his letter appeared in Latin and German. It was titled, "Concerning the Freedom of a Christian." Luther dedicated the German edition to the mayor of Zwickau, Hieronymus Muehlpfort.

1. "A Christian is free, lord over all things, and slave to no one."

2. "A Christian is slave to all things, and below everything and everyone."

Luther positioned those two statements prior to his interpretation of *"The Whole Sum of a Christian Life"* with 1 Cor. 9:19 and Rom. 13:8 (See NIV translation) as brief proof passages. To grasp such seeming contradictions as found in Scripture, one has to remember that each Christian has two natures: the spiritual internal new man, and the fleshly outward old man.

"We take a look at the internal spiritual man in order to learn what he has done to be called a holy, free, Christian man and it becomes clear that nothing external can make him free or holy. The soul has nothing else, either in heaven or on earth, than the holy gospel. It lives in the gospel and is holy, free, and Christian by the gospel.

"This is how we can be sure that the soul can get along without everything except the Word of God, and without the Word of God nothing can be beneficial for it. When the soul has the Word of God it needs nothing else, but it has enough in the Word: food, joy, peace, light, skill, righteousness, truth, wisdom, freedom, and everything good in abundance. ... But you might ask, 'What is that word which bestows such grace, and how should I use it?' The answer: Nothing else has happened than the preaching of Christ, as the gospel contains in itself, which is designed and has produced that you hear God speaking to you that all your life and works are nothing before God, but that you are for eternal ruin with everything that is in you. This means, that if you believe properly as you should, that you have to despair on behalf of yourself and confess that the passage from Hosea is true: 'O Israel, there is nothing in you except destruction; your help is from me only.' (Hosea 13:9 from the undated Luther Bible in German, issued by CPH. - William Beck's Bible translation, [An American Translation of the Bible] 1976, comes close to Luther's translation.)

"But so that you may depart and remove yourself from your own destruction, God places before you his dear Son, Jesus Christ. Through his living, comforting Word, he tells you to surrender yourself with firm faith to him and trust in him anew. Thus, all your sins are forgiven through that same faith. All of your destruction has been overcome, and you are righteous, real, at peace, holy, and with all of the commandments fulfilled, free of all things. This is as St. Paul says in Romans 1:17 "A righteous Christian's living is out of his faith" (TRANSLATOR's explanation: 'out of', from the Greek: 'ek', which takes the genitive); and Romans 10 "Christ is the end and fulfillment of all commandments for those who believe in him." (Romans 10:4 - LUTHER's, transliteratin of the passage.)

This title page of the original printing of this writing,
reduced from the actual size
in the frame decoration: on top, the Saxon swords;
at the bottom, the coat of arms of the city of Wittenberg

He then goes on to show that the Holy Scriptures contain two central doctrines: the law, which prescribes good works, but does not give the power to do them, and the gospel, the word of divine promise. He describes the action of both and writes, "When man has learned from the Commandments how powerless he is and has understood that the law has to be fulfilled, he becomes terribly afraid of how he could possibly keep the law. Thus, he is truly humbled and looks at himself as being nothing at all. He finds nothing in himself through which he might become holy.

"But then the other word is set forward, the divine promise and assurance. It says: If you want to be rid of your evil lust and sin, which the Commandments compel and demand, then look to and believe in Christ, in whom you are assured of all grace, righteousness, peace, and freedom. As you believe, so you have. If you don't believe, you don't have. (The German: "glaubst du, so hast du; glaubst du nicht, so hast du nicht.") This is how the promises of God provide what the Commandments demand. They fulfill what the Commandments require, so that everything comes from God, both the Commandments and the fulfillment. He alone is the One who commands. He alone also fulfills. These, and all of God's Word, are holy, true, right, peaceful, free, and full of goodness. The result is that whoever clings to these with a true faith has his soul united with God so completely, that all of the excellence of the Word also becomes the property of the soul. In this way, the soul - holy, right, true, peaceful, free, and full of all goodness from God's Word - becomes a true child of God through faith. This is as John 1:12 (Luther's own paraphrasing of the passage) speaks: 'He has given to them that they may become God's children, all who believe in his name.' "From this it is easily understood why faith has the power to do so much, and that no good work can be like it. ... This is the Christian freedom, the one true faith ("der einige Glaube"), not that we might continue to do nothing or to do evil, but that we do not need a single work to gain holiness or blessedness. But since Christ, our Bridegroom, with whom we, by faith, are united, is a King and Priest, so all Christians are kings and priests. Who then can fully understand ("ausdenken") the honor and the highness of a Christian? Through his kingdom he has mastery of all things. Through his priesthood he has God's mastery, for God does what he asks and wants as is written in the Psalms: "God does the will of those who fear him and hears their prayer" (Psalm 145:19 LUTHER's paraphrased translation) This honor he attains is only by faith and not by any work. Thus, a man can clearly see how a Christian is free from all things and is above all things.

"And since it is the common faith of all Christians which grants them such royal and priestly honor, therefore the distinction which the papacy draws between the priesthood and the laity is contrary to Scripture. The only distinction Scripture makes is between Christians as a whole, and those doers and stewards who are to preach to other Christians, since not all can be stewards and preach.

"But a Christian in this life is not yet completely spiritual, but still has flesh and blood, the old man, as a part of him. That old man fights against the new man and wants to imprison him with sin. Thus, all who belong to Christ have to crucify their flesh together with their lusts and desires. This is where the works begin. The inner man is one with God, happy and cheerful for the sake of Christ, who has done so much for him. His entire delight is that he, in turn, also wants to serve Christ freely out of love for God. But these works are not to be done with the thought that through them man becomes righteous before God. But a Christian does them out of free love, and he sees in his works nothing other than that they are pleasing to God, whose will he enjoys doing in the best way possible.

"So, in paradise Adam would not do his work to achieve righteousness, since he already had it. So, a Christian also will not become righteous and a Christian through the works he does. And if he had not been a Christian before, all of his works would be punishable and damning. Good holy works never produce a good holy man. But a good and holy man produces good and holy works, just as the good tree has to first exist in order to bear good fruit. In the same way, a good house does not produce a good builder, but a good builder makes a good house. Thus, whoever would do good works, must not begin with the good works, but with the person who is to do the good works. But nothing makes the person good except faith alone, just as nothing makes him evil except unbelief alone. And whatever seems good without faith, all of it is vain. So, to repeat, we do not reject good works as a whole. We only reject them when a person desires to become righteous and holy through them. Therefore, he who himself makes holy, robs God of His honor and falsifies "by God's grace".

"What's more, a Christian does not exist on this earth for himself alone; he lives among other people. So, he should be of the same mind as Jesus who had only our best interest in mind. Even though Jesus was completely free, for our sake he became a servant. So, a Christian will do as he sees in Christ. Though he is completely free he willingly makes himself a servant and thinks: 'Well then, my God has given to me, an unworthy, condemned man without any merit, the full riches of all holiness and blessedness. He has done this free of charge and out of pure compassion through and in Christ. Henceforth, I have need of nothing except to believe that this is so.

"Listen! I want to do what pleases such a Father, who has poured out on me his superabundant goods. I want to do so freely, cheerfully, and without pay. At the same time, I will become a Christ to my neighbor as Christ came to me. I will do no less than what I see he needs and is useful and blessed for him. After all, through faith in Christ I have plenty of all things.

"You see, this is the way love and desire for God flow out of faith; and a free, willing, and cheerful life of service for my neighbor, free of charge, flows out of love. For just as our neighbor suffers and is in need of our surplus, so were we suffering before God and in need of his grace." This Luther also demonstrated with several examples and passages from Scripture and in so doing puts the works of the papists to the test. He says that whatever work is not aimed toward serving one's neighbor and submitting to his will, as long as the neighbor's will is not in opposition to God, is not a good or a Christian work.

"From all of this comes the conclusion that a Christian does not live for himself but for Christ and his neighbor: for Christ, through faith; for his neighbor, through love. Through faith he elevates himself in God; from God he lowers himself through love and will always remain in God and godly love. ...

"Note that this is true, spiritual Christian freedom. It sets the heart free from all sins, laws, and Commandments, and surpasses all other freedoms, as heaven surpasses the earth. May God grant that we rightly understand and preserve this. Amen."

If the previously mentioned main reformation writings of Luther could be described as war trumpets blaring against the tyranny of the Roman papacy, then in this writing Christianity was hearing a still, soft whisper. In contrast to the new spring storms, it blew along pleasantly, warm, and smelling of paradise, and made the hearts alive. What a wonderful man who could compose such a pamphlet at such a time!

Luther sent this work directly into the dungeon which had enslaved Christians for centuries. In it they enjoyed calling the church the pope's enslaved bondwoman. He sent it along with a friendly letter to the man who had just sent his most bitter enemy against him with the declaration of the ban. It was a testimony against his and God's enemy, a testimony for the truth. It was a testimony that the man who gave it was not sounding the trumpet blare of battle to the nations against his enemies, because he wanted to fight nor because of personal animosity.

For Luther the bull remained what it was, a work of the Antichrist, and he treated it accordingly. Indeed, at first, he left the person of the pope out of it and assigned the blame for it to the one who had been most active in promoting it. In this way he was responding just like the others who refused to publish it, because Eck had not acted in a legitimate fashion. He issued a small publication entitled, "About the New Bulls and Lies of Eck," in which he explained he could not yet ascribe such an injustice to the pope. He wouldn't have sent such a bull through his most bitter enemy while Luther's matter was still pending examination and his appeal remained fully in place. He first wanted to see the original bull with its papal seal.

But immediately thereafter, he issued a document in Latin and German entitled, "Against the Bull of the Antichrist." In it he both defended some of the condemning statements in the bull and also took to task some of the distortions it contained. That he was not terribly afraid, which up to this point was the usual reaction to receiving a papal bull, he openly demonstrated to both his friends and his enemies. "Everyone should know," he wrote, "that a man who highly despised the insolent, heretical and deceitful bull is doing me no service. On the other hand, a man who holds it in high regard also gives me no grief. I am free through the grace of God; therefore, I will not take comfort in regard to these matters, nor will I be upset by them. I know well where my comfort and my courage lies, and it keeps me safe before people and devils. I shall do what I do. Everyone must answer for himself when he dies and faces judgment, and then he will understand my faithful warning. But so that no one can use the excuse that he does not know what to watch out for against such sacrileges and errors, I will tell you those things which are condemned in the bull and point out the blindness and the malice of the Roman transgressors."

Finally, he wrote, "If the pope does not retract and condemn this bull, and also punish Eck and his companions as purveyors of such a bull, then no one can doubt that the pope is the enemy of God, the persecutor of Christ, the destroyer of Christianity, and the true antichrist. Up to this time no one has ever heard of condemning the Christian faith when publicly confessed, as this hellish, accursed bull is doing."

In the Latin edition of this work he had gone into greater detail at its beginning than what he had said here in conclusion. There he wrote that he would try not to believe that Pope Leo X and his cardinals had produced this bull. This was not to protect the honor of the name of Rome, but rather because he would not exalt himself as someone who enjoys the good fortune of being condemned from such a high throne for standing up for the truth. "May everyone in Rome cling to whatever he wants. I hold the instigator of this bull, whoever he may be, to be the antichrist. And against the Antichrist I am writing this so that, as much as I am able, I will defend the truth, that truth which the issuer is trying to exterminate. First, so that he cannot hold against me everything that he maintains, I testify before God, our Lord Jesus, his holy angels, and the whole world, that I wholeheartedly declare myself innocent of the condemnation which has been declared in this bull. I condemn and curse such a bull as a malicious enemy and blasphemy against Christ, the Son of God, our Lord; Amen. Second, I maintain and hold tight with every confidence of my spirit to the articles which this bull condemns. I declare freely that all Christians, under the threat of the eternal curse, must continue to maintain these articles; and that all, who support this bull, are to be regarded as anti-Christian. In fellowship with the spirit of all who recognize and honor Christ I regard them as heathens and avoid them in accordance with the command of our Lord Jesus Christ. Amen. This is my retraction!"

A rally cry to Caesar, the other counts of Christendom, the bishops and doctors to not let themselves be insulted by such atrocious bulls, he left out of the German edition. Still, he again summoned Caesar, the counts, the nobility and the cities with the renewal of every aspect of his appeal, which he had made on November 17th. He summoned them to stand with him in his appeal and to dismiss the bull by not following it.

At the same time, he framed the pope as the accused, in that he allowed his appeal to be offered as if from Pope Leo:

"First, as from an atrocious power, a presumptive and unjust judge;

"Second, as from a hard-hearted, erring in all of Scripture, condemned heretic and apostate;

"Third, as from an enemy, adversary, and oppressor of all Holy Scripture;

"Fourth, as from a despiser, blasphemer, and abuser of the Holy Christian Church and of a free council..."

Luther had yet another response to the papal bull. On the 10th of November, a special public posting demanded the attention of the student body of Wittenberg. On it, Luther invited the young academics to attend a burning of the anti-Christian decretals at 9 AM. (The decretals were the books of papal rights, on which the popes would base particular claims.) At the appointed time the students arrived in large numbers in front of the Elstergate of the Augustinian Monastery. Many doctor and magisters, including Carlstadt and Melanchthon, were also present. An eminent magister arranged a pile of wood and set it on fire. After laying the papal decretals on the pyre, Luther also consigned the papal bull to the flames. He proclaimed in Latin, "Because you have grieved the Holy One, let the eternal flames destroy you." Then Luther returned to the city with his friends.

However, the students had not yet had enough. They wanted to make a greater show of their agreement with their bold teacher. While a large number stayed by the fire and kept it burning, others went back into the city. They gathered many of the books of Eck, Emser, and other papists and piled them on a wagon. A banner, one cubit in length, was waving from the wagon like a flag. Singing, they paraded through the city to the fire, where the books and the long banner shared the destiny of the decretals. But the next day, Luther admonished those students, strongly encouraging them to renounce the papacy with all their hearts by the salvation of their souls.

The place where their thought-provoking activity is said to have taken place is still being shown in Wittenberg. Each one of the previously mentioned writings was a bold action against the bull. The appeal to the pope for a future council was also an important step. But it would not be accurate to say that Luther was now proceeding from words to deeds. Still, the fire scene at the Elstergate was certainly eye-catching. It was not an act done in haste, but a carefully considered action. Many months prior to the deed, Luther had planned payback for the burning of his books, and after sincere prayer he followed through with that bold step. He did not regret it. As he reported to Staupitz, he rejoiced more in this than in any other deed of his life. This action was a personal declaration that he was free from that abomination of abominations, the atrocious Roman papacy, and it spoke louder than any words could say.

To justify his actions, he immediately issued a declaration in German and in Latin under the title, "Why the Books of the Pope and His Disciples Are Burned; Let It Be Shown, by Anyone, Why They Have Burned the Books of Dr. Luther." As a reason for the burning, he cited 30 errors in the papal books, and, as a summary of the papal decretals, the statement about the primacy of the pope. He carried this out according to the old custom, in conformity with the example of St. Paul (*perhaps referring to Acts 19:18,19*), as a baptized Christian, and a sworn doctor of Holy Scripture.

About the same time, a script appeared in Latin, and soon after in German, under the title, "Reason and Cause of All the Articles Which Were Unjustly Condemned by the Roman Bull." The Elector and others had expressed their desire for Luther to issue such a script. In it, Luther once again carefully discussed, fully and in detail, his statements in the same order as they had been condemned by Rome. He also issued a retraction here of individual statements, of course not in the sense that the pope desired. Thus, the statement was rejected in the bull under Number 18, "The indulgence is a divine deception of Christians and a lessening of good work and of a number of things, which are permissible, but not beneficial." Concerning this, he admits that he had indeed said this, but had not known better at the time. "But now that the holy father, the pope, has commanded me to retract and condemn this article, I will obey and say, 'I confess my error.' This article is not true and I now say so: The indulgence is not a divine deception, thievery, and robbery. It is a hellish, devilish, antichristian deception, thievery, and robbery, by which the Roman Nimrod and teacher of sin, sells sin and hell to the whole world. He sucks out and licks off all of their money for such unspeakable damage. If this retraction is not enough, I shall improve it another time." Also in regard to the following four statements, which the bull rejected, he had this to say: "To the honor of the highly intelligent bull, I retract everything which I ever taught about indulgences, and I am sincerely sorry from my heart for whatever I said good about them. ... Hence, it was right for my books to be burned. For this surely happened because I had yielded and served too much to the pope and his indulgence, and I personally condemn such teachings to the fire."

When the time during which all of these things took place, the 120 days allowance established in the bull, had passed and so Luther let himself be seen in Rome during the following weeks, a second bull was issued on January 3rd. In it he was unconditionally placed under the ban, along with anyone else who was uniting with him, no matter how high their position or reputation. All of them were declared to be condemned people.

Together with all of their descendants they all were declared as deprived of all honors, dignities, and possessions; and they were guilty for the sacrilege of insulting majesty. In addition, anywhere where Luther's teaching had been accepted, all priests were to declare Luther and all his followers as heretics, banned, and accursed, for three days. They were to preach against those heretics in the divine services. All places where Luther and his followers received shelter were to be placed under the interdict. This bull arrived in Worms, as Caesar Charles V was opening his first Diet.

Chapter 21
Before Caesar and the Empire

The hopes were high In Germany for the young Austrian noble, the twenty year old nephew of Maximilian. (Footnote: Karl V was born on Feb. 24, 1500, to Philip the Handsome of Austria, and Johannah, the daughter of Ferdinand and Isabella of Spain, the heir to the kingdoms of Spain, Naples, Sardinia, Sicily, Austria, Burgundy, Mexico, and Peru.) On October 22, 1520, he made his majestic entrance in Aachen. He rode on a stallion which was covered with golden brocade, followed by a company of five thousand riders. The following day as he was being crowned through the papal fiat, he accepted the title of the elected Roman Caesar. The German counts may well have been somewhat skeptical as they beheld that tender, slim figure of medium height and with pale beardless face, for the first time. A German he was not. They heard no German from him, and their German he did not understand. Karl likewise did not display the fresh and knightly presence with which Maximillian had deported himself. His eyes gave the impression of being tired and dejected. It was reported that he was completely under the control of his Secretary of State, Wilhelm von Croix, and his father confessor, the Franciscan Glapio. Glapio was a cunning old fox who knew how to furrow his brow, choose his words, and hang his cloak just as the situation demanded. In addition to his new authority, Karl's scepter also extended over the kingdoms of Spain and Naples, and over Sicily, where he could rule only as a Catholic count.

Still, men from both parties in Germany, even though their confrontations were becoming more violent, had high hopes for him. Hutten traveled to him in the Netherlands and one of his pamphlets showed Caesar's picture with the heading:

O Carle, Kaiser lobesan, Greif du die Sach am ersten an.
Gott wirds mit dir ohn Zweifel han.

Translated:
O Charlie, Caesar, man of praise, Attack the issue first, with haste.
God without doubt will bless your case.

"I will serve you day and night without pay or reward," Hutten called. "I shall arouse many a proud hero to help you. You shall be the leader, commander, and finisher." Caesar was also being encouraged in other areas: to dismiss the Franciscans, to rule with the nobility instead, to make Hutten and Erasmus his counselors, and to set limits to the ongoing pressure out of Rome, and also limits for the orders of beggars. Then he would have the nation on his side and have no need for the pope and the cardinals.

Luther had already written to Caesar in 1520. He made a heartfelt appeal for his own cause, since a huge effort was being made to destroy him along with the entire gospel. "After I had tried everything else, though in vain, it seemed right for me to follow the example of holy Athanasius. And so I turn to you, majestic Caesar, to see whether through your highness God will be gracious to me. Therefore, I beseech your majesty, Caesar, prostrate on my knees, that you will take not my person, but the issue of truth under the shadow of your wings. Protect me only until I have been given my hearing to see if I shall be found to be ungodly or a heretic. The only thing I ask is that neither truth nor untruth be condemned without a hearing and without having been disproved."

At that time, Luther did not get a reply to his humble letter, though he was easily comforted in this regard. Indeed, when Spalatin, who had journeyed with the Elector to meet Caesar wrote to him that there was not much to hope for from Caesar, Luther expressed his joy. He rejoiced that through this his friends had to learn that we are not to put our trust in princes. God had assigned the spreading of his gospel to fishermen, not to the mighty of this earth. But it was different for others. They understood that they would be disappointed in Karl. When the news arrived, that Caesar had allowed the hated bull to be executed in the Netherlands, which also was a part of his inherited kingdom, and that following his coronation Luther's books were supposed to have been burned in Cologne in his presence, there was good cause for suspicion.

Hutten, who had found little comfort in the Netherlands, lashed out in both German and Latin. He especially attacked the burning of Luther's works. Not satisfied with this, he began to press for a call to arms in Germany and personally tried to win the Elector of Saxony to his side. To his friend Sickingen, who was still putting his hopes on Caesar and greatly trusted in his own ability to influence the ruler, he held up the example of Ziska. Ziska was a wild leader of the Hussites, and had once been a terror to the papists. Soon there were rumors of a large war band being prepared to head toward Rome. The number supposedly included 35,000 Saxons, together with an equal number of Bohemians. Luther was not pleased with such efforts and reports, but increased his warnings against the use of force, asking that the matter be left to God and his Word. He even wrote the same to Hutten. When he invited Caesar and the entire nation to stand with him for his appeal, he was not calling for the use of earthly force. He wrote, "The world was overcome through the Word. The church was saved through the Word. It will be restored through the Word. The Antichrist, too, whose beginning was without (*a display of*) power, will also be trampled under foot by the Word."

But the legate was very much aware of Germany's frame of mind. Thus, Aleander reported to Rome that everywhere in Germany complaint and animosity were reigning, and Caesar would not remain ignorant of what was going on while he traveled through that nation. Although the legates were pushing Caesar to strictly enforce the bull in Germany, as elsewhere, the suggestion of the Elector Frederick did receive a hearing. For Caesar had responded to him in a letter from Oppenheim, dated November 28th. In it, he expressed his desire for this issue, which could cause so much confusion, to be set aside. Thus, he was prepared to allow Luther to receive a hearing before better understanding and highly educated authorities during the upcoming diet. He would also take care that no injustice would befall him there. The Elector was to bring him along and meanwhile should see to it that Luther would write nothing more against the papal authority or the throne of Rome.

Meanwhile the Elector had received news of the intentional burning of Luther's writings at Cologne shortly after he had departed. Without doubt, he also heard about what had occurred at the Elster gate in Wittenberg. With both events in mind he responded to Caesar on the 20th of December, that he was asking to be excused from his assigned task. He evidently wanted to avoid two issues: one, if what had happened to Hus were to happen to Luther, he did not want to be the one who would have delivered him to be executed; the other, as an Elector of the empire, he wanted to remain unconnected with Luther's cause.

However, Caesar had changed his mind before the Elector's answer reached him. As early as December 17th, he wrote to the Elector that he could leave Luther at home in case he did not wish to recant, or, if he wished to recant, he was to bring him only as far as Frankfurt. He wrote this because he had noticed that the ban against Luther had already expired, and the interdict had been posted in every location Luther would stop for lodging.

Caesar's change of mind we have to credit to the account of the Romanists' influence. They were afraid that the open testimony of Luther before Caesar and the empire would be a fresh disaster for the Roman throne. Luther also saw it that way and was saddened when he heard of how things had turned. When the Elector had asked him whether he was ready to appear before the diet, he had answered, "If I will be called, I will come as far as it refers to me, even if I would have to be carried there, should I be sick. Should Caesar call me, there is no doubt that God would be calling me. Should they resort to strength, as it appears, for they surely are not summoning me to instruct me, the matter must be committed to God." He was putting his trust in the One who had preserved the three men in the fiery furnace. He believed that, if God did not want to preserve him, "his head was a small thing in comparison to Christ, who was killed in utter disgrace." In conclusion he wrote, "You may be mistaken about me in anything save this, that I will flee or recant. I do not want to flee, much less recant, as surely as my Lord Jesus gives me strength.

According to the "Golden Bull", the German Caesar was to be chosen at Frankfurt, crowned at Aachen, and then conduct his first court business at Nuernberg. Because at this time the plague was threatening Nuernberg, the honor of hosting the first Diet of Karl V was allotted to the city of Worms. Caesar made his entrance in December. The authorities were summoned January 6th. But the diet was first convened January 28th. However, even before the opening, several issues dealing with Luther's matter had been attended to. There was heightened anticipation for him to appear before Caesar and the empire. Luther also declared himself ready to stand before Caesar, and the elector forwarded that information to him. But again, it seems that the little red caps intervened, and Luther had to patiently await further developments.

Meanwhile this delay was a time of restless activity for him. We have already been introduced to a number of his labors during these weeks. He occupied himself with the bull and with the " Emser Buck." The Roman theologian, Ambrosius Katharinus, had written a book, "Against the Ungodly and Highly Destructive Errors of Martin Luther," which Luther dismissed with a Latin essay. In the epilogue of this work, he dealt quite briefly with Silvester Prierias, who had again attacked him.

What's more, he continued his interpretation of the Psalms and issued an interpretation of the sermon texts for the Sundays in Advent. They were intended to be the first section of a postil, a book of family devotions, which he had begun to announce in 1519, acceding to the wish of his Elector and others. For those whose consciences were being pressured by their father confessors to turn over Luther's books, he who was always painfully aware of the need for conscience counseling wrote, "Instruction for the Confessing Children." Luther supplied the texts for the 26 pictures drawn by his friend, Lucas Cranach. Cranach had illustrated Christ and his humility in contrast to the pope and his pride. This work was later published in a booklet with the title, "The Passion of Christ and the Antichrist." (Footnote: This Passion has been reissued as a faithful copy and with a new foreword by Dr. C.F.W. Walther. See <u>Luther's Saemmtliche Schriften</u> by Dr. Johann Georg Walch, Vol. XIV, pp. 198-249) In addition, he preached twice daily during this time on Genesis, and on the Gospels. Finally, since the end of February he had been working on an edifying interpretation of The Song of Mary, intended for the nephew of Elector John Frederick. Then Caesar summoned him to Rome, away from all this work.

Meanwhile things were heating up at the diet. The bull of January 3rd had arrived. With it came a papal brief to Caesar, in which he demanded the immediate execution of the verdict and urged Caesar to use the sword. Caesar placed this brief before the Elector. On the 13th of February, the legate Aleander gave a speech three hours long. It concluded with the bull. He listed a good number of statements, which he said were sufficient in and of themselves. Because of such statements, thousands of heretics had already been burned. He protested the granting of a hearing at the Diet to one already condemned. He regarded the diet as being unable to judge in matters of faith, and demanded that Luther's writings be burned.

There was very little, if any sign among the authorities in attendance, that the speech had a powerful effect. The Elector of Saxony, who was ill, did not hear any of it. But the Romanists were burrowing like moles. Aleander had been given a lot of money and knew how to use it for bribery. For fifty guilders, one of Caesar's secretaries promised to pass on secret information. In one of his letters we read, "The counselors and scribes, even if they are ever so hostile toward the Roman court, dance to our tunes when they see money. Without this, nothing will happen."

Caesar's confessor, Father Glapio, was also present and was very busy. In an underhanded way he sought to gain something by exerting influence on Luther's Elector. But the Elector would yield nothing. And secret discussions held between Glapio and the Saxon Chancellor Brueck for a number of days in succession, likewise accomplished nothing, regardless how little Glapio requested. His actions had been intended to convince the Elector's Chancellor that Luther should recant because it would be in Caesar's best interest.

Among the concessions Glapio offered in these discussions was this one, that Luther would be given a hearing before impartial men in an advantageous location in Germany. But he did not include Worms among these advantageous places. Again, and again he emphasized that Luther should not leave the territory of his Elector. In this he was in agreement with the papal legates, who were vainly striving for Luther to be condemned away from Caesar's presence. They also persuaded Caesar to introduce an edict at the Diet, in which Luther was to be handcuffed as a heretic, without any further hearing. Discussions in regard to this edict bounced back and forth for seven days, during which the Elector Frederick also let his powerful voice be heard. Finally, a legal position for the good (a Gutachten") was established, which gave Caesar something to ponder. He had learned that Luther had too much support among the people to be dealt with so summarily.

As a result, he was to be summoned with a safe escort to face questions posed by men of learning, "whether he would or would not stand by the writings he had issued against our holy Christian faith." If he would retract these, then he would be given a further hearing on other points and issues. Thus, the issues would be disposed of reasonably. But if he did not appear or declined the request to recant, he would then be treated as a manifest heretic.

A self-portrait of Lucas Cranach

The outrage of the legates in regard to these proceedings was heightened, because the old grievances about the exsuctions out of the nation, and the encroachment of the Roman court and her ambassadors into the judicial work of the world, were again becoming evident. They listed 101 grievances, and the legates were horrified when even Duke George delivered his contribution of a full dozen grievances. And what type of language he used! In part, he denounced the same practices that Luther had named in his address to the nobility. In fact, he attacked the very matter of the indulgences which had begun this entire struggle. "The indulgence," he said, "is being sold for money. It is being praised in a most shameful manner, only to gather a lot of money, and because of this the preachers, who are supposed to proclaim the truth, instead bring forth a lot of deception and lies. The bishopric officials are just as zealous in the decision to rake in money. The poor have to pay, ... the rich are spared." In conclusion, he even requested a council and at this council "a general reformation."

There was no reference to the papal bull in the "Gutachten" (a legal document for the good in general) adopted by the authorities. The items which were to be given to Luther to recant were left so unspecific, that it was possible to reduce them to something very insignificant. Nor was there any definition of what was to be regarded under "other points and issues" concerning which a further hearing could be held. The same could be said about the idea of reasonable disposing. In view of the grievances, the Romanists could very well ask themselves what they should fear more, the victory if Luther would recant, or a stubborn refusal to recant. For if the first occurred, they had to be afraid that when they got to "the other points," with the monk as standard bearer, the entire diet, Duke George included, would stand against the pope. Then what?

But the authorities had spoken and Caesar yielded. He did make one more attempt to avoid extending an official imperial summons, when he asked the Elector Frederick to summon Luther. But when he would not agree, the official citation was completed on March 6th. It was signed by Caesar and the Archbishop Albrecht of Mainz, the Arch chancellor of the empire. It made no mention of recanting, but justified summoning Luther with the phrasing decided on by Caesar and the authorities, "on account of the teachings and the books," that had been written by him for some time. They needed information from him. The amicable address, "honorable, dear, devout" with which the summons began, was outrageous to the legate Aleander.

Carrying this summons and Caesar's accompanying letter, together with additional letters from the counts, through whose territory Luther would have to travel, was the royal herald, Kaspar Sturm. He proceeded to Wittenberg, where he arrived on March 26th, the Tuesday of Holy Week.

Luther had already received information, about what was decided for him at Worms, through Spalatin, before he had received the summons. He also replied immediately that unless he was convinced of some error, he would retract nothing. Indeed, if he were to be invited to Worms only for retracting, he would rather stay in Wittenberg. He could retract there just as well. But since he found nothing in the imperial summons about a request to retract, he immediately prepared for his journey. This was in order to arrive within the graciously allowed 21 days as stated in the summons. He celebrated Easter in Wittenberg. On Easter Sunday, he sent the finished pages of Mary's Song of praise, along with an accompanying letter to Prince John Frederick. On Monday, he sent the epilogue of his writing to Katharinus, to his friend Link. He began his journey on Tuesday. Together with his colleague Amsdorf, a noble student from Pomerania, and a brother of his order, Luther was seated in a covered wagon, supplied by the council of Wittenberg. He left the city amid hundreds of students, friends, and colleagues. Would he see them again? Who could say? Therefore, at his farewell he admonished his students to hold on tight to the teaching of the gospel. To Melanchthon he said, "If I don't return and my enemies murder me, I put you under oath, dear brother. Swear that you will not stop teaching and remaining in the truth of God's Word." His friends thought that they were seeing him for the last time.

However, anyone who saw Doctor Martinus Luther traveling toward Worms would not have gotten the impression that he was a heretic to be detested. He looked hardly to be the one, whom the pope had condemned anew in his Maundy Thursday bull, a man who with his adherents was on his way to his funeral pyre. The imperial herald in a coat of armor with the royal eagle on his chest did not look like an executioner. In Leipzig, the council received the doctor with the customary honorary drink of wine. People were streaming together out of the cities and villages through which he traveled, in order to see that brave man. At the border of the territory of Erfurt, the rector of the university, riding at the front of a stately train, prepared a festive reception. Luther preached in the Augustinian church that Sunday. His sermon was based on the Gospel of John 20:19ff, about the peace of God in Christ Jesus. The church was so overfilled that the galleries crackled due to too much weight, which terrified the people inside. There was even a throng of people outside the doors, listening to his preaching. He then proceeded to preach at Gotha and Eisenach as well. When he fell ill at Eisenach, the mayor of the city sent him a "precious water flask" (Waesserlein), which revived him at least enough to continue on his journey.

Thus, Luther was in good spirits as he moved ever closer to the end of his journey. But his friends, as well as his enemies at Worms, were afraid as they waited for him to arrive. His friends feared that the safe conduct would not remain in place for Luther since he was a condemned heretic. They warned him, reminding him of the end of Hus, as they offered their opinion that if he were to come, he would be burned to ashes in Worms. But he replied,"Even if they were to kindle a fire all the way from Wittenberg to Worms that reached all the way to heaven, I still want to appear in the name of the Lord, step into the mouth of the Behemoth with its large teeth, and confess Christ and let him reign."

Shuddering, his enemies noted that Luther was actually coming to press his suit. At first, they had still hoped that an imperial mandate, which had already been posted on March 26th, and which demanded the handing over of all Lutheran books, might have motivated him to turn around on his journey. Actually, the imperial herald had asked Luther, when this mandate was seen posted throughout the journey, whether he still wanted to press on. But the hopes of the enemies were dashed. By this time his books had been loaded on a wagon and burned, not far from Luther. Thereupon Luther wrote to Spalatin from Frankfurt, where he was lodging at the Inn of the Crest, "I know that a royal command has gone out to frighten me. But Christ lives, and we shall enter Worms, despite the gates of hell. Hence, prepare an inn for us." When he received another warning from Spalatin, he replied from Oppenheim, "And if there were as many devils in Worms as tiles on the roof, I still wish to enter."

As Luther was writing this, there was another final attempt to keep him away from Worms. This was an attempt agreed upon by both his friends and enemies. It targeted his courage and awareness. But it was also shattered, because Luther was bound by his duty. Unexpectedly, an unusual guest, old Glapio, appeared at the Ebernburg castle, where Franz von Sickingen was having Luther's writings read to him, and from where Hutten had sent his angry and threatening letters to the legates. Glapio played the role of being a friend to both sides. He spoke about Luther as a man, whom even his bitterest enemies could not dissuade, unless he had first been convinced by the truths of Holy Scripture. He responded to Hutten's question as to what crime Luther had committed with a shrug of his shoulders. He did not know. He then suggested to those nobles how dangerous Luther's appearing in Worms actually was, and how much better it would be if the discussion with him would be held at the secure Ebernburg castle.

Actually, it was Būcer, the former Dominican, whom Luther had once met at Heidelberg, and who was at that time staying with Sickingen, who was sent to Oppenheim. There he extended Sickingen's invitation to Luther with the urgent message to consider the dangers threatening him at Worms and to accept the invitation. But Luther tore the net which Glapio had so cleverly spread as though it were a cobweb. He replied that the safe conduct under which he traveled would only last another three days. He had not been summoned to appear before Glapio, but before Caesar and the empire. He thanked his friends for their concern. "So," he said later, "I continued my journey in all simplicity, for if I had waited three days, my safe conduct would have come to an end, and they would have locked the gates. I was unafraid. Nothing scared me. God must be able to make a man so stupefied. I don't know if I would have been so cheerful today."

So, the enemies had to be ashamed because they had shouted, "He won't dare; he will not come." Luther came. On April 16th, at 10:00 AM, the watchman's trumpet resounded from the tower of the cathedral, indicating the arrival of a foreign procession. Thousands of people left their breakfast tables and hurried to the place where the procession could be seen with the imperial herald leading the way. A crowd of many shades surged around the wagon in which the Wittenbergers were sitting. It was made up in part by riders, like Justus Jonas, who had joined them at Erfurt, and others who had joined them along the way. The rest were those who had come out of Worms to meet him. Mothers lifted their children up high so that in the future they could say that they had seen that brave monk. Luther stepped down from the wagon before the inn which had been prepared for him, a house of the Johannites. He was not staying in the royal palace as Aleander had wanted, but near the residence of his Elector and next to the Elector's counselors von Feilitzsch and von Thun. As he stepped down from the wagon Luther said, "God will be with me."

By now his friends were also of good cheer, and the circle of friends grew. People were coming to and going from Luther's residence until late in the evening. Numerous high lords came by to get acquainted. Immediately upon his arrival, he had invited von Glapio to come for the discussion. Glapio responded that now it was too late.

And it was too late. Luther's taking a stand before Caesar and the empire could no longer be prevented. Already before breakfast the next morning, the summons arrived to appear at 4 PM. It had been brought by the imperial hereditary marshal, Ulrich von Pappenheim, who lived in the same house with him. It also became known in the city that the monk was to be given a hearing at 4 PM. As the hour drew near, a throng of people was so pressed together in the street that Pappenheim and Sturm, who were to escort Luther, preferred to lead him through the garden and then by side streets, to the royal palace where the authorities were assembled. The multitude had hurried there when they learned that Luther was no longer at his inn. It took considerable effort to clear away the crowd in front of the entrance. Curiosity had driven many to their roofs.

Following a two hour wait, Luther was led into the hall. It is said that just as he was about to enter, Field Marshal Georg Frundsberg tapped him on the shoulder. He is supposed to have said, "Little monk, little monk, you are now walking the path to take a stand, a stand the likes of which neither I nor many high officers have ever taken, even in our most pressing battles. If you are of right mind and sure of your cause, continue in God's name and trust that God will not forsake you."

Caesar sat on his throne under a purple canopy in the center of the large hall with his brother Ferdinand next to him. Six electors and about 200 high lords were arranged by rank, sitting on both sides. A brilliant court-state ("Hofstat") sparkled around the throne. The simple monk from Wittenberg stepped into this assembly, and excitement spread throughout the large hall. When it had quieted down, the hereditary marshal spoke. He reminded Luther that he was to speak only when he was asked a question. Next to the official from Trier, who had the same name as Luther's main enemy from Ingolstadt, Eck, lay a pile of books. The official then asked Luther a twofold question. First, did Luther recognize those books, which contained many evil teachings, as his own; and second, whether he wanted to retract them or defend them.

Before Luther could reply, his friend Schurf, who along with other lawyers had been assigned to him as legal consultants, called out, "Let the names of the titles of these books be given." And the titles were read off. Luther answered the first part of the questions by confessing that they were his books. But the second part of the question had surprised him. For one thing there had been nothing in the imperial summons about an immediate retraction, and we have heard that Luther would never have come in response to such a summons without more information. In addition, the question was posed in such a way that Luther would have had to speak out about all his writings with one and the same answer.

Luther knew immediately how to regard the huge importance of this moment. Thus, he humbly asked for time to think about it so that he could respond to the question without prejudice to the Word of God and his own soul. This request was granted after a brief discussion among the authorities. However, it was granted. At the same time the official who spoke, stated to Luther that he was unworthy of such permission, since he should have known from the imperial summons the reason for his appearance. A glance at the summons itself would brand the official's assertion as a lie.

So, Luther was dismissed. As he was leaving the building, a voice from amid the throng of thousands pressing against the building cried out, "Blessed is the body which has borne you!"

Caesar had truly imagined the dangerous doctor differently. He did not want to believe that this frail monk had written those books and stated that he would not make a heretic out of him. With that he told the truth. In any event, ten heads, like the one that was on Karl's shoulders, could not have produced such books.

"I shall not retract one line, if Christ will be gracious to me," Luther wrote that evening. Christ was gracious to him.

The time granted for consideration ran out the following evening. The lanterns were already burning when Luther was allowed to enter the hall, where all of the seats were occupied for the second time. He had been kept waiting for two hours in the compact antechamber, where he had remained in good spirits all the while. After having reproached him again for asking for time to consider, in which he was accused of acting unworthily as a Christian, let alone a learned professor of theology, the official repeated the question. He did so in a more direct manner than the way in which the second question had been posed to him at the first hearing, in both Latin and German. Luther was to answer whether he wanted to defend some of the books he admitted being his own, or if he wanted to retract some of them. The day before Luther had answered quite timidly so that only those standing nearby could hear him. Now every muscle contraction had disappeared. With a modest yet loud voice that was audible throughout the hall, Luther responded with a longer, carefully prepared speech. He expressed his respect for the assembly with slightly bended knees.

He began by asking for forgiveness in case he, a simple monk, should offend through his inexperience against the custom of the court. He again admitted that he was the author of those writings. Then he divided them into three classes. Those in the first class, which simply dealt with faith and customs, he could not retract without condemning the truth, which his enemies themselves confessed. Those in the second class he likewise could not retract, for they had been directed against the unutterable tyranny of the Roman papacy. It was destroying all of Christianity, but especially the nation of Germany, both spiritually and physically, in deplorable fashion. If he were to retract these, he would be opening doors and windows for this to continue. Concerning the third class of books, which he had directed against individuals who defended the tyranny of Rome and against enemies of wholesome doctrine, he confessed that he had been too harsh. But he also was unable to retract these, because if he did he would help the tyranny and ungodliness which he had been fighting against. "Have I spoken evil? Then prove that it is evil! "He went on to plead, for the sake of the grace of God, that they defeat him with the writings of the Prophets and Evangelists, if he had erred. Concerning the unrest which might come about as a result of his teaching, as he had been reminded yesterday, he did not wonder. After all, this is the path which the Word of God takes as Christ had prophesied. However, he warned young Caesar that care must be taken, lest a rule of calamity result from trying to achieve peace, by condemning divine truth.

Caesar would later have reason to reflect on the penetrating truth of this warning. He would be troubled, while in his solitude at the monastery of St. Just, for in the battle against pure truth he had drawn the short straw. However, at this time and later he would be unable to be confronted with such truth. In spite of the oppressing heat of the questioning, Luther obeyed a request to repeat his entire speech in German. Then the Trier official, after getting advice from the assembled authorities, turned to him in the name of Caesar. He accused him of indiscretion and of avoiding the question. He explained that Luther's statements had already been condemned by the Costnitz Council, so retracting would be superfluous. He should now give a simple answer, one without horns and without a cloak.

To this Luther responded as follows, "Since your royal majesty and your grace desire a simple answer, I shall give you one without horns or teeth: Unless I am convinced by the testimony of Holy Scripture or with clearly illuminated reason – for I believe neither pope nor council alone, since it is clear that they have often erred and contradicted each other – I am held by the power of the passages of Scripture I have quoted. My conscience is held captive by the Word of God. I can retract nothing, nor do I desire to do so, because it is not safe but dangerous to act against conscience."

As once the other Eck at Leipzig had pressed him about the councils, so this Eck at Worms did the same, and Luther responded to him. The official also held him directly to this kind of questioning and asked him once more to express himself very clearly on the point whether he meant that councils can err. But Luther stood firm and replied that it is evident that councils have erred a number of times. The Council at Costnitz had erred against a number of clear passages of Scripture. When Eck interjected that he could not prove it, Luther replied that he would prove it in many ways.

Enough had been heard. Irritated, Caesar put an end to the matter. Yelling and unrest began in the hall. It had become night. "I cannot do anything else. Here I stand. God help me. Amen." were Luther's last words. Immediately he stepped out of the hall, led by two escorts. He did so as the Spaniards hissed and scoffed, amid the burgeoning turmoil of the Germans who believed he had been arrested. When Duke Erich von Braunschweig offered him a refreshing draught of Einbecker beer in a silver pitcher, Luther said, "As Duke Erich remembered me today, may our Lord Jesus Christ remember him in his last hour." It is reported that those words were remembered by Duke Erich in his last hour, as he was seeking comfort of the gospel from his noble son.

"I have gotten through it! I have gotten through it!" Luther cried outstretching his hands straight up, as he cheerfully and in a good mood entered his inn where his friends awaited him at 8 o'clock. In front of everyone he told Spalatin that if he had a thousand heads, he would allow all of them to be chopped off before he would retract.

Caesar also considered the matter ended. The very next morning he explained to the Diet that he was in agreement with the Council of Costnitz. He declared his intention to send Luther immediately back to Wittenberg in accordance with his letter of safe escort. He would then attack him as a hardened heretic.

But the matter would not be resolved so quickly. The monk had pleased many very well. Immediately after the hearing, his Elector had drawn Staupitz into his room, and with deep emotion had said, "Pater Doctor Martinus has spoken well before the distinguished Caesar and all of the imperial counts and authorities in both Latin and German. He is far too bold for me." The Landgrave Philip of Hessia sought him out in his inn and extended his hand to him in bidding him farewell with these words, "You are right, distinguished doctor, so help you God." Many others who visited him during the following days expressed similar positions.

Immediately following these events, Worms heard and read about a secret alliance of 400 nobles who would stand between the Romanists and Luther with their swords, and of 8000 soldiers who would be raised. The words, "Bundschuh, Bundschuh, Bundschuh" (a shoe made up of a sole strapped to the foot; also, a symbol and name of the Peasant Confederation during the Peasant Revolt of 1525) were on the poster of the one who reported this news. They were supposed to mean that farmers would be enlisted for the counts on Luther's behalf.

A note is said to have been found even in Caesar's chamber, which read, "Woe to the land whose ruler is a child!" The visitors to Luther's inn were more numerous than before. "Before Luther will be suppressed by the power of the pope, a hundred thousand people will lay down their lives." Such words were issued forth from Worms in those days. Both short and long reports and discussions about how Luther was dealt with were spreading throughout the land, and were being read with keen interest. When he left Erfurt on his journey back to Wittenberg, someone called after him, "All of Germany will go to combat for you in regard to the holy strife!"

It is possible that the threats of 400 knights and 8000 soldiers and the

"Bundschuh" were an exaggeration. Perhaps they had even been promoted by Luther's enemies to have him appear to disturb the peace of the empire. In any event, it was apparent that using force with an immediate attack against him, would lead to a bloody battle. That would not have bothered the Romanists. Aleander had openly declared, "If you Germans will cast off the Roman yoke, we shall make it our business for you to kill each other until you are destroyed in your own blood." Aleander was even now busily inducing Caesar to immediately dissolve any dealings with Luther. But the legate had no crown to lose, as did Caesar. When the authorities sought permission from Caesar to continue correspondence with Luther, he yielded. Such correspondence was slated through the following Wednesday.

The Archbishop of Trier was appointed to chair this session. On April 24th, at 6:00 AM, Luther was ordered to appear in the court of the German order of knights, the residence of the Archbishop. His friends Spalatin, Schurf, Amsdorf, and Justus Jonas stood at his side. With moving words, the speaker for the commission, the Baden chancellor, Hieronymous Vehus, described to him the confusion that would come from his writings. He cited the pamphlet about Christian Freedom, and how he, by standing firm in these writings, would make it impossible to promote other writings, in which he had written many good things.

The testimony concerning the councils was also brought up again. But here again Luther stood firm. He did not bow before the authority of the councils. He threw back the accusation of causing unrest with the same arguments he had used in the assembly of the Diet. He wanted to be bested by Scripture. The official Eck later contested the rightness of this request. He had been called in by the archbishop to continue the debate, after the rest of the commission had removed themselves. The theologian Cochlaeus, whom Eck had requested as a witness, injected himself. He had looked up Luther at his inn during the afternoon. When after considerable idle talk he challenged that Luther give up his claim for safe conduct, one of the present nobles almost laid hands on him.

The diet had still not abandoned its hope for success. As Vehus reported, Caesar even extended the time of Luther's stay in Worms for two more days. The discussion continued the next morning, and again in the afternoon. Luther was to submit to Caesar, the empire, and to a future council. But all attempts, even when they were thought to have attained their goal, failed because of Luther's persistent insistence that Holy Scripture would have to decide for the council what true teaching is. Even in a last discussion, which the archbishop at first conducted under only four eyes, and then with Spalatin in their company, Luther was led to conclude with these words, "I ask your electoral grace to grant me your gracious leave from the royal majesty of Caesar to go home again. For I have now been here for ten days, and nothing has been accomplished in regard to me."

Thereupon the archbishop rode to Caesar, while Luther paid a sick call to the Knight, Hans von Minkwitz, to whom he had given the Lord's Supper on the day of his first hearing. "I shall leave again tomorrow," he told him as he said farewell.

It was before 6 PM, scarcely three hours after separating from the Archbishop of Trier, when Dr. Eck and a secretary of Caesar appeared at his inn. They reported that Caesar was granting him 21 days of safe escort. He was to arrive home before those 21 days expired, and was also to abstain from preaching and writing during his journey. Of course, there had been no shortage of attempts to get Caesar to refuse the safe escort. The Elector of Brandenburg had involved himself in that regard. For that reason, as Luther reported, he had gotten into such a heated argument with the Elector Ludwig of the Palatinate, who disagreed with him, that both of them had been reaching for their daggers.

But Duke George had decisively declared that the German counts would not permit the disgrace of a breach of safe escort. In fact, at the conclusion of Caesar's first diet, Caesar himself had rejected this demand. The safe escort was secure. Luther relayed his thanks for this, as well as his gratitude for the gracious hearing he had received before Caesar and his empire, and said, "As it pleased the Lord, so it has taken place. Blessed be the name of the Lord." He went on to explain that he would always submit to Caesar, and was ready to endure anything for Caesar and his empire. He reserved for himself only this, that he would be allowed to preach and confess the Word of God freely and without restriction. Caesar's representatives shook hands, bidding farewell to the man, who up to these last comments had stood firm and unshakable in defense of the majesty of God's Word.

But now what? It could be seen that after the safe conduct had expired, Caesar, with the majority of the authorities on his side, would stop at nothing to stop Luther. And Luther himself was ready to endure anything. But how would the Elector conduct himself in this matter? Would he allow the upright man, the honored light of his university, to fall? Or would he leave himself, his country, and his people to fate for the sake of this man? His nephew, King Christian II of Denmark, was said to have bargained with Luther during those days, but they could not come to terms. Yet the Elector was not without advice. His plan was already in place. That same evening, he secretly informed Luther that he would be set aside. And he allowed himself to be satisfied with that.

Luther had entered Worms as a celebrity. He left it again in all quietness, in the forenoon of April 26th. "Nothing else was accomplished here than this: Are these books yours? Yes. Do you want to retract them? No. Then be gone!" This is an account from Luther himself, to his friend Lucas Cranach, in a letter of April 28th. (LV, 7, p.17)

Soon the imperial herald, Sturm, who had escorted Luther from Oppenheim to Friedberg, returned to Worms. He carried a letter from Luther, which was directed to Caesar in Latin, and to the authorities in German. Once again, several days passed. On April 30th the authorities were faced with Caesar's question what they should do with Luther. When the authorities left the decision to Caesar to make his recommendations in the form of an edict, he assigned the task of drawing up such a document to Aleander. Then Worms heard the surprising news that Luther had been attacked on his homeward journey, and had been taken away.

Who could have done that? Since some guessed that Aleander was the instigator, he became afraid of Luther's followers, especially those from among the people. Aleander, on his part, guessed correctly that it was the Elector, and wrote to Rome that the fox had hidden his monk. Still others believed that Earl Wilhelm von Henneberg, an enemy of the new doctrine, had taken him captive. As fast as the wind, the news about that gallant man's disappearance flew throughout Germany. "Is Luther still alive or have they murdered him?" wrote the artist Albrecht Duerer in his daily diary in Nuernberg. "This I do not know. He has suffered so much for the sake of the Christian truth, and because he has punished the unchristian papacy. O God, is Luther dead? Who will be the one to present the gospel so clearly? Oh God, what might he have written in the next ten or twenty years? Oh, you upright Christians, help me to mourn this God inspired man, and beg God to send us another enlightened man."

Caesar could only welcome this turn of events. He could now justify himself formally to the pope and his followers, and post an imperial alert about Luther, without fear that someone would respond by laying hands on him, so that a bloody battle would ensue. So, he allowed the question as to who had organized this kidnapping of the monk to resolve itself. He also took his time for issuing an edict. After a large number of the authorities, including the Elector Frederick and the Elector of Palatinate, had left Worms, the papal legate relayed news of a letter from the pope to the four elector counts and several other lords, who had escorted Caesar to his living quarters, after the Diet sessions. This news was passed on to them on May 25th.

Then Caesar laid out before them the edict which Aleander had drawn up. The Elector of Brandenburg immediately explained that the edict was exactly what the authorities had in mind. As far as the Diet was concerned, another formal resolution, which had already been resolved, concerning which Luther had been summoned, was regarded as superfluous. Thereby the "<u>EDICT OF WORMS</u>" was accepted.

The next morning, Caesar signed it and hung upon Luther the title of heretic, condemned by the pope, who preached rebellion and misled the people into bestiality. Indeed, as a devil in human form under the ban and double ban of the empire, no one should any longer supply him with food, drink, or shelter. What's more, anyone who captured him should deliver him as a prisoner to Caesar.

As written, this was the decision with the unanimous counsel of the electors and authorities. The certification of this bungled piece of work was dated retroactively to May 8th, when all of the authorities were still present.

Chapter 22
Patmos

When Luther received the news about this edict, he was quite safe. He was enjoying excellent protection at the Wartburg, the old castle residence of the late Duke of Thueringia, situated in a wooded area on top of a small mountain. But how did he get there? Let us return all the way to the day on which Luther had released the royal herald with letters for Caesar and his empire.

He had traveled from Friedberg to Hersfeld. "The abbot," he wrote, "sent his chancellor and chamberlain out to meet me while still a mile away. He personally welcomed me to his castle, and with many riders escorted me into the city. The magistrate awaited me at the gate. I was served wondrously, and was well housed in the monastery. Over my objections, I was obligated to preach a sermon the next morning at 5 o'clock. The next day, the abbot escorted us up to the forest and had his chancellor serve a farewell meal to all of us in Berka."

He also received a big reception in Eisenach, where he was again compelled to preach a sermon. But when the rest of his co-travelers continued on their way to Gotha, Luther, accompanied only by Amsdorf and Brother Petzensteiner, paid a little visit to the village of his family's origin, Moehra. There a large number of his relatives from the area gathered together. He spent the night with his uncle Heinz, who along with many other friends and relatives heard a sermon which Luther preached under the big Linden tree the next morning. The relatives accompanied him to the Altenstein Castle, which belonged to the knight, Burkhard Hund.

Soon it was time again to say farewell. As the evening shadows were extending over the area, the wagon rolled slowly over the bumpy road. It came to a lonely site in a narrow hollow, three fourths of an hour from Altenstein. Suddenly, they heard the sound of hoof beats and the clanging of weapons, as a troop of armored riders galloped toward the wagon. They harshly commanded the driver to stop with an aimed crossbow as added persuasion. The monastic brother was allowed to go, for he had immediately proceeded to flee without bidding farewell. Luther was torn out of the wagon, but they left the openly enraged, and complaining Amsdorf, and the shocked driver unharmed. The riders raced away into the forest so quickly that their captive had to abandon his gray hat. They appeared to be heading in the direction of Brotterode. They then seated Luther on a spare horse, and threw a rider's cloak over him. They rode late into the evening until about midnight, when the entrance of the Wartburg castle opened to receive the exhausted rider and his captors.

Luther was gone. He who had been cursed by the pope and outlawed by Caesar was being vainly sought by his enemies, who even resorted to fortune-telling, as they tried to pick up his tracks. The only information the wagon driver could supply was that the riders had set out in the direction of Brotterode, to the east. But the Wartburg was located north of the place where the attack had occurred. The other witness to the kidnapping, Amsdorf, could not give more information, and Brother Petzensteiner even less. Those who could have had something to say, like the castle captain, Knight Hans von Berlepsch, and Burkhard Hund, who carried out the kidnapping, remained as silent as a grave.

But soon a bearded knight, iron-clad and armed, could be seen walking to and fro within the confines of the Wartburg. He prowled around the woods, looking for strawberries. He was even seen taking part in a hunt. He once stopped at the inn of a neighboring village, accompanied by a fellow knight, and later visited the monks in the monastery. There, it is reported that this man, who could stroke his beard like any other knight, chose to take part in a conversation on spiritual topics, including, well, that Luther person. He became quite animated about the subject, until his companion stated that it was time to leave. It became apparent that this was a man who, upon noticing a book in a house, could not resist taking a look at it. If anyone were to ask who this strange knight was, the answer was, "Squire George." One could tell that he was a noble by the golden chain he wore around his neck. One could also tell that this was no usual house knight because of the first-rate attention which the valiant captain of the castle allowed him to receive.

Of course if an outsider could have observed Squire George in his room, his curiosity would be piqued. He would sit for hours, reading a book. If a person would have peeked over his shoulders, he would have seen at one-time Greek letters, and another time, Hebrew letters. He even spoke many times in those two languages. If one could have eavesdropped on conversations he had with his host, he would have heard much discussion about spiritual matters. It wasn't long before he sat all day long at his table, writing, writing, and writing. Sometimes he wrote letters to the court preacher, Spalatin. Carried by royal messengers they were either addressed to Spalatin, or to be forwarded by him. They were addressed "from the area of the heights," or "from the realm of the birds," or "from my place." They gave an indication of the site where the writer was staying as from his "Patmos" or from his "wilderness."

"I have been," it was stated in one of those letters, "taking part in a hunt for two days, so that I might get a taste of the bittersweet air of the high nobility. We caught two rabbits and a few poor partridges. In truth, it is a worthy occupation for the idle. I have even had theological ideas amidst these nets and hounds. Even though viewing such things has entertained me, the intended purpose of these activities also filled me with sadness and compassion. For what other meaning can be derived from these images then that the devil through his godless huntsmen and hounds, the bishops and theologians, secretly hunts and traps the innocent small animals. The image of simple and believing souls appeared very lifelike before me. Then something horrible was added. I had kept a poor little bunny alive and was hiding it in the sleeve of my coat, and trying to move a small distance away. Nevertheless, the hounds sniffed it out, slashed its hamstrings by cutting through the cloth of my sleeve with their teeth, and finally killed it. The pope and Satan frustrate my efforts in the same way, since in their rage they destroy souls that have been saved."

He also sent out letters to Wittenberg, to Melanchthon and others. In them, he asked how things stood in the church and with his personal friends. He also requested that they send him certain writings, which he had to leave behind unfinished.

One of these writings, as we recall, was the "Magnificat," or the "Interpretation of Mary's Song of Praise." He once again turned his attention to this interpretation and completed it. Here he wrote in a very tender fashion about God's compassion. He also wrote about faith and different kinds of fruits of faith, especially about the fruit of humility. It is noteworthy that in the addendum, Luther could still write to Duke Johann Frederick, "May the same Mother of God obtain for me the spirit through which I might profitably and thoroughly interpret her song." Then in his conclusion of the interpretation he wrote, "We shall leave it at this and ask God for a true understanding of the Magnificat. This song not only enlightens and speaks, but burns and lives in one's body and soul. God grant us such through the intercession and will of his dear Mother Mary. Amen."

From this writing, it becomes sufficiently evident that at that time Luther was still far from removing the idea of Mary as being next to, or even above Christ, or calling upon her as a help in time of need, as one was accustomed to react under the papacy. But those reflections of the intercession of Mary were attached to him like glue, as reminders of earlier days. He would later do away with them completely. Luther would in later years have good reason to point out how difficult it was for those who had grown up under the papacy, to rid themselves of papal behavior.

Prior to sending Spalatin the completed "Magnificat" he had sent a continued edition of his interpretation of Psalms, Psalm 22 in particular. While at the Wartburg, he worked on other psalms as well. These included the 68th, the 37th, which he interpreted for his congregation, "that poor little flock at Wittenberg," and the 119th, which he translated with some brief commentary. He added that last mentioned psalm to the writing he had published under the title, "About Confession, Whether the Pope Has the Power to Command it." He dedicated it to the knight, Franz von Sickingen. In it, he praised private confession as a precious thing from which one can derive great comfort.

Woodcut of Luther as Squire George
according to a portrait by Cranach

But he warned against viewing it and practicing it as a work commanded by the pope, without whose authority, as it was claimed, a person could not obtain the forgiveness of sins. Concerning his enforced stay in hiding he wrote, "I can no longer function. I have been shoved away from my purpose. Now they have the time to change what a person cannot and should not, nor should want to tolerate. If they are not changing, then someone else will change them, for which they will not be grateful, for he does not teach like Luther, with letters and words, but in deeds." Thanks and praise be to God that his fear of an aversion to the Hemp-god of Rome had been lessened.

Luther had begun another work at Wittenberg which was still incomplete. This was the Postil, the book of family sermons, which he now requested to be sent to him at the Wartburg, so that he might continue his work from where he had left off. The first section, the Advent Postil, had already been printed at the time when he was traveling to Worms. But now he wanted to change that partly completed plan and issue the Postil in German. He first completed the interpretations of the Epistles and Gospels of Advent in German, and sent them to the printer. When the printing was once again delayed, he continued his work with great energy, and by the end of September, he had finished the second part up to the Epiphany Festival. In a unique manner he would issue the Postil, so as to allow the Gospel sermon to immediately follow that of the Epistle. Later editors would be the ones who would separate them into a Gospel Postil and an Epistle Postil.

This work, which Luther began in this manner, was one of the most important and richly blessed works, which he would ever bring to light. For at that time very few preachers had the ability, even if they had the desire, to preach a proper Gospel sermon. With this Postil, they were now being offered a treasure trove from which they, with little effort, could mine the rich resources of wholesome doctrine gathered in simple and plain language. And in case they could not even do this, as happened far too often, they could simply read to the congregation that which they were unable to preach freely.

From this usage Luther's Postil was rightly called the "Church Postil." Thousands harvested the best lessons from this book, lessons which they then presented from the pulpit. Thousands of the listeners would draw instruction and edification from it in their homes, as one might draw water from a well. Thus, the blessings which were bestowed were immeasurable.

For the completed Postil, "a short instruction of what was to be sought and expected in each Gospel lesson," was printed ahead of the gospel. Luther had planned this already by this time. As early as the second edition he included this introduction along with his dedication to the Count of Mansfeld. If he had not done so, it would have been delayed even longer. In addition to the two sections of the Postil, Luther had issued only one sermon for those designated for the Postil, to allow them to go out with a singular message. With it, as he described it, Luther was dipping a sample out of the middle of the barrel for his dear Germans.

One of them was a sermon on the Gospel, for the 14th Sunday after Trinity, "about the ten lepers." In it he wanted to lead people away from the false commentary of the papists, who wanted to prove the necessity of oral confession from the words, "Go and show yourself to the priests." Because of the various other labors he had undertaken at the Wartburg, and later on at Wittenberg, Luther was hindered from continuing this work without interruption. So, the Postil, which Luther described in a writing of 1527 as "the best book" that he ever produced, would be completed much later.

Part of the time at Wartburg which Luther could not use for working on the Postil, he used to refute a scholarly writing issued against him by the Lyon theologian, Latomus. Although he had no reference materials at his disposal at Patmos, using only his Bible, he turned this work into one of the most thorough treatments of the doctrines of sin and grace, Law and Gospel, which we have received from his pen. A comparison of quotations from church fathers issued by his opponent he could not achieve due to his lack of books. And so, he submitted them to his friends in Wittenberg. He also urged them to do something for the gospel and put an end to the serpent whose head Christ had crushed.

The pope would again receive his share. While he was at the Wartburg,

Luther learned that the pope had included Luther among the heretics. He did this the previous Maundy Thursday, condemning Luther by name in his famous "Lord's Supper" Bull. Luther, in a writing seasoned sharply with salt and pepper, expressed that he wanted to present a New Year's gift to the "most charming, tender, and highly learned throne." "Who knows," he scoffed, "perhaps you will yet give even me a cardinal's cap, a bishopric, or a good parish. It is time for me to acknowledge that I am indebted to you, and will serve you, by helping to spread this bull and make it available to everyone. Therefore, I shall not only translate it into German, but I will include some notes along with it. But I will not hide the great effort I will put into translating it and adding the notes to the margins. That way, if you decide to reward me, you will look at my efforts properly and not merely reward me with a cardinal title without a tax. For I tell you, although that bull was produced in a Latin nation, yet it is so un-Latin that it might have been drawn up by a kitchen boy. But while I might not do enough you might consider it to be sufficient. I shall improve on it another time. New Year's Day has so quickly passed, and I wanted to bring this gift with me. Take care, my favor and grace, you charming, friendly and holy seat."

Luther was now also punishing the theologians of the University of Paris from the Wartburg. They had declared a long list of statements from Luther's writings to be pestilential heresies. Melanchthon had already defended Luther. Now Luther was personally dishing out punishment from the Wartburg by simply translating his statements and their verdict, and with a short prologue and epilogue, handing them over for printing.

However, he announced the most important work he was undertaking at the Wartburg in a letter of December 18, 1521, to his friend Lange, declaring it with the words, "I want to translate the New Testament into German." If this activity was the prime reason for the postil project to come to a standstill, we have nothing to complain about in exchanging the former for the latter. For, though the Church Postil produced many blessings, the profit which the reformation and the Church of the reformation have gleaned from the Bible translation by Luther was far greater. Bear in mind that there had been German translations of Holy Scripture prior to Luther's. But all of them suffered in two areas. First, they were produced from the terribly inaccurate Latin version, the Vulgate, and in addition to the mistakes in the Vulgate, more mistakes were added in translating it into German. Second, the language of the older German Bibles was so un-German, that they simply could not serve for the good of the people.

Luther's friend Lange had begun a translation of the New Testament from the original Greek that same summer and issued a translation of the Gospel of St. Matthew. In the before mentioned letter, Luther urged him to continue his work. But though Lange's knowledge of Greek was up to an accurate understanding of the text, his German could not compete with

Luther's. There was no other German theologian as skilled in the German language as Luther, to provide the German people with an accurate German Bible. Even though he had at first complained about his inactivity, without the forced leisure of the Wartburg, Luther would never have gotten to this work so quickly. Thus again we have reason to admire the wise guidance and dispensation of God, in regard to the exiled Luther.

Luther very zealously applied himself to the completion of this difficult task. As he went on, he became even more aware of its difficulty, even considering the idea of returning to Wittenberg in secret to carry on his work in some small cell with his friends' support. But nothing came of it. So he kept on working alone. He did this so diligently that he completed the entire New Testament during his stay at the Wartburg.

The type of language Luther used for his German Bible was, as he had used in his earlier German writings, not the German, that existed at that time in the established idiom of the day. This means it was not simply Meissen German, but rather the verbiage of the Saxon governing offices, which was used to write to the princely courts of Germany. It was in the middle of High German (referring to southern Germany which included the Alps), and Low German (referring to the lowlands of the north). But the words Luther used were not those most commonly found in books; they were the words that could be heard from mothers in their homes, children in the streets, and by the commoner in the market place. Yet he also put his stamp on the language with his mighty yet tender, and heavy yet moving, wondrously rich spirit. Thus, Luther became the patriarch from whom the highest masters of the German language would learn.

While Luther was restlessly occupied working with these various tasks from his elevated seclusion, the active business below the Wartburg, from which he had been torn, did not stop either. The Edict of Worms was being published in various areas, and many may have thought that the Wittenberg monk had been removed as a result. The belief was that he would not dare to come out of hiding and again play his part for pushing the wheels of history in forward direction.

Among the many who were breathing much easier as the news of Luther's removal sped through the nation, was the Archbishop of Mainz. On the one hand, he now had the hope that peace would rule in his territory. We discovered that in order to maintain peace, he commanded those, who would preach against Luther, to be silent. On the other hand, he now also understood that he had rid himself of the anchor which had been hindering him from pursuing his interests. For his pockets had been hurt the worst, when Luther spoiled the business of the sellers of indulgence. Just as previously, so now the bishop needed money, a lot of money. He needed money amounts which his regular sources of income could not supply.

But now the well, which had been sealed by Luther, was again to be opened. He had assembled a rich treasure of relics in Halle. They included such rarities as the alleged pieces of Moses' burning bush, thorns from the Savior's crown of thorns, dregs from the wine at the wedding of Cana, plus the pitchers in which the water had been changed into wine, even entire corpses of the saints. These treasures were now put on display in Halle, and the archbishop issued a summons inviting the people to come. In doing so they would acquire a rich indulgence with a devout viewing of those sacred artifacts and a donation of alms to the church foundation.

The news of this new grace collection also moved on to one whom the archbishop had not intended it to reach, the man in the Wartburg. Luther had already bitterly regretted the fact that he had tiptoed so gingerly at Worms. While there, he had remarked that if the situation would not change, he would have to throw the windows wide open. Now he wished that he had opened them. Luther believed that if he once again appeared before them, the idols would get to hear something different. Thus, when he heard about the new idolatry in Halle, he quickly came to a decision of what he would do. He had announced to Spalatin in October that he would publicly attack the indulgence idol of the cardinal.

The realization that the outlaw was loading his gun against such a high clerical lord and empirical count was just registering outside of the Wartburg. From various directions hasty efforts were made to hinder the expected well-aimed volley from the lofty Wartburg. An ugly letter arrived from Spalatin with the news that the elector would not tolerate the publication of any writing which would disturb the public peace. Luther angrily replied that he would not tolerate such a veto. He would rather lose Spalatin, the count, and the entire world. He had taken on the pope, why would he give way to his creature? In fact, he had already sent the finished work to Spalatin so that he could bring it to Melanchthon for possible changes prior to publication.

But news of what was to come had already reached the court of the elector in Mainz. One day that threatened prelate's trusted counselor, Capito, appeared before Melanchthon with his friend Stromer. In answer to his question as to what may have brought such lords before him, they replied that they wanted to visit their friends, and to see the famous Wittenberg. But soon they began, although with hesitation and reservation, to get to the point. But Melanchthon provided them with small comfort as he explained to them that they had come to the wrong craftsman. He had no role to play in this business. In this case they would have to deal with Luther's own conscience. For when they came straight to the point as to what they wanted, Melanchthon would not allow himself to become a mediator.

But Luther had also found out that Albrecht allowed no peace to the priests who desired to get married. Even though Luther was aware that the publication of his work had been delayed, he nevertheless located the archbishop and wrote him a letter on December 1st. He wrote this letter in downright plain German.

"Now your Electoral Grace," he wrote, "has again set up his idol in Halle. This idol will cause the poor, simple Christians to lose money and soul. Perhaps your Electoral Grace thinks that I am no longer a part of the game, that I want safety for myself and shall subdue the monk in myself, by way of the imperial majesty. That I shall allow. But your Electoral Grace should know that I desire to do what Christian love demands, in spite of the threatening gates of hell. I will neither endure it, nor remain silent, if the Bishop of Mainz pretends that he neither knew nor understood that it was proper for him to teach, when a poor man requested to be well informed, yet he, the archbishop, proceeds without shame forever and ever, as if there were profit in it for him. I do not want to be insulting. A person has to sing and listen differently. Therefore, it is my humble petition to your eminent grace, that your eminent grace must not let the poor people be misled and robbed, but that you show yourself as a bishop, not a wolf. God still lives; let no one doubt this. God also is skilled to oppose a Cardinal of Mainz, even though many Caesar's were to support him. Your Eminent Grace surely should not think that Luther is dead."

"Therefore, be it finally announced to your eminent grace in writing that if that idol is not removed, I must tell the entire world the difference between a bishop and a wolf. May your Eminent Grace conduct himself in accord with such information. Secondly, I ask that your eminent grace would stand back and peacefully allow the priests, who desire to get married to avoid unchastity."

Then, in case this would not be accepted, he threatened to expose the shame of the bishops. "I shall not remain silent," he added, "and if I should fail, I hope that you bishops will not sing out a little song of joy. In regard to this I shall await your Eminent Grace's proper and quick reply within 14 days. For after the 14 days my pamphlet against the idol in Halle will go out, if I have not received an agreeable response."

An answer arrived from the archbishop in support of the truth within the requested 14 days. "Dear Doctor," it began. "I have received and read your letter, dated the day of St. Katherine. I have accepted it in a positive way and have changed my plan completely. The reason for which you wrote such a letter has been removed for some time. I shall, if God wills, conduct myself in such a manner as it applies to an upright, spiritual, and Christian count. This is as God grants me his grace, strength, and reason. For these things I faithfully pray and ask others to pray for me."

That is the way in which an archbishop, cardinal, and elector responded to the monk banned by the pope and outlawed by Caesar. It was also soon reported in Wittenberg that the archbishop had released a priest, who had been imprisoned because of his marriage, and allowed him to return to his parish and his spouse. In fact, the archbishop himself was now preaching in such a way that it was being said, "Albrecht is going to join on the path of preaching the gospel and is now also continuing independently (independent from Rome) on this pathway."

What kind of pathway was this?

Chapter 23
Disruption at Wittenburg

During the first days after Luther departed from Wittenberg, life went on following the path Luther had set for it. The university continued to function in lively fashion. A letter from that time contained the comment, "There are over 1500 students here; each one of them, whether going or standing, is carrying a Bible with him. All are unarmed and there is great harmony among these brothers in Christ. Here are Saxons, Prussians, Poles, Bohemians, Bavarians, Swiss, French, Thueringians, people from Meissen, and from other areas. The whole city is unmistakably occupied and taken over by students."

The twenty-five-year-old Melanchthon stood at the head of the faculty. The burden of responsibility rested heavily on his shoulders. He had longingly hoped for Luther's return, since upon hearing the news of his hiding, he had written, "Our precious father is alive!" He strove to set a good example in his call as professor. The mediators of the Bishop of Mainz attended his lectures in which he was teaching First Corinthians. He was also working on his exhaustive lectures about living the Christian faith, the <u>Loci</u>. As these pages appeared in print, Luther received them with great joy. Luther was constantly concerned about this gifted co-worker because of his weak body. And so, even now, he encouraged him, in whom he had placed almost too much hope, to take good care of himself. Melanchthon received a new assistant in the person of Justus Jonas, who had moved from Erfurt to Wittenberg shortly after the Diet of Worms. The Pomeranian theologian, Johann Bugenhagen, also began to teach at the university. Matthaeus Aurogallus stepped in as a professor of Hebrew. Amsdorf was put into Luther's pulpit. However, Luther's wish that Melanchthon would also be called to preach remained unfulfilled. Johann Agricola of Eisleben, who was also active in teaching at the university, was assigned to be the Catechist for the instruction of children.

The one person on this list of co-workers, whom a person could have expected to have an especially close connection with Luther in this outward work, was Carlstadt. After all, he had been Luther's fellow soldier at the Pleissenburg. Their common enemy, Eck, had placed him along with Luther in the first bull. But instead of a closer unity ever increasing estrangement developed between the two. The fault for this was Carlstadt's. From the beginning Carlstadt had been jealous because of Luther's fame. Having been placed in Luther's shadow at Leipzig resulted in Carlstadt's cooling relationship. Luther's journey to Worms and everything connected with it added nothing to the healing process. The fact that shortly after Worms the Elector temporarily lent him to the King of Denmark, after he refused to allow Luther to go there, simply testified to the fact that Carlstadt was dispensable.

But now that Luther had been removed from Wittenberg Carlstadt could hope to advance to the forefront, the place he formerly had to yield to Luther. Already that summer he returned to Wittenberg after a very short stay in Denmark.

From this time on, some amazing news reached the prisoner at the Wartburg. Carlstadt was stepping forth as a reformer. Immediately upon returning from Denmark on June 19th he posted theses for a debate to be held on the 21st. It was to be about the unmarried state of monks and the sacrifices connected with monastic vows. He followed up on the 24th by issuing a German document in regard to monastic vows, and then five days later he gave an extensive explanation of his theses. The second of these theses stated, "No one who is unmarried should be called to a spiritual position." He substantiated this statement out of St. Paul's words of I Timothy 3:2, "Now the overseer must be above reproach, the husband of but one wife." (NIV) He said, "Here, the marriage of priests was commanded, just as it had been commanded to the Levites under the old covenant." Thus, we see two things about Carlstadt which would later become even more clearly recognizable. He showed an unhealthy tendency toward excess, and an unhealthy transfer of Old Testament practices and laws to New Testament Christianity.

In a second edition he threatened to publicly attack some of the bishops, if they would continue to persecute married priests. In the German edition he saw no problem in applying Old Testament laws concerning vows to contemporary New Testament living. In addition, he posed a question as to how images should be considered, and declared that all pictures were objectionable for divine services. In this work he went on to declare that confession of sins was useless, leaning toward the position that all visible and outward divine services are useless. In an attack on pilgrimages to a holy grave he asserted, "The flesh of Christ counts for nothing," as Christ says, whereas the Lord in John 6:63 (NIV) clearly did not mean his own flesh when he said, "The flesh counts for nothing."

Luther could not agree with the excessive expansion of doctrine. He could neither acknowledge the false statements nor some of the statements which were correct when they stood by themselves, but were supported by false premises. In fact, he had issued some of those statements himself, some time ago, which Carlstadt now was misapplying. He now also sent his own corresponding explanations to Wittenberg.

But in this case, debate and writing were not allowed to take their proper course. Indeed, it was in the same Augustinian monastery, where the fire kindled by Carlstadt first flared into flames as the monks began to make use of their rights. Thirteen of them had resigned, and some wanted to take up a profession and get married. On the other hand, those who remained in the monastery were persecuted, mocked, and threatened by citizens and students. Marriage of priests was already taking place outside of Wittenberg. Parson Bernhardi from Feldkirchen had done so. We had made his acquaintance earlier, as the one who had become the Provost at Kemberg.

Luther had much earlier stated that priests should be allowed to marry, and those for whom the single life posed questions of conscience should take up an orderly married life. We read a few pages back, how he had expressed himself to the Archbishop of Mainz from the Wartburg. However, when he heard about what was happening in Wittenberg he could not help being concerned that those monks who renounced their vows may have done so at the expense of peace of conscience. Rather, they took this step, as they had been brain-washed by Carlstadt's teaching about their rights. Therefore, Luther sought to help them and others by writing, "About Monastic Vows." He dedicated this work to his father, whom he had once hurt so deeply by taking his own vows. He explained that his vow, because of the damage it had done regarding his filial obedience, was not worth the value of a wild plum.

At the same time this booklet provided additional instruction for his monastic brothers on another issue. For a one-eyed monastic preacher named Gabriel Zwilling, (translated "Twin" into English) had begun to preach against the adoration of the host and the mass for the dead. He also demanded that in the celebration of Holy Communion, the cup be offered to all communicants. The consequence of his preaching was that most of the monks refused to conduct a mass after the papal fashion.

Since his Prior Held did not want to allow such a practice as Zwilling requested to start, mass in the monastery church was discontinued entirely.

When Didymus' (the Greek word for "Zwilling") sermon first became known, the university had intervened and set up a commission which was to deal with the monks. Carlstadt, Jonas, and Melanchthon were a part of this commission. When this commission could not reach agreement, a new commission was sent to the monks a few days later. This commission had issued a "Gutachten" for the Elector on October 20, 1521, confirming that the main issue of the monks was correct. They asked the Elector to reinstitute the distribution of the Sacrament of both kinds to all communicants and to discontinue the sacrifice of the mass, especially the mass for the dead. Melanchthon, too, stepped forward in October, with 65 theses against the sacrifice of the mass. But the Elector refrained from carrying out the Gutachten's requests. He, in turn, asked the writers to wait until others had the chance to come to the same understanding. He also asked them to consider the fact that, if masses were to be discontinued, the church would lose the biggest portion of its income.

Now Luther also spoke out. He issued a pamphlet, first in Latin, then also in German, dedicated to the Augustinians in Wittenberg about "This Misuse of the Masses." He sent it to Spalatin to be forwarded to Wittenberg.

Where Luther stood in regard to the entire matter, and what he wanted to accomplish with this work, can be gleaned from the opening words of the address where he said, "I have been informed, both by word of mouth and in writing, dear brothers, that you are the very first to begin to do away with the abuse of the mass in your assemblies. This gave me great joy as an action, which I believe the Word of God is working in you, and which you have not received in vain. Yet along with this joy I have a great concern, a concern out of Christian love which never fails. I am concerned that not all of you are of the same stability and good conscience, as you are taking such a huge first step."

With this work, as with his work on "Monastic Vows", Luther wished to make sure that the brothers would undertake their actions, which he considered proper, with good conscience and absolute conviction that what they were doing was correct. Toward the end of his work he also hoped that they would carry out their work with consideration for the weak ones, who were in their midst.

This was exactly the admonition which the monastic brothers needed. Prior Held wrote to the Elector on November 12th, that the people were being stirred up toward hatred through the sermons preached in the monastery church, even to the point of violence against the brothers. Thirteen monks had left the monastery and were inciting the people and the students against the prior and those monks who remained, so that they faced great danger. The movement also spread from the monastery church to the city church. There the priests who were saying the masses were driven away from their altars, after the mass books had been ripped out of their hands. It had been reported that the students, who had participated in this riot, had been carrying unsheathed knives under their cloaks.

On December 4th, threats were posted on the church doors. The monks who desired to read masses were mocked and persecuted in other ways. The senate even set night watchmen for the monks, since an attack by the students was feared. It was thought that the instigators of such unrest were outsiders, especially Erfurt students. The Elector was also requested to punish the guilty. But the very university committee which was to examine the issue could not come to an agreement on the main questions, namely, what was to be done with the masses. At last each party submitted a "Gutachten." The one, signed by the university rector plus Carlstadt, Melanchthon, Amsdorf and others, the Elector had rejected as mentioned earlier. The other one, the opposite view, sought protection for the mass.

During those stormy December days, a strange rider dismounted at the home of Nicolaus Amsdorf. He must also have needed to speak with Magister Phillippus, for Melanchthon spent many an hour in private and confidential conversation with that bearded man, clad in gray riding clothing. He did not allow himself to be seen in the city, but remained in hiding for three days in Amsdorf's home. Then, at the end of those three days, as a rumor was being spread throughout Wittenberg that Doctor Martinus was in the city, he quietly hurried off the same way he had come.

The rumor had been true. The gray rider was indeed Luther. He had been able to stand it no longer, and so together with a companion had taken steps to gain personal insight into the situation at Wittenberg. He had spent cheerful hours there in his circle of friends. "Everything that I see and hear pleases me very much," he wrote to Amsdorf. "May God strengthen the spirit of those, who want things to go well." Yet, he mentioned two concerns which prohibited his joy.

Instead of sending them on to Wittenberg, Spalatin had held on to Luther's works about the vows of the monks and the abuses of the mass. Luther now demanded their immediate publication, or else he would write much more strongly.

The second concern was that he had heard that people in Wittenberg were going too far. Immediately upon his return to the Wartburg he took up the task of writing a warning against such disorderly activity. That work appeared soon after under the title, "A True Admonition to All Christians to Watch Themselves against Insurrection and Rebellion." In it he wrote, "Those who read and understand my teaching correctly do not cause insurrection. They have not learned that from me. But what can we do about those who engage in insurrection, and using my name, boast about themselves? Isn't that exactly what the papists are doing with the name of Christ? They not only do what Christ has forbidden but also that which destroys Christ. But as I have said, the devil seeks such a cause, to slander this doctrine as much as he can. But if you say: 'What shall we do?' ... Let your mouth be a mouth of the spirit of Christ, of whom Paul reminds us above, our Lord Jesus Christ will overthrow him with the breath of his mouth. That is what we are doing as we confidently continue what has been begun. We stay active with sermons and publications about the pope's and the papists' bullying and treachery among the people. We will do so until he is exposed in his nakedness, is recognized for who he is, and will be ruined in disgrace throughout the world.

"Take a look at my actions. Did I not break off more of the power of the pope, the bishops, the priests, and the monks, using only my mouth? Without the whirl of a sword I have done more to this day to reduce his power than all Caesars, kings, and counts. How can this be? This is as Daniel 8:25 says, that this "King shall be destroyed, but not by human power," (LUTHER's translation explanation) and as St. Paul says, 'He shall be overthrown with the mouth of Christ' (II Thessalonians 2:8 LUTHER's translation explanation). Therefore, you must not desire a physical insurrection. Christ himself has begun one with his mouth which will be too much for the pope to bear. Let us follow his example and carry on in the same way. It is not our work which has been set in motion in this world. It is impossible for anyone to begin and carry out such a work by himself. It has come this far without my planning and counseling, it shall also continue to proceed without my counsel, and the gates of hell will not prevent it. Another pilot is at the helm. The devil has been afraid of these years for a long time and has smelled the roasting from afar. He often would very much have liked to kill me. Now he would like an insurrection, so that the spiritual insurrection would come to dishonor and be prevented. But it will not and shall not help him, as God wills. He must be overthrown without a hand, only by mouth; nothing will prevent it. Look around, be active and help to put the holy gospel to work; teach, talk, write, and preach that human laws are nothing. So, let us carry on for another two years, and you will see what will be left of pope, bishops, cardinals and all the infectious and worm-infested papal government. It will vanish like smoke."

He also demanded such teaching to continue for the sake of the weak. "For," he said, "there are some who have never heard such things before and would like to learn, or they may be too weak to be able to grasp it. A person should not trample them, or rumble over them, but instruct them in a friendly and gentle manner, pointing out reason and cause. When they cannot grasp it right away, have patience with them. You cannot be too strong against the wolves; you cannot be too gentle toward weak sheep."

Even before this work of Luther was published, the Elector had expressed himself with similar thoughts. He had informed the people of Wittenberg that the matter "should be debated, should be written, read, and preached about." Therefore, he had decreed that for the present time all people should abstain from any new form of church service.

Now it was Carlstadt who kept the ball rolling in the wrong direction. Until this time the foundation lords were the ones who kept holding on to the Roman mass. The foundation lords also were the majority of those who had asked the Elector to protect the historically traditional practices. But Carlstadt was one of the foundation lords. For quite some time he had abstained from conducting masses, and his partners had substituted for him whenever it was his turn. Since he was so strongly attacking the mass from the pulpit, in addition to the beforementioned writings, they explained that they would no longer take his place. So, he announced in his Sunday sermon on December 22nd, that he would personally conduct a mass on New Year's Day, but it would be an evangelical mass with the distribution of the bread and the wine. At once steps were taken to prevent him from carrying out his intent. But he headed them off. As soon as Christmas, he preached his sermon "About Receiving the Holy Sacrament." He then went to the altar, blessed the bread and the wine in German, and distributed them both without any previous confession of sins. He distributed them to all who desired to receive them. He did the same on New Year's Day and the following Sundays, and the people no longer bothered about the other masses.

There was more to come. On Day of St. Stephen, December 26th, he announced his engagement to an impoverished noble maiden, Anna von Mochau. He did this in the presence of Provost Jonas, Melanchthon, and other professors. At the same time, he performed a marriage of a pastor to his lady cook. He wanted his own wedding to be conducted in an especially festive manner. He even issued a written justification for it, and invited the elector to the wedding. Six resolutions from a large Augustinian convention which had convened in Wittenberg during those days were attached to his written justification.

Melanchthon, who had also spoken out in favor of stopping the sacrifice of the mass and similar abuses, now began to view all of the actions of Carlstadt and Zwilling with increasing alarm. Zwilling had also been traveling through the territory preaching rebellion. Melanchthon urged both men to be more careful with their actions. But he could no longer hold back the flood and so he reported soon after to the Elector. However, the water in this flood was to become even muddier and wilder, and the perplexity of Melanchthon bigger.

During all of this, as thousands of people including a growing number of the residents of Wittenberg were crowding the altar for Communion in both kinds, two weavers appeared. Their names were Markus Stuebner and Nicolaus Storch. Stuebner, who had previously studied in Wittenberg, was a guest in Melanchthon's home. These men boasted of incredible revelations by the Holy Spirit, which had been imparted to them in dreams and visions. They also claimed to have had conversations with God. They announced a much greater reformation than Luther's was happening. They wanted a reformation which would also attack secular authorities. During such a reformation all the godless and the pastors would be killed. Among the things that would be discontinued was infant baptism.

They had already preached the same things in Zwickau, where preacher Thomas Muenzer had begun a storm against established order. He had won a large following. Storch and Stuebner were among his followers. The swarmers of Zwickau had even chosen 12 apostles and 72 disciples from their number, and had caused all kinds of other disorder. When the city council of Zwickau had begun to oppose, and it had led to further insurrection, Muenzer and Stuebner had escaped to Bohemia. Storch had stayed behind. Nicolaus Hausmann, a friend of Luther and the first pastor of the city at that time, had taken a stand against his activities and summoned him to take responsibility for his actions. Instead of appearing, Storch moved to Wittenberg. He was accompanied by Stuebner, who had returned to Germany during that time.

Melanchthon did not know what to think about these new prophets. He and others had discussions with them. When they asked who had given them the authority to preach, Stuebner answered, "Our Lord God." When he was asked whether he had written any books, he replied, "No, our Lord God has forbidden this to me." As early as the first day of their arrival, Melanchthon gave a report to the Elector, "I have heard them myself. They tell such wondrous things about themselves. I cannot very well describe how much all of this affects me. Indeed, I have good reason why I don't want to despise them. This much is substantiated that there are many spirits in them. However, no one can easily come up with the right assessment except Martinus." Since Stuebner had also appealed to Luther, a request was made to the Elector to allow Luther to come to Wittenberg. If this were to occur, Melanchthon hoped to find relief from his inability to give good counsel.

Upon hearing this report, the Elector found himself in a great quandary. He, too, was afraid of acknowledging or rejecting them. Their existence in his territory made him very uncomfortable and he felt that, if he would permit them to remain, he would lose property and people. Yet, he did not have the keenness of mind to discern that they were swarmer's.

(Translator's note: *These swarmer's were often translated with the word enthusiasts, usually meaning "religious enthusiasts". Swarming happens in a beehive, when the bee population succeeds in hatching a new queen. Usually the hive then splits into two bee populations, which weakens the hive considerably in the midst of honey producing time. The old queen then has to move out with all her old followers and find some other place - perhaps some hollow tree trunk - to set up a new kind of a bee-nation. Since every beehive allows for only one reigning queen, the new queen will claim ownership of the old hive. Sometimes there may be as many as 3, 4, 5, even 6 new queen cells being developed by the bee population at the same time - for whatever internal problem the hive may have to resolve. At least some of these new queen cells could hatch at the same time. These will fight it out to death for gaining supremacy of the hive. As this new internal reorganization is going on, you really temporarily try to stay away from that hive. I think that this is what Martin Luther had in mind when he referred to false prophets at work in electoral Saxony {perhaps like the "super apostles" in Corinth during the Apostle Paul's ministry(?)}. A beekeeper will carefully watch for any such new queen capped larvae, which are a little longer than ordinary worker bee capped larvae cells. I learned such operation of bee hives, by starting to take a few lessons at first, and then operating a few beehives for a few years, pursuing such a project as a hobby.*)

Thus he, the Elector, was fearful of acting against God by moving against them. "Unless I would understand this issue, I would rather take staff in hand and walk away before I would knowingly act against God," he said in a conversation on the matter. But he dared not allow Luther to return to Wittenberg. His cousin George (the count of Provincial Saxony) was already bending his ear. If he would at this time allow the outlaw, the one regarded as the primary instigator of unrest, to freely and openly become involved in the matter, especially at a time when Wittenberg was being viewed as breeding grounds for rebellion, he would have to be afraid of the imperial army coming against him. The imperial troops, Caesar's representatives, were stationed at Nuernberg. Duke George wielded strong influence for their going into action. They would be breathing down his neck.

The only one who was not puzzled about the Zwickau prophets was Luther. He wrote to Melanchthon in a calm manner that he found nothing about the self-proclaimed prophets that could not also be produced by Satan. They should prove their calling. Their reasoning against infant baptism would not stand up under examination. Those people, who did not move him in the least, could not induce him to come to Wittenberg. He also wrote to Amsdorf that they should not allow themselves to become confused by the new prophets. It would be better for them to test the spirits to see whether they are from God. But he wrote to Spalatin that the Elector should not, by any means, stain his hands with the blood of those Zwickau prophets.

While this was going on, the establishment of a new order kept progressing in Wittenberg. Carlstadt produced a new congregational constitution, which was adopted by the city council and the university. According to it, the entire church system was to start out on a new foundation. A congregational treasury was to be established from all of the church's possessions and receipts. From it, the poor of the congregation were to receive support, partially through alms and partially through interest free loans. The education of gifted poor children would also be funded from this treasury. Begging should stop immediately. In addition, all pictures should be removed from the churches, and only three altars allowed to remain. Holy Communion would be administered strictly according to the words of Christ, by which the communicants could take both the wafer and the cup into their own hands.

But Carlstadt was not finished. With Zwilling's support, he incited the people against the mass, confession, and pictures in his daily evening services. He urged the congregation to rise up against these abuses. When a fully authorized agent of the elector told him to stop, he cited his office in the foundation church and his doctorate, maintaining that he was standing on the Word of God. His sermons and those of Zwilling affected the hearers so much, that they attacked the pictures. The people threw them forcefully out of the church, chopped them to pieces, and burned them. Confession stopped almost completely.

During this wild madness against external things, the pastoral care of the healthy and the sick was being ignored to a shocking degree. Carlstadt also neglected his teaching office at the university. His despising of his educational responsibilities, which he demonstrated plainly both in word and deed, caused many students to move away, saying that they wanted to learn a profession. Carlstadt and Zwilling traveled through the people's homes and allowed common persons to serve as interpreters of Scripture. Professor More urged the city's citizens, both men and women, to take their children out of school. He was doing this, begging and pleading both in the school and in the church yard. He kept on, until the school finally became completely empty and the building was converted into a bakery.

The consequences of these actions were being felt outside of Wittenberg as well. Some counts forbade their subjects to attend school at the University of Wittenberg. They demanded that those already enrolled leave, in order to protect against the expansion of Carlstadt's basic theses into their territory. The imperial government also spoke out, and the Bishop of Meissen stated his intention to send out preachers to counter the sermons of this new movement. That would have amounted to pouring oil on the fire and finally actually causing murder, arson, and burning. At this time, the hard headedness and forcefulness of the foundation lords of Wittenberg, who would not sufficiently defend the traditional customs, were truly adding to the stormy environment.

The news about what was happening traveled to the Wartburg. It brought the wish that Luther had expressed, to ripen to its conclusion. He wanted to return to Wittenberg. First, he took up his pen once again and wrote a sharp correction to the people in Wittenberg. He reproached them for forgetting about faith and love and substituting minor things. He wrote, "We still have many brothers and sisters living in Leipzig, in the territory of Meissen, and all around. We want them also to be with us in heaven. This movement was begun so quickly, - Shame! Shame! - and was reinforced with clenched fists. I do not approve of this at all. You must know that. If it comes down to your continuing this way, I will not be on your side. You have started this without me. See to it that you finish it without me. What you have done is not right, even if Carlstadt and others should have said so. You have started a burdening of many consciences in those who had received the Sacrament, and then attacked, torn down pictures, eaten eggs and meat. If they were to have to give an account of this to the devil while dying or during a panic attack, they would not know a thing about it.

... It appears to me that those who have started this whole mess were only looking for their own praise."

Luther had hit the bull's-eye with these words. But he was not a man who would accuse a drowning man of thoughtlessness, or light-mindedness, and then let him drown. Since the council and the people were now calling to him, and he saw the need and the danger to which his brothers had exposed themselves, he considered it his duty to save what could be saved. He was rightly angry with his Elector, because he had not granted a hearing on account of fear for man and self-justifying desires. He wrote to him by the end of February. His intent was not merely to deliver a sensitive rebuke. "Your

Electoral Grace for a long time has been collecting sacred relics from all nations. But now God has listened to your lust and has sent you, free of charge and effort, a whole cross with nails, spears, and scourge. (Footnote: He meant the cross of the Wittenberg unrest with this reproach.) But he concluded, "I don't have any more time. I will be there myself, if it is God's will. Your Electoral Grace need not concern yourself with me."

This letter upset the Elector. He now took immediate steps to prevent Luther from carrying out his intentions, being afraid of the consequences. That the Elector would start to oppose him Luther had known in advance. So, he put on his traveling garb in order to remain unrecognizable on his journey, and on March 1st he set out for Wittenberg.

Chapter 24
The Smothering of the Disruptions at Wittenberg

The day before Ash Wednesday, two students from Switzerland walked into the Bear's Inn, located just outside the city limits of Jena, while Shrovetide was being celebrated in the city. The two students were on their way to Wittenberg to study Holy Scripture. They met a traveler inside this particular guest-haven, a rider who had taken off his knightly garment. He was sitting at a table, immersed in a booklet. During ensuing conversation this knight showed an impressive familiarity with the popular professors at the university. He also knew that Luther was not currently in Wittenberg, but would be arriving shortly. As one of the students cast a glance into that rider's booklet, he noticed that it was a Hebrew book of Psalms. When the students expressed their heartfelt wish to meet the man who had taken on the entire authority of the priesthood, the inn keeper informed them that Luther had been in that very inn two days ago. However, a little later he called one of them outside and told him that the man who had shared a table with them was Luther. When this student whispered what the manager had told him into the other student's ear, he said that he must have misunderstood him. The inn keeper might have said that his name was Hutten.

As two other business men arrived, one of whom was carrying a copy of Luther's commentary of the gospels and epistles, the knightly stranger also engaged them in conversation. One of them made the statement that he would give his last ten guilders if he were allowed to make confession before Luther. The knight paid their bill for the evening meal and after supper was again alone with them as they were caring for their horses. They thanked him and voiced their opinion that they believed him to be Hutten. Meanwhile, the innkeeper once again stepped in as the mystery man called out to him, that he had entertained the nobility that evening, since these Swiss men thought him to be Ulrich von Hutten. The inn keeper replied, "You are not, but you are Martinus Luther." This seemed to amuse the knight who replied, "They think I am Hutten, you say I am Luther; soon I will be called Marcolfus." He then had a farewell drink and threw his knightly tabard over his shoulders. He shook hands with the students and said, "When you get to Wittenberg, please greet Doctor Hieronymus Schurf for me." When they asked, "From whom?" he said, "the one who is coming is extending his greetings." Then he went to rest for the night. The next morning, he resumed his ride in the direction of Wittenberg.

When the students went to relay the greeting, they found their acquaintance from the Bear's Inn in Jena, in the room actively engaged in conversation with Melanchthon, Justus Jonas, Amsdorf, and Dr. Schurf.

Luther had returned to Wittenberg on March 6th. On the day before he had written a detailed letter to his Elector from Borna. The evening before leaving the Wartburg, he had received the Elector's last letter, with which he objected to his coming out of hiding. The Elector asked him to consider that his emerging from hiding could result in a dangerous showdown with the imperial army, and especially with Duke George. Luther answered:

> "It was enough, your Electoral Grace, for me to submit to your wish for this past year in my service under <u>Y</u>our <u>E</u>lectoral <u>G</u>race (from now on Y.E.G.). The devil knows very well that I did not do so because I was scared. He got a good look at my heart when I entered Worms, to realize that if I had known that there were as many devils focused against me as there were clay tiles on the rooftops, I would still have leaped into their midst with great joy. Now Duke George is in no way a match for a single devil. Since the Father of inexhaustible compassion has made us joyful lords above all devils and death through the gospel, and has given us the sure confidence so that we may address him as 'Most Precious Father'! ... your electoral grace can easily see that it is highly insulting to this Father, if we fail to trust him in this, that we are also lords over the wrath of Duke George. I know this much about myself, that if all the current doings were to take place in Leipzig, I would still ride in. I would do so, even if (Y.E.G., forgive my foolish words) it were to rain Duke Georges for nine days, and each one of them were nine times angrier than this one. He considers my Christ a straw man. My Lord and I may endure that for a little while. But I do not want to hide from Y.E.G., that I have prayed and wept for him more than once that God would enlighten him. I shall pray and weep for him once more, after that, never again. And I plead that Y.E.G. will also help with prayers spoken by yourself and others around you, that the verdict against him might be turned away from him, which - O Lord God - is pressuring him constantly. I would throttle Duke George quickly with one word, if this could be accomplished thereby.

> "This is being written to Y.E.G. along with this letter of information that I am coming to Wittenberg, so that Y.E.G. may know that I am coming to Wittenberg under much greater protection than under your Electoral protection. In addition, I do not think that I shall want the protection of Y.E.G. In fact, I think that I will protect Y.E.G. more than you can protect me. What's more, if I would know that Y.E.G. was able to protect me and was willing to do so, I would not come. No sword should advise, nor could advise or assist in this situation. God must work by himself without any added human worry and contribution. Therefore, the one who believes more, he will protect more.

> *Since I sense that Y.E.G. is still very weak in the faith, I can in no way regard Y.E.G. as the man to protect or rescue me. Since I will not follow Y.E.G, Y.E.G. is excused before God, were I to be captured or killed.*
>
> *"Y.E.G. should regard yourself within the realm of human activity as follows: namely, as Elector obey the higher authority, and let the imperial majesty rule in Y.E.G.'s cities and lands, as far as body and property are concerned, as it should be the case for the sake of empire orderliness. You should not defend or oppose, or desire opposition or hindrance to the authority that exists, if it should want to arrest me or kill me. For no one has the right to destroy or oppose the higher Government power except the One who instituted that power. To do otherwise is rebellion and is against God. But I hope that they will use sound reason to recognize Y.E.G. as born in a little higher crib, than that they themselves should imprison me. If Y.E.G. will keep the gates open and give free electoral escort, should they themselves or their ambassadors come to arrest me, Y.E.G. will have been satisfactorily obedient. But should they be so unreasonable as to order that Y.E.G. lay hands on me personally, I shall then let Y.E.G. know what to do. I shall stand up for Y.E.G.'s safety of body, property, and soul in reference to my problem, whether Y.E.G. believes it or not.*
>
> *"With this I commend Y.E.G. to God's grace. It is a man other than Duke George with whom I am dealing. He knows me quite well, and I intend no evil against him. If Y.E.G. would believe, then you would see God's glory. But because Y.E.G. does not yet believe, therefore you have not yet seen. Love and praise be to God eternally. Amen.*
>
> *Transferred from Borne by message carrier ("Geleitsmann") on Ash Wednesday, 1522.*
>
> *Y.E.G.'s submissive servant, Martin Luther."*

What should the Elector do? He just had to let happen what he would have liked to prevent. But he wanted to have it from Luther in writing, that he had indeed returned to Wittenberg without his permission. He wrote to his adviser, Hieronimus (Jerome) Schurf, "After extending our gracious greeting you are to talk and deal with him so that he declares to us in writing, indicating for what cause and reason he has returned to Wittenberg, adding that this occurred without our permission. He should also include something that he does not wish to be a burden to anyone. May his message be fashioned and finished in such a way that we may send it to several of our lords and friends to preserve respect."

Luther complied, in full harmony with his Elector's urging. He even amended the letter he had written, when the Elector desired several changes, after receiving the first copy of his letter. (Footnote: See LV, Vol. 7, p. 29 ff.) The Elector could now show written proof to whoever was supposed to, or desired to, read it, that Luther returned to Wittenberg in order to smother the disruptions which had developed there, and, in general, in order to prevent rebellion. By doing so he had held his elector's grace or disgrace of second importance, and "behind his back and without his knowledge, will, favor, or permission, he had returned to Wittenberg and again taken up residence."

# #

On the Wednesday after Invocavit, after Luther had explained his reappearance, as his Elector had requested, he was already in the midst of the work which no one else could have achieved. On Thursday, he had arrived as a knight. On Sunday Invocavit, first Sunday after Ash Wednesday, he once again stood in his pulpit in the city church, dressed as a monk. Still, his outward appearance had undergone a few changes since his farewell right after Easter, the previous year. The good treatment he had received at the Wartburg, which initially had caused him to be physically ill, later proved to be good for him. He looked stronger and healthier, and carried himself with his head held high. He had kept the falcon-like glint in his dark eyes.

His form of speech was firm, unlike the forceful attacking preachers of the previous weeks, as he proceeded to calmly, yet powerfully and with all seriousness, tell his children what they needed to hear. But this was much more than could be said in one sermon. He preached eight days in a row in response to questions, which had plagued the citizens of Wittenberg during the recent months. (For these eight sermons, see LV, Vol. 17, 18. p. 186 ff.) He told them outrightly how they had especially been loveless and neglectful toward their weaker brothers and had harmed consciences. He proclaimed that they had taken into their own rowdy hands what should have been left to the working of God's Word, and that they were not to continue such sinful way of life. "You have heard," he said, "that no one is to be dragged to or from the gospel by his hair, but to simply preach the Word freely, and let it do its work without our input as to what it should and will accomplish. For I can herd no one into heaven, nor club him in that direction." "You have so misapplied your actions that it would have come as no surprise for thunder and lightning to smash you to the ground. If you do not stop what you are doing, then neither king, nor Caesar, nor anyone else will have to drive me away from you. I shall flee from you myself, without being forced. I may quite frankly say that none of my enemies, though they have done much evil to me, have given me as much grief as you, my friends, with these your recent actions. You have truly stabbed me to the heart."

Once again, the Word, through which Luther wanted to see everything done, proved its amazing power. When the eight days were over, the wild waves in Wittenberg, whose thunder had reached Luther's ears all the way at the Wartburg, had become calm, and there was once again peace in the city. People could again draw a deep breath of fresh air. The council gave the man, who had brought help to resolve the crisis, cloth for new clothing and a refreshing drink.

Even Gabriel Zwilling, one of the main stormy preachers, became reasonable and regained Luther's trust; but not Carlstadt. To be sure, Carlstadt was quiet at first, but inwardly he was boiling. Although Luther showed all possible patience in his eight sermons and attacked Carlstadt's person as little as he had Zwilling, the sins which he had to punish were especially Carlstadt's, and his pride was deeply offended.

The time had come for a number of the newly established practices to be reversed. The tearing down of pictures had to stop. When the Lord's Supper was celebrated in the city church, only the papal sacrifice was left out and the reception of the cup was left up to the communicants. This continued until the members of the congregation, out of their own conviction, stayed completely away from the one altar at which the old customs were still practiced for those who attended. Then this misuse came to an end all by itself. (Footnote: In the castle church all of the papal abuses continued for a longer period of time, including the private mass which had been discontinued for good in the city church.)

Luther understood Carlstadt very well. He did not trust him. It was soon discovered that he was about to distribute a book in which he attacked Luther. The book was confiscated by a decision of the university, without any action by Luther. Luther truly wanted to spare Carlstadt. This can be seen from the fact that Luther offered a substitute to Carlstadt's book seller, who had suffered much loss from his association with Carlstadt. Luther simply offered to give one of his own writings to the publisher. But Carlstadt's true feelings also came to light the same day on which his book had been suppressed. He lied to Luther, to his face, stating that he had never written anything against Luther. Yet, he noticeably started drawing back, stopped all his writing for a while, and moved out of Wittenberg into the country for an extended period of time.

The Zwickau prophets achieved just as little as Carlstadt. When Stuebner again showed up in Wittenberg several weeks after Luther's return, Luther met with him. (*See pp. 193ff. and 197ff. to review about their kind of reformation*) Luther remained as firm toward these swarmer's, as he had toward the papists, insisting that Holy Scripture is the only source from which we are to draw divine truth. Since Stuebner spoke of new revelations and his call to proclaim them, Luther challenged him to prove its divine origin and his call from God by means of signs. After threatening to do just that, Stuebner retreated and left the city that very day never to be seen there again. Nothing he had said had been established by any sign. Claus Storch was another person who appeared later in Wittenberg. He also met with Luther. When he soon saw that he would accomplish nothing more there, he moved away, dressed in his spectacular soldier'suniform.

But Luther was not yet done with the swarmer's. He had quenched their flames in Wittenberg. But he also wanted to extinguish their wild fire at its center, in the area of Zwickau. He could not put his plan into motion at once, for during the ensuing Lent and Easter seasons, his professional responsibilities at the professor's lectern and in the pulpit left him no time for travel. Even so, even during this time, he remained active by dealing with those troubling questions by means of various writings.

So, he wrote a treatise, "Receiving the Sacrament in Both Kinds and Other Renewals." He wrote an epistle ("Sendbrief" in German) to Knight Hartmuth of Kronberg, in which he held the enemies of the truth responsible for the disaster which was threatening to descend on Germany. (Footnote: See LV, Vol. 2, p. 163 ff.) In both works he seriously warned against denying the truth, which was now being despised and persecuted.

In the writing about both kinds he wrote, "In conclusion I see that there is need for a good admonition to those whom Satan is now beginning to persecute. There are those among them who think they may avoid the danger of being attacked by saying, 'I don't stand with that Luther, nor with anyone, but stand by the holy gospel. Actually, such a confession does not help them one bit. It is the same as denying Christ. Therefore, I plead that they be cautious. It is true that by body and soul you do not say: I am Lutheran or papal. For neither of those two died for you, nor are they your master, but only Christ. You should confess yourself to be a Christian. But if you confess that Luther's teaching is evangelical, and the pope's unevangelical, then you must not throw Luther away. If you do, you are throwing away his teaching, which you recognize as Christ's teaching. For you can see that the tyrants do not go around seeking to destroy Luther, but they want to destroy the teaching. They attack you because of the teaching and then ask whether you are Lutheran."

In the conclusion of his letter to Hartmuth of Kronberg Luther noted, "I have also undertaken to Germanize the Bible. That was necessary for me, lest I may well have died in the error, thinking that I am learned." We also find him continuing this work in Wittenberg, the work he had begun at the Wartburg. Here he also had access to that for which he longed so much during his "Patmos", namely, the help of his friends, especially Melanchthon. With his file (in reference to a carpenter's file) poised to begin, he resumed his work, and as soon as a piece had been properly shaped it went to press.

This work was interrupted when Luther left Wittenberg to carry out his intention to further deal with the swarmer's. Before many hearers he preached at Borna, in Altenburg, in Zwickau, and in Eilenburg. At Eilenburg, Zwilling had celebrated his reforms on the first day of the year, just as he had done in Wittenberg. After he had preached wearing the robe of a student, he had given the Sacrament in both kinds into the hands of the people without any previous confession.

In Zwickau, the crowds who wanted to hear Luther were so large that he preached one of his sermons from a window of the courthouse, while the people standing below were pushed together in this spacious area. (Until at least the year 1997 that building was so designated.) Twenty-five thousand people from the surrounding area were said to have assembled there. In Altenburg, steps were being taken to assign a gospel preacher to a parish church. The Elector's choice fell on Luther's friend, Link. He began his work in spite of the opposition of the choir lords in that area. He then also got married the following year.

There were storms developing in Erfurt just as had happened in Wittenberg. The reception that had been given to the monk, who had once wandered that city's streets as a beggar, was replaced by a confrontation between the angry priests and their opponents, the students, and citizens. A prepandary ("soloist"or "cantor") who had taken part in Luther's reception, was now kicked out of the choir with slander, as he was attempting to sing his hourly prayers. This premeditated revenge by the priest against a member of the university was punished by the students with a general attack against the clergy. They broke windows, destroyed furniture, emptied wardrobes and basements, cut open much of the feather bedding, and emptied the feathers into the streets in the air. Throughout the city it seemed like it was snowing.

Those events kept being repeated. The university had been getting a bad reputation with the result that many students and a number of professors moved away. Luther had heard about this while at the Wartburg, and expressed his concern. He remarked that such devil's work would give rise to the disgrace of the gospel. Strong sermons were later preached from the pulpits against the papacy, and just as had happened in Wittenberg, they gave no consideration to the sparing of the weak. But now there was a zealous attack directed especially against the honoring of the saints. Luther's old friend, Lange, who had also left the monastery, desired Luther to come to Erfurt, and to guide them in the right direction.

But Luther considered such a journey ill-advised. Instead, he sent "A Letter, or Instructions about the Saints" to the Christians of Erfurt. (Footnote: See LV, Vol. 7, p. 34 ff.) In it, he expressed his joy that the light of grace had also dawned on the brothers at Erfurt. But he also noted that quarrels and dissension had erupted among them, caused by several sermons about unnecessary matters. Now he admonished them that they must not forget the central truth in the pursuit of desires for lesser things. They must not allow Satan to set his evil into motion.

Yet, the people of Erfurt were given the pleasure of seeing Luther in their city and hearing him preach in October of that same year. Accompanied by Melanchthon and other friends, he arrived and was again welcomed and lodged with high honor. The fermentation of rebellion was still considerable in the city, and Luther approached the problem with great gentleness. He avoided any possible kind of sensationalism, and his three simple sermons, preached in the so-called St. Michael's Church, contributed quite a bit toward calming people's minds. Later that afternoon, after his concluding sermon, he returned to Weimar. He had been so invited by Duke Johann, and he delivered sermons there four successive days. He then returned to his work in Wittenberg.

Chapter 25
Planting and Watering

The entire New Testament had already been printed even before Luther's trip to Erfurt. Three printing presses issuing 10,000 sheets a day had accomplished the swift production. Thus September 21, 1522, was recognized as the birthday of the German New Testament. The first edition appeared as a large volume without naming the translator, the printer, or the year. It was made up of the New Testament text with forewords and marginal notations. Illustrated with woodcuts by Cranach, it was being sold for one and one-half guilders. In spite of the high cost, and in spite of, or perhaps because of, the ban against purchase in many locations, the available books were soon sold out, and a new edition was already needed in December.

The book had been strictly forbidden. Deliveries were confiscated by the authorities in Bavaria, Mark of Brandenburg, and Austria. Duke George was also one of them. In addition, he requested that his faculty in Leipzig issue a "Gutachten" in regard to this book. This "Gutachten" was issued January 6, 1523. It declared that this translation contained many mistakes. In addition, the forewords and marginal notes were full of heresies that had been declared as such for a long time. They declared that the ban was justified. Emser had also a writing in hand in which he wanted to prove "for what cause or purpose Luther's translation of the New Testament was being forbidden to the common man with apparent references, where, how, and in which places Luther's translation falsified the text, etc." But the 1400 mistakes, which Emser claimed to have found, were mostly aberrations from the mistake-riddled Latin translation, places where Luther, in agreement with the Greek text, had correctly translated them into German. When it was learned that the Lutheran translation could not be taken from the people by issuing bans against it, they attempted to sweep it away with the news that Emser had also issued a translation. His work, however, was copied almost word for word from Luther's translation, incorporating only the previous errors from the Latin edition.

But none of that helped. The New Testament was now in the hands of the people and was being zealously read, and portions were memorized by men, women, workmen, servants, and maids. Soon there were reports that simple lay members were going toe to toe with priests and monks, defeating them in personal debates. Luther had addressed the various bans that same year with his writing, "About Worldly Authorities, How Far a Person is Obligated to be Obedient." (L.V, Vol. 27.28., p. 85 ff.) He opined that not a single leaf should be handed over to such tyrants. But if they were to take the books by force, a person ought to endure this, and leave the judgment of such tyrannical fools to God.

Even before the New Testament editions had been circulated, Luther had already started with the Old Testament. He translated the first five books before Christmas. Then, while Luther, with the help of Melanchthon and Aurogallus, the professor of Hebrew at Wittenberg, was still carefully reviewing and improving the work, this section of the Old Testament went to print at the beginning of the year. The next year, two other parts of the Bible appeared, including the books up to the Song of Solomon. The rest of the books would finally appear years later. We shall find our translator, who had begun this work of translating the Bible while staying in a castle, translating again, but in another castle.

After his return from the Wartburg the applying of God's Word to hearts and consciences of people in all walks of life was Luther's preferred work. But this also called for thorough interpretation. As such Luther kept supplying for his German people in their own language. He kept presenting it both with his preaching but now also in print. It was also beginning to produce good fruit, even as Luther garnered all his hope from it.

At the onset he preached twice every Sunday in the city church, in addition to daily preaching during the week. In the main services he would use the text for the given Sundays. In the other services he continued to focus on entire books of the Bible. As a result, already in 1522, he had introduced I Peter and followed with II Peter. He presented the Epistle of Jude, the five books of Moses, and I Timothy. He had been preaching for the sickly city pastor, until he passed away in 1523. He continued, though less extensively, until Bugenhagen arrived from his homeland of Pomerania and filled the position. Most of his sermons were being diligently recorded by his hearers and sent to the printer. Sometimes this was with his approval, and sometimes not. These included his sermons on I Peter in 1523, and II Peter and Jude in 1524. During this same period his individual sermons were printed in Wittenberg, Basel, and Strassburg. The printers made quite a profit, especially considering that Luther took no payment for them.

In order to promote healthy preaching in other places, Luther also resumed his work on his Church Postil. When he delivered the update to the printer, he learned that a type-setter had stolen over half of the manuscript, and allowed it to be published hastily in Wittenberg, producing a sloppy result. Yet the Postil for the first half of the church year was printed in Wittenberg that same year under Luther's supervision.

Luther also stayed active in his classroom duties, developing his students into proper teachers of Scripture. He especially concentrated on teaching them about the prophets, with Melanchthon and Bugenhagen standing at his side in this scholarly interpretation of Scripture. Melanchthon explained the New Testament writings, and Bugenhagen the Psalms.

As the congregation grew in its understanding and was strengthened through this faithful work, it was now possible to continue the restoration of a pure church service for the congregation. One piece of sour papal dough after another was being swept out of the Wittenberg congregation. An example was the Corpus Christi Festival, which had also been abandoned at the elector's residence at Torgau. Since the foundation lords of the castle church were tenaciously hanging on to the sacrifice of the mass, Luther, after having exercised a great deal of patience, issued a work about "The Abomination of the Low Mass" (or, Private Mass – "Stillmesse" in German). Some stormy confrontations and broken window panes still took place despite all of Luther's efforts at appeasement. But then the foundation lords, who had still been depending on their Elector's attachment to his and their predecessors' foundation, finally gave in. The abomination was left out for the first time for the Christmas Festival of 1524.

During the previous year, the confession of sins which had been eliminated under Carlstadt and Zwilling, had been reinserted into the service. Regular communion announcements to the pastor were also to take place, and the communicants were to stand together in a special section of the church.

Luther had actually designed an illustration of an evangelical service already in 1523, as he wrote "About Orderliness in the Church Service" and "Form of the Mass." In these works, he had retained customs and traditions as much as possible. He simply removed the offensive parts and substituted improved sections for them. He was especially concerned that congregational participation in the church service, which had been almost entirely removed under the pope, was rightly restored to the congregation. Thus, he retained the old Scripture lessons (historic pericope) which we still use to this day, but he demanded that they be read in German. Furthermore, he replaced the Latin hymns with German hymns, in which the congregation could sing along. He encouraged his friends to write German hymns, and when this failed to bear enough fruit, he reached for the strings himself.

He had written his first hymn in 1523, "Dear Christians, One and All, Rejoice". Then, there appeared three collections of German hymns in 1524. The first of these contained only eight hymns, four of them by Luther. They included "From Depths of Woe I Cry to You", "O Lord, Look Down from Heav'n, behold", and "Flung to the Heedless Winds." Besides these, there were three hymns by Paul Speratus. One of them was "Salvation unto Us Has Come." The second collection increased to include 18 hymns. The third collection, called, "Spiritual Hymn Booklet," contained 24 hymns by Luther along with their melodies. These hymns of Luther, plus another 12, which would be added later, were freely composed. Some of them were taken from the Psalms and hymns of praise of the Old and New Testaments, and others were composed from German songs already available, sections of which were translated from the Latin with some lines added.

At the time, Luther himself very likely did not realize the value of the gift which he had bestowed on Christendom in Germany with these hymns. Oh, how they sounded out! How they echoed a thousand-fold in cities and villages, in churches and schools, in homes and huts, in the fields and in the forests during those spring days of the reformation! Even those places where the preachers of the gospel were commanded to be silent, the gospel truth was being sung into the hearts of the people through these gospel hymns. Soon the Wittenberg nightingale lured other singers, and thus a rich treasure of German hymnody was added to those hymns of 1524, which have remained as most precious jewels.

When he issued his songbook, Luther not only had his eye on the congregation but also on the young people in school. Melodies had been written for them in multiple voice settings, even adding a few Latin hymns. But his concern for the schools went even farther. Carlstadt and his co-workers had turned the city schools into empty seats. Now they were being restored. For that reason, Luther sent out an encouragement in 1524, "To the Mayors and Councils of All Cities of Germany, that They Erect and Maintain Christian Schools." (Footnote: See LV, Vol. 4, p. 67 ff.)

Luther recognized that a large danger for the Christian congregation lay in neglecting its youth. "On that account," he wrote, "I beg all of you, my dear lords and friends, for the sake of God and those poor youth, that you do not fail to pay attention to this. So many fail to see what the prince of this world has in mind. This is an important issue, which applies to Christ and the entire world. We must aid and counsel the young people. When we do so, there also comes help and counsel for ourselves.

"What has anyone learned in the colleges and monasteries up till now, except how to become asses, blockheads, and bullies? After 20 or even 40 years of continuing higher education have been provided they still didn't understand German or Latin. It is true that before I would wish for schools and monasteries to stay as they are today, with no other method being used to teach young people how to learn and live, I would rather that a young lad would learn nothing and remain ignorant. It is my sincere opinion, prayer, and desire that these donkey barns and schools of the devil would either be swallowed up by the earth or be changed into Christian schools. But our God has richly favored us with this grace, in giving us so many able people to teach and freely nurture our young people. Truly, we must not throw God's grace into the wind and allow him to knock on our doors in vain. He is standing at the door. If we open the door to him who is good to us, blessed is the person who answers. If we fail to see him passing by, who can bring him back again?

"Let us look at the former lamentable condition and the darkness in which we were living. I treasure the fact that Germany is hearing so much more of God's Word now than ever before, for a person doesn't even get a whiff of such a thing from past history. If we were to allow this to pass on without giving thanks and honor, then we would need to be afraid that we would experience an even more horrible darkness and plague. Dear Germans, buy while the seller is at the door; reap while the sun shines and the weather is good; make use of God's Word and grace while it is here. You need to understand this, the Word of God and grace are like a traveling, refreshing shower. It will not return to where it once was. It was with the Jews. But it is gone, now they know nothing. Paul had brought it to Greece. Gone, it is gone again, and now they have the Turks. Roman and Latin lands also had it. Gone, it is gone again, and now they have the pope. You Germans dare not think that you will have it eternally. Your ingratitude and despising will not allow it to remain. Therefore, reach for it whoever is able to reach. Hold on to it whoever is able to hold. Lazy hands must receive a time of evil.

"Since it is the biggest crime, need, and reason for sorrow that there are not enough proper teachers, you must not wait for them to grow up by themselves. You won't be able to carve them out of wood or stone. God will not perform miracles in answer to your assumption that you can get God's goodness through others. Therefore, we need to do our part, to spend the effort and the money to produce and train them ourselves."

Indeed, as Luther correctly emphasized, they also needed to have schools available at which the old languages, especially the original languages of Holy Scripture, were being promoted. "Let us listen to this," he wrote, "that we shall not preserve the gospel without the languages. The languages are the scabbards in which the sword of the Spirit is kept. They are the shrine in which this jewel is carried. They are the cupboard in which the food is stored. Yes, you may say, many fathers have been saved, who taught without (*knowing*) the languages. That is true. But you must also include the fact that they also often failed in the Scriptures. How often didn't Augustine miss the point in the Psalms and in other commentaries; Hilarius also; indeed, all of the others who have taken it upon themselves to interpret Scripture without (*knowing*) the languages?"

This admonition bore fruit. We hear about this or that location where existing schools were improved and new ones were built. Luther became the reformer of German education. What followed was that as new church constitutions were being adopted throughout Germany, there were also regular connections with the constitutions of the schools. This happened at a time when the papacy and the new rise in the pursuit of material things, things to fill the money sacks, were working hand in hand at large at the expense of the schools.

But there was a special reason why Luther turned to the government officials with his encouragement. Congregations as we know them did not exist. Luther was hoping for them at a future date, but now had to be satisfied with people coming to hear the gospel wherever it was being proclaimed. There was one such envisioned goal at Leisnig, on the Mulde River, which according to Luther, was to become a model for other congregations. But the sad story is this that its pastor had to give up due to hunger, and everything collapsed.

But Luther, in spite of all the setbacks he experienced, wisely learned to accept them. He still had many reasons to thank God for all that came into existence through the preaching of the gospel. We will be able to understand this even better as we study what powerful attempts would be made to hinder or to steer this reformation movement, which had arisen by God's will and guidance, in the wrong direction.

Chapter 26
Luther's Counsel for High and Low

There were three enemies, whom the devil was inciting to invade God's garden that was flourishing with so many lovely blossoms. He wanted the spiritual leaders, the secular lords, and the false brothers to turn it into a wilderness.

About the same time when Luther was leaving his Patmos to re-enter life at Wittenberg, the Bishops of Meissen and Merseburg, who up to this point had shown little concern for any purely ecclesiastical matters, decided to enter the fray. They arranged visitations to churches to warn the people about the "new teaching." Anyone who had already turned to that new teaching was to be disciplined. Such behavior was even being carried out in the territory under the Elector's rule. The Elector permitted the Bishops to go on, but Luther didn't. As people were troubled by what they were hearing from many other sources, Luther eased consciences with a number of writings. Examples of these writings are "About Human Teachings to be Avoided," "Against the False Position of the Pope and the Bishops," and "That a Christian Assembly and Congregation Has the Right and the Power to Prove All Teachings and to Call Teachers, Install Them into Office, and Put Them out of Office." (See LV, Vol. 13, 14, p 7ff.)

For those who were troubled by their desire to escape the sins of monastic life and forced celibacy, Luther provided aid with a sermon, "About Married Life," (See LV, Vol. 13,14, p. 251 ff) and with a commentary on I Corinthians 7, which he submitted to print, and in which he treated the subject matter directly and openly. He also lent a hand to those brothers who had quit the monastery by providing counsel and support, as much as his meager possessions and intercession could supply. When nine nuns secretly escaped by night from the convent Nimtzsch near Grimma, with the help of three citizens of Torgau, he praised the actions of those men in a public letter and admitted that it was he who had advised them to do so. He urged the nuns' relatives to take them into their homes, saying that if they refused, he would care for them personally. He also persuaded Spalatin to plead for money for their support. Soon thereafter other nuns also received their freedom, much to his delight. This happened partly due to his counsel. During the following spring he publicized the story of a nun. This woman had experienced pain in her convent in a number of ways and had finally been sequestered for life, but had escaped due to the carelessness of her nunnery's guardian.

Luther also rejoiced when his pastoral friends got married. This is what Bugenhagen did in 1522, and Link did it in 1523. Luther himself, accompanied by other friends from Wittenberg, made the trip to Altenburg for that wedding. Then he personally conducted the wedding service.

At first Luther made little personal use of that freedom which he loved to see others enjoy. To be sure, right after the burning of the bull he had stopped adhering to the strict monastic rule. In 1524, he traded in his last worn-out cowl for a cloak, which had been tailored for him out of a piece of brown cloth the elector had given him. He did this "to the honor of God and the joy of many others, and to spite and disgrace Satan." But he was still living alone in the deserted monastery, amidst all kinds of wants. The monastery had been abandoned, except for the former Prior Brisger. It lacked badly for income, supplied only what the lowest funds could provide, and offered a bad bed. He simply dismissed the thought of his own possible matrimony until close to the end of 1524. He, a man outlawed and facing death, did not wish to bind a woman's life to his own.

The Edict of Worms was still in place against him. He also had powerful enemies among the leaders of the imperial army. "Only dead, dead, dead, they shout," he had written at the Wartburg. Truly, what had been written to the Archbishop of Mainz shortly after he had been kidnapped had been completely fulfilled: "We have lost Luther, just as we had wanted. But I am afraid that if we shall not search everywhere for him with lanterns and bring him back, we shall barely escape with our lives." His arrival in the nick of time, by which he had calmed the storm and set those in Wittenberg and elsewhere free of their shackles, had not gone unnoticed. It had turned the opinion of many members of the imperial army toward favoring him.

But his bitter enemy, Duke George, had become even more bitter, because of Luther's writing to Hartmuth von Kronberg. For there the words could be found written, "One of them especially is 'The Waterblister N. (which letter was to stand for someone's **N**ame). She (namely, the Waterblister,) defies heaven with her big belly, and has renounced the gospel. He even intends to devour Christ like a wolf swallowing a mosquito. He allows himself to think that he has already taken no small slash out of his left spur, and keeps raging along for the rest. I have truly prayed for him with my whole heart. I have been close to feeling compassion for him and his atrocious assault; but I am concerned that his ill, long deserved, destiny is pressing him pretty hard."

The copy that George received into his own hands even had his printed name on it. Two days after receiving it, on December 28, 1522, he wrote a letter to Luther, in which he complained that he had been identified in that writing. As a result, he had been assaulted with outrageous words and heavy insults against his soul, his honor, and his good reputation. He closed, "It is our desire that you will answer us, as to whether you have sent out a writing to Hartman of Cronenberg, and whether you will admit this, as you would deem proper, to allow us to know how to address this issue, as is necessary for our honor."

Luther answered on January 3, 1523: "Stop fuming and raging against God and his Christ. Instead put my ministry first! Disgraceful count and Lord, I have received from <u>Y</u>our <u>R</u>oyal <u>D</u>isgrace the writing, together with the pamphlet or letter, which I was supposed to have written to Mr. Hartmann von Cronenberg, and had especially read the section to me, which Y.R.D. complained about as being weighty insults to your soul, honor, and reputation. The same booklet was printed a short time ago both here and elsewhere. Since Y.R.D. desires to know what I would admit in the same, my answer is short. It makes no difference to me whether it is received by Y.R.D. as acknowledged, laid down, seated, or having run full course. For whatever I manage or speak, either secretly or openly against you, I regard myself to be correct. I will, if it is God's will, defend it as correct. But God will surely have the ultimate power. For if Y.R.D. would be serious and not lie so impolitely that I came too close to Y.R.D.'s soul, honor, or reputation, Lady Disgrace would surely not blaspheme in such form as to damage and persecute the Christian truth. Still, this is not the first time that I have been lied about and been evilly represented by Y.R.D. I have the more proper cause to complain about insults to soul, honor, and reputation. But I have remained silent about all of those things, since Christ has commanded me to even be supportive toward my enemies.

"This I have done till now, with my poor prayer to God on behalf of Y.R.D. I still offer to serve Y.R.D. with everything that I am able to provide without any false request. If this is rejected I cannot do any more. I shall not therefore frighten myself to death for some 'Waterblister,' as God and my Lord Jesus Christ wills. May he enlighten the eyes and heart of Y.R.D. and make Y.R.D. pleasing to him, and turn you into a gracious and favoring count for me. Amen.

At Wittenberg on the 8th of St. John, 1523.

Martin Luther Wittenberg Evangelist by God's Grace" (*The St. John Festival is Dec. 27th. "The 8th, 8th days after, is Jan.3rd.*)

The Duke complained to the Elector, beginning a lengthy exchange of letters between the two cousins. George also called for help from the imperial army, but with a commiserating shrug of the shoulders was again referred to the elector. Count Albrecht von Mansfeld was called to deal with Luther on the matter. The only thing he was able to accomplish was that Luther explained that he had not arranged the printing, but was innocent of name calling and had not wanted to dishonor the Duke. He maintained that he had good reason to write as he did.

But what Duke George had again attempted as before, was to put the imperial army into harness. Now another attempted the same thing. Leo X had died, and Bishop Hadrian of Tortosa, an early voice among Luther's opponents, had now ascended to the papal throne as Hadrian VI. As he did so, he proclaimed that he accepted the honor only in order to lead the bride of Christ back to her former purity. When a new Diet was being held at Nuernberg in the fall of 1522, a papal legate arrived who insisted that they must get serious in their dealings with the monk whose teachings had already been condemned by church councils. He was said to be worse than Mohammed, and had been preaching polygamy and fleshly freedom. But the pope achieved no more than Duke George had achieved.

During the legate's visit, evangelical preachers were allowed to proclaim Luther's teachings unhindered in Nuernberg. No one wanted to hear any more about persecuting Luther, whose writings had opened the eyes of the German people to the abuses, which even the pope himself acknowledged in part. Furthermore, a resolution was adopted by the leaders of the professionals and was sent out as an edict from Caesar. It demanded that a free Christian Council be held within a year's time on German soil. It also established in descriptive form, how the parties should conduct themselves in their teaching in the meantime. The pope, who had addressed two letters to Luther's earthly rulers, failed to get any results. The legate expressed amazement publicly when he learned about the renewed position of the imperial diet and repeated his request that the Edict of Worms be enforced. He did so in vain. Things remained as they were.

The majority of the empire's professionals were in agreement with Luther, united against the pope, but not along the line of Luther's thinking. Luther, however, was satisfied with what he knew. He just assumed the support to be in favor of the gospel and in favor for himself, as he wrote "Against the Wrong Doers and the Falsifiers of Caesar's Mandate." He sent this to Ferdinand, Caesar's brother and also Governor and Archduke of Austria, as well as to the professionals. He also sent along the papal direction, which had been given to the imperial diet, and had been printed with marginal notes.

One complaint which the Archduke Ferdinand had expressed openly before the professionals was, that Luther taught that Christ was a natural descendant of Abraham. Luther responded by correcting this complaint in 1523 in his writing, "That Jesus Christ Is a Jew by Birth." Luther wrote the way he did, because he gave special consideration to the Jews during this time. He desired to persuade one or two among them that the promised Messiah truly did appear in Christ.

The conclusion of the transactions of this Diet was all the more meaningful and a cause for rejoicing. This was the case, because things happened during the Diet, which the papal supporters thought would be an advantage for them against the reformation. Franz von Sickingen, who had once offered Luther the Ebernburg as sanctuary, had emerged as a political reformer. Standing at the head of the nobility, he had wanted to begin a new order of things in Germany, and make a breakthrough for the gospel at the same time.

A private meeting with the Archbishop of Trier gave him a reason to start a fight.

But the archbishop received powerful support. Sickingen did not. His attack on Trier failed and he had to retreat to his castle. The besiegers entered into the fortress. The counts, who had defeated him were praying the Lord's Prayer, bare-headed and kneeling, at the death bed of the knight who had been fatally wounded by a bullet. Soon after this Ulrich von Hutten also died. He had not yet reached the age of 36, when he met his end on the island of Ufnau in Lake Zurich, where he had found a safe haven. The Romanists were striving so hard at the Diet of Nuernberg to turn the proceedings in favor of the Edict of Worms, so that at one point the Elector again considered the idea of letting Luther disappear. On the other hand, he considered that, if it would come to war, he would obtain Gutachten from his Wittenberg theologians. However, Luther immediately provided a decisive reply to both possibilities. He wanted nothing to do with a new Patmos, nor with a war on behalf of the gospel.

Picture of Franz von Sickingen
According to an old copper plate engraving

But the enemies, who had claimed that the anti-Caesar (Sickingen) was now dead, and that the anti-pope (Luther) would soon follow, did not succeed, as we have already noted. Instead, the real pope soon followed Sickingen. Hadrian was already dead in 1523, and Clemens VII took his place. He picked up and followed the thread of papal behavior which had slipped from the stiffened hands of his predecessor. When another Diet met in Nuernberg in 1524, another papal legate was present who diligently pursued the enforcement of the Edict of Worms. But once again this ambassador had little in his report to make his lord happy.

During the time of the diet there again was preaching against the pope in the city. As the Lord's Supper was celebrated, there were 30 to 40 men among the many thousands who received Holy Communion in both kinds. These were court employees of Caesar's governor. The adjournment of the Diet again displayed that it had wanted to satisfy the demands of both parties, who actually stood in opposition to each other, as distinctly as "yes" stands against "no." The Edict of Worms was acknowledged, but its enforcement held only the promise of possibility. Luther's teaching was to be examined further, and contestable statements in his teaching were to be presented at a meeting in Speier, at which the demand for a Christian council was also to be dealt with.

Becoming somewhat furious by this apparent contradiction, Luther found cause to have the two Edicts, the one of Worms and the new one of Nuernberg, be printed together under the title, "Two Imperial Disagreeing and Contradicting Commands against Luther."

It sounds shameful," he wrote in the foreword, "for Caesar and his counts to openly occupy themselves with lying. But it is even more shameful for them to issue contradictory orders at the same time, as you see here. They have commanded that I am to be treated according to the ban which came out of Worms, and this ban is to be seriously executed. But alongside this they declare that a contradictory command is also to be accepted, that a decision is to be first made at the Diet of Speier as to what is good and bad about my teaching. The result is that at the same time I am condemned, yet spared for the future verdict. The Germans are supposed to consider and to persecute me as one who stands condemned, yet they should wait and see why I am going to be condemned. Those counts must be drunk and daft.

"Now, my dear counts and lords, you are just hastening me, a single human being, to my death, and when that occurs, you will have won. But if you have ears that are actually able to hear, let me tell you something that sounds eerie. How would you feel if God valued Luther's life so highly, that if he could not live, none of you could be sure of your own life or position? His death would mean misfortune for all of you. Just go ahead, strangle and burn. I shall not resist, if it be God's will. Here I am. And I plead in a completely friendly fashion that, when you have killed me, you do not wake me up again to kill me once more.

"Still, I advise everyone who believes that God exists, to restrain himself from such a command. For as God has granted me his grace that I do not fear death, as I used to, I know that he will also help me, so that I shall embrace death, and do so willingly. Yet, they will not do it any sooner than the time when He, who has kept me alive through this third year against their will and far above my hope, can also very well spare me longer, though I do not highly desire it. But if they do kill me now, they will make it such a killing which neither they nor their children will be able to overcome. Concerning this, I would rather warn them in advance, for I truly do not wish it upon them."

The other participants were just as dissatisfied with the Nuernberg Edict as Luther. Caesar in whose name it was issued blustered all the way from Spain against it and forbade the assembly in Speier, with penalty of being treated as outlaws. Elector Frederic decided to deal with it according to his own conscience. He later allowed the beginning of the German service in his residence. The pope was guiding matters in Rome. It was decided, if possible, to prevent the diet which had been set for Speier. It was even suggested to take the Office of Elector away from Frederick.

But the legate Campeggi now used a malicious plot aimed at an open division of the German realm. His purpose for which he had been unable to move the imperial diet, he now established with a minority. Under his leadership, Ferdinand of Austria, the Dukes of Bavaria, and a large number of German bishops or their representatives conducted a sixteen day private conference at Regensburg. The participants of this conference agreed to strictly carry out the Edict of Worms. The poor objects of these leaders would soon experience what that meant. Soon the blood of martyrs was flowing and wooden pyres were burning here and there throughout the German territories.

But there were far greater dangers than those caused by the opposing counts and the counseling lords for the reformation. These dangers came from one who proclaimed even more decisively than Luther that they were fighting for the truth. "He is a worse enemy to me, indeed, to all of us," Luther wrote about a man who had wanted to overthrow the papal bastion by the use of force. His name was Carlstadt.

Chapter 27
The Allstedt Spirit

Carlstadt, as we noticed, had withdrawn himself listlessly after Luther's return from the Wartburg. He had secretly continued his activities only with spiritual brothers like Muenzer. But he could not bear to remain silent for long. He had been farming on his own property. He was hauling manure, dressed in gray farmer's garb, and was called "Neighbor Andres." This was not his piece of pie for very long. He reappeared in the public eye in 1523, with various writings in which he referred to himself as a "new lay member." In one specific work he offered information about "The Reason why Andr. Carlstadt Had Remained Silent for a Time." Once again "the new lay" applied himself against the institutions of higher learning, even though he received deposits to his account from his position in Wittenberg, and that even in advance. But since there was no hope for success in Wittenberg for this swarmer, he searched for another place to be active. The Orlamuende parish was by her location attached to the church foundation. Its charter stated that it was to be served by a permanent vicar. But this position was vacant, because the vicar had departed.

Carlstadt personally stepped forward as the preacher at Orlamuende. Then he had himself legally elected as pastor and accepted the election. He again practiced his reformation, tearing down pictures, altars, and crucifixes and reducing them to rubble. In one of his writings he attacked those who "Preached and Wrote about Offenses and Brotherly Love." It was evident whom he meant, especially since he specifically mentioned "the banqueters at Wittenberg."

Such was his makeup that he deviated into more and more questionable side streets of doctrine. He wanted Sundays to be observed in the Jewish way. False believers were to be punished by death, as it was claimed to have been commanded in Old Testament times. If they would not stop their idolatry, entire cities were to be destroyed. In 1524, Luther wrote to Chancellor Brueck, "Perhaps they will install circumcision again in Orlamuende." His swarming spirit also spoke out against infant baptism. He would not even permit his own newborn child to be baptized. In a writing of 1524, "Whether a Person Can Prove from Holy Scripture that Christ is Present in the Sacrament with Body, Blood, and Soul," he tried to prove just the opposite, for Christ said that the flesh counts for nothing. When Christ said in the words of institution, "This is my body, this is my blood," he did not mean that which he was handing out for eating and drinking. Instead he was pointing to his body and the blood in his veins. This, he claimed, is to be derived from the first capital letter of the Greek word for "this" (touto) and from the period before this word. (Footnote: However, the basic text of the N.T. originally had been written in many capital letters and without punctuation between letters. Luther rightfully criticized Carlstadt for this reason.) He called those from Wittenberg "new papists," and spoke about "sacrament slaves" and "sacrament gluttons." In order to protect his writing from the inspections which were in use in Wittenberg, he allowed them to be produced by an alley print shop in Jena.

In spite of repeated urging from Wittenberg that he return to his post in Wittenberg, Carlstadt continued to proceed with his disorder in Orlamuende, even gaining a following of preachers from other places. Disciplinary action had to seriously be considered against him. His behavior contributed to the circumstances under which Carlstadt's companion, Muenzer, who had settled down at Allstedt, carried on in the same way as Carlstadt, even worse. While he was openly preaching that the enemies of the gospel must be beaten to death like dogs, he was secretly stirring things up. He was contriving dangerously bloody plots which, if they were carried out, would have far-reaching consequences.

Luther recognized the danger with which Carlstadt and that "Satan at Allstedt" were threatening the work of the reformation. Though they and their friends pretended that they were truly serious about reform, they did not proceed with proper passages like Luther. Instead, they proceeded in line with their revisionist teaching. This unhealthy urging toward all kinds of rebellion was readily received among the people, among whom it had been bubbling and fermenting for a long time already. There was Carlstadt, who stepped into the spotlight while acting as Brother Andres, and Muenzer, who pretended to have secret conversations with God in the church tower, and who understood how to keep others well informed about his revelations, and was bravely demanding the blood of tyrants. Both of them were found to be appealing in the eyes of the people.

Melanchthon had not recognized the same spirit in the Zwickau prophets. However, Luther was more than capable of immediately providing instructions in Wittenberg about that spirit. In a letter to the elector, and to Duke Johann, which he also shared publicly, he declared himself to have nothing to do with their intrigues. He wrote, "It is now a special joy for me that those belonging to our group are not taking such action. They, the swarmers, want to be commended that they are not with us and that they have not learned or received anything from us. But they claim to be receiving it from heaven, and are hearing God himself speak with them as with angels. They say that it is a bad thing that Wittenberg is teaching about the faith, love, and cross of Christ."

With this description Luther had set forth, correctly and distinctly, the difference between the Allstedt spirit and the Wittenberg spirit. But at the same time, he reminded both counts to be on the alert against the exorcised

Satan. He had been running around in barren places looking for a resting place and finding none. Now he wished to fight on the side of good, under its umbrella and protection. He wrote that he had noted how this spirit did not wish to leave things up to the Word, but wanted to proceed with force. (See Matthew 12:43-45)

"What might this spirit bring about, if he were to gather the commoners for his cause? If they were to claim with impressive words, as they are wont to do, that the spirit is urging them to proceed with action and the use of strong muscles, I reply as follows: This surely has to be an evil spirit, who cannot achieve his success in any other way than by tearing down churches and monasteries and burning saints. Truly, this is what the cruelest bullies on earth might do, especially when they are sure of themselves and have no opposition. I would rate them higher if this Allstedt spirit were to move on to Dresden, or Berlin, or Ingolstadt, instead of creeping away to such a remote corner, and dread being in full view. It should have to stand in the open before its enemies and opponents to bear witness and provide answers. But he has smelled the roast. He had been clouted on the nose once or twice before me in my monastery at Wittenberg. Therefore, he trembles at the thought of such soup ... "They should be allowed to preach as bravely and vigorously as they are able and against anyone they desire. For it is understood that there must be sects, and the Word of God has to be met to do battle. If their spirit were true, they would not be afraid of us and would have remained. If our spirit is true we shall not be afraid of them nor of anyone else. The spirits must be allowed to present themselves at the same place and confront each other. Will some be misled in the process? All right, that is what happens in regular warfare. Where there is quarrel, and even battle, some fall and are wounded. But whoever does battle with words will be crowned the victor. But when they want to go beyond a battle with words, when they also want to break things up and strike with their fists, then your Electoral Grace must step in. Whether it pertains to them or us, forthrightly forbid warfare in your territory and say, "We gladly love to grant permission and see to it that you will be fighting with words so that true doctrine can survive, but refrain from using your fists, for that is our office, or get out of the country."

So Muenzer was given a hearing in August at Weimar. But when he realized that they were getting serious, he secretly fled from Allstedt and moved to Muehlhausen, where the former monk Pfeifer was his ally in thought and deed. But their circumstances soon developed that forced both of them to move on. Muenzer moved to southern Germany and Switzerland to continue his work there. In Nuernberg, where he now was established, he defended himself in a speech against Luther. Muenzer defended himself against the unspiritual and soft-living flesh of Wittenberg, for Luther had warned the city council of Muelhausen about him in a letter. (See LV, Vol. 7, p. 75 ff.) In this speech he used especially despicable words against Luther.

But the fire which the swarmer had kindled kept glowing in the stove that the same swarmer had abandoned. Luther traveled there in August, as he was responding to the elector's desire. When Luther preached against the murderous spirit of Allstedt at Jena, Carlstadt was present. Since Luther identified it as it was revealed through the attacks on pictures and the removal of sacraments, Carlstadt applied it to himself. Immediately following the church service, he sent Luther a letter saying that they should meet for a discussion.

Luther invited him to the inn where he was staying, the Inn of the Black Bear. Since he was just dining at a table with many guests, he asked Carlstadt to be seated among them. During the discussion, Carlstadt resented being put in the same company with Muenzer. He claimed that when Muenzer had urged Carlstadt and the people at Orlamuende to rise in rebellion, Carlstadt had replied to Muenzer in a letter rejecting such urging. Luther acknowledged this. In response, Luther pointed out that he had not named Carlstadt in his sermon. However, if Carlstadt believed himself to be under fire, he might consider himself to be just that. In any event Carlstadt belonged in the company of the new prophets. He had not shown himself to be openly honest in Wittenberg.

Carlstadt in turn accused Luther of teaching falsely about the Sacrament. When Luther asked him to prove it, he offered himself for a debate. He had not followed through with one in Wittenberg, which Carlstadt said was because he had not been allowed to write freely. But Luther promised him safe escort for the debate in Wittenberg and urged him to write freely against him. As a guarantee that he truly meant what he said Luther gave him a gold guilder. He furthermore supported his promise with a toast and a handshake. Carlstadt left with his gold guilder and immediately began to write.

In Kahla, where the fire was also burning, Luther found a smashed crucifix when he mounted the pulpit. So right in front of him, he had a piece of evidence, showing the spirit that had been active there. He calmly pushed it aside and delivered his sermon.

Those from Orlamuende had formerly asked him with a rather impolite letter to come. When he indicated that he would come, they had sent him a second invitation to Jena. When he appeared on the 24th of August, the local residents were quickly gathered from the harvest fields. Luther would not deal with Carlstadt, who was now his public opponent, and had accepted his guilder as such. Carlstadt left when Luther explained that if Carlstadt stayed, Luther would leave.

Now it was time for negotiations to begin. Luther was presenting their letter to the local residents. They protested against Luther that he was identifying them along with the swarmers. In so doing, however, they exhibited such a strong spirit of the swarmers that Luther recognized there was nothing he could do there. He climbed into his wagon and rode away. Let's listen to his own explanation as to what was going on there. He said, "Carlstadt had convinced me at Jena through his writing that I should not have mingled his spirit with that of Allstedt. But when I came to Orlamuende at the directive of the elector and was among his Christians, I found out what kind of seed had been sown there. I was glad that they did not shower me with dirt and stones, as some of them were giving me this kind of a blessing: 'Move on in the name of a thousand devils, and may you break your neck before you get out of the city.'"

When Carlstadt and his followers came out with yet another complaint against Luther to the Elector, his insolence caused the Elector to run out of patience. Carlstadt was ordered out of the country. He wrote two farewell letters, one to the men, the other to the women of the congregation at Orlamuende, and signed them: "Andreas Bodenstein, undebated and undefeated, driven away through Martinum Lutherum." The bells called the congregation together for the reading of the letters, and eyes were damp as they saw the writer fade into the distance.

We do not wish to follow Carlstadt through all of his travels hither and yonder. Wherever he went he would be welcomed at first, but then they were happy for him to move on. He was causing unrest everywhere and was party to other restless spirits. In Strassburg he was turned away by the council after a short stay. There he had again caused confusion because of the pictures. The Strassburg preachers sent a special messenger to Luther with a request for a Gutachten concerning his teaching, and Luther responded with an epistle to "the dearest friends of God, to all Christians at Strassburg." (See LV, Vol. 2, p. 78ff.)

Since the petitioners had made special reference to Carlstadt's teaching on the Lord's Supper, Luther reacted to it in his letter. "This much I admit," he wrote in response, "If Carlstadt or someone else had informed me five years ago that there is nothing but bread and wine in the Sacrament, he would have done me a great service. Truly, at that time I had to endure such deep despair, that I was wringing my hands and was physically squirming. I would have rejoiced to get out of that despair because I could see very well that in doing so I could have given the papacy the greatest pain. I even had two others write to me with more skill than Dr. Carlstadt, and they did not murder words according to their way of thinking. But I am held captive and cannot escape. The text is too powerful and does not allow the words of others to tear out its meaning. Yes, even if it were to happen today that someone were able to convince me with sound reason that only bread and wine are present here, I could not be allowed to be moved to anger as a result. Truly, I become more inclined for the cause with every breath. But the way that Carlstadt imagines this doctrine bothers me so little that actually, through it, my understanding grows only stronger."

But Luther would square off against Carlstadt even more in the writing, "Against the Heavenly Prophets about Pictures and Sacrament," which he now published in two sections. We shall treat the second section later. (p. 276). In the first section, he dealt mainly with the pictures and demonstrated the misuse that Carlstadt was promoting in the way he used the Old Testament Law. In the middle of his argument, he attacked his money hungry opponent, asking why he didn't hurl his coins away since they also had pictures on them. Carlstadt had been bearing false witness everywhere with his claim that he had been forced out by Doctor Luther and had been unjustly driven away by the elector. Luther turned this against him by explaining that Luther was exposing the crooked methods by which Carlstadt had landed at Orlamuende. He showed how all of the admonitions which had been sent to Carlstadt, to abstain from his raging and scattering of rubble, and to sever all ties with the swarming spirits, were without fruit. He pointed out that it would not be a credit to Carlstadt if the spirit, which was hovering around his spirit, was bringing about things that were even worse.

Carlstadt himself would clearly provide the actual proof of how correct Luther's verdict was. He did so when in 1525, he stood in a cemetery at Rothenburg, located next to the Tauber River. Dressed in farmer's clothing, he incited the farmers to rebel against the higher authorities.

Chapter 28
The Peasant War

At that time inciting the farmers to rebellion did not require a lot of skillful speech. Since the last decades of the 15th century the conditions for German farmers had been declining rapidly. Country people were being deprived of inheritance rights, and new taxes were being levied against them. They were being leeched by the nobles, by the merchants, and by the clergy: by the nobles through taxes and forced service; by the rich merchants through usury; by high and low priests through a hundred different ways of pilfering their purses. They were being pressed in the most demeaning manner, especially up the Rhine River, in "The Preacher Alley," as Maximillian used to call it. This was taking place even though crop failure and the plague should have earned them helpful support. Add to this that farmers at that time were far less satisfied with their lot than before, because serving their bellies was becoming ever more common.

True piety, which allows for Christians to serve the enemy and patiently accept injustice, was rare in German lands. Was it any wonder that the farmers of that time would look up with concealed anger and covetousness at the castles and monasteries, where festive and joyous revels were taking place? Was it any wonder that farmer's hands and fists were ready to reach out against those residing within the walls, and for the things, which were being hid in their cupboards, boxes, and basements?

So, we also hear that around the time when the 15th century changed to the 16th, farmers were plotting rebellion under oath. One such secret alliance was identified under the picture of a farmer's shoe, the "Slave Boot," on its banners. Another had its secret oath in this rhyme:

> *"What kind of business is this mess?*
> *The mighty and the priests oppress."*

from the German little rhyme:

> *Was ist das denn nun fuer ein Wesen?*
> *Man kann fuer Muenchen und Pfaffen nit genesen.*

A literal translation would be:

> *What kind of an existence is that?*
> *One can not survive because of municipals and priests.*

(municipals could refer to city governing under Roman law)

What would happen if the Allstedt spirit would insert itself into this mess and even add new throngs to its numbers? What could happen if they were presented with a caricature of the socalled pure doctrine of Christian freedom as though it (*a sort of worldly freedom*) were the gospel? What might a person expect if papal counts were to permit persecution on account of faith to be added to the other forms of oppression?

With fear and trepidation, Luther was watching all of this taking shape. As a farmer's son he understood that you don't fool around with "Mr. Omnes," the masses, especially at such a time. He wrote a true warning to that extent against the forceful oppression by higher authorities but also applied to the lowly (poor). He rightly dreaded the Allstedt spirit.

But his warning was in vain. A severe test stood before the reformation. It was already bursting forth. Already in 1524, flames were shooting into the sky here and there, and soon the skies of Germany were filled with a reddish glow from the horrible fire which threatened to devour everything that the Spirit of God had built up. Where the Black Forest divides the beginnings of the Danube and the Rhine Rivers, masses of farmers began to band together and lash out. Soon the wave of rebellion was sweeping across southern and central Germany. Both at the beginning and later, when the rebellion became a little more disciplined, the farmers were making their demands, and when they met opposition they threw weapons and fire-bombs.

But for others this was not enough. This was especially too tame for the arch-devil of Allstedt. Muenzer had now returned to Thueringia, and things became very serious. In Muelhausen, he was received as a master and a prophet, and he preached murder and fire without end, before the thousands of farmers who streamed into his audience. Weapons were being forged. Huge cannons were being cast. Soon smoke was rising from burning monasteries and castles. All of them, without exception, were supposed to vanish from the face of the earth. No grace was to be granted to their inhabitants. There were to be no terms offered, and none to be accepted. "Go! Go! Go!", Muenzer was urging. "This is the time. The evil ones are despairing like dogs. Go! Go! Go! Show no mercy, though Esau may suggest kind words. Don't consider the lamentations of the godless. They shall beg you as friends, crying, pleading like children. Don't let mercy prevail as commanded by Moses in Deuteronomy 7, and as revealed to us. Go! Go! Go! While the fire is hot! - Forge, "ping, ping," - on the anvil of Nimrod! Hurl the tower down to the ground. It is impossible for you to be free of human terror as long as they live. Don't let your swords, steeped in human blood, cool off. Go, while it is day!" Nor was Muenzer the only one who was fanning the flames. Pfeifer was also back again, and soon others would learn their language. Where the tidal wave passed by, farmers and citizens were forced to participate. Where they refused, blood would flow, and the red roosters were posted to the rooftops of monasteries.

If Luther had allowed himself to be put at the head when the movement had begun, how might that have turned out? The peasants in Bavaria, you know, had called for him. "The Twelve Articles," in which they had set forth their demands, were sent to him. He was to react to these. Among those who were being attacked by this erupting storm were his most bitter enemies. But Luther did not for a moment waver as to what position he must take. Indeed, even before he had learned of the actual uprising of the farmers and their ensuing work of blood and fire, he was writing at Eisleben, where he was asked after Easter of 1525, to help toward starting the rebuilding of a new school. He wrote an "Admonition toward Peace in regard to the Twelve Articles of the Farmers' Alliance in Swabia." (LV, Vol. 27, 28. p. 7ff.)

In it, he first confronted the counts and lords, the bishops and priests with the truth that they were driving the poor people to despair with their tortures, their lust for treasure, and their raging against the gospel. "If I now had the desire to avenge myself," he wrote, "I would laugh into my fist and watch the farmers, or perhaps even join them and make the situation even worse. May my God preserve me from such action as he has done till now." Concerning the Twelve Articles, he stated that some are fair and right. But the manner in which the farmers were demanding them cannot be blamed on his teaching, as some were accusing. Rather, the murderous prophets had penetrated among the people.

This he now brought to light as he turned his attention to the farmers. For them to call their gathering a Christian assembly, he described as a misuse of the name of God. The gospel teaches us to bless those who insult us, and the Christian way to be delivered from evil is to be derived from the Lord's Prayer. Truly, he declares that if they continue in their rebellion, they are worse enemies to the gospel than are the pope and Caesar. Their first article, in which they requested the right to choose their own preachers, he declared to be valid. He rejected the others or referred them to those who were better acquainted with the law. In conclusion, he encouraged both sides to deal with each other in peaceful manner.

However, shortly after he offered his response, Luther learned how the peasants were acting, and that there was already a full rebellion in Thueringia and Saxony. He then played a different role. Yet there were still some farmers in those lands who had been affected by the storm, but still wanted to be dealt with. Perhaps he could still accomplish something there. But there was no time to lose. The waves were swelling higher and higher. It was estimated that the number of rebels who had assembled had grown to 35,000 within the count's territory, and there was danger that the number was growing. Luther decided on short order to throw himself personally into that tidal wave. He traveled from Eisenach right into the middle of this boiling cauldron of rebellion and with his sermons tried to call those farmers to reason, but in vain.

"About the Thueringian farmers," he reported, "I found out for myself that the more a person admonishes and teaches, the more stubborn, proud, and furious they become. In every instance they acted intentionally and daringly, as though they wanted to be killed without any grace or compassion." Thus, he was forced to give up his last try, which he had dared at the risk of body and life. He returned to Wittenberg, and once again took his pen in hand. He issued a new work and gave it the title, "Against the Murdering and Robbing Rabble of Farmers." In it he urged the authorities to do their duty, to take up the sword and start brandishing it, since every other effort had been spent in vain. (LV, Vol. 27,28, p.44f)

That is what happened. Count Albrecht of Mansfeld had already scattered a horde of rebels in all directions. Now Landgrave Philip of Hessia, who had quelled the rebellion in his own territory, moved in to help. On May 15th, "Muenzer and his sword of Gideon" was attacked from behind his bulwark of wagons, and he and his poorly equipped farmers were defeated. Half of those farmers were slain during their flight. But Muenzer, who had been hiding out in a bed, was taken alive. He, together with Pfeifer and other ringleaders, were beheaded at Muehlhausen. The rebellion was also extinguished in Swabia and Franken with heavy use of force, and the courts delivered ter-

Picture of Thomas Muenzer according to an old woodcut
Muenzer's Execution site in the background

rible verdicts against the conquered.

There was one man who had succeeded in calming his farmers with his words. That man was Elector Johann (1486-1525). The Elector Frederick had not witnessed the bloody conclusion of the Peasants' Rebellion. He had fallen asleep May 5th at Lochau, quietly and peacefully as he had lived, a true "Peace-rich." (This is a play on the German names, "Friedrich" [Frederick = "Peaceful" or "Peace-loving"] and"Friedreich" ["Peace rich"] with the addition of an extra 'e' in the second syllable, the second syllable being then pronounced with a long "i" [as in the word "Third Reich" = Kingdom] referring to Hitler's description of his Germany].)

Frederick the Wise (in office 1486-1525)
According to a painting by Cranach

He had just received Communion from his father confessor, as it had been instituted by Christ. His body was ceremoniously laid to rest. However, the ceremony was not papal. Luther, who had been called back from his trip among the farmers, preached two sermons in memory of the count on the text of I Thessalonians 4:13-18. Martin Luther had never spoken with him directly, but the Count lovingly remembered him during his final hours.

Neither side thanked Luther for his position during the Peasant War. The papal lords and their adherents were describing his having addressed the consciences of the counts and so took part in stirring up the rebellion. The vicious accusation, which Luther had discredited in his "Admonition toward peace", was brought up repeatedly. Especially Duke George, in whose territory the hordes of Muenzer had led a campaign of fire and murder, now acted as though these hordes were made up of Lutherans. He therefore turned his sword against innocent people just because they were Lutherans.

On the other side, because Luther had at a later time urged the authorities to smother the rebellion with the sword, the conquered held this against him. They expressed themselves blasphemously that, when Luther had seen how it was going to end, he had hung his garment into the wind and washed his hands, like Pilate had once done.

But regarding both reactions Luther knew what to do. In his "Epistle about the Harsh Pamphlet against the Farmers" he conceded absolutely nothing he had written. (S. LV, Vol. 27, 28, p. 53ff.) He only spared himself from the misinterpretation that he had wanted to speak against the lords, who even after the rebellion had been smothered, were raging against those who were conquered with very cruel and bloody verdicts. He pleaded as intercessor for some individuals who had been misled.

Even Carlstadt was seeking refuge under his wings. He had at first been as good as executed by the very farmers in the region of Rothenburg whom he himself had incited. He was subsequently being sought as cause of the rebellion. He came to Luther for help in his time of need, nor had he overestimated Luther's generosity. After Carlstadt had given a somewhat satisfying explanation, the Elector forgave him on the strength of Luther's intervention and allowed him to settle as a quiet village resident. He had promised to no longer preach or write but to remain "eternally silent and support himself only by his labor."

When this former despiser of baptism conducted his own child's baptism the following February, Luther was present as a guest. The sponsors were Melanchthon, Jonas, and Luther's wife.

Chapter 29
Luther's Marriage

One of the nuns who had escaped from the Nimtzsch convent that Easter night of 1523 was Katharina von Bora (Katharina will henceforth be identified as Catherine, Cathy, or Kate). She had been in that convent from the age of ten. She hailed from an old, but poor family of the nobility. When Luther's teaching penetrated through the trellis and into the cells of the convent, she, together with the other sisters of the convent, learned to consider their station in life in a new light. Nine of them had desperately pleaded that their families take them out. But their petitions fell on deaf ears, until Luther personally interceded on their behalf. He assigned the task of their liberation to the former Councilman, Koppe of Torgau. He, in turn, brought them safely through the territory of Duke George on the third holiday of Easter. They traveled to Wittenberg in a covered wagon. To this day a slipper is on display at Nimtzsch, supposedly lost by Catherine during her flight.

"You might ask what I will do with them?" Luther wrote to Spalatin at that time. "First, I shall write to their relatives to take them in; if not, I shall seek to find a home for them some other way; for some have made a promise to me. Some of them I shall marry off, if I can."

His intercession with the relatives seems to have borne no fruit. Thus, those poor women had to be housed somewhere else. Catherine of Bora was warmly welcomed to the home of the city secretary, Philip Reichenbach. She stayed there for two years, "quietly and well."

When Luther wrote that he would marry some of that "poor lot of women" off, he did not think that he himself would offer his hand to one of them. And if he would have had some idea after meeting them for the first time, his choice would not have been Catherine. He "suspected that she was proud and arrogant." Instead, he brought her to the attention of a young man of Nuernberg by the name of Baumgaertner, who had been considering her toward the end of 1524.

Luther implied that another suitor had stepped forth and if Baumgaertner wanted her he should not waste any time. As far as the other suitor was concerned, he was Dr. Glatz, pastor of Orlamuende. Catherine could not warm up to him and asked Amsdorf to help so that she would not be forced into a marriage with him. At the same time, she did not hesitate to make it clear that if Amsdorf or Luther would have her, she would not resist. The declining of a suitor, whom she had to consider favorable since the match-suggestion was coming from Luther, her benefactor, was no doubt difficult for poor Katherine.

Luther according to a painting by Cranach, 1525

Thus, it is understandable for her to make her offer, by which she gratefully expressed her warm regard for Luther. Luther, who himself was of an honest and frank nature, may well have been moved by the open honesty of this woman who had been abandoned.

In 1525, when the springtide of rebellion was raging, Luther began to note that the devil seemed to have it in for him personally and wanted to see him dead. He wrote the following in a letter, "If I could send a spiteful message to the devil, I shall take my Kate as my wife before I die, as I am hearing that they are carrying on." Soon afterwards he challenged the Archbishop Albrecht to enter marriage by sending this message, "If my marriage may prove to strengthen his Electoral Grace, I shall soon be ready to gallop ahead of his Electoral Grace as an example. For I have in mind, before I leave this life, to find myself in a state of matrimony, which I regard as commanded by God, even if it were no more than an engagement marriage like that of Joseph." He later spoke of his intention, "I had completely decided this within myself, before I took a woman as my wife, to honor the state of marriage. Were I to be unexpectedly dying or lying on my death bed, I would have allowed myself to be wed to a believing maiden and would have thereupon given her two silver chalices as evening and morning gifts." That he had truly made the right choice following his heartfelt prayer is a given in Luther's case. He later expressed that very thought with the words, "Friend, do as I did. When I wanted to take my Kate, I prayed to the Lord God about it with all solemnity. You do the same."

Katharina Luther, nee v. Bora, according to a painting by Cranach

When Luther learned that slander was being spread in regard to his relationship with Kate, he hastened to carry out his decision. Since he must have been afraid that some of his friends might try to talk him out of it, he consulted none of them for advice. He did all he could to prevent the most fearful one among them, Melanchthon, from finding out. On June 13th, he invited Pastor Bugenhagen, Provost Jonas, the professor of law Dr. Apel, and also the artist and councilman, Lucas Cranach and his wife, to an evening meal. Thus, in their company and with them as witnesses he entered into marriage with Katharina von Bora according to the customary practice. The bridegroom was in his 42nd and the bride in her 27th year of life.

The following morning the newlyweds hosted the witnesses of their marriage with a hardy breakfast. The gift of an excellent wine came from the municipal magistrate. On the 27th of June, Luther and his wife Kate, who were now living in the monastery building, invited a number of friends for a wedding supper, to which a festive procession to the church was attached. The guests: Spalatin, Amsdorf, Link, Koppe and others, but especially Luther's father and mother, were asked to confess themselves on behalf of his marriage before God and the world, and represent him honorably. The city magistrate and the university also took advantage of the situation to make a public statement. The first sent a keg of Einbecker bier and 20 guilders, the other a stately silver goblet as wedding presents. The goblet, which is now in possession of the University of Greifswald, has the inscription at the bottom:

"The laudible University of the Electoral city of Wittenberg honors Doctor Martino Luthero and his virgin bride Kethe v. Boren with this wedding gift."

Display of the Wedding Ring pertaining to Martin and Katharina Luther

Wedding rings were most likely not used in Luther's marriage ceremony. Yet two rings are still being displayed in memory of the occasion. Catherine may have given one of them to Luther later as a remembrance of their wedding day. It is skillfully finished in filigreed and raised gold-work. Besides a ruby, it shows the image of the crucified Savior, the instruments of torture, and the dice of the soldiers. On the inside flat surfaces is the inscription: D. Martino Luthero Katharina v. Boren, June 13, 1525.

The other ring consists of two ring-bands which may be joined to each other. The mountings of the two jewels, a diamond and a ruby, display on the two facing flats, situated alongside each other, the first letters of the names of the wedding couple: M.L.D. [Martinus Luther Doctor] and C.v.B. [Katharina von Bora]. The inside of one of the bands displays the inscription, WHAT GOD HAS JOINED TOGETHER, the inscription inside the other continues, LET MAN NOT SEPARATE.

Thus, the marriage took place on June 13th, and was publicly announced with much cheer on the 27th. There were many, both friends and enemies, who were shaking their heads, but Luther just let them do so for as long as they could keep it up. In his Kate, God had given Luther not an angel, but a faithful, upright woman, and he thanked God for the treasure he had in her. It did not bother him that his enemies were reminding people of the legend that the antichrist would be born from a marriage of a monk and a nun. He

A view of how the other double ring fits together

knew that the antichrist did not need to be born to exist. Luther, the reformer of the Church, became a husband and father, who also set an example for how to reform Christian family life, another reformation that was needed.

Luther had made no concession to the antichrist as a married man. His first publication as a married man served as a witness for this purpose. It was the book, "The Bondage of the Will," or, "That Free Will Does Not Exist." (*in reference to conversion and salvation. So Justus Jonas titled this writing of Luther.*) This book was published against Erasmus of Rotterdam.

Chapter 30
Erasmus of Rotterdam

When Luther published his book, "About the Babylonian Captivity," a counter treatise appeared, of which Henry VIII of England claimed authorship. This lustful tyrant considered himself to be a great theologian. As a reward for this treatise, in which he with unbelievable coarseness and conceit hurled himself at Luther as a snarling, demonic wolf, and an incorrigible heretic, who was already in the devil's belly, Pope Leo X gave him the title, "Defender of the Faith." The pope also promised that anyone who would read this royal work would receive ten years worth of indulgence. In his reply, which Luther first published in Latin in 1522, and later in German after Duke George had seen to it that Henry's work had been translated, Luther carved him as though splitting off wedges from a block of wood. Luther played him so well that the king sent a complaint to the Elector Frederick through a special ambassador. "I knew very well," Luther wrote shortly thereafter, "that I would deliver a blow to many a person's head with what I would write against the king of England, that ill-bred and poisonous Thomist; except it also gave me pleasure and was necessary for a number of reasons. No one knows what I am doing now, but it will be realized later."

The Elector, as was his manner, merely dismissed the matter with a wave of his hand and reminded the king of the style of his own treatise. On the other hand, that twirler of a big club, Eck, came to the defense of the ill-amused King Henry. Luther took no notice of him. But Henry VIII had won over another avenger, a man, whom many honored as the king of the intellectual worlds, the genius Erasmus of Rotterdam.

Erasmus was a very gifted man, was well educated, but at the same time frivolous and with an ambitious wit. At the time when Luther appeared on the scene Erasmus was by far the most celebrated intellectual in the western world. His many journeys were like triumphal processions in which counts and bishops, universities and magistrates, vied against one another to display their high regard for him. He drew his regular annual salary from a number of high ranking persons. In addition, many gifts of money and valuables flowed toward him. At the same time, he had accumulated large debts because of a number of foolish donations to schools and to the Roman church. He was also the one who brought the first printed edition of the Greek New Testament to the market in 1516. Next to this, he had published commentaries on the books of the New Testament. But in the process, as those commentaries testify, the center and star of Holy Scripture, Jesus, the Savior of poor sinners, and the righteousness that comes by grace alone through faith, had remained hidden from him. What he really seemed to have wanted was to build a kingdom of intellectuals, which would extend to other nations, Erasmus himself holding the uncontestable royal scepter as dictator of such a world of science.

Suddenly, to his dismay, up popped the Wittenberg monk, a man who knew nothing about being celebrated by the giants of the earth, as was customary for Erasmus. Erasmus did not know nor did he want to know this man who would divert the entire stream of spiritual activity and behavior into a new, wide river bed, and who threatened to leave Erasmus sitting high and dry. Soon thousands of people would be singing the praise of that bold Augustinian, as though there had never been an Erasmus. The star of this genius would fade throughout the world in comparison with the glowing reformer. What should he do?

Should he support Luther? His ego would not allow it, and it could even become dangerous. He had no desire for a martyr's crown. His gifts and annual salaries were things that Luther never thought about. But he did not want to fall out of favor with the higher lords. Should he begin to support the issue that Luther was attacking? He did not want to do that either. He himself had spitefully tilted against clerisy and scholastic wisdom.

Hence, he first attempted to position himself as superior to both sides, and to apply the brakes to both of them. When he was entreated to render a verdict on Luther's books he side-stepped the issue by explaining that he did not read them; thus, he could neither support nor reject them. Yet at Cologne, before the Diet of Worms, in a conversation with Elector Frederick, he had explained that Luther had sinned in regard to two issues, namely, that he caused offense to the papal crown and the bellies of the monks. But when the papal ban against Luther became public knowledge, he made it his top priority to write to Pope Leo X, asserting that he had neither commonality nor acquaintance with Luther's writings and that he was restraining himself to his own writing only, so that he would not make things worse in the polemic quarrel.

But in acting this way he made both sides despise him. The Romanists as well as the Lutherans saw Erasmus either as a coward or a totally senseless individual who had no conviction whatsoever, or indeed as both of these. The latter, no doubt, was the correct assessment. While at the Wartburg Luther had already offered his judgment that Erasmus knew nothing about divine grace and shunned the cross. He later wrote about him, "He has brought in the languages and has called us away from godless studies. Perhaps he will die with Moses in the land of Moab. He is not able either to show what is good, or lead anyone into the promised land."

However, Erasmus could not maintain his position over an extended period of time, at least not if he did not want to completely disappear from the dance. When the crowned benefactor, Henry VIII, pressured him repeatedly to step up as his avenger and write against Luther, he finally yielded with fear and trembling. He wrote a book about "Free Will" against Holy Scripture and against the teaching of Luther and regarding the total corruption of man by nature. He began by explaining that in all things he submitted to the resolutions of the church. He regarded those as more certain than when an individual relies on Scripture, which is lacking in clarity. He continued by saying that if a person would take a closer look, he would discover that he was unable to believe anything at all with the firm confidence of heart, as we find it to be with Luther. Concerning free will he then taught that man has the ability to turn toward God's grace or to turn away from it, essentially the teaching of the ancient heretic, Pelagius. With the statement, "The die has been cast," Erasmus sent his concoction, called "Diatribe", to his lofty benefactors.

Luther had gotten wind of this writing's coming into existence even before it appeared. He had anticipated that the learned genius, Erasmus, would produce something brilliant, if not in regard to the issue itself, then in regard to its execution. How amazed he was when, in September 1524, he got to see the book! The scrawling in regard to such a fertile subject was so pitiful and lamentable that Luther had to make every effort in his decision as to how to respond. That is how in December of the following year Luther came into the spotlight with his reply in very good Latin, "About the Enslaved Will," or, as Jonas entitled it in his translation, "That Free Will Does Not Exist." ("Dass der freie Wille nichts sei" – literally: "That the Free Will is nothing.") In the introduction, Luther explained that he was at this time answering the book of Erasmus, which he had almost disdainfully left unanswered. He added that his reason for this was that his friends had reminded him that many people might allow themselves to be fooled, due to the author's popularity, and so he looked at his response as his duty to his office and to make clear what he owed in regard to this book, even though it didn't deserve it.

He begins by showing how reprehensible it was for Erasmus to leave everything in doubt, holding Scripture responsible for its darkness, whereas in truth it is bright and clear. "You are reading falsely concerning the issues," he wrote, "because you do not read the Scriptures diligently or do not pay attention." Going on, he blames Erasmus that in other matters, such as the teaching of the eternal election, he tears open the lock and the door, even though here God reserves secrets, which God did not want to reveal. "Why," he wrote, "did you not let yourself remain unconcerned and also direct others to leave such things unexplored? There are things that God wills to be hidden from us and of which he does not speak in Scripture. Here it would have been proper to put your finger over your lips, to meet with awe what is hidden, to worship the secret counsel of God's majesty, and to say with Paul, 'But who are you, O man, to talk back to God.' ... (Rom. 9:20 [NIV])

"But then you continue: Who will improve his life? I answer: no one! Nor is anyone able to do so; and in regard to any life improvement which occurs without the Spirit, as you speak about it, God is not interested, because it only produces hypocrites. But the elect and the upright will improve themselves through the Holy Spirit; the others will remain unimproved. ... Furthermore, you say: who will believe that God loves him? I answer: no human being will believe it or is able to believe it. But the elect will believe it. The others who will be condemned in unbelief, are angry, and blaspheme, just as you are doing here. Therefore, there will be some, who will believe. But for you to say that through these teachings door and window are opened to godlessness: let this be the case! May those belong to the leprosy of which I spoke above who are to be acknowledged as evil. Nevertheless, through this teaching the door to righteousness is being opened, at the same time the entrance to heaven, the way to God for the upright and the elect.

" 'What does it profit then, or for what is it necessary to proclaim such a thing, since there seems to be so much evil derived from it?' I answer: It would be enough for a person to say: God wants it to be proclaimed, but we are not to search for the purpose of God's will, but worship him in simplicity, and honor God, that he who alone is just and wise treats no one unjustly. He does not treat anything foolishly or approximately, though it may seem different to us. The believers are satisfied with this answer.

"But before we do anything else, two things must be tended to so that this teaching may be proclaimed. The first is the humbling of our pride and the recognition of the grace of God; the other is the Christian faith itself. First, God has certainly promised his grace to the humble, that is, to those who lament their misery and fall into despair on their own. But man cannot be totally humbled until he knows that his salvation is completely and fully removed from his own powers, counsels, resolutions, will, and works; derived completely from another source, namely, only from God's action, counsel, will, and work. For as long as a person carries the opinion that he is capable of the smallest effort for his salvation, he remains confident in himself and does not totally despair. Hence, he will not be humble before God, but retains for himself some sort of place, time or any kind of work, or hopes or wishes for at least something, whereby he will finally reach salvation.

"But whoever believes that this originates completely and fully from God's will, despairs for himself, does not make a choice, but waits for God to work, he is closest to the grace to be saved. Thus, this is being proclaimed for the sake of the elect that they are saved, after they have been humbled and reduced to nothing in this way. The others strive against this humbling. Indeed, they condemn the fact that they are being taught to despair of themselves. They want something, even if it were the very smallest thing, left to them, that they might do it. These remain secretly proud and enemies of God's grace."

With these examples the basic thoughts are offered throughout the book about how man's will can contribute absolutely nothing toward his conversion and salvation. On the contrary, God's grace alone has to produce the wanting and accomplishing and has to give and preserve the faith. Indeed, it is exactly this, that God has taken our salvation entirely out of our hands and laid it in his own hands, which supplied Luther with powerful comfort.

"Yes, I confess," he wrote in conclusion, "that even if it were possible, I would not want free will to be given to me, nor anything else placed in my hand, by which I could try to achieve my salvation." For, he says, if we had to preserve our salvation over and against so many enemies, no man would be saved. "But now," he continued, "since God has removed my salvation from my will, and has laid it on his own will, and has also promised to preserve me not through my working or running, but through his grace and compassion, therefore I am secure. I am sure that he is faithful and will not lie to me. He is also powerful and great so that no devil, no opposition can topple him or steal me from him. 'No one,' he says, 'can snatch them out of my hand.'"

This powerful treatise received widely different reactions outside of the papal church. One opinion, which Calvin claimed somewhat later and which is maintained to this very day, is that in regard to this teaching, Luther had abandoned his position later in his life. On the other hand, others have attempted to water down the content of this book, claiming that Luther had not really meant it in the way in which it was written and only wrote this way against Erasmus in the heat of battle. None of that is true. Rather Luther himself emphasizes in this book that he is not drifting in doubt like Erasmus, but that he is speaking in all seriousness and is fully convinced.

Luther never took back any of what he had here written. To the contrary, he later referred to this work and to his Catechism as those of his writings he would like to see preserved, even if the others were to disappear. He also confessed this work before his students during the last years of his life. And he could do so because there is no truth to the statement that Luther taught any of the terrible things that some have read into this book. However, it is certain that much of what Luther presents in this excellent work, which approaches the impenetrable depths of Scripture and corresponding Scriptural doctrine, is heavy food which not everyone can take. Luther writes about it, "Therefore, take heed that you do not drink wine while you are still a suckling babe. Each doctrine has its measure, time, and age."

Chapter 31
The Spreading of the Reformation

The spring season of the reformation, during which the seed of the gospel was sown, was stormy as we have seen. But the crop sprouted, and the storm which Satan had previously unleashed, now produced the result that the plants were sinking their roots deeper into the soil, waiting for the time when they would produce blades and then ears. It was happening now, especially in cities outside of the territory of Saxony, that a growing number of gospel preachers could water the seeds which Luther had planted with his testimony. We have already heard about Nuernberg, and Strassburg as well. The gospel was also being welcomed in Magdeburg, in Frankfurt on the Main River, in Ulm, in Hall of Swabia, in Breslau, and in Bremen. The landgrave, Philip of Hessia, asked for a brief lesson about the disputed points of doctrine as he traveled along a stretch with Melanchthon. In July he commanded that the pure gospel was to be preached in his territory. The following year he, the son-in-law of Duke George, declared that he would yield his country and his life before he would give up the gospel.

The reformation also made inroads into Mecklenburg, and in Hamburg there was the beginning of "the search for God's Word." But a special bit of good news came from Prussia. There two Catholic bishops had changed over to the Lutheran doctrine already during 1523 and 1524. When in 1525 Margrave Albrecht of Brandenburg became the first Duke of Prussia, this region got its gospel ruler. Even before his installation he had applied to receive Lutheran preachers. Luther now wrote about him, "Because he gave place and honor to the gospel, it provided him with place and honor, much more than he could have wished."

The gospel had gotten a foothold earlier in Riga, Reval, and Dorpat, as well as in Danzig. Most of those listed cities and territories had contacted Luther personally and received counsel, encouragement, and comfort from him in his friendly replies. This is how he responded in 1523 to the "chosen dear friends of God, to all Christians at Righe, Revell, and Tarbthe (Riga, Reval, and Dorpat)". To those of Riga, who had asked him "to write something Christian for them," he sent an interpretation of the 127th Psalm in 1524. And when he found out that rabble rousers were also at work in their territory, he sent an encouragement to "all dear Christians in Latvia, and to their pastors." (LV, 3 writings)

The blessings of God which he was pouring out on Germany were also overflowing to the countries outside of Germany. Immediately after the Leipzig debate, during which Luther had been pressed to comment on the Costnitz Council, two priests from Prague had approached Luther with wishes of good fortune, including gifts. The rumor had been spread repeatedly that Luther would flee to the Bohemians if he could not remain in Germany. Luther himself admitted that he would have liked to visit the Bohemians. Luther's teaching was being accepted here and there. But the spread of the gospel was hindered when a Roman inclined group gained the upper hand. The fact that Luther was conscientiously guarding against gaining followers through compromise of the truth for the good in general becomes evident in connection with the false teaching the Bohemians held regarding Holy Communion. He severed his relationship with them, after he had in love vainly instructed them with a treatise, "Concerning the Adoration of the Holy Body of Christ." (LV, Vol. 25,26, p. 206 ff.)

The Petersen brothers, who had studied under Luther in Wittenberg, had carried the gospel to Sweden as early as 1519. The fact that the influence of Wittenberg had been realized had become evident by way of the encouragement of Christian II of Denmark. This has already been mentioned. Hans Tausen, who had also sat at Luther's feet, had been active there since 1524, at first facing strong persecution.

In the Netherlands, the powerful words of their order's brother from Wittenberg had entered the cells of the Augustinian monks and had gained brave souls for the truth. The Edict of Worms was being strictly enforced by the Domina Margaretha, Caesar's aunt. On July 1, 1523, two confessors of the Augustinian order, Henry Voes and John Esch, were publicly burned in front of the city hall in Brussels, the capital. Luther expressed their martyr's deaths in hymn which began:

> *By help of God I fain would tell*
> *A new and wondrous story,*
> *And sing a marvel that befell*
> *To His great praise and glory.*
> *At Brussels, in the Netherlands,*
> *He has his banner lifted,*
> *To show his wonders by the hands*
> *Of two youths highly gifted*
> *With rich and heavenly graces.*

At the conclusion he sang:

> (10) *Their ashes never cease to cry,*
> *The fires are ever flaming,*
> *Their dust throughout the world does fly,*
> *Their murderous shame proclaiming.*
> *The voices, which with cruel hands*
> *They put to silence living*

> *Are heard, though dead, throughout all lands*
> *Their testimony giving,*
> *And loud hosannas singing.*

(11) *From lies to lies they still proceed*
And feign forthwith a story
To color o'er their murderous deed:
Their conscience pricks them sorely.
These saints of God, e'en after death
They slandered and asserted,
"The youths had with their latest breath
Confessed and been converted;
Their heresy renouncing.

(12) *Then let them still go on and lie,*
They cannot win a blessing;
And let us thank God heartily,
His Word again possessing.
Summer is even at our door,
The winter now has vanished.
The tender flowerets spring once more
And he who winter banished
Will send a happy summer.

(The whole hymn LV, Vol. 25, 26, p. 278 ff.)
(A translation from German to English of all 12 stanzas of this hymn is printed on p. 190 in *The Handbook to the Lutheran Hymnal,* copyright 1958 by Concordia Publishing House.)

Luther held the pope responsible for the execution. When in 1524 the deceased Bishop Benno of Meissen, who had died at the beginning of the 12th century, was granted sainthood, Luther reacted. He issued a written response, "Against the New Idol and Old Devil, Who Is to Be Elevated at Meissen." He stated that this is Hadrian's way. He burned the real saints at Brussels. Now, he is elevating Benno in their place, yes, the devil himself.

The persecutions in the Netherlands had not at all reached their end with the execution of the two Augustinians. Luther comforted the oppressed with an "Epistle to the Dear Christians in Holland, Brabant (Belgium), and Flanders." (LV, Vol. 7, p. 48 ff.)

Another Augustinian brother from Antwerp, Heinrich von Zuetphen, had at first been snatched away from his native land, away from his persecutors. He later proclaimed the gospel, first in Bremen and then in Dithmarschen. He then was gruesomely butchered by a bunch of farmers who had been riled up by the monks. Luther dedicated one of his works to his martyrdom. (LV, Vol. 25, 26, p. 248 ff.) It was previously attested how some counts in Germany, who were enforcing the Edict of Worms, were persecuting Lutheran subjects even to the point of taking their lives.

It was regrettable that Luther had to experience the retreat of some of his friends during those years in which the reformation was blossoming in the midst of the spring storms. Some withdrew into silence. The behavior of his spiritual father, Staupitz, pained him the most. He withdrew to Salzburg, unable to endure what the gospel had caused. His friend, the Archbishop of Salzburg, arranged a place for a quiet retreat away from the city. He became an abbot of a Benedictine monastery and a vicar under the archbishop. He died two years later, in 1524. Luther loved him but also lamented him for having left.

Chapter 32
In the Home of the Reformer

Having journeyed through areas, to which the wider influence of the reformation had become extended, we return to electoral Saxony. There we begin by looking at Wittenberg, and in Wittenberg at Luther as a man and at his immediate surroundings.

Luther received the former monastic buildings as a residence. The Elector John presented it to him as a gift, while Luther was still living there with his monastic brothers, even though it was unfinished. This is where Luther lived with his Kate. The "Luther chamber," which is still being displayed, was very likely used as the living room. For a study, Luther used a small chamber, located over the water in the moat. It was later removed for a military purpose. When he was busy there at his desk, his wife Kate often sat with her husband. He later related how she would try to start a conversation. It is likely that she would ask questions like, "Honored doctor, is the grand master of Prussia the brother of the margrave?" But the grand master and the margrave were the same person. He talked with her about his work and his struggles. Sometimes he read this or that to her, things that were being written to him. He only locked himself in when his work was truly pressing. We can understand how this had been necessary. When visiting his residence, one could find tables, chairs, benches, stools, window seats, and wherever one could lay something, covered with all manner of work.

Working in his garden, which was attached to his home, offered Luther some relief. He would get seeds for it from Link at Nuernberg and from Lange at Erfurt. Some of his produce from that garden would also help his friends. He would tell Amsdorf when he was harvesting some vegetables for the kitchen. He also began to learn how to work a lathe, along with his classroom assistant, "Wolf" (Wolfgang Sieberger). He ordered tools for this work from Nuernberg. He wrote to Link, "If the world will no longer feed us because of the Word, we will want to take care of ourselves with work by our own hands."

However, he did not have the skill to make serious use of hand tools. God provided for his needs in another way. His wife Kate had plenty of opportunities to show that she understood how to save and manage the home very well. The doctor's income was quite modest. He took nothing for his considerable work at the parish church, plus he took no honoraria as stipends for his lectures. His writing, for which he could have received fine pay, his publishers got for free. All he got for them was a number of free copies to give away. Thus, he had nothing except his wages, which his elector raised to 200 guilders after his marriage, and whatever the city council would give him for maintaining and improving his home. Still he enjoyed giving things away and would offer free lodging. He had welcomed his wife's aunt into his family, "Aunt Lene", who had been in the convent with Kate. The result was that in spite of all of the saving which "Lord Kate" achieved, the doctor often found himself in financial embarrassment and went into debt.

On July 7, 1526, the married couple received a special kind of treasure in their monastic residence. On that day their first child, Luther's "Little Hans," was born.

In July of the following year it appeared as though Mrs. Kate would become a widow, and little Hans, whose father treasured him with tender love, would become an orphan. From January on Luther felt tormented, suffering from blood rushing toward his heart. On July 6th, he suddenly experienced such a strong and oppressive panic attack that he thought it was the end for him. He had Bugenhagen come, made his confession, received absolution, and commended himself to God. Toward evening he lost consciousness and his body was turning cold. After recovering somewhat under the care of the physician who had been called, he prayed and asked those friends who were present to pray with him. He commended his Kate and his precious little Hans, who had been brought to him, to the Father of orphans and caretaker of widows.

Finally, after continuous massaging had helped him to work up a sweat, the danger passed.

Immediately after this episode the university was temporarily moved to Jena due to the approach of the plague. When the plague actually broke out in Wittenberg, Luther stayed there and assisted Pastor Bugenhagen. He honored several students, who had also stayed, by arranging a special lecture for them. Soon eighteen bodies were buried, not far from his home, near the Elstergate. But he remained cheerful and high spirited. "We are not alone," he wrote, "but Christ together with the holy angels, and your prayers, and those of all the saints, are with us."

Luther published a letter he had written to a friend in response to the question, whether it is proper for a Christian to flee during the outbreak of the plague. He explained who may flee and who may not, and how those who had to stay should guard themselves from the contagious disease. (LV, Vol. 6, p. 116 ff). In November the plague even entered his home. Two of the female residents, one of whom was the wife of the physician Schurf, were infected. "Little Hans" was also sick for a number of days. On top of that, Mrs. Kate was approaching her second delivery.

On the 10th of December, after the three patients had recovered, she gave birth to a daughter, Elizabeth. However, she was already taken from them on the 3rd of August of the following year. "Elizabeth," he wrote to a friend, "bade us farewell in order to go to Christ, through death to life;" and to another, "She has left behind a wondrously ill, yet strongly female heart

Picture of the Luther Home, formerly the Augustinian Monastery

for me." In her place another daughter was born on May 4, 1529, named Magdalena.

In the meantime, by the beginning of 1528 after the plague had passed, the university had returned to Wittenberg. In the midst of a number of deep seated spiritual problems, Luther gave his highest priority to his office of teaching. He lectured his students on the Prophets, Ecclesiastes, and the Song of Solomon, as well as the first letter of John, the first letter to Timothy, and the letter to Titus. He also served his congregation by word and example. We noted how he had served as example of self-disowning love during the plague.

As he had faithfully stood in support of Pastor Bugenhagen at that time, the entire relationship between Luther and his dear "Doctor Pommer" was an overall pleasant one. Not only did Luther regard him highly as a friend, but also as caretaker of his soul. He diligently sought comfort from him, confessed his sins to him, and was absolved by him. He also joined with the congregation for listening to his sermons and for attending the Lord's Supper. During that time, he also stood faithfully at his side, assisting in the pastoral office, and continued to build the congregation with his counseling. During following years, Bugenhagen, because of his special gifts of administration in church life, was often used in other places. Luther maintained the pastoral office for him during his absence.

In 1527, the Church Postil was expanded through Magister Roth of

Picture of the Family Room in the Home of the Reformer
(Most likely their living room)

Zwickau. With Luther's approval, it included the publication of the gospels of both the Trinity Season and the Festival half of the church year. This addition was derived in part from notes which had been taken during his sermons, and in part from earlier printings of his sermons. Luther personally had issued an interpretation of the prophets Jonah, Habakkuk, and Zechariah, along with a number of the Psalms. He also was continuing to work on the German translation of the Old Testament as a whole. It was with much love and care that the Prophets, of whom Luther complained that they were resisting and did not want to let go of their Hebrew, were finally brought to the point that they too, were speaking German to the German people. But Luther was also hindered in this, his dearest occupation, by a number of other tasks. He could very well speak with Paul, "I face daily the pressure of my concern for all the churches."

Pastor Bugenhagen of 1543
according to Cranach
In the so-called
genealogical book in Berlin

Dr. Martin Luther according to a painting by Cranach in 1528

Mrs. Martin (Kate) Luther according to a painting by Cranach in 1528

Chapter 33
For the Congregation's Participation in Worship

The situation in electoral Saxony had changed considerably since Elector John had taken his brother's place. Luther's relationship with his new earthly leader was completely different from that with his former leader. He had dealt with Frederick only through the mediation of Spalatin, except for the exchange of some letters. The mediator was no longer needed, and he was released from his service to the court in accordance with his long-held desires. He became a pastor in Altenburg, where Link, who had been called to Nuernberg, had served. But Luther communicated with the Elector John the same way he had with Count John, in writing, and now also face to face as conditions allowed or permitted.

Luther's work kept continuing the same way, as God had begun it in electoral Saxony. Here, too, John conducted himself differently than his brother. In Wittenberg, the magistrate, in conjunction with the University under Luther's measured leadership, had formed church organization without any serious hindrance or specific sanction from Elector Frederick. Now, in response to the command of the new leader, the improvements continued. Up to this time, the hymns for the church service were sung by the pastor and choir in Latin, except for a few German hymns that were sung by the congregation. Now Luther was to design and produce a Sunday church service entirely in German. Luther asked the Elector for two men, gifted in music, to assist with the musical parts of the service. Their names were Johann Walter and Konrad Rupf. The resulting service was approved by the Elector, and was used for the first time as a church service in the city church on October 29, 1525, the 20th Sunday after Trinity.

The sermon remained the main feature of this divine service. In the city church there were three sermons each Sunday: on the Epistle in the morning at 5:00 or 6:00; on the Gospel of the day at 8:00 or 9:00, and on the Old Testament in the afternoon. Luther wrote the song of praise for Holy Communion. He based it on Isaiah 64:1-4, "Isaiah, mighty seer in days of old...." He also composed the melody. For the introduction to Holy Communion, he wrote a reconstruction of the Lord's Prayer, adding an admonition for worthy reception of the Lord's Supper. As a liturgy for Baptism, he used his Baptism pamphlet of 1526, in a somewhat altered form. It had originally been produced in 1523. He retained exorcism in his revised pamphlet, but in a shortened form. That part would later gradually fall into disuse. But on the whole that Baptism pamphlet, with a few additions and minor changes, is the form for Baptism in the Lutheran Church to this day.

In addition to the Sunday services, morning divine services were held Monday through Friday. On Saturday, an evening divine service was held, during which students would sing Latin Psalms. Books of the Bible were being interpreted continually during services and in classrooms.

Luther was not yet able to organize a congregation in the way we understand a congregation, a place for those who seriously desired to be Christian and confess the gospel in word and deed, and give their signature for it. In addition, it was not a congregation like ours from which someone who did not conduct himself as a Christian, when he refused to heed an admonition, could be excluded or put under the ban according to the command of Christ in Matt. 18. He wrote, "I cannot and also do not wish to organize such a congregation or assembly, for I do not yet have the people or individuals for it, nor do I see any who are striving for it."

In general, as we have already mentioned, the conditions under which Luther had to labor, and what he could expect were completely in line with then existing situations. Due to the horrible management of the Roman clergy, from the pope all the way down to the village vicar, the church life among the commoners had been completely shattered. Nearly all priests were unskilled men who were neither capable nor willing to give Christian counsel to the people. The dues which the members of the parish paid had either been forced through the coercing of their consciences or simply taken, contrary to the granting of carnal freedom. The brutality and wickedness among the masses were truly hair-raising. Added to this was the fact that next to the gospel, the spirit of Carlstadt and Allstedt had penetrated into people's hearts. No wonder then, that where papal power ceased and the accustomed shackles had fallen, soon loud complaints were being heard regarding the disdainful abuse of the produced freedom and the neglect of the preaching office. Many of the noble lords, including those who were papal-minded, also knew how to take advantage of the new conditions. They forcefully claimed the ownership of monastic properties, despoiled them, and had little or no concern in regard to the source from which the preachers were to receive their living.

The wisdom with which Luther assessed these conditions deserves our highest amazement. He did not hope for the church to flourish as a result of rapid reconstruction of the church's outward existence, for which the right people had not yet appeared. Instead, he put his hopes in the continuing action of the Word, which creates new people. But there was only one way for this to happen, and Luther pursued this way, fully aware that he would have to account for emergencies as a result. He permitted the secular counts who wanted to wrestle with those things to step in as emergency bishops and do what no one else was doing. That the worldly and the spiritual governors had to stay separate he knew well and clung to that division. He constantly distinguished between what belonged to the realm of government and that which the current needs and the law of love put into the government's hand. He never yielded the right and duty of the congregations to call and support preachers and to apply Christian discipline. But when the congregations did not carry out their responsibilities, the use of the means of grace would not cease and allow everything to go to ruin because of this.

Chapter 34
Church Visitation in Saxony

The Elector John of Saxony applied himself faithfully in the office of "Emergency Bishop," for which Luther served as his right hand man, or his head, or both.

If the preaching of the gospel was to continue to exist and to spread, preachers would need to be trained. For this reason, special attention was given to the university. An electoral commission had to plan a site and station for the necessary start, and money was spent to carry it out. The money was available now due to the reduced number of church endowment lords.

Luther had alluded to these new guidelines, in fact so urgently that he excused himself in a letter of October 31, 1525, to the Elector, (LV, Vol. 7, p. 102 ff.) stating that he had pressed too hard to install new order in the university. In the same letter he alerted the count to the need of a general church visitation in his land. He pointed to this, "That the parishes everywhere are in such miserable condition; no one gives; no one pays. Gifts and soul-pennies have fallen. There are no stipends, or too little. Hence, the commoner honors neither preacher nor pastor. If no determined order and important support is established by your Electoral Grace for the parish and the pulpit, there will soon be no parish estate. Nor will there soon be schools or students, and the Word of God and services will be swept away. For this reason, may your Electoral Grace allow himself to be used by God and become his faithful tool to provide comfort, also for your Electoral Grace's own conscience, because it is through our being asked and demanded by God himself, that there is a pressing need to establish orderly procedures."

The Elector followed through immediately and invited the doctor to let him know how he thought it should be carried out. Luther answered with a letter, dated November 30th. (LV, Vol. 7, p. 106 ff) He suggested dividing the entire territory of the count into four or five districts, and to send two visitors into each district to assess the situation. Where it was discovered that the parish did not have enough money to support the preacher, the members of the parish should be urged to raise the missing part by way of adding an annual tax." Along with this,"he wrote," attention would also have to be given to the old parish lords, or those who were under-performing, but who were otherwise upright and not against the gospel.

They were to either read the gospel out of the Postil themselves, or if they are not adept at preaching, would have to be held responsible to have those same portions read by someone else."

With such new procedure the execution of those suggestions was expedited right away at the beginning of the following year. They had Spalatin visit the district's office of Borna, and Frederick Mykonius, the office of Tenneberg. Furthermore, Luther published a work under the title, "German Mass and Order for Divine Service Undertaken at Wittenberg," as a description of the nature of the divine service in the city church. The Elector directed the pastors to hold to this form. Earlier they had been directed to live in Christian manner, to preach the gospel, and to administer the Sacraments according to the way Christ had instituted them.

As complaints increased, Luther approached the Elector again in November 1526. He reported that if the older clergy wanted to go to the devil so badly, then at least the youth should be saved through instruction in Christian schools and the preaching of the gospel. When he visited the count in Wittenberg, he even forced his way into the count's bed chamber, and with tears, laid the heartfelt need before him.

At last visitations were being carried out seriously. Melanchthon was included among the visitors who were named in February 1527. As the visitation had been going on for several weeks in Thueringia, they had gained insight into the highly deplorable situation. Melanchthon was then given the task of coming up with a plan to continue the visitations. It was carefully reviewed several times, with input from Luther and Bugenhagen. Finally it was published with a foreword from Luther under the title," Instructions from the Visitors to the Parish Lords in the Electorate of Saxony. These "instructions" set forth the basic teachings of the Christian faith and the chief parts of Christian congregational life, in a concise and simple manner. Special emphasis was placed on building and maintaining Christian schools for the rearing of Christian youths. Visitors were installed anew in July 1528. This time Luther was also to be included. From among the four districts into which he had divided his territory, the Elector directed Luther and Jonas to the area of the Elector's district and to the Meissen offices, which included the offices of Torgau, Grimma, Eilenburg, Hainichen, and Dueben. Three other visitors who were not theologians were added to this team. They began carrying out this task in October, and Luther went into action as the true model for a visitor. He kept his eyes and ears open for everything. Wherever the commission went, the elders of the congregation were assembled. They were asked about the conduct of the pastor up to that point in time, about the management in the congregation, and about their own understanding. The preachers were also tested about their knowledge and ability to teach. In these fact-finding visitations their findings as a whole looked abominable. In fact, in nearly every place the papal mass with its audience had been destroyed. Many pastors were completely unable to write a sermon and had to be directed to preach "according to the contents of the Postil." It now became clear how great a need there was for such a book.

Ignorance was even greater among the people. Terribly brutal behavior and indifference became apparent. Luther reported, "Things are terrible within congregations in that the farmers learn nothing, know nothing, pray nothing, and do nothing except abusing their freedom, do no confession, no communion attendance. They behave as though they had been set completely free from religion." They had to establish a rule that from this time on no one would be allowed to take the Sacrament who could not at least say the Ten Commandments, the Confession of Faith, and the Lord's Prayer. Luther also had reason to complain about the attitudes of the electoral office holders, in that they, according to their own judgment allowed themselves to deviate from the Elector's instructions, and as a result only added to the confusion. Luther also took to heart the neglect of the youth. In order to provide them with some help, the sextons were to be held responsible to have the children at least memorize the Ten Commandments, the Creed, and the Lord'sPrayer.

The following example may show us how kindly the great doctor dealt with the poor people during these visitations. One time he was asking and instructing some poor farmers about the Christian faith, as he was accustomed to do during the visitations. After one had recited the First Article, Luther asked him what 'almighty" means. "I don't know," he replied. To which Luther said, "Yes, dear man, I and all the learned men also do not know what the power of God and his omnipotence are; but you simply believe that God is your dear Father, your faithful Father, who wills, is able, and knows how to help you, your wife, and your children in all your needs."

Regretfully Luther could not finish the visitation in his area. Not only was he forced to take a break due to an extended period of illness, but there was also an important need for him to return to Wittenberg. With Melanchthon doing his visitation in Thueringia at the same time, dissatisfaction had arisen among the students, so that over 100 of them were moving out. On top of this, Bugenhagen was absent in order to straighten out evangelical church procedure in Braunschweig, and after that in Hamburg, while Luther had to substitute for him in Wittenberg. Thus, Luther received the elector's order in March 1529, to let another theologian take his place as a visitor and to remain in Wittenberg. Yet later he continued to do personal visitations in individual locations, of which Torgau was an example.

Chapter 35
Luther's Catechisms

However, the things Luther experienced while serving as a visitor would yet produce an overall glorious and valuable fruit for the Lutheran Church of all time. He summarized those things in the foreword of a pamphlet which he published in 1529, with the words, "Dear God, help! I have repeatedly seen the misery that exists because the common man does not know anything about Christian teaching, especially in the villages. Regretfully, many parish lords are so unskilled and neglectful in regard to teaching. Yet, all have been called Christian. They have been baptized and enjoy the Holy Sacrament. Still, they don't know the Lord's Prayer, or the Creed, or the Ten Commandments. They live their lives like domesticated animals and sloppy sows. Now that the gospel has come, they have learned how to abuse their freedom." Because of this "abominable and miserable need" he now considered himself "forced and compelled" to carry out a plan, which he had been considering for some time, but the execution of which had remained unfinished up to this point.

Bringing the chief parts of Christian doctrine to the people through sermons had been Luther's primary objective from the beginning of his teaching career, as we have seen. What's more, already in 1520, he had presented on fourteen quarter sheets, "A short form of the Ten Commandments, the Creed, and the Lord's Prayer." He had written in its foreword that it had not happened without a special orderliness from God, and that it stands as established fact for a common Christian to learn and to know the Ten Commandments, the Creed and the Lord's Prayer. Those three parts are the minimum of what a Christian needs to know. He again issued this work two years later, with somewhat expanded content, under the title, "Prayer Booklet." This book was spread widely in many editions.

In 1525 appeared "A Booklet for Lay People and their Children". It contained the alphabet, the text of the Ten Commandments, the Creed, the Lord's Prayer, and the words of institution for Baptism and the Lord's Supper.

But none of these booklets were a "Catechism." Others besides Luther had recognized the need for such a book, and in February 1525, Luther informed a friend that Jonas and Agricola had been assigned to produce a "Boys' Catechism." But soon Luther must have come to the decision to undertake this important task himself. In a letter to that same friend during the second half of the year we find the words, "I am postponing the Catechism; for I would like to complete everything in one project." He then pointed this out again in a "German Mass" that "a course, a plain, simple, and good Catechism" is of foremost importance. Years passed and the Catechism was still postponed. But now the abomination, the terrible need which he had experienced, when he served as visitor, impelled the reformer to no longer delay his Catechism. On the 3rd of March, he could write to his friend, the one to whom he had earlier commented about the Catechism, "I am still not finished with the Catechism, dear Hausmann, but it will be finished soon."

Soon after this Luther's Large Catechism did appear under the title, "Deutsch Katechismus." It was immediately translated into Latin, and a second edition, which appeared the same year, contained the newly added "Short Admonition in Regard to Confession." Before the short foreword of the first edition, Luther placed an even longer foreword in the edition of 1530. In it he specifically dealt with the subject of how necessary it is to keep on using the Catechism. He wrote, "There is good reason why we strongly urge the use of the Catechism, and both wish and beg you to use it." After pointing out the negligence of many of the parish lords, he continued, "On top of this, the hateful blasphemy and the secret evil alliance of complacency and boredom are lashing out. They claim that many are of the opinion that the Catechism is a plain and simple teaching which they read once and know it. Then they throw it into the corner and immediately are ashamed to read it any longer. This is what I say about myself: I am a doctor and preacher too. Yes, I am as educated and experienced as any of those who carry so much arrogance and complacency. Still I act as a child, to learn, to read, and to recite word for word every morning, if I have the time, the Ten Commandments, the Creed, the Lord's Prayer, the Psalms, etc. Besides this, I have to read and study every day, but I still cannot continue as I would like. I must remain a child and student of the Catechism and I like it that way."

After writing the Large Catechism, Luther also produced the Small Catechism in 1529. The first edition is no longer available in its original Wittenberg printing. After a later printing in Erfurt and Marburg, it appeared under the title, "The Small Catechism for the Common Parish Lords and Preachers." (Footnote: The later editions put the Greek word "Enchiridion", which translated means "Handbook", (from the Greek "in the hand" before this title). Here the same five chief parts were found as in the Large Catechism; plus the morning and evening prayers, the prayers before and after meals, and the table of duties with the little verse:

Let each one here his lesson learn,
God to such home will bliss return.

Ein jeder lern sein Lektion
So wird es wohl im Hause stohn.

Our English version now prefaces each part with the words: "As the head of the family should teach it in all simplicity to his household."

For the parish lords and preachers, who according to title and foreword were to be the first to have the booklet in their hands, a marriage pamphlet was added. It is noteworthy that in the first editions the Address to the Lord's Prayer was missing. It was added with an explanation in the edition of 1531. The second edition, which was also issued already in 1529, contained a few additional statements. In the Fifth chief part the question was added, "How can eating and drinking do such great things?" The answer to this question was also new. An explanation of the first table prayer and the directive for Confession, which appeared in two sets of wordings, were also new. This edition also contained three woodcuts. They were a picture of the worship of the golden calf under the First Commandment, an illustration of creation under the First Article, and a picture that presented the proclamation of the gospel together with the third chief part. This edition included a copy of the Baptism pamphlet in addition to the marriage pamphlet. In 1531, the questions and answers for Confession were added between the fourth and fifth chief parts. The questions about the Office of the Keys and the Christian Questions were added later by others. The Doxology of the Lord's Prayer, "for the kingdom, the power, and the glory are yours now and forever," Luther left out because of its regular use in church services at that time. In the Address of the Lord's Prayer he set the word, "Father," ahead of "our" in harmony with the common usage at that time, although he followed the newer practice in his Bible translation. Luther's retention of the form "Send away our debts" was later changed to "Forgive us our debt." The latter word is incorrect in that Luther wrote "debt" ("Schuld") in place of "debts" ("Schulden"). (Comment by the translator: *Cannot the word also be understood in its collective sense as though it were plural? I have always understood it that way.*)

With his Catechism, Luther wanted to provide a means whereby those things that needed to be learned could be brought "into the people, especially into the young people." They were first to be taught the text, then the understanding, and in the process, retain the form unchanged. For those who were not able to improve, Luther recommended the form which he presented. But till now there has been no one who has been able to improve this form, which is presented so short in this "Layman's Bible" (the expression stand for Small Catechism), so clearly, and so well. We therefore do well to allow no other book to replace this most glorious gift which God has granted to us through Luther, which is second only to the German Bible.

The blessing which grew out of the visitations and was further established with the Catechism soon proved its value. As early as the following May Luther could comfort his Elector with the words, "In regard to this, so does the God of compassion reveal himself even more graciously as he causes his Word to be so powerful, producing fruit in the territory of your

Electoral Grace. Surely the territory of your Electoral Grace has the very best and most of good preachers and pastors, more than any other territory of the world. They teach so faithfully and purely and so help to preserve a beautiful peace. Now tender youths, boys and girls, are growing up well trained in the Catechism and Scripture. It calms my heart as I see how young boys and girls pray, believe in, and speak about God and about Christ, more than all of the foundations (federations), cloisters, and schools were able to do before."

"Such young people in the territory of your Electoral Grace are truly a beautiful paradise, the likes of which is not seen in the entire world. And God is building all of this in the lap of your Electoral Grace as a sign that he is gracious and favors your Electoral Grace. It was as though he would say, 'Well, dear count Hans, therein I commend to you my noblest treasure, my joyful paradise, and you shall be their father, for I want to have them under your protection and governance, and grant you the honor to be my gardener and caretaker.' This is most certainly true." (LV, Vol. 8, p. 7ff.)

Chapter 36
Persecution of the Church within the Empire

The quiet development of this paradise within the Elector's territory proved to be a blessing during the political conditions which were developing. Immediately following the peasant war, the sky over the German lands was darkened with heavy clouds. First, both clerical and lay counts, who despised the gospel, vented their rage against those, who confessed the gospel. Among those who had been decapitated after the suppression of the rebellion at Wuerzburg were many whose only crime was that they had confessed their belief in the evangelical faith. At Bamberg, nine well-respected and peace-loving citizens were executed specifically because they were Lutherans. As for the actions of the bailiff Aichill who was ridding Swabia and Franconia of Lutherans, it was said: "He was especially busy against Lutheran pastors. He caught 'em, robbed 'em, tried 'em, and hanged 'em." He strung up forty evangelical preachers on the trees lining the street. We had earlier heard about the rage of Duke George. Caesar also reverted to the Edict of Worms. When he declared a Diet at Worms in December 1525, he reaffirmed that the former declarations had to be re-established. The clerical lords, the imperial government, and those preparing for the Diet also concurred, and it looked as though things were heading in a very unfavorable direction for the Evangelicals. Therefore, it was quite understandable for the two counts, who had publicly voiced their support for the Reformation, the Elector John of Saxony, and Landgrave Philip of Hessia, to begin preparations to counter the threat. The Elector's son, John Frederick, and Philip of Hessia met at the fortified castle Friedewalt to begin plans to unify all of the evangelicals in Germany.

A Diet had begun at Augsburg, but the attendance was so poor that none of those present wanted to address any of the important issues, and the estate lords tabled their meeting to May 1st of the following year, 1526, at Speier. The only action worthy of note was that the decisions declared in the closing statements of the previous two diets were repeated.

The deciding encounter, according to the counsel of the empire's estate lords, was to take place at Speier. Caesar promised his personal appearance and indicated that he would finally clean up the "damned Lutheran teaching." He urged a Catholic alliance to cling faithfully to the old faith and to eradicate the new teaching. This alliance was an expansion of one that had already been previously established by a number of dukes. Duke George and Cardinal Albrecht of Mainz were among these.

The opposition of evangelical dukes also determined to move forward. The alliance that had been approved the previous year, became reality in February of 1526, at Gotha. The Saxons approved it at Torgau, and so it is usually called the Torgau Alliance. The two leaders, John and Philip, immediately became partners in the alliance. The Elector's efforts were so successful that Duke Ernst of Lueneburg, Philip of Grubenhagen, Henry of Mecklenburg, Wolf of Anhalt, Albrecht of Mansfeld, and the city of Magdeburg joined at a meeting held in Magdeburg.

Luther was still expressing high hopes in 1525. He especially took note that two of his most bitter opponents, Henry VIII and Duke George, could possibly be won for the gospel through friendly encouragement. In fact, King Henry VIII was already leaning toward the gospel. Thus Luther wrote humble letters to both in response to the wishes of such "lofty and elite personages." Yet in them he surrendered nothing in regard to doctrine. He humbled himself and asked pardon from both rulers for anything, with which he may have offended them, and sincerely encouraged them to pay homage to the truth. (The letter to Duke George, LV, Vol. 7, p. 107) But in return for his humility, he received vicious kicks from both of them, immediately from Duke George, and later from the king. George made the accusation that God had punished Muenster for his evil deeds because of Luther. He added that God could well do the same to Luther and that he, the Duke, would gladly be the one to carry out such punishment.

When he learned of the alliance of the evangelical leaders, Luther wanted nothing to do with it. He wrote, "I do not like hearing about the alliance against Caesar, for I say that human blows will fail." Then in his writing, "Whether Soldiers Can Also Be Saints," he specifically emphasized that no one may use the sword against the authority of government, even if that authority is tyrannical and guilty of lying. Here God's Word stands, "Vengeance is mine, I will repay, says the Lord." (Dt. 32:35; Romans 12:19 - NIV) (LV, Vol. 5, p. 104 ff) This work was presented to Duke George without reference to the author or the city in which it was published. It is said to have pleased him so much, that he presented it to Lucas Cranach saying, "Look, here I have a pamphlet that is so good, truly better than Luther could ever have written." When the painter informed him, that Luther had written the work, even showing him a copy with the name of the author, the Duke is said to have angrily blustered, "It's too bad that such a wicked monk has produced such a good pamphlet."

Fortunately matters would take an unexpected turn so that the threatening storm cloud, which had begun to rise as the two sides were preparing for confrontation, would disappear on the horizon.

The Elector John had arrived at the Diet of Speier with a grand procession of seven hundred people. The Landgrave of Hessia also was adept at garnering respect. Both leaders had divine services held daily in their residences. Thousands of people crowded in on Sundays and Festival Days to hear their preachers. The inscription over John's door boasted the Saxon Elector's coat of arms, "Verbum Dei manet in aeternum" ("God's Word remains forever.").

The diet was ruled by a wondrous array of contradictory issues. The issues swirling through the diet included the need to carry out the edict, complaints against papal abuses, reminders of the dangers posed by the Turk to the empire's borders, and Caesar's new discord with the pope. It seemed as though everything would end in ruin, and the members of the new alliance began to lean on Saxony and Hessia in case things came to blows. But the moderates finally gained the upper hand. The fact was realized that to this point no one had actually enforced the Edict of Worms. A document stated, "If you wish to examine the letters, you will see that there is no count or bishop who has enforced the edict, or who has not been distraught at having to enforce it ad literam (to the letter)." How could they face the Turk if the Germans were taking up their swords against one another?

Thus, a decision was finally reached. They would send ambassadors to Caesar in Spain to request of him to set up a free council as soon as possible, to eliminate the confusion in the church and to permit the enforcement of the edict to be delayed until that time. Since in the meantime similar, even larger, allowances for concessions had arrived from Caesar in Spain, the diet produced a final decision regarding the empire. It said, "In accordance with this, we, the Electors, Dukes, and Imperial Estate Lords, including the ambassadors, have studied and compared and unanimously come to an agreement at this Imperial Diet. <u>We all</u>, including the subjects of our respective territories, <u>want to accomplish no less than</u>, in regard to the edict that went out from Caesar's majesty from the Diet of Worms, for the interval between now and the council or the national assembly, <u>having each of us live, rule, and act, as each of us would hope and trust to be able to answer</u> (*satisfactorily*) <u>to God and to Caesar's majesty.</u> (*The underligning and all italicized words are by the translator.*)

Thus, it was resolved that it be left up to the individual counts and leaders to conduct themselves in matters of faith, as the counts wanted to be held responsible before God. This historic resolution has served as legal basis for further development of the church ever since. It laid down the basis for the state church system, which has continued to this day.

Now the Germans showed how grateful they were for the concession which they had wrested from Caesar. They provided him with powerful support, both in Italy, and on behalf of his brother in Hungary. The evangelically minded field commander, Georg of Frundsberg, marched toward Rome with an army of German soldiers. During this march that old chief commander endured the mutiny of his mercenaries. Having suffered a stroke, he was left behind as the army continued its march. Rome was overpowered two hours before sunset on May 6, 1527. The troops had been deprived of their basic needs for a long time and were seething with rage. They showed it by the terrible plundering they visited on the houses and churches of this rich and luxury filled city. Soldiers, dressed in cardinal robes and similar garb, rode through the city on donkeys and cried out, "Luther should become the pope!"

We have seen how the Elector John, in harmony with the concluding decision regarding the empire, lived and ruled in his territory in such a way as he hoped to be able to give an account before God, and the majesty of Caesar.

We get a similar picture of the Landgrave Philip of Hessia. He likewise pursued a new structure for the church system in his territory. He summoned a number of the pastors of his territory, together with his appointees in the cities and the nobility, to a unifying meeting in Homberg. There a plan was submitted and adopted, according to which evangelical congregations were to be formed throughout the territory. The members of these congregations were to sign up in a register, call their own pastors, hold regular congregational meetings, and practice church discipline according to Matthew 18. The pastors, congregational officers, and representatives of the nobility were to meet annually with the ruler of their territory, when they were to choose visitors and conduct other business. The liturgy for the church service was adopted according to the form of the German Mass by Luther.

Luther, who was given the opportunity to read this plan, regarded such a decision to be premature, for the reasons we have already cited. The landgrave listened to him and did not permit the plan to be put into action. He instead began his reforms with the Saxon visitation pamphlet. In addition, he recognized the great value of his own evangelical school of higher learning. In 1527, he established the University of Marburg, to which he granted the income from the claimed monasteries. This was the first university that had begun without papal consent.

The reformation also proceeded in other areas, growing both in expansion and in depth. In the Franconian-Brandenburg area Margrave Georg also began evangelical organization and received good advice and preachers from Luther. (LV, Vol. 7. p. 141ff). Lutheran worship services were also being held in the territory of Braunschweig and in the cities of Hamburg, Goettingen, and Goslar. The Elector lent Bugenhagen to assist the first two of these named cities, while Luther was seeing to the entire parish office in the Wittenberg city church.

However, the leaders who were hostile to the gospel also continued to attack that gospel even after the Diet of Speier. In Bavaria, confessors of the gospel were martyred by fire and water. Among them was the preacher, Leonhard Kaeser, who was burned at the stake on August 16, 1527. Luther published a report of this martyr's death, which had been sent to him by one of his friends. He published it with a prologue and an epilogue by his own hand.

Luther also sent a message of comfort to the Christians in Halle after the death of their pastor, Winkler, who had been treacherously murdered. In 1528, he wrote them another letter, this one to encourage them to remain faithful to the truth. In its context, he pointed them to the terrible death of a Doctor Krause, who had slashed his throat on All Saints' Day in 1527, out of despair, because he had denied Christ, his Lord.

The Elector Joachim of Brandenburg also raged against the confessors of the pure teaching, even against his own wife Elisabeth. She was a niece of the Elector of Saxony. She had been imprisoned by her husband because she had received Holy Communion in accordance with the words of institution of Christ. She remained there until she fled to Saxony disguised as the wife of a farmer. She did so with the help of her brother, the exiled King of Denmark, and her uncle. She then lived at the Castle Lichtenberg near Wittenberg, where she was befriended by Luther. Her physician, Ratzeberger, also came to Wittenberg. He became one of Luther's trusted friends, and later the Saxon Elector's personal physician.

Duke George remained the same old hostile papist. He continued his oppression of his evangelical subjects and let it be known that he intended to take up arms against his nephew, the Elector, as soon as Caesar would command him to do so. He would never be reconciled with him as long as the Elector remained Lutheran. "Dear God," Luther prayed, "will that mad ruler not quit? If he is to be converted, my Lord Jesus Christ, then convert him. If not, then come soon to our defense against him." Matters had once again become personal between Luther and George. For Duke George had illegally obtained a letter from Luther to Link which contained remarks about the Duke. He demanded an accounting from the author of the letter. When Luther refused, George attacked him harshly with a public writing. In response Luther issued a brief work, "About Secretly Stolen Letters Together with a Psalm Interpreted against Duke George of Saxony." George responded with a printed, "Short Report in Regard to Several Insane Lies, Which Martin Luther Had Issued." In addition, he complained so loudly to the Elector that Luther was forbidden henceforth to allow anything to be printed against George or any other ruler without special permission, since peace with him had been restored again. Caesar Charles, however, remained the most dangerous political enemy of the gospel truth. He had made his peace with the pope again and immediately set sights toward the "extermination of the Lutheran sect."

These, and other signs of the times, produced sinister thoughts, especially for the politician among the evangelical leaders named Philip of Hessi. Otto von Pack, *a scam artist*, a dismissed chancellor and adviser to Count Herzog, one day found him in such depression. As the Landgrave began to share his concerns, he responded with considerable groaning. After some hesitation, he blurted out a tale of some communication that spoke of an alliance which was determined to wage war against the evangelical leaders. He personally offered to obtain and bring the proof documents for this plan in return for sums of wealth and security. In February of 1528, he actually presented the landgrave with a copy of a contract sealed with the Duke's ring. From it emerged the fact that the electors of Mainz and Brandenburg, the counts of Saxony and Bavaria, and a number of bishops, had allied themselves together to attack the Elector of Saxony. If he chose to resist handing over Luther and his followers, they intended to divide his territory among themselves. Then they would drive out the landgrave and transfer his land to Duke George. There were also accurate details as to how this plan was to be carried out.

Philip took immediate steps to counter this plot. He hurried to Weimar to inform the Elector of the danger, since he was the first target of this threat. Neither doubted the accuracy of the information. They immediately formed a military alliance and offered forces to head off the planned attack against themselves. The Saxon troops were already stationed in the Thueringian forest, and the Hessians deployed their officers and their troops, ready to do battle. It seemed as though the bloody conflict was going to begin. All of Germany was on the move.

It was Luther who stood firm against the avalanche of war. Though he did not doubt the accuracy of the information, he refused to permit the Elector to fire away. Instead, he gave his "Gutachten" for the attack to be waited out and to call upon Caesar for protection, but not to go beyond forming the alliance. The other Wittenberg theologians agreed, and the leaders yielded, the Landgrave reluctantly of course. He only gave in when he was convinced he could not rely on John's cooperation.

But when Philip, acting on Luther's advice, published the document agreement, which Pack had provided, the German counts were amazed. Duke George responded quickly in writing, claiming the document to be a gross forgery. Other counts submitted similar excuses. The Landgrave was forced to arrest and condemn Pack, clearly in order to clear himself of any suspicion. He would later admit that he had allowed that traitor to lead him astray, who had shown himself on previous occasions to have been guilty of other such activities. The Evangelicals, especially Melanchthon, loudly lamented that their good work had been stained through excessive haste.

The damage, however, was not curtailed. The bitterness of the Roman counts had increased. That bitterness was being fostered by Caesar's Vice-Chancellor, Waldkirchen, who in the spring traveled from city to city, and from court to court, in an effort to promote the pope's agenda. Rome also reminded Caesar that he should not permit it that future generations would have to read that swarms of heretics had infested Germany under the greatest Caesar.

Woodcut of Philip of Hessia by Brosamer

Chapter 37
The Protéstants

Two Imperial Diets had been scheduled to take place at Regensburg. Nothing happened. One of them had too few people in attendance. The other one was cancelled by Caesar. But a new Imperial Diet was arranged for February 21, 1529, at Speier. The mere announcement of this Diet spurred a higher level of interest. Those involved were warned that the absence of delegates would not matter. Some of the main issues that were to be on the agenda included the renewal of the churches, the call to arms against the Turk, and the disruption of the peace.

As early as the beginning of 1528 Luther had made his thoughts known about the war against the Turk. He had addressed the entire German nations with his work "Concerning the War against the Turk." He sincerely urged all of his people to faithfully and unanimously rally under the banner of God and Caesar, and to advance into battle against the terrible enemy of Christendom, as this was proper for pious counts and their subjects. In it, he sharply scolded those counts who had no respect for Caesar's banner and begrudged Caesar his honor, wanting to be the heroes themselves. He had bitterly mourned the fact that neither Caesar nor the counts were paying attention to their duty to protect their subjects. But for them it was Luther and the gospel who were the Turk.

Those last words were actually being endorsed by the Diet which was assembled at Speier. The imperial delegates arrived at the appointed time. The clerical counts, or their authorized representatives, appeared in very large numbers. The Diet was opened punctually. Immediately the delegates commissioned by Caesar issued the suggestion that the adopted motion of the Diet in 1526, by which the enforcement of the Edict of Worms had been left up to the judgment of the individual authorities, was to be legally rescinded and actual contrary measures be adopted. The members of this committee, to which these suggestions of Caesar were assigned, were by majority of Caesar's opinion. Thus, a recommendation was made which agreed with the imperial directive as follows: Those who had enforced the Edict of Worms should continue to do so. In those territories where the Edict was not honored, there would be no more renewals, and no one should be hindered from reading or hearing the Mass. Rights and income were not to be taken away from the ecclesiastical orders through the ban or a counter ban. Those sects, which were opposed to the Sacrament of the true body and blood, were in no way to be tolerated any more than the Anabaptists.

It was not difficult to guess how the vote of the diet would go, for the evangelicals were very much in the minority. In those days the report from

Speier was "Christ is again in the hands of Caiaphas and Pilate." Thus, it was no surprise that the original position (of Worms) was adopted without change.

It was a foregone conclusion that the evangelical proponents would not submit to this resolution. Even papal cities raised their objections against rescinding of the resolution of the Diet of 1526, for they had also benefited from the peace it had brought them. If they would support the new resolution, the hands of the evangelical proponents would be tied, and the Roman bishops would be free to begin to recapture what they had lost.

Still, in spite of all proposals to the contrary, and in spite of the passionate statement from the Saxon delegate Minkwitz that the Evangelicals would never agree to this resolution, the Catholic majority remained immovable. On April 19th, King Ferdinand appeared at the Diet and declared that the resolution had been adopted as proposed. After further explaining that he was carrying out Caesar's order, Ferdinand and the imperially commissioned delegates left the assembly hall.

After hearing that announcement, the evangelical estate lords immediately withdrew to a nearby room and held a short meeting there. They then returned to the assembly hall where the other estate lords were still gathered and read a protest against the majority resolution. They argued that an attempt to overturn a unanimously adopted resolution of an official Diet through a majority resolution is absolutely invalid.

They added that they would continue to adhere to the previous resolution and conduct themselves accordingly. They stated that especially in matters that pertain to the honor of God, and the salvation of souls, each man would have to give an account before God for himself. Finally, they requested that if the resolution to which they objected was entered into the official minutes of the diet, their protest should also be entered. The protesters were John of Saxony, Philip of Hessia, George of Brandenburg, Ernst of Braunschweig-Lueneburg, and Wolfgang of Anhalt. They were joined by fourteen imperial cities.

But King Ferdinand decisively rejected also this petition. Hence the "Protéstants" took it one step farther. On the following Sunday, April 25th, with all solemnity, they presented a "Document of Appeal" in which they, dissenting from the majority, appealed to Caesar for the next free council or a congress of the German nation, as the previous Diet had stated.

The total hostility of the Catholic majority moved the establishment of an evangelical defense alliance ever nearer. As a result, Saxony, Hessia, and the cities of Nuernberg, Ulm, and Strassburg drew up a contract already at Speier. The delegates were to discuss its implementation further when they would meet in Rotach in June.

Luther took little note of the terrible resolution of the Imperial Diet. When he was informed of the Alliance, he disapproved of it for two reasons.

First, he believed that a Military alliance against Caesar was one against the higher authority, which had been established by God. It was therefore not permissible, even though that authority was again as tyrannical now as it had been years before. In addition, he regarded the alliance to have grown out of human fear and trust in man's ability, rather than out of trust in God.

How different his confidence was! He expressed it in the words of his heroic hymn, "A Mighty Fortress Is Our God," which he had written at this very time when the most horrible rumors had progressed all the way to Wittenberg. Luther also wrote the hymn's melody. But he had still one more objection to the alliance, namely, the participation of a city like Strassburg. In order to understand his objection, we need to turn our attention to something else of great importance that happened during that decade.

Chapter 38
The Swarming Sacramentarians

We had previously learned how Carlstadt had falsified the real presence of Christ's body and blood as early as 1524, and how the teaching about the Sacrament had become a bone of contention between him and Luther. Luther had issued a detailed refutation of Carlstadt's error in the second part of his work, "Against the Heavenly Prophets." The false teaching had appeared publicly at the beginning of 1525. From the onset, Luther had described it as a piece of the swarmer's spirituality, for which "Mrs. Hulda," the human intellect, played its role. (for "swarmers" *See translator's note pp. 222-223*). It was that very thing, that Carlstadt abandoned the Word of God and put reason in place of it as its "madam" master, which was the most dangerous of what Carlstadt was teaching concerning the Sacrament. "Dr. Carlstadt," he wrote, "had now become more insane than the papists ever were. The papists have always been quick in taking passages out of Scripture, even though they used them incorrectly. And so, the papists still confess that in the Sacrament it is not reason which is to be followed, but God's Word. But Dr. Carlstadt prattles on and gathers together everything that reason can reveal, teach, or judge on the subject." Where that reasonable approach must lead Luther explained, "Because they are going down the path, on which they have no desire to honor God's Word with their faith or what they read by the simple structure of the language, but with sophistic reason, measuring and mastering it with pointed subtlety, you shall see that they shall actually come to the point where they shall deny that Christ is God. For according to human reason, it sounds just as foolish to say that man is God as to say that bread is body. Since they deny the one, they will very soon also deny the other. This is exactly what the devil is looking for. He has led them away from Scripture and into their reason in order to restore all heresy.

Earlier he had written, "Let's say that a person wishes to deal with faith by first carrying our thinking into Scriptures, and then to direct Scripture according to our thoughts, only looking for that which the majority holds in its common mind. Then no article of faith will remain. There is no one in Holy Scripture (i.e. of those *who belong to the Christian Faith Family, the Church*) whom God has not placed above reason. (*By cancelling the two negatives in this statement, it would read, " ... For everyone has been placed above [beyond] reason by God in Scripture."*)

This is a basic element which reveals Dr. Carlstadt's error. He talks about faith and the Word of God in a way which reason happily and willingly accepts. Yet it sets itself against the whole of God's Word and the articles of faith." What was especially reprehensible to Luther was the way in which

Carlstadt was using Holy Scripture. He did not let Scripture stand as it is, but took from it or added to it as it pleased him.

Thus, Luther turned Carlstadt's use of "... The flesh counts for nothing, ..." (John 6:63 NIV) against him in this writing, "Against the Heavenly Prophets." He states that Christ does not say, "My flesh is of no use," but, "The flesh is of no use." With this statement Jesus is not openly referring to his flesh, of which he says so much more, "... My flesh is real food ..." (John 6:55 NIV).

In contrast, Luther puts forth a simple statement. He wrote, "Where Holy Scripture sets forth something to be believed, a person is not to stray from the words as they are stated. He is not to turn from the context in which they occur, unless an expressed article of faith forces a different interpretation or different setting for the Word. Otherwise what would the Bible become?" Carlstadt would make an application of a spiritual union with a reference which, in context, talks about a physical union. He did so to make it fit his own reason, or to not have to submit himself to such a passage of Scripture. Luther then sent him packing with the statement, "It would be good and pleasant for me to also do this, which I could well do when a passage proves too difficult for me, a passage which speaks of physical actions and beats me over the head to make my brain reel, that I could add to it and say, it does not apply to me; he is speaking of spiritual things. Then I would be free and would not need to give any explanation as proof. It would be easy to be a heavenly prophet. Then, if I would be forced to provide proof, I would stand there like butter in the sun. I would sweat a few drops on this account and reply that it seemed correct to me. Thus, this passage (*I assume Luther is here referring to I Corinthians 11:24, See NIV*) of Paul stands as solid as rock. (...Now, let him who is a devourer of iron rip out a notch with his bare teeth; I shall watch."

Everything which Luther had applied to Carlstadt in his writing, "Against the Heavenly Prophets," also put Luther in contention with another opponent. This opponent was Zwingli.

Ulrich Zwingli had been the preacher in the huge cathedral of Zurich, Switzerland, since January 1, 1519. Previously he had been a pastor in Glarus, then a military chaplain in two Italian campaigns, and then the assistant pastor in Einsiedeln. He, too, had delivered powerful testimony against the wrongs of indulgences, which the indulgence peddler, Samson, was selling in Switzerland. From the very first day of his service in Zurich he had explained how he wanted to make Scripture the foundation of his preaching. He immediately began to interpret the Gospel of Matthew from his pulpit. He had won the Council of Zurich to his side by way of public debates, and with their support, the public divine services were restructured according to Zwingli's understanding. They had done away with processions and Corpus Christi Day. Communion was set free to be celebrated in both kinds. Monks and nuns were allowed to leave their cloisters. Priests had gotten married, as had Zwingli himself. There had also been some stormy confrontations, and only through the intervention of the government had the destruction of images been avoided. But Zwingli himself, and then with the approval of the council, had proposed the removal of the images and crucifixes from the churches. Mass was completely discontinued on Maundy Thursday, 1525. In its place there was the distribution of the host and the wine to the members of the congregation. They knelt in their places in the pews, and the preacher and the church council members carried around the wafers on their plates and the wine in wooden chalices.

But this particular type and sort of distribution is not the only peculiarity we find in the Zwinglian type of Holy Communion.

When Carlstadt had emerged with his new doctrine of the Lord's Supper, he had found acceptance here and there. In this context Luther had been informed that Carlstadt's behavior had had an impact in Strassburg. In Reutlingen, Pastor Hermann had taken Carlstadt's side, while his colleague, Alber, stood with Luther. Alber was exchanging letters with Zwingli, and Zwingli responded to his friend in Reutlingen on November 16th. What he had taught earlier in vague terms, he presented here in clear form. He stated that the breaking and eating of the bread in the Lord's Supper is purely symbolic, as Christ was to have indicated in the words of institution: "This is my body." The sense of the little word "is" was to be understood as "signifies."

Just like Carlstadt, Zwingli also supported his doctrine with the passage of John 6:63, which has nothing at all to do with Holy Communion. Through the urging of the author, copies of this letter were sent to more than 500 people. One of those copies came into Luther's hands. An open confrontation between Luther and Zwingli took place when Luther issued his work, "Against the Heavenly Prophets", for Zwingli also took a hit in that work. And when he wrote his book, "About the True and False Religion," in March 1525, what he had written to Alber could be found in that work, almost word for word.

When a controversy arose between Zwingli and a papist, who was the city secretary at Gruet, about this teaching presented in his book, Zwingli asserted that he had recent special enlightenment from God in a dream. It took place on April 13th, while he was sleeping in the morning. It seemed to him as though a person had stood next to him and asked why he was not using the words of Exodus 12:11 (NIV) against his opponent. Those words state, "For it is the Lord's Passover." He then woke up and remembered this direction with thanks to God. It was clear to him that he had received this reference in a miraculous way. It showed how the Holy Scripture used the little word "is" for "signifies," in that the Passover Lamb was not truly the passing over of the Lord, but it only "signified" this.

That this "enlightenment" could not have come from God we can easily see. In that passage Scripture does not use the word "passah" in regard to the passing over of the Lord, but Scripture uses it in regard to the Passover Lamb itself. Thus, in this passage not only is "is" used for "signify" as little as in any other usage, but this passage contains no figurative language at all. But Zwingli remained adamant that a divine revelation had been given to him in this dream. He tells the story himself in a "Postscript" for that particular book. From that time on he personally availed himself of that passage, loving to cite it and its false application in defense of his error.

That Latin "Postscript about Holy Communion" Zwingli issued in German at the beginning of 1526, after a "Clear Instruction about the Evening Meal of Christ." In these writings he sought, in part, to prove through the premise produced by human reason that the real presence of the body and blood of Christ in Holy Communion is impossible. He did so by adding other passages of Scripture to support the idea that Christ's words of institution were to be taken figuratively. He said that since Christ's body had left earth and ascended into heaven it could not be on earth. He claimed that it was impossible for a real body, as Christ had, to be in various places at the same time. What's more, if Christ's flesh and blood were present in Holy Communion, you would be able to see and to taste his flesh. For these and other reasons he posited that in the words of institution it is clear that a person must take the word "is" as "signifies", just as in other passages of Scripture. He cites as an example where Christ says, "I am the vine"(John 15:5 – NIV) and "I am the gate for the sheep," (John 10:9 - NIV) where the true meaning of the word is, "I signify the vine," etc.

Thus, we essentially see the same attitudes, which we found in Carlstadt. However, since Zwingli contended his mastery over Scripture through his reason, it stands out even more. Now what Luther had declared in opposition to Carlstadt concerning the danger of the theology of human reason found its confirmation in Zwingli. He applied the same method of dealing with the doctrine of Holy Communion to other matters of faith. Both in the book, "About the True and False Religion," and in another writing issued the same year, "About Baptism," he would not allow the efficacy of baptism for the one being baptized stand as valid. Baptism was to be merely a sign of belonging to the people of God. He also claimed to bring amazing insights to light regarding the person of Christ and his work of redemption. And he described inherited sin as a frailty of human nature.

Luther also recognized the "other spirit" with which Zwingli would speak and warned his listeners about it in his sermons. Bugenhagen was the next one to write against Zwingli. But it soon became apparent that some more powerful intervention was needed. Zwingli was rapidly gaining followers in southern Germany. Capito and Butzer were doing the same in Strassburg, while in Basel Oecolampad published a work in the spirit of Zwingli. He likewise denied the real presence of the body and blood in Holy

Communion. Carlstadt had erred through a false reference to the word "this" (as in "This is my body") and Zwingli had distorted the words of institution by misreading the little word "is." However, this new contester directed his thoughts to the word "body" and explained that this word stands for "picture or sign of the body." "Mrs. Hulda, mistress reason" stood by his side, not satisfied with the fact that the body of Christ can be present in many places at the same time.

In addition to these three false teachings concerning the words of Holy Communion, a fourth was added around the same time. This came from Caspar Schwenkfeld of Schlesien, and his partner, Valentin Krautwald. They simply turned the words of institution around and alleged that Christ had meant to say, "My body is this," that is, bread or food, and "My blood is this," that is, wine or a drink, as Christ had spoken elsewhere, "My body is the true food and my blood is the true drink." And in the days, that followed two more false teachings were added.

We shall soon see that Luther was not merely an observer who didn't involve himself with these sacramentarians of many colors. It was immediately apparent to him that he would have nothing to do with their doctrine. He quickly understood that these men of reason were evil enemies of the truth just as much as the papists. There were two reasons why he had not already produced a detailed refutation against Zwingli and his allies. First, he didn't have the time to spare. Second, he had already left no doubt as to what he taught and believed about the Sacrament in his writing against the Bohemian brothers, "About the Worshipping of the Holy Body of Christ,"

Picture according to an old copper plate
M. Huldricus Zwinglius, Reformatur et Pastor Ecclesia. Tigurina

as well as in his writing against the "Heavenly Prophets."

At the same time, he was certain that he could not remain silent in regard to the teachings of Zwingli and Oecolampad. And he also wrote to the Strassburg preachers, Capito and Būcer, who had tried to keep Luther out of the public fray against them in a friendly face to face conversation. He had replied to their messenger, "I ask my dear gentlemen of Strassburg to diligently continue to talk so that they won't mistake the light of reason for the light of the Holy Ghost. A person can easily make a mistake in this and, when that happens, it is of the devil. My conscience is quiet and safe by remaining with the Word. If we were permitted to thus make a martyr of Scripture, nothing sure would be left for us. I will always look at those who maintain that the body is not present as being outside of the faith. I take note of the fact that they believe that I will not yield out of shame and pride. They are certainly mistaken. They say that I am also a human being. This I admit and, even though I stand all alone as I am, I will still not be easily moved away from Scripture." So Luther recognized Zwingli and his followers as enemies. As long as they held to their position, peace with them was impossible.

Oecolampad had sent his writing to a number of his friends among the brothers in Swabia. But instead of being won over to his side, they, 14 in all, with John Brenz as their leader, responded with a refutation under the title, "Swabian Syngramma." Luther wrote a foreword for its German edition which was obtained by Agricola. "Well," he wrote, "since I still don't have the time to give special consideration to refute this spirit, I shall confess my faith with this introduction. Those who are willing to take this warning to heart, I counsel in truth that they be on their guard against these false prophets, who call our God a baked God, a God made out of bread. ... Still, they are a patient, pliant people. First of all, this sect is so fruitful that within one year they have acquired five or six heads. First there was Carlstadt with his tuto ("this"); the next was Huldrich Zwingli with his significat '("signifies")'; the third was John Oecolampadius with his figure corporis (picture of the body); the fourth inverts the text; the fifth proceeds to replace the words; the sixth has not yet been born and tosses dice with the words; the seventh may also yet appear and shuffle the cards. Each one wants to become the master in this field."

"Therefore, I shall render my judgment. I know that it is true, though it will cause them great grief. For in this case I understand the faith and the devil very well. There are two reasons for their error: one, this doctrine is a very clumsy thing in the light of reason; two, they believe it is unnecessary for Christ's body and blood to be in the bread and the wine. Since they have tinted glasses over their eyes, they come trudging up to Scripture to see how they can add their reason to it and to pull the Scriptures in line with their opinion. There it stands revealed. There the words cannot be understood as they are simply stated. One must stretch them and bend them. "Finally," he declared, "If God grants me the time I shall write about this myself." In accordance with this announcement, later that year there appeared from Luther's pen a "Sermon about the Sacrament of the Body and Blood of Christ against the Swarming Spirits" in which he further distinguished between the "two reasons for the error." (LV, Vol. 5, p.5 ff.) Zwingli responded with a sermon,"Friendly Forbearance and Declining". ("Fruendliche Verglimpfung und Ableinung"; in Swiss-German speech. *"Ableinung" is assumed to be the same as "Ablehnung", namely, "Declining", as in declining a call. If this is what he meant with Ableinung, then "Verglimpfung must have meant something like "misconstruing" or "Comparing".*) But Luther was already prepared with a longer work which he issued in the spring of 1527 under the title, "That These Words of Christ: 'This is my body,' Still Stand Firm against the Swarmers' Spirits." (LV, Vol.17, 18 p. 7 ff.)

"The common proverb is so true: 'The devil is a skilled, thousand-fold expert.'" So Luther began that book. He first states that Satan has ripped Scripture apart and twisted it through various kinds of false teachers, until "no one allows himself to be satisfied with it, but everyone digs himself a hole in whatever direction his snout is pointing." So, it was claimed that Scripture is not enough, but "the councils and orders of the fathers and commentary have to be added to it." Then the devil did away with Scripture completely. Now that Scripture has again been brought to light, the devil has sown his seed in secret, "so that while we battle against human vanity in front of us, they fall upon our army from behind. They raise rebellion and rage against us, so that we might all the more easily fall between two enemies.

"But he will not leave it at this. He begins with the least, with the Sacraments, even though he has already ripped up Scripture into ten pits and misleadings in regard to the same issue. But he will continue to attack more articles, as his eyes are already glistening with the idea that baptism, inherited sin, and Christ are nothing. There will once again be such a <u>trashing</u> of Scripture, *(or, such a pile of junk [like, perhaps, in your attic] – the German "Geruempel")* with so much discord and so many hordes, that we might also say with St. Paul that the secret of evil is already at work. It is truly the same devil who is now attacking us through the swarmers with their blasphemy against the holy, highly honored Sacraments of our Lord Jesus Christ. They want to turn it into a mere eating of bread and drinking of wine for a 'meal-sign' or a memorial for Christians. So, they dream it up, or find it pleasing to them, that the Lord's body and blood should not be present, even though the bare and clear words stand there and say: Eat, this is my body; which words still stand there, firm and unbitten by them.

"I have, truly and with all diligence, opposed Carlstadt in regard to these issues. Thus, whoever does not want to err should help himself from that work against such a demonic spirit. But my dear swarmers despise me so gloriously that they do not regard me as worthy enough to give a diligent response. Thus, I shall now once again take a stand against the devil and his swarmers, not for their sake, but for the sake of the weak and the simple. For I have no hope that these teachers of heresy or swarming shall be converted. If that were possible, surely, enough has already been written for them to be converted. It has never been heard that a person who invented a heresy was ever converted.

"Even though I shall convert no master swarmer, yet if it is God's will for me to set forth the truth clearly and dry enough before their eyes that there will be no lack of their students being turned away, or the simple and the weak to be strengthened, preserving them from the poison. If I do not succeed in this as God wills, then I will at least with this have given witness and have confessed before God and the entire world that I am not in favor of these blasphemers of the Sacrament, these swarmers. I have never been for them, nor will I ever be for them, if it is the will of God ("ob Gott will,"). I will have washed my hands of the blood of those souls they have stolen from Christ by misleading and murdering them with such poison. I am innocent of this and have done my job.

"Thus, to despise the devil, I shall once again assert no more than the one passage, 'This is my body,' in regard to the Meal. I shall see what the swarmers have taken away from these words. The main reason for doing this is that they are slippery and inconsistent, turning themselves around and over into a thousand corners every time I ask them in God's name to stick to this passage and answer correctly. The other passages I shall leave for another time."

He then gave direct attention to this passage and his opponents' assertions. He shone the spotlight so thoroughly on the entire matter that he could truthfully conclude with the words: "I will leave it at this for now, until they come again. For the passage, "This is my body," still stands firm against all of their swarming. Praise to God, this is what I have upheld with this current writing. God grant that they will be converted to the truth. If not, then they will have to write useless ropes with which they will tie themselves up and deliver themselves into my hands. Amen."

While Luther was writing his book, Zwingli was also busy with a paper in Latin. He directed it straight at Martin Luther under the title, "An Amicable Commentary about Dealing with the Evening Supper." When Luther's work, "That These Words, etc." had reached Zwingli's hands, he responded immediately in German under the title, "That These Words of Christ: 'This Is My Corpse' etc. Will Have Their Own Old Meaning Eternally and What M. Luther with His Last Book and the Pope's Understanding Did not at All Teach nor Prove." Oecolampad also came out with a counter argument, from which it became apparent that he had not allowed himself at all to be convinced through Luther's work, just like Zwingli.

After receiving these writings Luther knew immediately what he would do. One more time he would highlight, in detail and thoroughly, his own teaching and the objections of his opponents, and then let them rest under the judgment of God. And so, in March 1528, appeared his large "Confession About the Supper of Christ." He explained its contents himself with the words: "I want to take up three points in this publication.

"First, we have given a warning from our side with proof that this swarming spirit did not at all respond to my basic statements.

"Second, to deal with the passages which teach about the holy Sacrament.

"Third, all of my articles of faith testify against these and all other heresies. This is so that they may not one day or after my death boast that Luther held to the same teaching as they, since they have already made that claim in a number of articles."

This confession about the holy Lord's Supper was Luther's most detailed, most thorough, and most careful of all of his works. He wrote like a person who was speaking his last words. He began by placing his pen to paper in the spirit of Psalm 25:21, "May integrity and uprightness protect me, because my hope is in you ... O God." He concluded with the words, "What I have spoken here is not enough. My books will give sufficient witness, especially those which have been issued during the last four or five years. And so I ask all upright hearts to be my witnesses. May they pray for me that I might remain firm in the faith to the end of my life. If I say anything other than what God wants, I declare that it is nothing. I confess openly that it is untrue and inspired by the devil. To such an end please help me, my Lord and Savior, Jesus Christ, blessed eternally. Amen."

His chief enemies would not allow themselves to be converted even through this writing. Zwingli and Oecolampad at once issued responses. They even dedicated them to the Landgrave Philip of Hessia, and to the Elector John of Saxony. They hoped to win both leaders over to their side. Truly Zwingli expected that in a little while all of Germany, France, Spain, and Italy would come over to his cause. In this hope, of course, he had miscalculated. Nevertheless, many took his side, especially in the southern German cities. Strassburg, Ulm, Constance, and Lindau embraced the doctrine of the Swiss theologians. The division which Satan had brought into existence was never healed. This applied especially to the leaders. And that is what Luther had foretold with saddened heart.

Finally, Carlstadt also fled to be sheltered under the wings of the Swiss. With the permission of the Elector he had moved to Kemberg and was working as a grocer. However, the condition under which he would be allowed to return to Saxony, namely, that he would remain silent, was unbearable for him. Since he was no longer allowed to speak publicly in Saxony, he slipped out of the territory, leaving his family behind. He did so after beginning to fight against Luther's doctrine and to deride it. He had already rescinded his retraction. Now he traveled around Holstein and Friesland, preached against the pastors of Wittenberg, and led many astray. He especially raged against his benefactor Luther, and he did so with venomous hostility. When he was no longer safe in Friesland, he moved to Strassburg. We later find him in Basel and Zurich. Zwingli and Oecolampad were full of admiration for him and testified that he was far from being a sectarian. But even in Switzerland it took a long time before he found rest. He found rest at last as a preacher and professor of theology in Basel, where the former destroyer of images, but now lay member, lived out the rest of his days as a Zwinglian.

Chapter 39
The Marburg Colloquy

Since the Swiss cities of Strassburg and Ulm were included among the cities, which, together with the Lutheran counts, had protested against the imperial conclusion at Speier, we now understand the second concern that Luther had with the alliance. This is the alliance to which the Protéstants had agreed and concerning which there was to be more discussion at Rotach. He informed his Elector that if a person were to ally oneself with those people, he would also be allied with their false teaching and would become party to their strange sins. Melanchthon, who at Speier had agreed to allow the Zwinglians to be included, realized his error and now stood with the rest of the Wittenberg theologians on Luther's side. The Nuernberg theologians and the city's magistrates also recognized that a person could not join with the Zwinglians without sinning.

As a result, the Elector John was convinced of the rightness of his theologians' position and acted accordingly. He did, of course, send his representatives to Rotach, but with strict instruction to only listen and then to report back to him. The result was that nothing was accomplished at Rotach. A second meeting, which was to be held at Schwabach, did not materialize, and the delegates from Strassburg and Ulm who did appear had made their journey for nothing. When the Landgrave attempted to negotiate with the Elector via letter, he also failed to get the Elector to agree.

Philip, who had anticipated this resistance, had already taken steps in the meantime to achieve his goal of bringing the geographically higher cities into the alliance. Already at Speier, when the arguments against joining with the Swiss were being offered, he had thought about a reconciliation between the two sides. He had written to Zwingli about it and spoken to Melanchthon face to face. When Melanchthon heard of how the Landgrave suggested the meeting with Zwingli should take place, he immediately objected. When Philip also found Luther to be completely opposed to the idea, he shared his plans with the Elector in a letter.

The Swiss and their allies had a different reaction to this plan. They were already halfway counting Phillip as their own and hoped to win him over completely to their side through a discussion in his presence. Indeed, their hopes went even farther. Their overestimation of Philip's intent for the council of the evangelical counts let them nourish their hope that winning the Hessian would also draw in the Elector of Saxony and the Margrave of Brandenburg. Zwingli's eager willingness to participate in the Landgrave's plans was especially based on the fact that the two were very similar in two respects. Both were politicians. Luther had always been afraid of Philip's political acumen, and Zwingli's politics would cost him his life. In addition, both of them lacked a tender conscience when it came to differences in doctrine and matters of faith. That description also applied to those from Strassburg, who had earlier appealed to Luther by subtly covering up their differences in doctrine, and who would now have been willing to enter into an alliance with the Lutherans without establishing doctrinal unity.

The theologians from Wittenberg understood Philip of Hessia sufficiently to know that their convictions were not in line with his understanding. They would have loved to have their Elector refuse their participation in the colloquy. But, even though he strongly shared the conviction of his theologians, this Count could not respond to the Landgrave's pressure with a resounding, "No!" With the Elector's consent Philip thus extended a formal invitation to a "friendly non-debatable discussion," which was to take place at the castle in Marburg on St. Michael's Day. Luther still held no hope that such a discussion would bear fruit. Already ten years earlier he had learned in Leipzig that such negotiations between avowed opponents would bring little gain and all sorts of regret. Still, he did not want to appear as the one who was unwilling to pursue peace, so with a resisting attitude he yielded to the ongoing pressure of the Landgrave. He would, as he wrote to him, render the service he had sought. He must have known very well that Luther would not yield to Zwingli; and if they would not yield, they would part without producing any fruit. (* S. "LV," vl. 7, p. 138ff.)

Zwingli was afraid that the Council of Zurich would hold him back from the dangerous journey through hostile Catholic territory. Hence, he departed as the night shadows began to fall without taking leave of anyone, not even saying anything about it to his wife. He traveled through Basel, where he took along Oecolampad, and through Strassburg, where he took along Būcer, Hedia, and Counselor Sturm. They arrived in Marburg on September 29th. The next day the Wittenberg men arrived. This group was made up of Luther, Melanchthon, Cruciger, and Mykonius of Gotha. Luther had left the wagon at the Inn of the Bear, but like the rest accepted the invitation of the Landgrave, who was hosting all those invited with a brilliant reception in his castle. As Luther was walking up the steps to the castle he is supposed to have spoken Latin words on every step, "This is! This is!", as though he had wanted to keep those words firmly fixed before him. Two days after the arrival of the men from Wittenberg came Osiander of Nuernberg, Brenz from Hall in Swabia, and Stephan Agricola from Augsburg. Numerous other guests arrived who had wanted to attend the discussion. Carlstadt had also sought to be admitted. But the Landgrave made his admission dependent upon the agreement of the men from Wittenberg, and they denied it.

The day after the arrival of the men from Wittenberg the Landgrave had arranged a preliminary meeting with the leaders of the two sides. This included Luther and Oecolampad, and Melanchthon and Zwingli. The actual colloquy took place on the 2nd and 3rd of October. Zwingli had asked that anyone who wanted to listen should be allowed to attend. But Luther properly objected. He knew that the ability to properly evaluate both sides of this discussion would require educated minds. This was especially true because, as in this case, the arguments on the side of reason would easily win victory for themselves. It almost sounds like a joke in regard to Luther when it was alleged, as often was the case, that he had no confidence in his own position. The fact that he was more concerned that the listeners would properly understand the situation is shown as follows. Zwingli wanted the Latin language to be used for the discussion. But some of the lords, who had to be in attendance, had little if any acquaintance with that language. Luther wanted the discussion to take place in German, which everyone could understand. So, the Landgrave decided that the number of listeners would be limited and that German would be used.

At 6 o'clock, on the morning of October 2nd, the actual discussion began. It opened in one of the finest rooms of the castle when Chancellor Feige addressed the participants of the discussion with a speech. Then Luther, who was seated with Melanchthon, Zwingli, and Oecolampad at the same table, spoke first. He wanted not only the doctrine of Holy Communion, but the entire sum of Christian doctrine to be thoroughly pursued. He wanted the assurance that it was clearly understood that he was concerned not only with the main issue of the dispute, but, as he had explained in his writings, that he had found other issues among his opponents which were not completely pure. But Zwingli made the appeal that he had already discussed those things with Melanchthon, and that this meeting had been called for a debate about Holy Communion. Oecolampad explained that he knew of a difference between himself and the men of Wittenberg only in regard to the teaching of the Lord's Supper. And so the discussion proceeded directly to that topic. Luther was the spokesman for the Wittenberg men. Melanchthon would only jump in here and there with brief remarks. On the other side, Zwingli and Oecolampad spoke interchangeably. As this discussion of the doctrine of Holy Communion began and Luther was preparing to speak, he took a piece of chalk out of his pocket. He lifted up the velvet table cloth and wrote on the table with plain letters the words, "This is my body." Those words stood fast for him and would continue to stand fast. He did not want to allow himself to be separated from these words by anything.

On the other hand, Zwingli and Oecolampad continued to refer to the words of Jesus in John 6, which they applied in an entirely false manner. They always offered their proofs by way of reason; namely that if the body of Jesus were a true body, it could not be in many places at the same time and that the physical presence of the body and blood of Christ was unnecessary. Therefore, the words, "This is my body," (I Corinthians 11:24 NIV) are to be understood figuratively. They supported this idea with other passages in which Scripture does speak figuratively. They referred to this as the testing of Luther's explanation of Holy Scripture.

Luther, however, held fast to the point that the words of the Sacrament did not need any explanation, but were to be taken as they are stated. He added that a person may not pursue what they were discussing; it had to be left up to Christ how he could be present with his body and blood in the Supper, and to trust in his omnipotence that he would also verify what he had promised in his words of institution. The "bronze wall" which Zwingli always wanted to build out of John 6:63 (NIV), "the flesh counts for nothing," Luther demolished using one little word, "my." He stated that Christ did not say, "My flesh counts for nothing," and that it would be a terrible thing to say that Christ's flesh counts for nothing. Luther also did not allow himself to be handcuffed by quotations from the church fathers. A man dare not let go of God's Word for the sake of the fathers.

So, the debate proceeded, back and forth, all day Saturday and all day Sunday. The only break was observed during the morning hours of Sunday, during which the divine service was conducted. Luther preached clearly and powerfully about righteousness through faith in introducing the gospel, without reference to the doctrinal dispute. That dispute continued during the rest of the morning, and when evening began to approach it was obvious that no agreement would be reached. So, the debate was brought to an end. Throughout the discussions the speakers on both sides had made strong efforts to remain polite. "Dearest lord," "Doctor," "Sir," "You Loved Ones" were forms with which they addressed each other. Only once did Luther become forceful. For when Zwingli again injected the passage of John 6 and Luther had again explained that it didn't belong in this discussion, Zwingli had countered, "No, dear doctor, this place is breaking your neck." That hit Luther like a blow to the head. He became rude and sharply replied, "You are not in Switzerland now, but in Hessia. Here necks are not broken that way." But Zwingli offered that he had used the expression as a figure of speech which was common in his homeland, and the Landgrave also added calming words to this encounter.

Now that the discussion was to end, Luther declared once more that he would remain in his faith. He asked Zwingli's pardon, if he had been too harsh. He too was made of flesh and blood. Zwingli also asked Luther's forgiveness for the harshness that had escaped him, asserting that he had always been minded toward peace and concord. At that moment tears came to his eyes. That was the outward conclusion. But the gap between them had not been filled, and they also expressed that fact to each other. In gratitude for his opponent's civility, Luther spoke the following farewell, "We shall let you go and commend you to the righteous judgment of God. He will decide who is right. Pray God to convert you." Oecolampad replied, "May you also so pray, for you are in need of the same."

Then Counselor Sturm of Strassburg stood and addressed the landgrave who had attended the entire colloquy with great interest. "Highborn count, gracious lord," he said, "Luther raised some issues at the beginning of the discussion which might be understood by some as rude or accusatory for an honorable city like Strassburg. He implied that we were not teaching correctly about the Trinity, original sin, justification by faith, and others. If I were to remain silent, then we, who were appointed by our city council to be present here, would return home and be considered to be guilty of and burdened by not only one, but two or more false teachings. I therefore ask of you, gracious count, to grant Martin Butzer the chance to respond to this accusation." That took place. After Butzer had explained what was being taught in Strassburg, about such things, Luther was to testify as to whether he was correct. But Luther opined that he did not wish to be the preceptor (professor) of Strassburg and could not give such testimony since he did not know how it might be misused. When Butzer then made a plea for Luther to accept them as brothers, Luther replied that he could not. He said that they had a different spirit than he. He stated that if a person simply believed the Word in one place only to criticize it and abuse it in another, then they could not be of one and the same spirit.

The Landgrave would have liked to have the discussion go on, even though what he had desired to be accomplished was not accomplished. But he had to admit that little more could be expected. What's more, it was reported that a dangerous illness, called the English Sweat, was approaching. As a result, he decided to continue negotiations in private and allowed the colloquy to end.

But before the theologians journeyed home from Marburg, the landgrave succeeded in entering their names under a mutual confession. On the 4th of October, Luther wrote to his wife,

"Dear Sir Kate, know that our friendly discussion at Marburg has come to an end. We are united on most issues except that the contrarians wanted to retain mere bread in the Supper and to confess Christ spiritually in it. Today the Landgrave was asking whether we could be united, or even if we cannot be united, nevertheless, be brothers and regard each other as members of Christ. The landgrave is working mightily in that direction. But we do not wish to be called brothers or members. To be peaceful and kind, this we do want."

That is how it was. After Philip had talked with them individually he brought the parties together once more on Monday. Luther made himself available to draw up a number of articles, in regard to which they could allow themselves to be considered united. That is how the 15 Marburg Articles came to be. They dealt with the Trinity, the Person of Christ, Original Sin, Faith and Righteousness, the Word of God, Baptism, Good Works, Confession, the Higher Authorities, Ceremonies, Infant Baptism,and Holy Communion. Luther had chosen clear and plain words without rudeness. The last article reads as follows: "For the 15th point, we all believe and hold regarding the Supper of our dear Lord Jesus Christ that both kinds be used in accordance with the institution. In addition, we hold that the mass is not a work with which one can derive grace for another, dead or alive; that the Sacrament of the Altar is a Sacrament of the true body and blood of Jesus Christ, and that above all the spiritual participation of the same body and blood is needed by each Christian. The same way in which the Word of the Almighty God was given, so the use of the Sacrament has been given and established in order that weak consciences be prompted to faith and love through the Holy Spirit."

These, then, were the Articles, concerning which unity was declared, and the Landgrave was of the opinion that he had finally achieved his goal. Yet, he still believed that what was missing was for the parties to recognize each other as brothers, and he continued to strive toward that end, as was stated in the letter. Zwingli and his allies also pleaded for such recognition, with Zwingli tearfully extending his brotherly hand. But Luther could not do the same because of the chasm that remained. If he had, he would have done that for which he had admonished the Swiss to regard those as brothers, whose doctrine they had rejected. He declared that they must not have much regard for the teaching which they themselves were holding.

For Luther his doctrine was divine truth. He could not call someone a brother who, when faced with the clear words of Scripture, was persisting in rejecting the truth. He stood by his statement, "You have a different spirit than we," and rejected the brotherly hand. May God reward him as a faithful witness of the truth (see Matthew 5:12), who without regret for the friendship of man or the favor of princes paid honor to the divine Word. If Luther had softened at Marburg and yielded, he would have driven a blade through his life's work and would have allowed himself to be driven from the fortress from which he had defied the papacy. He would have agreed to give the lordship of God's Word over to human reason, the lordship he had victoriously taken away from the pope and councils. The words of his heroic song, "The Word they still shall let remain," would now have been sung with bitter disdain.

His steadfastness was not hampered by his brothers. They were completely of the same mind. The following words were added to the fifteen articles as a conclusion:

"In so far as we have not, at this time, reconciled with each other on the issue as to whether the true body and blood of Christ are physically present in the bread and wine, nevertheless each side should show Christian love to the other. They should do so as much as each conscience can endure. Both sides should diligently beseech the Almighty God so that he, through his Spirit, will confirm in us true understanding. Amen." The Lutherans had insisted on the inclusion of the words, "as much as each conscience can endure," and Luther wished to acknowledge the love shown as merely the love which a Christian even owes to his enemies. The Landgrave also achieved the agreement that the heavy war of pens would not be renewed, and Luther personally saw this as an asset. The Marburg Articles went to print immediately after the signatures had been added at the bottom on October 4th.

Luther reported on the proceedings and their conclusion to his congregation in Wittenberg from the pulpit. He praised the friendliness of his opponents and declared that it had gone much better than they had expected. "But," he said, "the fact that Christ's real body and blood are there in truth, they still cannot believe. They wish to be our brothers. We had to reject them in this at this time and could not consent. If we were to receive them as brothers and sisters, we would have to consent to their teaching. As much as we did not like to deny them, we showed that we would show love to them until God would bring them closer to us, for we should even love our enemies. Whoever wants to report this in an evil way let him do so. They remain in their belief. May God enlighten them. They patch together, adorn, and soft-pedal the idea that they are not denying the presence of the true body and blood of Christ. Thus, they sound like they are of the same mind with us. They confess that those who go to the Lord's Supper truly partake in the body and blood of Christ, but spiritually in that they have Christ in the heart. They do not want to allow the participation in the physical elements. We have put upon their conscience the fact that we have God's Word and his text in our favor, which they do not. Therefore, the issue stands as hopeful. I do not say that brotherly unity exists, but a charitable, friendly unity. This is what they lack and seek from us in a friendly manner and we will serve them. And may you now diligently pray that it will also become brotherly."

The report of his opponents sounded different. They boasted, as Luther had cautioned, that they had overpowered the Wittenberg men at Marburg. This did not agree with the fact that their own followers had vilified them because of the concessions which they had granted to the Wittenberg men in the Marburg Articles.

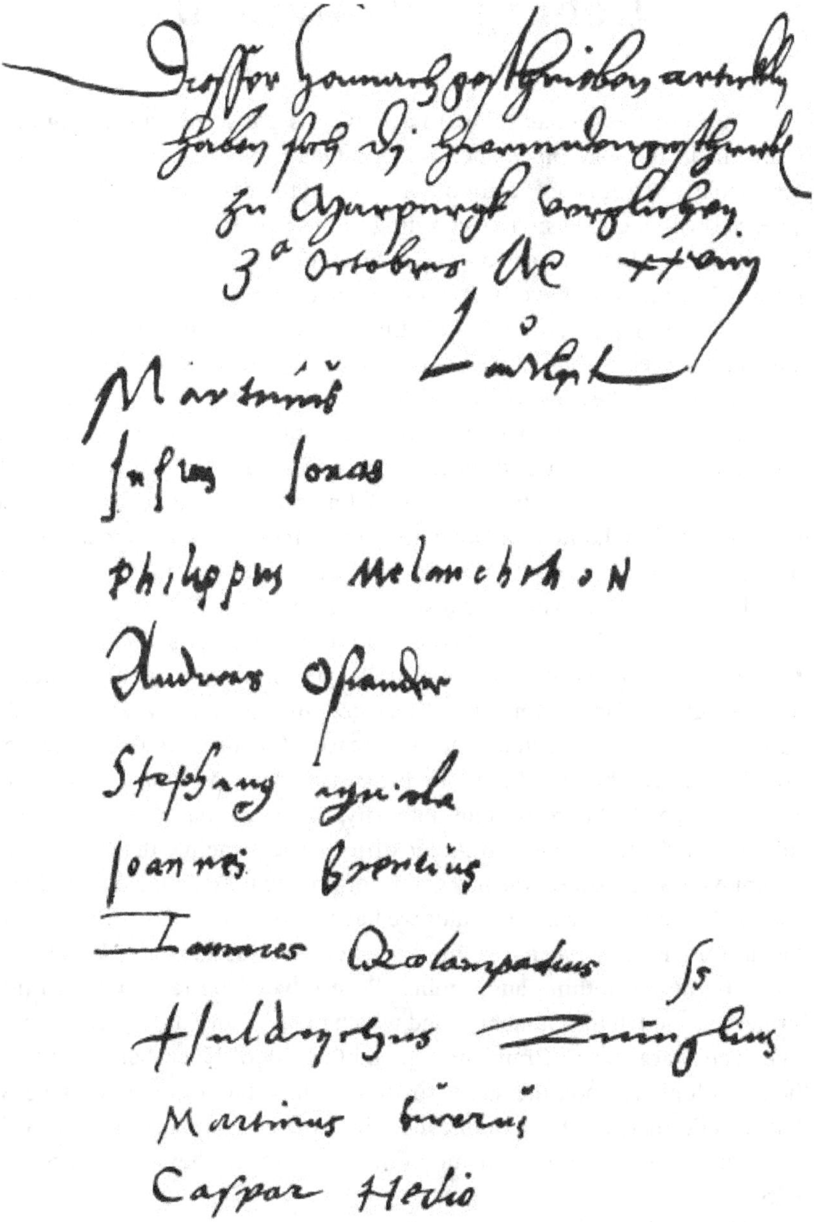

[Handwritten text, approximately:]

Dieser hernach geschriben artickel
haben sich die hernachgeschriben
zu Marpurg verglichen.
3ª Octobris Ao xxjx

Martinus Luther
Justus Jonas
Philippus Melanchthon
Andreas Osiander
Stephanus Agricola
Joannes Brentius
Joannes Oecolampadius
Huldrychus Zwinglius
Martinus Bucerus
Caspar Hedio

Facsimile of the title and the signatures of the Marburg Articles

Chapter 40
Coburg and Augsburg

Philip of Hessia had failed to achieve his goal. Yes, a meeting of the Evangelicals did take place once again in October at Schwabach. But only representatives from the Elector of Saxony and the Margrave of Brandenburg appeared with a confession. According to the requests of the counts, membership in the Alliance was contingent on signing this confession. These articles, 17 in number, have been known since that time as the "Schwabach Articles." (LV, Vol. 17,18, p. 266ff) Luther had drawn them together for the counts from the Marburg statements, while at Schleiss on his journey home from Marburg. They had requested his presence at Schleiss.

Since the real presence of the body and blood of Christ in Holy Communion had been clearly and specifically confessed in the 10th Article of this confession, the cities of Strassburg and Ulm withdrew. At yet another meeting held in Schmalkalden in November, the Landgrave had to recognize the failure of his attempt, drop his plan, and be satisfied to join the Lutherans.

Even so this Alliance had also lost its value for Philip because of the position which the Elector had taken by following Luther's advice. That was in regard to the question of whether it was permissible to mount armed opposition against Caesar. Luther had answered that question with a resounding "No!" in a number of Gutachten. His reason for this was that the Elector would have seen himself bound by his conscience. As long as Caesar was the Caesar, you had to respect his authority. He would have lost his authority only if he had been deposed from his office. The principle that power could be removed with power was not valid, for no one may be his own judge. If Caesar should become a persecutor we have no right to oppose him, no more than a count in turn may assist him in persecuting his subjects. We are to be strong by doing nothing and hoping. These were the ideas which Luther further outlined in his Gutachten and which the Elector considered to be correct. The Margrave of Brandenburg, and the city of Nuernberg, along with their theologians, took the same position. Thus, the armored alliance was disavowed. Instead, they commended themselves to trust in God regarding their concern for what Caesar might do, from whom they could expect the worst.

Had Luther regarded it proper to encourage war against Caesar he would have been very effective. This was shown when, immediately after the time at Marburg, news of the terrible siege of Vienna by the Turks reached the German people. In response, Luther preached a powerful warlike sermon against the Turks, in which he urged all Germans, young and old, man and wife, servant and maid, to defend themselves and to risk their money and property, body and life against the enemy in the name of God. He urged all of them, without exception, to aid Caesar. He did so even though he was aware that the hand which would remain free through the loss of the Turks may well then be turned against the Evangelicals. In fact, even as Philip of Hessia wanted to take advantage of the situation caused by the Turkish threat by denying any kind of help for Caesar until he agreed to peace with the Evangelicals, Luther would not yield. He patiently went about sowing his seed. He continued his visitations and in so doing kept up his spiritual care for the field, which he had begun. He left it to God what kind of weather he would provide.

#

On February 24, 1530, Carl V was ceremonially crowned as the Roman Caesar in Bologna. In accord with this event, he swore his oath to serve as the defender of the papal throne. Nevertheless, he announced on January 21st, from the same city where he was crowned, that a Diet was to be held in Augsburg on April 8th. That sounded very conciliatory. "Caesar Carl will personally appear in Augsburg in order to settle all issues," Luther wrote to a friend. In the statement he had released, Caesar had recommended to "allay repugnance, commend past wrongs to our Sanctifier, and that all of us be diligent in that each one be open minded, and have the intent and aim to hear, understand, and to live in reconciliatory manner." Caesar's brother had also begun to correspond with Elector John, and he was aiming toward an amicable agreement. How serious he was we can derive from Ferdinand's own letters. For example, he had written to Caesar, "I shall negotiate as long as possible and not decide anything. But even if I should have reached a decision there would still remain enough pretexts for its correction."

However, even though the Evangelicals could expect little in the way of goodness and love, the upright Elector felt it was his duty not to let the opportunity for a public confession before Caesar and empire go to waste. And so he issued a written request on March 12th, the first day after he had received the invitation to the Diet. In it he asked that those counts who were his spiritual brothers personally attend the Augsburg Diet with him. The next day, "since it is very likely that such a diet was desired rather than a council," he directed his Wittenberg theologians, Luther, Melanchthon, Jonas, and Bugenhagen, to set up the articles "about issues in which our divisions... show themselves clearly, "in accordance with the instructions from the royal invitation. They were to be prepared to personally hand over their work to the Elector by Oculi Sunday (the 3rd Sunday in Lent). He commanded such so that he and his brothers in the faith would know what they would be able to concede in good conscience at the Impirial Diet. He also requested that the theologians Agricola and Spalatin, along with the men of Wittenberg, except for Bugenhagen who as pastor had to remain at home, join the Elector when he set out for Augsburg. If it happened that the preachers were not allowed to appear at the Diet, then they, especially Doctor Martinus, should stay at the Coburg. This was so that the count could get their advice and opinion" as quickly as possible as situations would be developing."

Jonas, who was doing visitations, was recalled immediately, and the Wittenberg men went to work. They handed the results of their labors over to the count at Torgau a few days after the determined date. Their work was in the form of individual essays along with a copy of the Marburg -Schwabach Articles.

The Elector and his company began their journey on April 3rd. They arrived at the Coburg on the 15th. Easter was being celebrated there, and Luther preached twice on the first day of the festival, and once on the second. Melanchthon immediately made use of the time at the Coburg to lay out the confession, using the Torgau Articles as its base. Melanchthon, Jonas, Spalatin, and Agricola joined the count on April 23rd, when he resumed his journey to Augsburg, where he was expected to arrive before the end of the month, as Caesar had directed in his letter. The Count would have especially liked to have had Luther with him, but he did not dare to risk it. In the letter, which the count received from Augsburg, it was clearly implied that the appearance of the "outlaw" would have caused great difficulty for the Elector, for Luther's name was deliberately excluded in the invitation. This was the wording: "Yet, we herewith exclude anyone, whom your Electoral Grace may have in his company and would bring to this location, who has either transgressed against the peace of the land that was established by the Imperial Majesty and / or the Holy Empire, and has fallen under a penalty or penitential correction, which we are not authorized to reconcile." However, in order to have him nearby and to be able to receive his advice, the Elector arranged for Luther to remain at the Coburg. As the rest journeyed on, Doctor Martinus was brought to the fortress above the city during the early morning darkness. While he was in quiet hiding he was again to grow a beard, as he had done at the Wartburg.

The largest residence in this castle had been prepared for this valuable guest, and he had a key for every room. The room which he used as his living room is on display to this day. The count, who was concerned for his doctor's health, had arranged the best of care for him.

Luther's table partner from Wittenberg, the 24-year-old Magister Veit Dietrich, was provided as a companion. What's more, Cyriakus Kaufmann, a Wittenberg student who was a son of Luther's sister, was with them. Besides these quiet guests there was also a small force of soldiers occupying the castle. They were often known to make so much noise that Luther had to insist that they would provide the quiet that his work required.

In regard to that work for which he would be spending his time, Luther wrote on the very first day of his stay at the Coburg, "We have arrived at our Sinai. But we wish to make a Zion out of it and build three shrines at this place: one for the Psalms, one for the Prophets, and one for Aesop."

Since the chest with his books had not yet arrived, he could not begin the construction of those shrines on that day. He therefore took a tour of his new surroundings, which he called "the wilderness," "the desert," or "Gruboc" (Coburg written backwards). He also referred to his location in his writings as "out of the kingdom of the birds," or "out of the imperial diet of the Malt-Turks," since an army of jackdaws, crows, and other birds had roused his attention by playing their games before his eyes. "They are great and mighty lords," he wrote, "but what they desire I do not know as yet. However, this much I have gathered from one of their preachers. They intend to carry out a powerful campaign and battle against wheat, barley, oats, malt, and all kinds of rye. Many of them will become knights and do mighty deeds."

"And so, we sit here at the Imperial Diet. We listen and watch with much pleasure and love how the counts and lords, along with other elements of the empire, sing and revel so cheerfully. But it really makes us happy to note how knightly they wag their tails, wipe their beaks, and overrun the defenses as they conquer and apply their honor against the rye and the malt. We wish them luck and health, that in the end they may be perched on the lath of a fence. But I believe that this is no different from what the sophists and papists do with their writing and preaching. I must have all of them before me in one group so that I may hear their lovely voices and sermons in order to recognize them as a useful nation which consumes everything on earth, and how they cluck to pass the time."

As soon as his books arrived he started on his planned work. By the end of May, he could report that he had almost finished the translation of the prophet Jeremiah. He wanted to have the rest of them translated by Pentecost. So, we find him occupied at the Coburg in the same way as at the Wartburg, translating the Bible for the German people. When he got to Ezekiel he began with a special edition of chapters 38 and 39, the prophecy of Gog and Magog. He did this with marginal notes. This is how he explained the actions of the Turk, that furious enemy whose wrath visited upon the German people went straight to his heart. So, he wrote to Jonas on the 20th of June, "I can hardly be more amazed at how Ferdinand, who is able to forget about the Turk, can even forget about the misery of his own subjects. If so many people were killed or enslaved because of me I would perish in one hour, especially as my own conscience would accuse me of my neglect." With the exception of Ezekiel, which remained unfinished, all of the prophets had been translated by the time he left the Coburg.

The second shrine was being built for the Psalms in that Luther had the 118th and the 117th printed with commentary. (See LV, Vol. 11,12 p. 141 ff.

And Vol. 3 p. 1 ff.) He claimed the first of these as his own in his dedication to the Abbot Frederick in Nuernberg. He wrote, "As much as the entire book of Psalms and the Holy Scriptures are also very dear to me, as they are my only comfort and life, nevertheless, I come to this psalm and state that it must be mine by name. Its words have proven their worth to me very often. It has helped me from many great needs, from which neither Caesar, kings, wise men, or saints could have helped me. It is more precious to me than the honor, possessions, and power of the pope, the Turk, Caesar and the whole world. I would never have the desire to trade this Psalm for all of them together."

Luther also occupied himself with the Psalms, as he presented an interpretation of the first 25 Psalms to Veit Dietrich, which Dietrich wrote down and which his sons later had printed.

The third shrine Luther erected was for the old writer of Greek fables, Aesop. He translated a number of Aesop's tales into German, because he believed that a person could find in them the best teaching, warnings, and instruction in very simple words, for anyone who knows how to use them.

But that was far from all that Luther produced by pen at the Coburg. Soon after his arrival we found him occupied with an "Admonition to the Spiritual Leaders Gathered at Augsburg for the Imperial Diet." Copies of this work reached Augsburg as early as June. So, Luther, who had to keep his person at a distance, sent his powerful spirit forth among the people, with whom he once again desired to have a very serious discussion. In it he admonished the bishops not to allow this opportunity, which God was giving them through this Imperial Diet, to blow away with the wind.

He addressed them as follows: "We do not need an Imperial Diet, advice, or a master. We know that you cannot do better; indeed, you do not understand how to do it as well. It is not that we are perfect ... but we have the correct rules ... for ourselves." He showed them that they blasphemed by looking at his teachings from the wrong perspective, and that they ought to be more grateful for them than they would admit. "In summary, we know and you know that you are living outside of the Word of God, but we have the Word of God. Therefore, it is our highest desire and most humble plea that you give honor to God, and that you become aware, repent, and improve your ways. If not, then take me to yourselves. If I live, I will be a plague to you; if I die, I will be your death. For God has appointed me against you. I must, as Hosea says, be a bear and a lion for you on your way to Assur (*Assur referred to the power country north of Israel, namely, Assyria. The overall meaning was that God had sentenced the 10 Northern Tribes of Israel into the captivity of no return. Ephraim in Hosea 13 was another name for the northern kingdom of Israel.*). You will have no rest under my name until you either improve or fall." He also prayed to God that he would help them find the knowledge of the truth through his Spirit. But if they remained stiff-necked and went to ruin on account of this, he did not want to be guilty of their blood.

Luther issued some additional short writings from the Coburg. First among them was his letter, "About Interpretation and the Intercession of the Saints." (LV, Vol. 17, 18 p. 273 ff.) In it he defends the small word "alone" in his translation of Romans 3:28. In this regard, he explained the basic principles he followed in his translating the Bible. At the same time, he showed how little cause the papists had to find fault with his interpretation. "I know well," he wrote, "and they know less than the miller's donkey what sort of skill, diligence, reason, and understanding is involved in good interpretation, for they have not tried it. If I were to ask them how the first two words of Matthew 1, "liber generationis," should be translated, none of them would have been able to respond with a single cackle. Yet those great colleagues now stand in judgment over my entire work." He then told how his New Testament had been copied nearly word for word and distributed under someone else's name in the land of Duke George, while his translation had been strictly forbidden. But their bombastic style and the brazen manner, in which those people wanted to be his master, he turns against them by demonstrating that he doesn't have the need to be mastered by the papists. He wrote, "As Paul boasts against his so-called super apostles, so I will boast of myself over and against these asses. They are doctors? So am I. They are preachers? So am I. They are theologians? So am I. They are debaters? Me too. They are legates? I also. They write books? I also.

"And I shall go on with my boasting. I am able to translate the Psalms and the Prophets. Not they. I can interpret. They can't do that. I can read Holy Scripture. They can't do that. I can plead. They can't. And I shall now digress. I can handle their own dialects and philosophy better than all of them put together. I know for certain that none of them understand their Aristotle. If just one of them can correctly grasp a preface or chapter in Aristotle, I will let myself be chastised. I am not exaggerating. For from my childhood on I was taught and I learned every bit of their skill and know very well how deep and wide it is. Hence, they know very well what I know and that I am adept in everything that they can do. Still these unsavory people deal with me as though I were a newcomer to their skills, as if I just arrived this morning." Therefore, he would not be mastered by them. "If there is any mastering to be done, I shall do it myself. If I don't do this, let them leave my interpretations alone. May each man do whatever he wants for himself, and may he be successful."

Another precious little treatise from the Coburg is the pamphlet, "That Children Should Be Kept in School." (LV, Vol. 4. p. 107 ff) Here Luther appeals to the heart of Christians by pointing out how necessary Christian schools are and how important it is for children to learn. "Truly, the Gospel and Christendom," he wrote, "must remain until the Day of Judgment, as Christ says at the end of Matthew, 'Behold I will be with you till the end of the world.' (Luther's own paraphrasing) But through whom is the gospel to be preserved? Neither oxen, nor horses, dogs, nor swine shall do it. Nor will wood or stones. We humans will have to do it. For this office has not been assigned to oxen and horses, but to us humans. But from what source shall such humans be taken except from those who have children? If you don't want to raise your child to do this, nor another and so on, if no father or mother will give his child for this purpose, what will happen to the spiritual office and profession?"

But if the children were to learn something, there had to be schools. "I would like to see," Luther wrote, "from what source will pastors, teachers, and sextons come after three years. Are not we the ones who need to take action? Do not especially the counts have to apply themselves so that both elementary schools and schools of higher learning be correctly established? If they don't, there will be such a shortage that three or four cities will have to be assigned to one pastor, and ten villages to one chaplain." Then he shows that there should also be decently educated people for other offices and occupations. At the same time, he complained bitterly how earlier, when the pope was ruling, all money chests were open. But now, when it is made clear that schools needed to be maintained for the sake of Christ, all money chests are locked with iron chains. In this context he prayed for a short period of blessing, lest he would have to endure punishment for such ingratitude. He closed, "Come now, my dear Germans, I have told you often enough. You have heard your prophet. God grant that we follow his Word to the praise and thanks of our dear Lord for his precious blood, which he so lovingly offered for us. May God protect us from the terrible vice of ingratitude and of becoming forgetful of his kindness. Amen."

All these and other writings Luther was producing at a time when he was enduring weeks of physical and spiritual suffering that made all labor nearly impossible for him. (In the "Luther Public Library" ["Luthers Volksbibliothek"] we also find the following treatises from this period: "A Retraction about Purgatory," (Vol. 25,26p. 167ff.) - "About the Keys," (Vol. l. 3, p. 62ff.) - "Admonition in Regard to the Sacrament of the Body and Blood of Christ," (Vol. 1, p. 65ff.) He was suffering from blood pressure, surging to his head and roaring in his ears. He nearly fell into unconsciousness a number of times. As a result, he had to lay Ezekiel aside for a time and apply himself to easier tasks. Once he wrote, "It is now already the third day that I have no desire, nor can I look at a single letter. It doesn't work any longer. Getting older is adding to this." He had already chosen a spot under the cross in the chapel where he should be buried, if the end of his life were to come while he was at the Coburg. He often asked the pastor for help, to absolve him from his sins and serve him with the Sacrament.

He sought strength by daily meditating on God's Word and diligently spent time in prayer. Veit Dietrich reported how he daily spent as much as three hours in prayer, during prime time, which was usually scheduled for in-depth study. "Good God," he said, "what a faith bespoke his words! He pleads before God with such reverence and faith and hope that it seems as though he is talking with a father or a friend."

Luther experienced deep grief when he heard the sad news that his aged father had passed away on May 29th. He had sent him a letter of comfort when he had heard that his father had become seriously ill; and he heard the news of his passing away on June 5th. (LV, Vol. 7, p. 158ff) "Yes, my father is now dead," he said to Veit Dietrich after he had scanned the letter. He then retreated to his chamber with his book of Psalms to seek comfort from God's Word and in prayer, plus relief by way of many tears. "It is right and proper," he wrote to Melanchthon that same day, "that I, his son, weep for such a father, through whom the Father of mercy created me, and by whose sweat he fed me and developed me into the person which I happen to be. Yet, I am happy for this, that he has lived at this time and has seen the light of the truth. God be praised in all his works and counsel eternally. Amen." Now Luther also shows himself to be a man of strong faith even in his pain. He did not allow his sorrow to be noticeable from the next day on. Veit Dietrich wrote to Luther's wife, "He forgot about his father during the first two days, even though it caused him great sorrow."

Luther was also distracted from his work through many visits while he was at the Coburg. He was actually considering having his residence changed so that the "pilgrimage" would stop.

One of his visitors at the Coburg was the renowned theologian Urbanus Regius, who met him for the first time at the end of August while traveling through the area. He called that day which he spent in Luther's presence "the most precious day of his life." We will later refer to a visit by Martin Būcer shortly before his stay at the Coburg came to an end.

In the midst of this busy time, in addition to the previously mentioned publications, Luther found time to carry on extended correspondence (for a selection of these Coburg letters see LV, Vol. 8, p. 7-44). It was simplest for him to send letters to those at his home. Two of his students, Hieronymus and Peter Weller had been living at his home during his absence. Luther wrote friendly letters to both of them. In one of those on June 19th, he included the well-known letter to his little Hans, who was a student of Hieronymus Weller. The following is this letter.

"Grace and peace, my dear little son!

"I love it when you like to learn and are diligent in prayer. Keep doing so, my little son. When I come home I will bring along a nice little funfair.

"I know of a pretty, cheerful garden, to which many children go with golden coats. They pick up many apples under the trees, pears, cherries, yellow and purple plums. They sing, skip around, and have fun. They have ponies with golden bridles and silver saddles. So, I asked the man who owned the garden, whose children they were. He said that these are the children who love to pray, study, and are good. I then said, 'Dear sir, I too have a son. His name is little Hans Luther. May he also come into this garden so that he could eat those nice apples and pears and ride such nice ponies and play with these children? 'The man then said, 'If he likes to pray, study, and be good, then he can along with Lippus and Jost (Philippus and Jodocus, sons of Melanchthon and Jonas). Then when they all get together they may make music with pipes, drums, and lutes, and may also dance and shoot with little crossbows.'

"Then he showed me a well-maintained meadow in the garden which had been made for dancing. Pure gold pipes, drums, and neat silver crossbows hung there. But it was early and the children had not eaten yet. I could not wait for the dancing, so I said to the man, 'I want to go quickly, dear sir, and write about all of this to my son, little Hans, that he will diligently pray, study hard, and be good, so that he will also be able to come into your garden. But he also has an Aunt Lene. He has to bring her along too.' Then the man replied, 'So shall it be. Go and write to him.'

"Therefore, dear little Hans, learn and pray bravely, and tell Lippus and Jost that they should also learn and pray. Then you will also come into the garden. For now I ask the Almighty God to keep taking care of you. Greet Aunt Lene and give her a kiss for me.

The year 1530. Your dear father, Martinus Luther."

His dear wife was also regularly writing to her Sir "Doctor." She sent him a picture of his little daughter, Magdalena. He pasted it across the table on the opposite wall of the dining room so that he might be cheered by looking at it.

Augsburg! He would have very much liked to have gone there with the rest. "But there was the One who had told me," he said, "be quiet, for you have a bad voice." Yet that one, the Elector, had also clearly stated that, if his presence would be necessary, he would be asked to come. At least we often read in Luther's earlier letters how his anticipation regarding his summons kept increasing. This is how he wrote on the 19th of June, "I am sitting here in this wilderness and there is little hope that I shall be called to the imperial diet." The next day he wrote to Jonas, "If I am called I shall go without any doubt. Yet I am considering whether or not I should go without being summoned." A little more than a week later he expressed the same idea to Melanchthon, "If I should hear that your situation is turning bad and even becoming dangerous, it would be difficult for me to restrain myself from flying to you to take note how frightfully the devil's teeth are surrounding you." (See Psalm 22:13 [NIV].)

Though Luther was not permitted to travel to Augsburg to defend the truth, he approached God all the more diligently with his fervent prayers for the sake of the victory of the Gospel. "He was holding <u>the rod and the staff</u>

of God in his hand. He stood face to face with God and lifted his holy and heavy hands in supplication to the Lord Jesus Christ that he would move strongly to weaken the papacy. He cried to God day and night that he would preserve and strengthen those true descendants of Joshua, those German knights, with his Spirit; that he would comfort them and surround them with his angels to keep watch over those men, who together with the angels were arrayed on the battle field at Augsburg against the antichrist for the honor of his name, the holy gospel, and his Kingdom..." wrote old Mathesius. Veit Dietrich once heard him pray, "I know that you are our God and Father. Therefore, I am certain that you will defeat the persecutors of your children. If you do not do so, the danger is looming for you as much as it is for us. The entire cause is yours. We have just been compelled to face it and become involved in your name to attack him (namely, the Antichrist). May you then preserve it (your cause)."

But Luther continued to stand faithfully alongside his brothers in faith, who were at Augsburg, as he encouraged them. This he did as the drama continued to unfold. When the Elector and his theologians had arrived on May 2nd, they learned that Dr. Eck had shown his hostility against the Evangelicals by drawing 402 statements from their writings and sending them to Caesar. He had also seen to it that they were distributed in the German language.

According to these statements he blamed the Lutherans for having fallen away from the faith in nearly all of their teachings. The plan of Melanchthon, which he had largely developed already at the Coburg, did not lend itself well for refuting these accusations. What was now important was to show that basic Lutheran teachings were the same as Christians of bygone ages had taught and confessed, and then to also show clearly which were the chief teachings of the Roman church, from which it was necessary to turn away.

Therefore Melanchthon, with the help of the other Saxon theologians, Jonas, Spalatin and Agricola, took great care to provide much greater detail for the Apology than had been planned. (*Apology actually meant "defense". At that point in time at the Empirical Diet in Augsburg the Wittenbergers were defending the Lutheran teachings over against the Roman teachings*). However, the document was also to serve as the confession of all the Evangelicals before Caesar and the Empire.

The Elector sent this plan to Luther at the Coburg on May 11th, along with a letter which read, "Since you and our other scholars at Wittenberg had drawn up your articles in line with our gracious thought and desire, articles which are controversial in their religious nature, we want you to be aware that Magister Philip Melanchthon has now revised them further and has put them into the form which we have now sent to you. It is our gracious wish that you will not consider it burdensome to review and ponder them. Deal with these articles and write down your notes on the margins, or by adding or subtracting from the wording in line with your thoughts, whether you find them acceptable. Luther responded on May 15th: "I have reviewed Magister Phillipen's Apology. It pleases me completely and I do not know how to improve or change it. It would also not be proper, for I cannot proceed so gently and quietly. May Christ, our Lord, aid us so that it will yield much and great fruit as we hope and pray. Amen."

The Elector had yet another question for Luther to answer. Caesar still had not appeared in Augsburg, but was continuing to conduct the empire's business at Innsbruck. Yet it had already been reported that he would confront the evangelical officials with a request that they do no preaching at Augsburg. How should they respond to such a request? The old Electoral Chancellor Brueck decisively advised them not to agree with it. It was different with Luther. He wrote to the Elector that they should humbly make another appeal to Caesar for him not to forbid the preaching without a prior hearing. "If this does not help, then the authority has the right to be obeyed. We have done what we should do and are therefore excused." This "Gutachten" was not in keeping with the Elector's thinking. "I don't know," he is to have said, "whether my scholars are fools or I." So when Caesar actually did make his demand from Innsbruck, he sent it back.

But that did not solve the problem. Caesar finally left Innsbruck on June 6th, and was ceremoniously led into Augsburg on the 15th in glorious procession following the various guilds. He ordered the four counts of Saxony, Brandenburg, Lueneburg, and Hessia to appear before him that same evening and repeated his request concerning the preachers. When the Landgrave explained the counts' refusal to comply, Caesar became angry and remained determined for his will to be done. At that point, the Landgrave George stepped forward. He explained that before he would abandon this teaching and the Word of God, Caesar would have to sever his head from his body. Caesar responded in an appeasing manner, "O Lion of a count, not your head, not your head," and finally dismissed them. They then allowed their preachers to calmly carry on with their preaching during the next four days. They only yielded when the Catholic preachers were also commanded to cease preaching, and Caesar established that there would only be Scripture readings. But even before this they had let the procession of the elevated host pass by without participating, in spite of Caesar's repeated requests.

Luther knew nothing about what had transpired. Since receiving the Elector's letter, he had received no others from Augsburg, and he complained bitterly about it. "I don't know if I should think that you are indifferent or disrespectful, since you know how I thirst for letters from you while in this desert," he wrote to Melanchthon on the 5th of June. On the 7th, he continued, "I see that you all decided to make me a martyr by way of your silence. So be it. Thus, I inform you that I shall compete with you from now on by remaining silent." He called his friends in Augsburg "Squire Silencers." Yet messengers repeatedly arrived from Augsburg on their way through the Coburg. Each time his conversation with them went as follows, as he later complained, "Are you bringing a letter?" The answer, "No." "How are the Lords faring?" The answer, "Well."

The first letters to arrive from Augsburg after several long weeks of silence made no mention of things going well. Melanchthon was full of heavy concerns. He expected dangers from the papists, from Caesar, from the Swiss, from the Landgrave, who he still feared would assert himself on behalf of the Zwinglians. He begged Luther to write an urgent letter to the Landgrave, and Luther did so. He affectionately urged the landgrave not to share in the sins of those people. Since Melanchthon also understood how angry Luther was about his silence, and the silence of the others as well, and would be sending his messenger back empty, he found even more to grieve about.

But now the letters were coming from Augsburg quickly, one after another. So Luther could no longer sustain his silence with which he had wanted to punish his friends. He discounted any justification for Melanchthon's concerns. On June 20th he wrote to Jonas, "Philip allows himself to be burdened by his philosophy and nothing else. For this matter is in the hand of Him, who so plainly assures us that no one shall take them out of my hand." Eight days later he wrote to his depressed friends personally. "From the depth of my heart I despise your sky-high worries which are consuming you, as you have put it. It is not the enormous size of the danger, but the enormous amount of unbelief that rules in your heart which is to blame. If our stance is wrong, we shall recant. But if our stance is true, why should we recant, in contradiction to his promise and make a liar of the One who bids us to be as calm as we are when we sleep?" He wrote, "Cast all your worries on the Lord." "The Lord is near to all broken hearts that call upon him." "Is he saying these things into the wind? ... It is your philosophy that is torturing you, not your theology."

During the time which passed between those two letters, the hands of the clock were moving on and were being watched with trepidation. Caesar had opened the Imperial Diet on June 20th. In the presentation which was offered by the Palatinate Count, it was pointed out that if there had been obedient submission to the Edict of Worms, the error would not have been that damaging. But all kinds of ungodliness had come forth because of the disobedience. That type of blame did not sound very encouraging to the Evangelicals. But the opening speech also offered the encouragement, "That everyone, in connection with the declaration of the Imperial Diet, take responsibility to kindly offer his thoughts, opinion, and understanding of the declared error and schism, and to also avoid any possible abuse when writing in German or in Latin. On Wednesday, the 22nd, it was declared that Caesar would consider the entire case on Friday. Therefore, having everything in its proper order was very important.

As he was preparing the confession, which was being written in Latin and German, Melanchthon had been making improvements all along. This was his practice in everything that he wrote.

On Thursday all of the Evangelical Counts, Heralds, Counselors, and Theologians met. The "Apology" *(See the note on p.303)* was read in Latin and German and both copies were signed. On Friday, the time of the Imperial Meeting was spent on other business. The papal side would have much preferred that the public reading of the Confession would have been denied. This mirrored the desire they had had years earlier already, when they tried to undermine Luther's taking the witness stand at Worms. But the evangelical representatives insisted that the public reading be allowed on Saturday afternoon.

In order to limit the number of listeners, Caesar insisted that the reading be held in a hall within his own living quarters at the bishop's palace, instead of in the large hall of the Imperial Diet building. And so it was. The Saxon Vice-Chancellor, Christian Beier, read the German copy of the Confession from 3:00 PM to 5:00 PM in Caesar's presence. He did this with such a loud voice that all of the 200 people who were in the hall, and the numerous listeners who had assembled in the courtyard outside the hall, could understand everything.

Luther was overjoyed when he received the news of this huge event. "Jonas wrote to me," he said to a friend, "that our Confession which Philip had prepared was read in Caesar's own living quarters ... and those in Caesar's party are already talking about their answering. Many are inclined toward peace, and are standing against the sophists, Faber and Eck. In the presence of two witnesses a bishop is said to have made the comment, 'That is the pure truth. We cannot deny it.'" And to another Luther wrote, "I am filled with grateful joy to have experienced this hour in which Christ has been publicly proclaimed in such a large assembly with the most beautiful Confession through so many joyful confessors. Now that Word is fulfilled, 'I will speak of your statutes before kings.' It will also be fulfilled, 'and I will not be put to shame.'" (Psalm 119:46 – NIV)

And to the Elector Luther wrote, "Our opponents are of the opinion that they have done very well in having the royal command of his majesty forbid preaching. But those miserable people do not realize that through the reading of the written Confession more preaching has been done than might have been accomplished by ten preachers. Isn't this a beautifully fine jewel of wisdom that M. Eisleben (Luther) and others have to remain silent; but the Elector, together with the other counts and lords, stand up with their written Confession, and freely preach before the royal majesty of Caesar and the entire empire as well. This is happening right under their noses, and they have to listen to it and not speak against it. I might say that truly the rule against preaching was broken as a result ... for Christ will not be silent at the imperial diet, and though they may be sort of reckless, yet they had to learn more from hearing this Confession than they could have heard from ten preachers for a whole year."

The impressions which the confession made in Augsburg were varied. Some, who had been led to believe terrible things about Lutheran doctrine, had been brought to a better understanding. Others were embittered, especially because of how things had worked out. It would have been great for them if Caesar had immediately reached for his sword. "If we were Caesar," a furious papist was heard to have said, "we would turn this black ink into bloody red rubrics." To which another responded, "as long as the red would not squirt under your eyes." The Archbishop of Mainz counseled peace. In their letters Luther's friends had described him to be doing so. This resulted in Luther writing him in a printed letter to give such advice as that of Gamaliel (Acts 5:34ff [See NIV]) to his friends in faith. "But if neither peace nor unity results," he wrote, "and if they reject the advice of Gamaliel and of the Apostles, and the example of the Jews, then let go whoever does not wish to remain, and whoever rejects the Confession let him be angry. Such a one will find plenty of the anger and discord for which he contends."

Caesar also wished to avoid the type of violence against which Luther warned, even though the papal delegates would have liked to drive him in that direction. He recommended instead that a refutation of the Confession be prepared in his name. After that would be read, he would make his final decision on this entire matter. A commission of Roman theologians was appointed, which included Eck and Wimpina, Tetzel's old friends. They went to work immediately. It took them a long time to produce anything. When they finally handed in their refutation, Caesar found it so abominable that he shredded and rolled the 280 pages to such an extent that only twelve pages remained. Those lords had to revise their work five times. When, on the 3rd of August, their "Confutation" was finally read in the same hall in which the "Confession" had been read, it was still so excessively deplorable that Caesar was ashamed to give a copy to the Evangelicals. Nevertheless, he required them to submit to this refutation of their teaching; if not, he would have to move against them as is expected of a Roman Caesar, the protector and administrator of the church.

The result of this requirement was becoming apparent almost immediately with a small example. When Philip of Hessia learned about this, he requested that Caesar release him from the Imperial Diet. When his request was denied, he rode off without permission on the 6th of August. Soon it was reported that he was gathering troops. Caesar was not ready to use force at this time, nor were a number of the Catholic leaders. Since the Turk was still at the border, new negotiations were introduced. Seven men were chosen from each side, who" were to take up the entire matter and have friendly discussions among themselves." When Luther heard that news he first was amazed, but then he expressed his disapproval. He couldn't imagine anything that could still be conceded from the Confession, that "soft-treading document," nor did he consider any negotiations from the papal side as honest. "I know indeed,"he wrote to Augsburg, "that through these negotiations you will always eliminate the gospel. But I am afraid that if we do not do what they want they will later blame us for having broken our word. In summary, I have complete dislike for this negotiating, because unless the pope wants to give up his papacy, it is totally impossible. It was enough for us to have given an account of our faith and have searched for peace."

In another letter he wrote, "I hear that you, sure of being disappointed, have undertaken a noble task to try to unify the pope and Luther. But the pope does not wish it and Luther begs to decline. Therefore, take care lest you spend your efforts in vain. If you are able to accomplish your goal contrary to the will of both, then I will soon follow your example and reconcile Christ with Belial."

When this great commission could not find unity and when any possibility for success was frustrated by Duke George who added himself to that commission, it was reduced to three members from each side, also excluding that enemy of peace by this welcomed deportment. The Evangelicals had, with some disapproval, allowed themselves to be ready to negotiate. So, Luther also warned his friends to be on full alert. "Should it happen," he wrote, "that you would concede anything against the gospel, you will not do it by the grace of Christ. Have no doubt that they will lock the eagle (the gospel) in some kind of a sack, and don't doubt for a minute that Luther will come to set this eagle gloriously free. As surely as Christ lives, that is what will happen."

What Luther had indicated gently, namely that his friends might be brought to the point of taking something away from the truth, others were saying more openly. They spoke of how they had strong fears of this happening, and the evil suspicion was voiced most loudly against Melanchthon. So complaints were brought to Luther's attention from the direction of Nuernberg. Landgrave Philip had also expressed such a fear in a letter to Luther. Here Luther again had to intercede. He wrote to the people of Nuernberg, "I have committed this matter to God. As such I regard it as having kept this issue under my own control. Thus, no human being will take anything away from me, nor could anyone ruin this, as long as Christ and I remain as one." He also comforted Melanchthon in regard to the evil slander which Melanchthon had received, though he was not without fault.

In the meantime, the futility of any continued negotiations was becoming even more clear. The Elector also wanted to take his leave. He was staying only to answer the decisive opposition of Caesar. When the information arrived from Caesar that the pope was willing to grant the demand for a council under the condition that until it convened, everything would go back to the former manner of doing things, the confessors rejected that condition without hesitation. Caesar held this against them and declared that he wanted to take up arms. Just a little earlier he had written to the pope, "It would now be the use of force that would produce the most fruit."

As negotiations were again renewed, once again reports of a lack of trust were being circulated against Melanchthon and his partners at Augsburg. Luther realized that he would need to have a very serious word with them. "Many important men on our side are bringing me some very frightening news," he wrote to Jonas by way of Nuernberg, "as though you have betrayed everything and would concede too much for the sake of peace. Therefore, Jonas, let me know very soon if something has happened in the meantime, something I don't want. I am almost bursting with wrath and indignation. I plead with you to break off the negotiations and come home. They have the Confession. They have the gospel. They may allow it if they so desire. If they do not, then they may go to their own home."

Although in a loving way, Luther wrote similar sentiments to Melanchthon, who had been the reason for the before mentioned apprehension. Melanchthon had openly expressed his concern that the Catholic bishops would be given certain allowances over the Evangelicals. He had already here shown that he was striving to find doctrinal formulas which both parties could accept without damage to their conscience, that both would apply common sense through those statements. In light of this Luther had written to him as early as August 26th, "You write that you had forced Eck to confess that we are justified through faith. O, if only you had not forced him to lie." Such an example of bungling was sharply condemned by the determined men. Baumgaertner, the delegate from Nuernberg, reported to his home city, "At this Imperial Diet no one has up to this point done more damage to the gospel than Philip."

But before the two letters which Luther had sent through Nuernberg had been forwarded, they had become unnecessary, and the people of Nuernberg sent them back to Luther. For on the 22nd of September Caesar announced a temporary closure of the Diet. He explained that the "Confession" of the group, which had departed from the pope had been refuted. They would be given time to reconsider their return to the unity of the church until the 15th of April, the following year. Truly false practices were to be inspected until a council would be held within a year. In the meantime, nothing new was to be printed in regard to matters of faith, hearing of confession of sins in cloisters was to be allowed, and the opposite side should draw no one into its sect.

The Evangelicals did not accept this closing statement. They rejected having been declared a sect. For proof that their "Confession" had not yet been refuted, they referred to the Apology of their "Confession," which Melanchthon had produced in response to the written "Confutation". Chancellor Brueck was delivering it to the Palatinate Count Frederick, in order to deliver it to Caesar. In response to a wink of an eye from King Ferdinand, who had spoken to Caesar in secret, that writing was returned to Brueck. Caesar wanted to hear nothing about a justification. When on the next day the Evangelicals held fast to their rejection, they were told that nothing would be changed. If they wished to accept the statement of closure it was there to be had. If not, then Caesar and his followers would undertake the destruction of their sect without delay.

Even then the Evangelicals held fast to their position. They welcomed the time permitted to think about terms. In any event, they would have an opportunity to consider what else could yet be done. They were finished at Augsburg.

Picture of "Elector John The Steadfast" (in office: 1525-1532) according to a painting by Cranach

The Elector immediately took his leave from Caesar. He accepted his farewell with tears in his eyes. "Cousin, cousin, I would not have foreseen your falling into your dear prince's displeasure." ("Ohm, Ohm, das haette ich mich zu euer Liebden nicht versehen.")

Immediately after that, the Elector left Augsburg, a city which he had honored with his presence. He had spent every moment as the model of a loyal count who gave to Caesar what belonged to Caesar, and every moment as a steadfast Christian who gave to God what belonged to God. Counts Ernst and Franz of Lueneburg and Wolfgang of Anhalt also began their homeward journey that same day.

So what Luther had already requested in his letter of July 15th, finally happened. He had written, "Always back home, always home!" Two months later, the returning traveler, Elector Prince John Frederick, visited him at the Coburg and Luther greeted him in the way one welcomes the first swallows. (A lengthier footnote is attached on the next page, p. 312.)

The Count then offered to take Luther along home with him, but Luther graciously declined. His reason was that he would rather stay to receive the others and to wipe the sweat off their brows after their hot bath.

Exhilarated, Luther now informed his Kate that he hoped to be with her again within 14 days. The news of how the Imperial Diet concluded for the Protéstants did not depress him. "He shall speak with them in his wrath," he wrote. "They want to have it this way that things happen to them according to their will. We are excused and have done enough. Their blood comes upon themselves."

To his Elector, however, he sent a letter of comfort on October 3rd. "I rejoice in my heart," the letter read, "that your Electoral Grace has come out of the hell at Augsburg by the grace of God. And though human disgrace is seen as extremely sour along with their god, the devil, we do hope that God's beginning grace will also henceforth prove all the stronger and in greater measure for us. Truly they also are in the hand of God, just as much as we are. Make no mistake about this. They accomplish nothing nor do anything unless God wants it that way; they also shall not kink one hair on our heads or on anyone's head, unless God himself does so by his power. I have committed the matter to my Lord God. He has begun this, this I know. He will also complete this. This I believe."

The elector and his company arrived at the Coburg on the day after the date of this letter, and Luther traveled with them on the 5th of October. He took along with him the beard which he had allowed to grow on his face while he was in his "wilderness." They rested in Altenburg until the afternoon, and Luther preached. But Melanchthon was already once again hard at work. He wanted to reverse that well-calculated lie in the closure of the Diet, the lie that the evangelical Confession of Scripture had been refuted. He wanted to do a thorough job of it in his Apology of the Confession, which was intended for later publication. As he was still writing while at table that Sunday, Luther took the quill out of his hand and reminded him that God can also be served by celebrating and resting. The following Sunday Luther preached once more in the elector's residence at Torgau. From there he returned home to Wittenberg, safe and sound.

(At this visit John Frederick brought along a precious ring for Dr. Luther for sealing letters. He had the ring made for him. The coat of arms, which Luther had chosen for himself on an earlier occasion, had been engraved in stone on this ring. Luther had personally explained his seal in a letter to his friend, Spengler, in Nuernberg: "The first shall be a cross, black, within a heart, which was to have its natural color. It was such, so that I would be reminded that it is faith in the crucified one which saves us. If a person believes from his heart he is justified. Though it is a black cross, it mortifies and should also hurt. Nevertheless, it will allow the heart to retain its color; it does not spoil its nature, that is, it does not kill but keeps alive, for the righteous will live by faith, but it is by faith in the crucified. Such a heart should be centered in a white rose. This indicates that faith gives joy, comfort, peace, and, in short, is set in a white, happy rose, for the peace and joy is not as the world gives. Therefore, this rose should be white and not red, for the color white is the color of spirits and all angels. Such a rose is set into a sky-blue field, so that such joy in spirit and faith is a beginning of our future joy in heaven. It is already now comprehended therein and grasped through hope, but not yet revealed. And around such a field is a golden ring. It shows that such salvation in heaven lasts forever and has no end. It is also precious above all joy and possessions, just as gold is the grandest, most precious metal.")

Luther's Letter Seal   Luther's Coat of Arms

Chapter 41
The Turk, God's Peace Corps for the Reformation

While the Saxon contingent was traveling home, Caesar continued the Imperial Diet at Augsburg with a Catholic majority. It was finally declared to be over on November 19th. Caesar did not make a single concession from his earlier decision. However, setting April 15, 1531, as an end to the period of thinking things over had also not changed. He would have liked to use force immediately, but even among the Catholic representatives there was no agreement on this point. Still, the Imperial Chamber Court established the decision to attack the evangelical counts immediately if they were to violate the terms of the closure. The procedures for executing that closure had already been decreed, namely that the Evangelicals were to return the church properties of which they had assumed ownership. In order to secure even stronger support for Caesar's commands, his brother Ferdinand was to be chosen as the King of Rome. The Catholic Electors were won over to this plan with persuasive well-sounding arguments. The election was finalized on January 5th, despite the documented protest by the Saxon Elector.

In order for them to give further consideration in regard to their stand toward Caesar and Empire, the representatives of the Evangelicals had been allotted "think it over time". However, the instructions that had been given to their Imperial Chamber Court made it necessary that they come to a common understanding among themselves immediately. Hence the following met on December 22, 1530, at Smalcald: The Elector of Saxony, Duke Ernst of Lueneburg, Philip of Hessia, Wolfgang of Anhalt, Counts Gebhard, Albrecht of Mansfeld, and delegates of George of Brandenburg along with a number of other cities. The first decision in respect to the forthcoming procedures was that those bonded would be "allies with counsel and aid for one another." On the other hand, it was not fully clear what would be done, if Caesar would carry out his threats and take up his sword. The lawyers asserted that their understanding was that Caesar, per se, did not possess unlimited power. Thus, if he should overstep his authority, the individual leaders were allowed to enforce the law with their own military defense, to confront Caesar's attempt in accord with Caesar's own recognition of their rights.

But before they made any further decisions they wanted to hear the "Gutachten" of their theologians. These theologians had not been confronted with the matter before in this light. As a result, when Luther, Melanchthon, and Jonas submitted their "Gutachten," it was structured so as to declare that as theologians they were unable to render a verdict. It was a question for them whether Caesar's authority was such as was claimed by the lawyers and then whether the current situation could be judged under Caesar's claim. Thus, they would have to leave any decision up to those who practiced law. According to Scripture they would be unable to prevent the counts from proceeding under such a decision.

To those of Nuernberg, who were rather shocked by this "Gutachten" Luther wrote: "I have said my piece. I give advice as a theologian. If the lawyers can show that this is permissible under their laws I leave it up to them. Let them proceed according to the law. The lawyers and the experts must take this responsibility upon themselves." This was not what Duke George and the leaders of Nuernburg wanted. Nevertheless, all the rest met again in March 1531, at Smalcald, and formed a Military Alliance for the purpose of jointly defending themselves, should one of them be attacked on account of the Word of God. Of those in attendance who were not able to join this Alliance immediately it was expected that they would do so soon thereafter. Since those, who were living in the higher regions (that is in southern Germany), had provided a somewhat satisfactory confession regarding the Sacrament, their cities were allowed to join. More meetings were held during that year. Soon this newly established Alliance existed as a power that demanded respect. Their fame as a new Alliance spread so wide that even Catholic imperial counts and foreign governments sought some sort of association with this alliance. However, this new Alliance did not provide the connection they sought mainly for political reasons.

Luther now allowed the lay people and the rulers to function. He did not write against them, but he made sure that his German Christians clearly understood how they were to regard the issues of the situation at that time. He did this with two editorials issued at the beginning of 1531. The first he titled "Regarding the Presumed Edict of Caesar, Issued after the Imperial Diet of 1530, Comments by Dr. Martin Luther." With the word "Presumed" he referred to the closure of Caesar's edict. In his introduction, Luther stated that he did not wish to hold the "upright Caesar" responsible for it. His loyal and submissive German heart caused him to express himself in that manner. During all those years he put only the best construction on the actions of the head of the highest form of government, and he did so with affectionate intent. "Pray especially for Caesar, this admirable youth," he had written to one of his friends from his residence at the Coburg. From that same location he had written to the Electoral Prince, "Yes, Caesar has an upright heart, worthy of all honor and virtues. One cannot assign him too much honor in regard to his person. But, dear God! What can any person do against so many devils, unless God assists with his power."

Luther wanted to aim his blows against the powerful opposing lords, whom he saw as the real "crooks and criminals", namely, the pope and his legate. He did not want to oppose Caesar whom he pictured as the pious Carolus, as a sheep among wolves. He described the edict as a work full of lies and malice. "First of all," he wrote, "they boast that our Confession stands refuted by the holy gospels. This is such an obvious lie that they themselves know it is a disgraceful falsehood." In regard to the producers of the edict he said, "God blinds them to such an extent that they cannot put down a single word without slapping themselves in the face and exposing themselves. Truly, I could not rebuke or disgrace them as strongly as they disgrace themselves with this deplorable lying edict."

In regard to himself, he would not allow it that he be forbidden to bear witness. In the beforementioned introduction he referred to his doctorate. He stated that in his pursuit of that degree he had to take an oath to teach Holy Scripture faithfully. "In my pursuit of such teaching," he went on, "the papacy fell into my path and wanted to keep me from witnessing. As a result, it was obvious that what was happening to the papacy would get even worse. They shall not be able to defend themselves against me. In God's name and through my call I shall tread upon the lion and the cobra and trample the great lion and the serpent (Ps. 91:13 [See NIV]). This was ordained to begin during my lifetime and will be completed after my death. St. John Hus prophesied about me as he wrote from his imprisonment: 'They shall now roast a goose (Huss = goose); but in a hundred years from now they will hear a swan sing, whom they will have to endure.' So it will be, God willing."

"This is my comment regarding the edict. If I live and someone inflicts me with a somewhat deeper scratch, I can gently finger-nail the itch and rub it (German: " ... krauet mich jemand, so kann ich es noch bas jucken und kitzeln."). In the meantime, let no one be frightened because of this edict. May our God put an end to such blasphemy and sanctify his name again so that his kingdom may come and his will be done. Amen. Amen. May the blasphemous papacy and everything connected with it fall into the abyss of hell, as John proclaimed in Revelation. Amen. Whoever would be a Christian, let him say so. Amen."

The other treatise which Luther produced in response to the imperial diet he entitled, "A Warning from Martin Luther to His Dear Germans." He stated that he had encouraged the church leaders toward peace at the Imperial Diet. He had also asked God to help them in that regard. But they were like Pharaoh and kept at it until there was no longer any hope for them. They just kept escalating their quarrels with threats and defiance. "Oh well, perhaps it will come to war or rebellion. In regard to this I am bearing witness before God and the entire world that we, who are being despised as Lutherans, did not counsel or encourage to such an end, nor did we give any cause for this. But through it all and without ceasing we prayed to God and called for peace. ... We have taught and lived quietly until now. We did not draw a sword, burn anyone, murder or rob as they have been doing all along and still are doing. Since we have a clear conscience in regard to such conflict, and the conscience of the papists is guilty ... hence let things happen and proceed in the worst way, be that war or rebellion as God's wrath shall decree it. If it should result in rebellion, my God and the Lord Jesus Christ can rescue both me and those with me. Should he not rescue us, thanks and praise to him.

"I have lived long enough, have well deserved death, and have begun to verbally avenge Christ my Lord against the papacy. They shall properly feel Luther after my death. As to what is happening now ... should I be murdered by such papal and church rebellion, I shall take with me a whole heap of bishops, priests, and monks. So, it shall be said that Dr. Martinus was taken to his grave with a great procession. He is a doctor above all bishops, priests, and monks. Therefore, they shall also go with him to the grave on his back. That is how the event will be told and sung. For it is safe to calculate that whoever kills Luther in the rebellion will not spare many of the priests. And so, we shall pass away together. They, in the name of all devils, will be heading to hell. I, in God's name, will go to heaven." Secondly, we know that they will not start such a war in God's name. ... We shall speak a blessing over them, a blessing such as follows. As holy as you are on God's behalf and as great a reason as you have to go to war, so great may be the fortune and the victory which God gives you. Amen.

"Thirdly, since it did not seem proper for me to go to war or to counsel or to incite for war as a spiritual preacher, I have most diligently up to this point been counseling much more for peace instead of war. The whole world has to testify such about me. Since our enemies do not want peace, but war, if it comes to this that a war does take place, I shall then also lay down my pen and be silent. I will no longer throw myself into my work, as I would do in the following rebellion. ...

"Furthermore, if there will be war according to God's plan, I do not want to have scolded them, nor let them be scolded as rebels, namely those who decide to defend themselves against the murdering and blood thirsty papists. Instead I shall let it go on and let it happen. When they shall call it a defensive emergency, I shall direct them to take action justifiably and so rightfully defend them before the judges. ... It is not that I desire to incite or arouse anyone to such defensive opposition, nor justify them. That is not my office, even less is my judging or rendering a verdict. A Christian knows well what he is to do. He is to give to God, what belongs to God and to Caesar, what belongs to Caesar. But he is not to give to the blood hounds what does not belong to them.

"O what a disgraceful imperial diet, the likes of which has never happened before or been heard of! ... What will the Turk and his entire realm say about this, when they hear of such incredible events in our kingdom?" Luther went on to shed light on all of the procedures during the Imperial Diet and the bloody recommendations, with which Caesar was intended to be won over. "But," he said, "what dramatic consequences would have resulted, if Caesar had started it with murder as had been urged with devilish and papal advice. That would have produced an imperial diet where not a single fingernail would have remained of either bishops or counts, especially in such dangerous times."

However, if Caesar were to start a war against the Evangelicals, how

Picture of Caesar Carl V
according to a copper plate by Behams in 1531

should the subjects of the papal counts, who would be drafted for this purpose react? In this regard Luther replied, "This is my true advice. If Caesar should call for some to serve and to wage war against us on behalf of the pope's purpose or against our teaching, as the papists are currently maliciously boasting and defying, I do not agree with Caesar in regard to this. In such a situation no person should permit himself to be drafted for war or be obedient to Caesar. Instead such a person can be certain that God clearly forbids him to obey Caesar in such a situation. The first reason for not obeying Caesar in going to war in such a case is this: you as well as Caesar took an oath in baptism to uphold the gospel and not to fight against it. ... The second reason is that you in such a war are taking it upon yourself, making yourself a participant, and are indebted before God for all of the abominations which have been committed by the papacy and are still being committed." He then followed through further on this topic and concludes, "If you are to be advised about this, you have enough of a warning herewith that in such circumstance you should not be obedient to Caesar or to your count. If you follow this advice, good; if not, then let it be and proceed boldly to the fight. Christ will not be afraid of you and shall, God willing, remain in your sight. Should he remain he will give you plenty of fighting. In the meantime, we shall see who will overpower the other and hold the field!

"This I want to tell my dear Germans as a warning, and, as I said earlier, I also testify that I do not want to incite anyone to war, rebellion, or self-defense but I advise only peace. But wherever our devils, those papists, do not wish to keep the peace, but with hardened, abominable impenitence rage against the Holy Spirit, still want to go to war, and as a result get bloody heads or even fall, I want to have given witness publicly that I did not do this nor did I cause this. They want it that way. Their blood will be on their heads. I am innocent and have done my work faithfully. Henceforth, I shall let him be judge who will judge, should judge, and can judge. He will not hesitate nor fail. To him belongs the glory and honor, thanks and praise, eternally. Amen."

That was a valiant word from a faithful German to his dear countrymen during those dangerous times. It surely made a strong contribution for clear understanding for both friend and enemy. Caesar did not deserve the great confidence which Luther expressed toward him in this treatise.

A German count, Moritz (or Maurice) of Saxony, whose thinking was less upright and noble than Luther's, did know Caesar better. A few years later he repaid that spiteful Caesar with his own coin in the Smalcald War. (Note: In service to Caesar, Moritz had been obligated to deal treacherously with his own blood relatives and brothers in the faith in Saxony. But unexpectedly he changed his loyalty, marched against Caesar and defeated him in 1552. - According to the *Lutheran Cyclopedia* ©1954 by CPH, St. Louis, MO)

The reason why Caesar and his brother did not succeed during Luther's days to overpower Germany and hand it back to the pope was the Turk. The authorities in Constantinople were well informed about the gross disunity in the German nation. The question of whether Caesar had reached terms of peace with Luther had been put before the ambassadors of Ferdinand, and the appropriate language which the Sultan directed against the king obviously had to have been downright uncomplimentary. The king also knew what the Turk knew, namely, that a strong defense was impossible without a united nation. For that reason, it was Ferdinand himself, who urged his brother, Caesar, to bring about a better agreement with the Evangelicals.

The time limit which had been given to the Evangelicals had passed quietly. Now Caesar began to take steps toward a closer relationship. When the Evangelicals explained that they would agree to nothing until the procedures, which had been attached against them, had been knocked down, they were dealt with as they demanded. At that time Suleiman Pascha moved toward the boundary with 250,000 men. He inquired about the way to Regensburg, where the German leaders had once again assembled since the 17th of April.

The king was still carrying on correspondence with the empire's enemy. Even though there was some possibility of reaching a favorable conclusion, there was no improvement in the unification of his people within the Empire. The Protéstants were also not in agreement in regard to several points, namely whether they should insist: first, that everyone who might join with them in the future be included in the overall peace; second, that in the article about the (proposed free) council they should insist on including the words, "according to the pure Word of God." Luther advised them to ease up on both points, lest the hope for peace be jeopardized. It was his opinion that the added stipulations would not change anything in later discussions, and that gracious peace should not be rejected because of some sharply and accurately sought details.

Peace was finally achieved at Nuernberg on June 23, 1532, according to which, "No one was to insult the other in regard to his faith, nor insult him for any other reason, or assist someone else in using force against him; but everyone was to treat the other (the opponent) in true friendship and Christian love until the time of the joint, free Christian council." Both of the previous stipulations were omitted in accordance with Luther's advice. This peace was confirmed by Caesar at the Imperial Diet on the 2nd of August, in spite of the strong opposition of some counts, especially Duke George. In return for this peace, the Evangelicals had promised to provide Caesar with strong assistance against the Turks.

It was high time. The Turk had already marched through Hungary as though it belonged to him. While the heroic Nicolas Jurischitz was holding the enemy from advancing further, a German army of 80,000 gathered near Vienna. The Evangelicals especially had provided more for the prepared defense than they had promised. How amazing the sight of such an army was to Suleimann, who had set his hopes on the disunity of the Germans! He declined to engage in battle and gave the order to signal retreat.

Luther greatly rejoiced over this new development regarding the Turk. He especially wished every success to "dear, upright Caesar."

Soon after the confirmation of the peace of Nuernberg, the gallant Elector John entered his eternal peace. He had a stroke on the 15th of August, while he was participating in a hunt at Schweinitz. Luther was quickly sent for. On the 16th, he found him still alive, but unconscious and saw him depart before the day had ended. The following Sunday the body of the count was interred next to the body of his brother. Luther preached the funeral sermon on 1 Thessalonians 4:13-18. Let us pay attention to some of his simple, heartfelt words, spoken at the graveside of his dear "Duke Johannsen." "We should diligently give thanks to God for the grace that he took hold of our dear Elector through the death of Christ and embraced him with his resurrection. You know what kind of death he experienced at the Imperial Diet at Augsburg. I do not wish to praise him for his highly virtuous character, but let him remain as a sinner, as are all of us. We are also reminded to go along the same path and desire to hand over to our Lord many large sins that we might remain under the forgiveness of sins. Therefore, I do not wish to make our dear, territorial lords so very pure, even though he has been a very upright, friendly man without falsity. In him I have never, throughout my life, sensed a degree of pride, wrath, or jealousy. He could forgive and bear everything easily and was gentle beyond measure.

"I shall proceed past this his virtuousness. If at times he failed as a commander, why should we wish to hold that against him? A count is also a human being and is surrounded by ten devils all the time, whereas an ordinary man is plagued by only one devil. All of this, we shall now leave alone. Let us remain in this that we praise him like St. Paul praised his Christians, namely, that God led him to be with Christ. We do not want to view him in regard to his temporal death, but in connection with Christ's death and the count's spiritual death, with which he imitated Christ. For all of you know how he died like Christ two years ago at Augsburg. He suffered the real death not only for himself, but for all of us, when he had to swallow all of the evil soup and poison which the devil had served him; that is a truly horrible death with which the devil grinds a man. There our dear Elector confessed Christ's death and resurrection publicly before the whole world, and he remained true to that confession. He risked his land and his people. Indeed, he put his own body and life on the line. So should we now seek comfort for ourselves that Christ died, and our dear count was captured and fell asleep in the death of Christ."

Following the peace agreement at Nuernberg the outward work of the reformation took a new powerful upswing. It proceeded under the new Elector John Frederick of Saxony, as it had begun under his predecessors. Provisions for preachers were being tended to as proper arrangements were made. The monastic properties were assigned in part to the church and in part for the common good. Efforts toward more strict discipline were being pursued in congregations. There was still cause for complaint regarding the populace due to their intemperance and gluttony. Thus, even Luther himself felt compelled to direct his public preaching at those, who during the time of church service gave offense with their loud carousing in the bars. Luther also knew how to speak of the "amassers of goods on their farms," the "Squires in the villages," and the "city bullies," who only wanted to hear what their ears were itching for. Among those who loved to hear the Word, he also recognized many despisers of that Word. When in 1535 his old friend Link expressed the desire to return to Saxony, he answered him, "How would it be if I myself would wander in your direction or go into exile?" His advice regarding difficult questions continued to be in demand. But now he, as well as Melanchthon, was being spared from directly participating in visitations.

The work of the church in Hessia was conducted in a similar fashion. Urban Regius served as the watchman for the same work in Lueneburg. The directive to the church from the Duke usually began, "We, by the grace of God, Ernst, Duke of Braunschweig and Lueneburg, and Urbanus Regius, the doctor of Holy Scripture, bid...etc." Diligent work also continued in the territory of Mark Brandenburg. Since 1532, the territory of Anhalt had been won for the reformation through the joining of the three brothers, Georg, Johann, and Joachim. Luther's friend Hausmann became the court preacher there, and Luther himself carried on regular correspondence with those three "righteous counts of Christian and princely character."

Wuertemberg was likewise incorporated into the religious peace in 1534. With the help of Philip von Hessia, Duke Ulrich had regained ownership of his territory, of which Austria had previously deprived him, through a "coup de main." Luther had protested this action of Hessia, but Philip would not take back his actions. When Ferdinand acknowledged what had happened in the form of a peace agreement, Luther recognized it as a gracious unfolding of God's providence. The reformation was formally installed there under the leadership of the active theologian Schnepf. The University of Tuebingen became a center of Lutheran theology.

Reformation was also happening in Pomerania at that time. Duke Barnim had already been a friend of Luther for quite some time. We saw him earlier near Luther at the Leipzig Debate. Now, in conjunction with Duke Philip, his nephew, he borrowed Bugenhagen from Wittenberg, who was talented and experienced in such matters. In spite of opposition from some nobles and distinguished spiritual leaders, an evangelical church system was put in motion throughout the territory. Duke Philip then married the sister of the Saxon elector. Luther officiated, using a form which had been introduced by him.

Chapter 42
A Free Christian Council (?)

The same time that the papal trash was being swept out in Pomerania, Pope Clemens VII died in Italy without having held the proposed council. He had announced its convening already in 1532, but he had postponed it on the day of his death. His successor was Paul III, who assumed the papal throne in October, and appeared to be eager to take the issue of the council more seriously. During that same year he sent his delegate, Cardinal Vergerius, to Germany in order to make arrangements with the German counts, as to the location where the council should be held. The papal ambassador also arrived at Wittenberg on November 6th. He, together with his 21 horses and one donkey, was honorably welcomed into the Elector's castle by the castle's commander. That very evening he invited Luther for a meal, and when he declined, Cardinal Vergerius extended an invitation to Luther and Bugenhagen for breakfast the next day.

Early in the morning, as he was about to meet the papal legate for the first time since 1518, Luther asked for his barber. It was the Sunday after "All Saints." The barber came. When asked why he had requested a shave so early, Luther replied, "I am to come to the holy father, to the pope's messenger. Therefore, I have to adorn myself so that I might appear young. Then the legate will think: 'Oh, Luther has caused so much misfortune and is still so young, what will he do in the future?'" When he had been shaved he put on his best clothing and put his golden chain around his neck. When the barber commented, "Dear Doctor, that will anger them," Luther opined, "That is why I am doing it. They have angered us more than enough." As he was seated on the wagon with Bugenhagen on the way to the castle he joked, "Behold, here come the German pope and Cardinal Pommeranus. They are God's tool and work."

While in the Cardinal's company in the course of table conversation he played, as he himself reports, "the annoyed Luther", blaming the Cardinal because they were not at all serious about holding a council; "and," he continued, "if you do indeed hold a council you will not deal with sound doctrine but with useless things: caps and bald heads, eating and drinking." "He has hit the main issue," the legate said to the man next to him. But Luther went on, and reminded them that the papists truly needed a council. "We," he said, "do not need a council. Through the Holy Spirit we know what we believe. But if you desire it, then hold a council. I will come, God willing, even if I were to learn that you were to burn me." "Where should the council be held," the legate asked. "It makes no difference to me," Luther fired back, "in Mantua or Padua or Florence." "Would you come to Bologna?" Vergerius asked further. Luther responded, "To whom does Bologna belong?" The legate answered, "The pope." Luther replied, "Great God, did the pope steal this city as well? Very well, I will even come to you there." Vergerius then said, "The pope would not refuse to come to you in Wittenberg." To which Luther answered, "Very well then, he shall be welcomed by us." The legate continued, "How would you like to see him, with an army or unarmed?" Luther responded, "However he wishes, we shall receive him in whatever manner he arrives." When asked whether priests were also ordained here, Luther replied, "Of course! The pope does not ordain any for us." Then, pointing to Bugenhagen, he said, "There sits a bishop whom we have ordained."

After the meal the legate rose from the table. As he was mounting his horse he called to Luther once more: "See to it that you keep yourselves prepared for the council." "Yes, my lord," Luther countered, "with this, my neck and my head."

So, Luther parted from the legate, who himself converted to the Lutheran doctrine ten years later. However, that discussion at the table lets us plainly see how the situation had changed dramatically since 1518.

Conditions improved even more for the Protestants during the following years. The Smalcald League was gaining more and more members. Both Pomeranian counts, Ulrich von Wuertemberg, and a number of cities joined. The League which originally was to last for six years was renewed to last ten. Two foreign kings now also seemed to have taken a political leaning toward the League.

One of these was King Franz of France, Caesar's old enemy. Quite suddenly he wanted to become Lutheran. He talked about reformation, and wanted Luther and Melanchthon to come to France. Melanchthon wanted to go. When the Elector refused to allow the visit, and reproached him for having entered so deeply into negotiations, Melanchthon became quite upset. But the Elector was surely correct. He wanted to avoid disrupting the peaceful unity that existed in the empire by bonding with Caesar's enemy. Without any reservation did the Count express himself why he did not want to have Melanchthon head into such an assignment, "It is no small concern that should Philip go to France he would leave so much unfinished business behind him, that Dr. Martinus and the other theologians would not be able to handle all obligations at Wittenberg.

The other royal foreigner, who was leaning toward the League, was King Henry VIII of England. He had planned to divorce his wife Catherine in order to marry a lady of the court (Anne Boleyn). Catherine was an aunt of Charles V. The reason he gave for his action was that his conscience would not allow him to justify his marriage, since the queen had been the wife of his late brother. Hence his marriage was not permitted according to Scripture. Since the pope, not wanting to make an enemy of Charles V, would not honor the divorce, Henry renounced the pope. He then sent negotiators to the universities throughout Europe in order to win a "Gutachten" in his favor.

The theologians of Wittenberg were also approached for that purpose. However, they responded that the king would have to keep his spouse. In 1535 the king's ambassadors arrived at the Saxon court, and they also approached the Smalcald League. Negotiations were conducted into the following year. They revealed the fact that the king was united with the Lutherans only because he also was an enemy of the pope. Nothing became of this union, and the negotiations had already gone on far too long for Luther. At the beginning Luther had supported the king's entreaty, in which he expressed his desire to deal personally with Melanchthon in England about doctrine. But later he became convinced that the king was a Lutheran just as little as the pope. Luther regretted the expenses which the Elector had to bear as a result of these negotiations.

In place of these negotiations another movement for peace came into existence in 1536.

Chapter 43
The Wittenberg Concord

One of those who sought Luther while he was at the Coburg castle was the before mentioned Martin Būcer (pronounced, "Būzer"). It happened this way. Būcer had previously sought a connection with the Lutherans at Augsburg. Since he did not succeed, the southern German cities of Strassburg, Constanz, Memmingen, and Lindau had drawn up their own so called Four-Cities-Confession. But Būcer did not give up. After Būcer had discussed things by mail with Melanchthon and Regius, he approached Luther with a number of articles, which he sent along with Regius. Since neither Luther nor Regius answered him, Bucer just headed in the direction of Coburg by horse. He arrived there on a Sunday evening. The next morning, he went to the castle. He reported, "Luther invited me to lunch there, and after lunch we engaged in conversation." However, Luther didn't want to hear about the unification articles in Būcer's form, which anyone could understand in his own way.

"The next day," Būcer went on, "I again came for lunch, as he had directed me. After we had eaten, we again talked about this business. Finally, he did not want to be persuaded that our preachers had taught sufficiently in regard to what we had discussed in confidence. He remained of the opinion that it was necessary that our preachers first lead our people back in the right direction. He added to this that in order to avoid offense he did not want us to change our minds instantly. I agreed to admonish those of our party accordingly." Referring to Luther in person, Būcer wrote, "I discovered that this man truly fears God and seeks to honor God from his heart."

Luther on the other hand soon commented, "There is hope that the Sacramentarians, at least those from Strassburg, will soon be reconciled to us. After all, Būcer had been sent specifically to discuss this church business with me at the Coburg castle in confidence. And, if what he told me is not deceptive, - I had admonished him to keep everything out in the open - then this hope is not a trifling matter." Būcer kept on doing his work. It is to be said in his favor that the points in regard to which he attempted to persuade his own people, seemed to them to be too Lutheran. Particularly the people of Zurich refused them. But soon the two leaders of the reformed, namely Zwingli and Oecolampad, were quite quickly called out of this life.

The people of Zurich instigated the Catholic canton in their area to an eruption of an old rancor, as they responded to a political ruling. That mountain canton simultaneously took up arms and stormed Zurich. The battle ensued on October 11, 1531, near Kappel, and the people of Zurich were defeated by a much larger force. One-fourth of them were killed on the battle field. Zwingli, who had gone along as a field chaplain, lay under a tree, critically wounded. Two enemy soldiers called out to him, "Do you want to confess and call upon the mother of God?" When he shook his head in reply, the captain Unterwalden delivered the death blow. The next day his body was quartered, burned, and the ashes strewn into the wind.

An image of Martin Būcer
according to an original woodcut by Reusner

Luther was deeply moved by the news of these events. He saw the end of Zwingli as a judgment of God, just as he had also viewed the end of Muenzer. Six weeks later Oecolampad also died.

Būcer would not allow himself to be diverted from his goal, in spite of the critical comments Luther repeatedly expressed about the Sacramentarians. Once again, it was Philip of Hessia who offered to help. In accordance with his arrangement a discussion took place between Būcer and Melanchthon, at Kassel December 27, 1534. At that meeting Būcer confessed his agreement with the statements Luther had sent, statements in which Luther's doctrine was set forth clearly and distinctly as never before. Melanchthon knew Luther well enough to be sure that Luther would do everything possible to avoid an appearance of extending the hand of fellowship without a true agreement in doctrine. As a result, he was deeply concerned that the negotiations for unity would end with even greater differences. What's more, he himself was plagued with doubt in regard to the disputed doctrine. He even went so far as to write to a trusted friend that he had served as "messenger of a foreign doctrine" at Kassel. The lectures he gave after his return from Kassel were not at all to Luther's liking. They sounded almost Zwinglian. It was therefore all the more joyful to the Wittenberg team, as to how Būcer wanted himself to be understood.

Nevertheless, Luther did not jump to a quick conclusion. He studied and carefully weighed the explanations which Būcer had provided and the formal confession he submitted, with which the people of Augsburg had already declared themselves to be in agreement. After such a conscientious study, Luther made it known during the last days of January that, since they now desired to teach according to the Augsburg Confession, he personally could not oppose a union. Since they clearly confessed that the body of Christ was being distributed truly and in essence, received, and eaten, he was satisfied with their wording.

Still, the final adoption of the concord was to be delayed until the troubled waters on both sides had settled and the distrust that remained here and there had disappeared. He also desired that the matter be adopted not only between Būcer and himself, but also between a larger number of persons on both sides. This was because just as he had not wanted to give up his conviction to others, so he also did not want to pressure others to accept his conviction. Since he had now become more confident in regard to this issue, Luther would also be participant with heart and hand. He expressed his sincere readiness for actual unity in one faith and confession during those days with these words, "Nothing more cheerful has happened to me during this entire time of the renewed rising of the gospel after the deplorable schism than this, that I may finally hope for, indeed can even see, a concord. When this concord stands established I shall sing with joyful tears, 'Lord, now you let your servant depart in peace,' for I shall leave peace behind for the church. Be assured that as far as things pertain to me, I shall do and endure, faithfully and cheerfully, anything and everything that is possible for the completion of this concord."

There were also steps being taken to set up, if possible, a meeting for many to participate for the purpose of formally recognizing each other. Since Luther was quite ill at that time, a place had to be chosen which was more suitable for Luther. The Elector decided upon Eisenach as that place.

Hence, invitations went out for a meeting at Eisenach on May 14, 1536. But when the people from southern Germany were already under way, it was realized that Luther was too weak even for a trip to Eisenach. What's more, some circumstances had quickly developed which were throwing the goal of establishing the concord into question.

A writing of Zwingli which had survived appeared in print. In it not only did Zwingli's teaching about the Lord's Supper stand forth in stark nakedness, but the editor also extended a ready hope to the "Christian King" of France, to whom the writing had been addressed, that in the next life with Christ and the saints under the old covenant, he would also find the presence of wise heathens: Socrates, Aristides, and others. Zwingli's follower, Bullinger, had praised this work in the foreword as Zwingli's swan song in which he surpassed himself. Furthermore, about the same time there appeared a collection of letters by Zwingli and Oecolampad, which was introduced with a foreword by Būcer.

But Luther did not back down. Instead he asked all the more that, in order to make it possible for him to attend, the meeting might be held at Grimma. But the people from southern Germany now had decided to travel straight to Wittenberg, where they arrived on May 21st. When the two men from Strassburg, Būcer and Capito, visited Luther at his home the next day, a Monday, Luther did not give the slightest indication that he would hide his thinking, which had risen anew in his mind. He emphasized that an external unification without an inner unity would make it an evil a hundred times worse. It would be better to leave the issue where it was at that time. Būcer responded that Luther's suspicion was unfounded. Those letters, which included his own letter in the preface, had been published by the printer's own decision, and without his own knowledge or desire. However, they were completely sincere in regard to the concord, which could have been adopted already, if there had not been a prevailing misunderstanding on both sides. But that was not good enough for Luther. He wanted the other side to disavow what they had previously taught. He would then also acknowledge where he had been too harsh in his writings. The other side should confess their agreement that the ungodly also receive the body of Christ in the Lord's Supper. If they could and would desire to do this, they were to consider this once more with their friends among themselves and give their answer the next day.

The afternoon of the following day, all of the representatives of both sides again assembled at Luther's residence. Būcer, who was the spokesman for the southern Germans, then explained that they believed and taught with a united voice that unworthy guests also receive the true body and blood of Christ in the Lord's Supper, and as a result, those who drew near without faith, received the Sacrament unto judgment. Only among such godless people, who falsified the words and institution of Christ, could they not accept the actual benefit ("wahrhaftige Geniessung") of the body and blood of Christ. He repeatedly explained that as far as the rest was concerned, they did not make the presence of the body and blood in the Lord's Supper contingent upon the faith and unbelief of those who receive it. In the event that they had still not expressed themselves clearly enough, they welcomed further questions to be addressed to them.

When they, each and every one of them, had personally testified in answer to questions that they taught exactly like Būcer and were in complete agreement with the Augsburg Confession without any reservation, and asked again to be received into the fellowship of faith, the Saxon theologians withdrew into an adjacent room with Luther. After a brief discussion Luther returned, and with a joyfully uplifted voice and beaming face, said, "Honorable lords and brothers! We now have heard the answer and confession of each of you that you believe and teach that the true body and the true blood of the Lord is given and received in the Lord's Supper and not only bread and wine. In addition, you confess that this administering and receiving truly takes place and is not imagined. You take offense only in regard to the godless; yet you confess, as St. Paul says, that the unworthy receive the body of the Lord where the institution and the words of the Lord are not falsified. Therefore, we do not wish to quarrel. Since this is the way it is with you, we are at one. We recognize and accept you as our dear brothers in the Lord as it pertains to this article. We shall want to discuss the public open writing of this concord later, when the other articles will also have been treated. Philip shall now put this article into writing."

Everyone listened to these words with folded hands, Būcer and Capito with tears in their eyes. After exchanging handshakes all around, further discussion was postponed to the next day since it had already gotten late. The meeting was adjourned.

The rest of the points about baptism, absolution, and the power of the office of preaching were taken care of on Wednesday without any difficulties. The next day they were celebrating the Festival of the Ascension, for which Luther preached a powerful sermon with Mark 16:15 as the text, "Go into all the world and preach the good news to all creation."

On Friday, Melanchthon presented the document which he had prepared regarding the Lord's Supper, and it was accepted by both sides without any objection. On Sunday, Albert of Reutlingen preached in the morning, Būcer at noon, and Luther in the evening. The bonded union found an endearing expression with a joint Holy Communion celebration according to the Lutheran rite. In the evening, Būcer and some of his group celebrated "Gemuetlichkeit" (sociable comfort) while dining with Luther. An eye witness reported, "As now a number of comments were expressed about the sermons. Luther told Būcer that his sermon that day had pleased him very much. Yet, I am a much better preacher than you. Būcer replied, 'Yes, everyone who has heard you will testify to that and has praised your sermon.' 'Not that way,' said Luther. 'You are not to explain it as praise for me, for I know my weakness and do not know how to put together as ingenious and intelligent of a sermon as you. But when I step into the pulpit I see what kind of listeners I have. To them I preach what they can understand, for most of them are poor lay people and the simple yohmen (in German – "Wenden"). But you elevate your sermon too high and float it over their heads, with intellectualistic spiritual language ("im Gaischt, Gaischt"). Therefore, your sermon applies only to the intelligent. Those things my country folk, my yohmen, cannot understand. Thus, I behave like a faithful mother who offers her breasts to the mouth of a crying and nursing child and gives it milk to drink. From that milk the child is much better refreshed and served than if she would pour in a sugary drink or some other costly syrup from the drug store. Such practice every preacher should follow. He should take note of what kind of listeners he has and whether they can understand and grasp what he preaches, and not how educated he is.'"

On Monday all of the articles of unification, including the added statements regarding baptism and absolution, were signed by all of the participants. Later that same day, the guests set out on their homeward travels after heartfelt good-byes.

Luther and Melanchthon reported to the Elector that, "Bucerus and his fellow travelers have distanced themselves from their error, have acknowledged the same, have confessed the truth, have publicly recanted, and have turned to the confession and teaching of our church."

Chapter 44
Smalcald, (The Smalcald Articles)

A few weeks after the Wittenberg Concord the pope announced a council would be held at Mantua in May 1537. One of the reasons given for this council was "the extirpation of the poisonous Lutheran heresy." John Frederick immediately believed that it would be wrong to agree to such a council, a council which considered that the teaching to be evaluated was a poisonous heresy from the start. Since Luther and Melanchthon, on the other hand, continued to recommend sending representatives to such a council lest they give the impression that they did not want peace, the Elector directed Luther to put his doctrine into articles, as his foundation on which he would stand to the end. Then he was to lay those articles before other theologians to be signed. Such a confession could be presented at the council if need be. Luther immediately went to work. He was already able to place his articles before his Wittenberg colleagues and other friends during the season of Christmas. Having gathered their signatures, he sent the confession to the Elector on the 3rd of January.

It was divided into three parts. The first part summarized "The Sublime (lit. "Highness") Articles concerning the Majesty of God;" the second part, "The Articles Which Refer to the Office and Work of Christ;" and the third part had the heading, "The following sections, or articles, we may assess with learned and reasonable men, or among ourselves. The pope and his government do not care about these. For conscience is nothing to them. Money, honor, and power are everything."

Luther listed those doctrines in which nothing could be conceded; namely, the teaching that we are made righteous and are saved without our own merits, but only by grace through faith. "In regard to this article," he stated, "nothing can be yielded nor conceded, even though heaven and earth and whatever will not remain may pass away. This article contains everything we teach and live in opposition to the pope, the devil, and the world.

The mass was described as "the greatest and most horrible abomination since it directly and powerfully strives against this chief article." In regard to the discussion of this subject at the council, Luther wrote, "This article concerning the Mass will be the entire business of the council. Even if it were possible for them to concede to us all other articles, they would not be able to concede this one. As Campegius said at Augsburg that he would rather be torn to pieces before he would relinquish the Mass, so, with the help of God, I too would let myself be reduced to ashes before I would allow a servant of the Mass, be he good or bad, to be made the equal of Christ

Jesus, my Lord and Savior, or to be exalted above him. Thus, we are and remain forever separated and opposed to one another. They well understand that if the Mass falls, the papacy lies in ruins. Before they will allow this to happen they will put us all to death, if they can." (Part II, Article II, Paragraph 10). Then he goes on to set forth "the brood of vermin, which this dragon's tail, the Mass, has begotten."

Of the pope, Luther wrote, "that he is the true antichrist and contrarian Christ, who has exalted himself above and stationed himself against Christ, because he will not allow Christians to be saved without his power, which nevertheless is nothing." (Part II, Article IV, Paragraph 10) "Therefore," he concluded, "as little as we can worship the devil himself as lord and god, just so little can we endure this apostle, the pope or antichrist, in his rule as head or lord. For to lie and to kill, to destroy body and soul eternally, that is wherein his papal government really consists, as I have clearly shown in many books." (Part II, Article IV, Paragraph 14) To this he attached a reminder that the papists would not allow the smallest portion of this article to prevail at the council.

But at the same time Luther did not regard the articles of the third part this way, as though there were still doubts about them which the council needed to decide. He was not referring to the council as "the learned and reasonable men" in this part's title. He had no expectations that they would busy themselves with these articles. At the end he wrote, "These are the articles on which I must stand, and, God willing, shall stand even to my death; I do not know how to change or to yield anything in them." (Part III, Articles XIV,XV, Paragraph 3)

In no way did this confession tread as softly as the Augsburg Confession. It is noteworthy that of all of the theologians who signed it only Melanchthon did so with a reservation. He signed it, "I, Philip Melanchthon, also regard the above articles as right and Christian. But in regard to the pope, I hold that, if he would allow the gospel, then his supremacy over the bishops, which he possesses otherwise in accord with human law, would be allowed by us also for the sake of peace."

The Elector, on the other hand, expressed his unreserved gratitude to Luther for this concise and clear Confession. He declared that he would himself confess to it before the council and the entire world.

The advice of the evangelical representatives regarding their participation at the papal council was to be gathered at Smalcald. The Elector wanted Luther, Melanchthon, and Bugenhagen to take part in those discussions. The rest of the representatives wanted to bring theologians along as well. The Elector and his company arrived at Smalcald, on February 7th. Besides the counts and the city delegates about 40 theologians gathered there during the following days. One also had been sent by Caesar, along with a papal legate who carried a letter from his lord.

However, the main concern of the assembly was not in regard to the council, but in regard to the life of the man who stood a notch above all of them. Luther had been suffering from kidney stones for some time. He preached in the large city church on February 9th. That same day his pains were again noticeable, but improvement seemed to occur and the whole week passed quietly. The proceedings had not yet begun, and for Luther the idleness became burdensome.

On Sunday he preached again, even though his condition had taken a turn for the worse in the meantime. Now the pains became stronger and stronger. The doctors, one of whom had been summoned from Erfurt, tried their best. "They gave me drinks," he later related, "as though I were a big ox." External cures were also applied, but all in vain. The patient was only getting weaker. It seemed as though his life would end.

Luther himself was prepared to die with quiet submission in accord with God's will. The pains he had to endure were horrible. "If this continues much longer," he said, "I may even go out of my mind. If it were not for faith in Christ, it would not be surprising for me to take my own life with a sword." Still he remained patient and said, "Since we have been the recipients of God's goodness, should we not also accept the bad? As it pleases the Lord, so let it happen. Let the name of the Lord be praised. I have often contested against the pope and the devil, and the Lord saved and strengthened me in a wondrous manner. Why should I not calmly accept whatever he may do to me according to his will?"

Through it all, his thoughts were occupied with needs in the church. Tearfully he prayed to God that he would preserve the Word after his death." I am dying as an enemy of your enemies," he said, "a man under the ban of your enemy, the pope, with the result that your enemy will in turn die under your ban." He also expressed concerns for the University of Wittenberg. He was afraid that after his death the unity that existed would be disrupted. The anticipated separation from his wife and children was oppressing him heavily. He commended them to the Elector, who promised to care for them as for his own. But as he was growing ever weaker and had begun to vomit, he cried, "O dear Father, take this little soul into your hand. I will thank and praise you. Move on, little soul, move on in God's name."

Since there was no further change in his condition, the doctors considered it wise to send the patient to Gotha, where aid could be given for his restlessness as well as for a lack of medicine. Luther, the Erfurt physician Sturtz, Bugenhagen, Spalatin, and Mykonius boarded the Elector's carriage on the 26th of February. Another wagon was sent along carrying the necessary materials for medical assistance, especially coal pots for warming towels. They said farewell at the wagon, and Luther made the sign of the cross over them with the words, "May the Lord fill you with his blessing and with hatred against the pope."

It was feared that traveling in the carriage would cause the sick man pain, and that is what happened. But the jostling up and down in the carriage on the rough road through the hills also caused a different, completely unexpected result. It produced the emptying of the patient which had been missing. "Luther is alive!" "Luther is alive!" was the resounding in Smalcald not many hours later, in front of the house of the papal legate. This was the messenger who had set out from Tambach at 2:00 AM with the good news. That same night Luther had written the good news in a letter to Melanchthon, and had announced the reversal of his condition while it was still taking place. Luther also wrote to his wife right away. "I was dead and had commended you and the children to God and to my good lord, as though I would not see you again. I was very concerned about you, but I had committed myself to the grave. There have been so many sincere prayers to God for me, which have been offered tearfully by so many people, that it seems to me that I have been born again. Therefore, give thanks to God, and let Aunt Lene give thanks to the true Father; for you surely would have lost this father."

Unfortunately, that new found improvement would not last. At Gotha the pains recurred with such vehemence that the end appeared to be near again. Once again Luther submitted to dying. He assigned the task of comforting his Kate to Bugenhagen, asked forgiveness of the Wittenberg theologians, especially of Melanchthon, for whatever way he had offended them. He also sent greetings to the Elector and the Landgrave to tell them that they should not allow themselves to be disturbed by the hostilities of the papists, but bravely carry on in their work for the gospel. He also stated again that he had a good conscience in regard to his storming against the papacy. "Indeed," he concluded, "I am now prepared to die, whenever my Savior, Christ Jesus, so wills. Nevertheless, I would like to have lived until Pentecost, so that I would still be able to make public in print my harsh accusations, exposing to the whole world the Roman beast, the pope and his kingdom. If God lets me live I will truly do so, and no devil shall prevent me from doing so. But if I die, there surely will come after me those who will also not present him with a gift. Now I commend my soul to the faithful hand of my Redeemer, Jesus Christ, whom I have preached and confessed to the world." Then he made his confession and let Bugenhagen pronounce the absolution to him.

It appeared as though the wish that Luther had expressed at Smalcald, namely, that he would like to have died and been buried in his Elector's territory, was going to be fulfilled there at Gotha. But God had decided differently. The next morning Luther wondered why he was still alive. We would soon find him again in ecclesiastical debates.

Already at Smalcald, Būcer sent him news from Switzerland along with a letter from mayor Meyer of Basel. Luther replied to this letter in a friendly fashion and promised to do what he could so that a true union could also come to pass between them. At the same time, he asked that "the resting birds be not startled." Further discussions with Luther were impossible due to his illness. But Būcer, together with the Augsburg preacher Wolfhart, decided to travel and seek Luther, upon receiving the good news from Tambach. They found him still considerably ill in Gotha. Still, in his serious illness, he willingly permitted a meeting with them. Once again, he warned them against hiding things. Moreover, he stated that when he would be well again, he wanted to be faithful in presenting the Swiss with a treatise. Luther kept his promise even that same year. There were also further negotiations, and Luther continued to hope for a good outcome. He did so until he had to admit that the Swiss did not want to let go of the Zwinglian doctrine, and those negotiations died.

Finally, while still at Gotha, a decisive improvement set in for Luther regarding his sickness. Six stones, one as big as a bean, left him. In the meantime, the discussions at Smalcald were quickly concluded. The leaders explained that they were not being served with the sort of council which the pope had proposed. They would have to appear in a foreign country as the accused, and the pope would be both the accuser and the judge. They had requested a free council and would insist upon it. They sent the pope's letter back unopened.

The purpose for which Luther had written those articles was thereby rendered void. However, since there were already a number of signatures affixed to that fine and powerful confession, the issue was pursued further and others were also allowed to confess themselves with their signatures as adhering to the Lutheran teaching. Some signed while traveling. Most of them signed while they were at the meeting at Smalcald. Thus the Confession, which belongs to the symbols of our church, bears the name: "The Smalcald Articles. "What's more, a tract, which had been produced by Melanchthon about the primacy of the pope, had also been presented for signing and so was recognized by the theologians as a joint confession. In addition, the Augsburg Confession and its Apology had been taken up once again. The adjourning of that alliance conference reported, "Our learned men, who have discussed all the articles of our Confession in a Christian manner, agreed on all points as contained in the Confession and the Apology. There is only one article, the one about the primacy of the pope, which they have tabled for the time being." Finally the counts and delegated theologians confessed themselves there to the concord in a formal manner, that concord which had been established with the southern Germans in Wittenberg.

Let us now again return to Luther, whom we had left in Gotha. He was being brought to Weimar by way of Erfurt with special care. There Melanchthon, who was coming from the convention, caught up with him. Jonas and one of Luther's nieces had traveled to meet Luther. They rested in Altenburg at Spalatin's home. They arrived safely in Wittenberg on the 14th of March. Luther remained weak for some time. But before the month had ended, he again occupied his pulpit for Lent and Easter as a diligent preacher.

"John Frederick the Magnanimous" (in office 1532 – 1547)
according to a painting by Cranach

Chapter 45
Harvest Days During Stormy Weather

Longer threads were being spun in the empire, and new threads were begun, while Luther was tending to some of his duties in Wittenberg. When it became known that the Smalcald League had rejected the papal council, the active papists thought that now was the time for Caesar to be prompted to take action. In order to be prepared to have a united front in such a case, the counts, George of Saxony, Heinrich von Wolfenbuettel, and Erich von Kalenberg entered into an Alliance, which would later include King Ferdinand and Caesar. The Imperial Vice Chancellor Held, who had begun the whole movement, made an attempt to spur the Alliance into open battle. However, he fell into some disfavor with Caesar for doing so.

Once again, the Turk was on the move. The Imperial Forces could hardly do without the Smalcald Forces, especially if they should be challenged to open warfare. So, what happened was that instead of going to war against the Evangelicals, a new treaty was adopted in France at the beginning of 1539. In connection with this it was hoped that a side discussion might be pursued, aimed at peace regarding the ecclesiastical entanglements.

In addition, a favorable change had developed in the situation for the Evangelicals in the Dukedom of Saxony. Duke George had been called out of this life on April 17th. Luther had repeated differences with him ever since the Imperial Diet at Augsburg. They had stood opposed to each other as early as the appearance of both of his writings about that diet, "Remarks about Caesar's Edict" and the "Warning to His Dear Germans". The Duke had issued a response under a pseudonym, which Luther had countered with a writing that had been poured out of a salty brew under the title, "Against the Plotter of Dresden." In it he defended himself against the unjust accusation that he was starting a rebellion.

Since his Elector had admonished Luther about this sharp writing, Luther let go of the "knots and lumps", which George had still carried with him on his sleeve, and lapsed into silence. When George in 1532 had exiled a large number of evangelically minded subjects from Oschatz and Leipzig, Luther applied himself to comfort those who had been driven away and those who were still being threatened. (Footnote: "To Those Christians Who Have Been Driven Away from Oschatz" LV, Vol. 8, p.79)

The Duke interpreted this as a stirring up of subjects, and Luther again replied sharply. This quarrel once again was knocked down. Still, Luther had done something meaningful and had encouraged those oppressed brothers in the faith at Leipzig that God had already removed many of the bloodthirsty oppressors since the Diet of Worms. "Let us patiently wait a little while longer for what God will accomplish before ten years will have passed since the occasion of the Diet of Augsburg." While the ten years had not yet passed, Duke George had become a corpse. (Footnote: It is said that while the Duke lay dying in his bed he was vainly seeking rest and comfort by calling on the saints. A noble reminded him of his own proverbial statement, "Going straight makes the best message carriers." That noble urged him to go directly to Christ for his refuge, and as a result he is said to have called out, "Indeed, so help me, faithful Savior, Jesus Christ; have mercy on me and make me holy through your bitter suffering and death.")

His two sons had preceded him in death, one in 1537, and the other in 1539. Now death had claimed the father so quickly that he had not been able to make his last testament legal and binding. He had meant to exclude his brother Heinrich as his heir. He would assign his estate and his territory to Caesar and his brother Ferdinand, if Heinrich, who was a member of the Smalcald League, would not return to the Roman church and join the Nuernberg Alliance of Catholic counts. Hence not only was the ponderous enemy of the Lutheran doctrine gone, but, on the heels of the death of Duke George, Heinrich now permitted the Reformation to spread throughout the land immediately upon his taking office. Nothing stood in the way.

The evening before Pentecost Luther preached in the chapel of the Pleissenburg, where he had once debated with Eck. Luther and Jonas had been invited to the "homage" celebration. (The "homage" festival was the swearing in of the new head of government.) The next afternoon he preached once again in one of the city churches, which had been barred to him during the days of the debate with Eck.

That same year, the Electorate of Brandenburg joined the ranks of the Evangelical territories. When Duke Erich died in 1540, not only did the Catholic Alliance lose one of their members, but his widow welcomed the reformation in Braunschweig - Kalenberg. The countess herself was a dear personal friend of Luther and his wife, and Luther was helpful to her in reforming the church in her lands. It was not surprising that Caesar would be inclined toward a peaceful rule in Germany under such circumstances. A meeting at Speier to promise a "Christian equality" in religion was thwarted because of an epidemic. Nevertheless, such a meeting was held at Hagenau.

Melanchthon was delegated by the Elector to attend. But he only got as far as Weimar. From Weimar, a letter of the Elector came to Luther asking him to travel to Weimar immediately and bring Cruciger with him. Melanchthon had become ill and could not travel farther. Therefore, Cruciger was to go to Hagenau, and Luther as the count's advisor was to await the continued transactions in Weimar.

There was a special reason for Melanchthon's illness. The Landgrave

Herzog Georg „der Bärtige" von Sachsen, nach einem alten Holzschnitt.

A woodcut of Duke George, the Bearded

Philip of Hessia, who had not been enjoying a happy marriage with his wife, the daughter of Duke George, had the bad idea of marrying a second wife, a lass from the Saale River area, with whom he had fallen in love; otherwise, he claimed, he could not control himself. He declared that the advice he had received at his confession, which he had received from Luther and Melanchthon through Būcer, was in his favor. He then actually consummated the marriage with Margaretha of Saale on March 4, 1540. Melanchthon, who had been brought there by pretext, was requested to be present as a witness.

Luther had a good conscience about what he had done in this situation. He didn't hide his involvement in this matter for which he would be blamed as it had taken place at this time. It was also possible for him to justify his actions. But he did not want to do that. "I will," he also wrote soon thereafter, "hold in the strictest confidence what the Landgrave disclosed to me through Būcer's confession, even to my own disgrace. It is better to say that Luther acted foolishly ... than for me to reveal the real reason why we yielded to the Landgrave." The fact that he did not regard the actions of the Landgrave as justifiable he expressed repeatedly later.

This is the way he wrote against Hans Worst. "I know of a lady Landgrave in Hessia who lives there and should be called Mrs, and mother in Hessia ... I refer to the Duchess, the daughter of Duke George in Saxony. The fact that you counts are, in part, traveling on a road of planks (not as durable as a road of stone), you are responsible for having brought this about with your bad example, etc." So, when this entire affair became public knowledge with the dust flying, Melanchthon was plunged into angst and despair at the thought of his role in the matter and because of fear of the consequences, until he finally collapsed under his burden.

The condition in which Luther found his friend Philip was wretched. It seemed as though death had already accomplished its purpose, as though his senses had already ceased and his eyesight had been dimmed. The physician, once again the renowned Sturz, had reached the end of his skills. At this point Luther applied his. He stood in front of the window and prayed with all his might. He grasped all of the heavenly promises of his heavenly Father and insisted that his petition be heard. He received his answer. After he had prayed he again turned to the patient, who was beginning to show signs of life. When Philip asked that they let him go home, Luther said, "Not at all. You must keep serving our Lord God."

He had food brought to him and ordered, "You must eat in front of me, or I shall put you under the ban." Thereupon Melanchthon ate and recovered further, so Luther could write to his friend Lange, "We found him dead. He is alive through a miracle of God." Melanchthon himself later said that he would have died at that time had Luther not come.

Nothing was accomplished at Hagenau except that new negotiations for a meeting at Worms were being considered. Indeed, the discussion of religion had been begun at Worms, but it was again postponed to take place at a diet, which Caesar himself wanted to hold at Regensburg.

We know that Luther considered the efforts toward unity with the papists hopeless. He had expressed that very clearly in the Smalcald Articles. The accuracy of this conviction became very evident again at Regensburg. If ever the hope for a favorable result was evident, it was at Regensburg. The main figures in the debate for the Evangelicals were Melanchthon and the peacemaker, Būcer. On the Roman side were the well-intended, and for some time already, reform-minded theologians Pflug and Gropper; even the papal legate Contarini, who was present at the diet, showed himself more inclined than the other papists.

For those who did not look deeper into the matter, it actually did at first seem that things were heading in a good direction. The papists made concessions as never before on a number of important issues. But soon that wagon became mired down and could go no farther. It happened exactly as Luther had predicted in the Smalcald Articles. It was in the articles of the primacy of the pope, of the mass, and the like, that the Romans would not yield. At last the Evangelical representatives sent a message to Luther for his "Gutachten" for the plan they proposed, to gain his consent if possible.

Luther was once again in pain. Head problems, especially a draining ear, caused him much pain. Yet, as always, he was available for open and correct advice. Tolerance had been suggested. But Luther wanted to practice only one kind of tolerance, one in which not a single bit of the truth would be conceded or be forced into silence. Efforts for peace had already fallen apart at the diet due to the contrary position, which the Catholic leaders had taken against the joint statements of the theologians. Add to that the fact that the Catholic leaders, along with the pope, had declined the proposed tolerance request from the Evangelicals. The Protéstants, on their part, did not yield to the demands of Caesar. Yet one thing was achieved; the religious peace of Nuernberg (See p. 319) was confirmed by Caesar. The fact that this stayed in place at this time was due mainly to that nasty Turk.

Caesar did enter into an expressed agreement with the Landgrave. In it the Landgrave received full amnesty. He, in turn, promised not to permit the Smalcald League to unite with England or France. Because of this action, Caesar aroused great displeasure among the papists. The Elector of Mainz is said to have declared at the time that they were without protection and would have to seek another Caesar for themselves. Indeed, Caesar did not protect the papal shock troops when aggressive steps were being taken against those who were believed to oppose a religious peace. One such example was in motion, when the fanatic Duke Heinrich of Braunschweig wanted to enforce one of Caesar's suspended verdicts of the Imperial Chamber of Justice against the protéstants Goslar region.

For many years this powerful voluptuary had irritated the Landgrave and John Frederick. He had even been accused of starting the fire in the Elector's territory. He had made the accusation against Luther that Luther was referring to his own territorial lord as "Hans Wurst," in a blasphemous writing. Luther replied with salty words under the title, "Against Hans Worst." (LV, Vol. 29,30, p. 195 ff.) In that writing, Luther cleared himself of that accusation, but now attached that name to Duke Heinz in person.

Because of this breach of the peace, the Landgrave chastised Duke Heinrich with a surprise, when he invaded the territory of his opponent, who was waiting in vain for help from Caesar. After a brief siege, he captured the Duke's main city, Wolfenbuettel, and brought that entire region under his control. The Landgrave's court preacher preached the first Evangelical sermon in Wolfenbuettel, using the text of the unjust steward. The Reformation was imported into the whole area under Bugenhagen's supervision.

No explanation is needed as to how the Protéstants would boldly step forth at the next Imperial Diet at Nuernberg. Nevertheless, they did not succeed with their request for complete freedom to teach and to have the Imperial Chamber of Justice dissolved. On account of this they rejected Caesar's conclusions of his Imperial Diet.

Caesar aroused even more displeasure among the Romanists at the next imperial diet, which was held at Speier, in 1544. Since France and the Turk were united against him, Caesar knew well from whom he could expect the most powerful aid. He not only consented to continuing a truce with the Protéstants, but he also set up the prospect for an imperial meeting, in case a free Christian council would not soon take place on German soil. At this meeting, the professionals could bring the religious discord between them to a peaceful conclusion. The relationship between the Evangelicals and their Caesar was outwardly more amicable than ever before.

Of course, the dislike that Caesar held in his heart against the gospel and its adherents soon showed itself. This became evident as early as 1545. He had promised to bring about a free council. Now the pope was once again underwriting a purely papal council at Trident, and the German Protéstants were expected to peacefully accept this under the Caesar. How he then, as soon as his hands were free, would throw his Spanish mercenaries against the Evangelicals is recorded in the history books. But Luther's eyes did not have to watch. As long as he lived, there was rest and peace. The Turk, an enemy of Christendom, and the papal King of France still had to serve the gospel of peace in Germany with their saber rattling as God's global peace protectors.

Chapter 46
Later Life Labors

Having paid a great deal of attention to the political situations under which Luther spent the last decade of his life on earth, from now on let us turn to the smaller circle of the reformer's friends.

Since a school needs calmness to thrive and to continue to bear fruit, the two full decades of unrest could not have been very beneficial for the University of Wittenberg. The peace of the more recent years had to have been a special blessing for this school. And so it was. Luther personally complained about the disorder which was said to have ruled during the "pope's war." But when the calmer years came, this very important school benefited from the blessings of the peace. The theological faculty received a new status in 1533. During that year for the first time since 1525, doctorates were granted to Bugenhagen, Cruciger, and Aepin. The Elector, together with princely guests, attended the celebrations. During the summer of 1535 the fear of a plague was the reason for temporarily moving the university to Jena. But Luther calmly remained in Wittenberg and poked fun at those who fled. He implied that some of them must have had the boils on their school bags, the colic in their books, the scabs on their pens, the gout on their paper, or had contracted homesickness out of their mothers' letters. But the fugitives returned in February of 1536, and the Elector marked that year by opening new wells of income for the university. The accompanying charter (for the occasion) stated:

"God in his mercy has let his Holy Gospel-precious Word be revealed during these last times, through the teaching of the honorable and highly educated, our dearly devout and devoted Martin Luther, doctor of Holy Scripture, with correct and true Christian understanding for comfort and salvation for all people, for which we shall express praise and thanks to him eternally, and alongside other skills especially the languages of Latin, Greek, and Hebrew by way of excellent ability and diligence of the highly educated Melanchthon, for promotion of correct and Christian understanding of the Holy Scripture."

Holy Scripture, according to the statutes, was to remain the central issue for theological instruction. The interpretation of the dear Word of God would remain Luther's most beloved labor. Yet since his return from the Coburg, he was still hindered in many ways from practicing what he was teaching due to the weakness of his body. Roaring in his head and weakness of his heart caused him great misery. At times he could neither write nor read, and was often close to falling. As a result, the Elector was very careful as he wanted to spare this valuable man. He had admonished him at the Coburg to make sure to take care in regard to his health. During the following year he had to submit to rehabilitation for some time at the Pretch Castle, with the Stablemaster Hans Loeser, as much as that was possible for Luther. When he rode along in a cart for a hunt, he also took his Psalms with him and was doing some spiritual hunting. In 1536, the Count released him entirely from his responsibilities of lecturing in respect to theological writings or for any other work at the university. He did this by removing him from the theological faculty. Instead, the Elector gave him, and Melanchthon as well, an additional salary of 100 guilders.

Luther according to the painting by Cranach
in his so called genealogy record in Berlin

Nevertheless, Luther continued to interpret books of Holy Scripture before those youthful students as much as his strength allowed. So, during 1531-1534, he provided interpretations of selected Psalms, the 2nd, 51st, 45th, 90th, and the so-called Psalms of Ascent, Psalms 120-134, which were also published later from notes that had been taken. (Note: For the interpretation of the 51st Psalm see LV, Vol. 15, p. 61ff.) During the same years he had also lectured on the prophets Hosea, Micah, and Joel, the interpretations of which were printed later. In addition, we have an extensive interpretation of the letter to the Galatians from those years. It was issued in 1535 from notes that had been taken during his lectures. He even provided a foreword for this commentary. Luther had a special love for his work on this letter. He once said, "That is the epistle to which I am engaged. She is my Kate von Bora." He treated this interpretation with great thoroughness and referred to it as among the best of what he had written about Law and Gospel, and the righteousness through faith alone.

After the university's return from Jena, where it had fled because of the plague, Luther began his large interpretation of Genesis. With this he busied himself until shortly before his death. This became his last lecture, and at the same time, his most extended lecture. It was a treasure chamber in which he again collected the riches which he lifted out of the mines of the Word of God. At first, he did not want to let this interpretation be printed. He finally yielded to the pleas of his friends in 1543. Veit Dietrich prepared these lectures for printing from carefully taken notes. The first volume appeared in the spring of 1544 and included a preface by Luther. In it he wrote, "St. Jerome speaks correctly: 'Each one brings to the ark of the Lord according to his possessions, the ones gold, silver, and precious jewels, other skins and goat's hair. The Lord needs all of this and allows himself to be pleased with the good will of all those who sacrifice to do so and bring gifts to him, though they do not all bring the same gifts. Therefore, I am also satisfied that these lectures of mine are set forth in print for public use, and are being offered and sacrificed to God's temple as goat's hair." (See Exodus, chapters 25 to 36 for reference.)

Luther continued his activity in the pulpit along with his activity at his lectern. Shortly after his return from the Coburg he again had to step in for Bugenhagen, who was working at large from October 1530 to April 1532. Since Bugenhagen, in accordance with the Wittenberg pericopes, had been preaching on Wednesdays from the Gospel of Matthew, and on Sundays from the Gospel of John, Luther simply continued from where Bugenhagen had left off and interpreted the Sermon on the Mount, Matthew 5-7. All these sermons were also taken down in notes and set into print in 1532 (See LV, Vol. 9-11). For his Sunday sermons he interpreted from the Gospel of John, chapter 6:26-8:38. These sermons were published after his death.

He again preached from the Gospel of Matthew when he had to substitute for Bugenhagen, who was working for church order in Denmark from 1536-1539. During that time Luther interpreted Matthew 18-24. During those same years, shortly after his severe illness at Smalcald, and prior to Bugenhagen's departure around Easter, he preached on John 14-16. These sermons were published a year later from notes that had been taken. Sermons on John 17, which Luther had preached during Bugenhagen's absence in 1528 and 1529, appeared in print as early as 1530. (Note: For the sermons on John 14-16, see LV, Vol. 19-23) An interpretation of Psalm 110, which he must have delivered in sermons after Easter of 1538, he published personally the same year. (See LV, Vol. 29 and 30) In his conclusion of this interpretation he called this Psalm "A special core and quintessence of all of Scripture, the likes of which none other foretells so richly and completely, as it portrays the Lord Christ with his entire kingdom."

Luther substituted for the absent city pastor not only in the pulpit, but also in private ministry. With a great deal of personal devotion, he made himself available to the sick in the congregation. Even when a plague threatened to break out again in 1538, and talk was again heard about moving the university and, when many citizens wanted to flee, Luther openly stated from the pulpit that he would remain, preach, and visit the sick, and even a hundred plagues could not cause him to flee. Concerning those who would forsake their relatives, friends, and neighbors, he threatened to burn their wood and let their savings be distributed to the poor.

We might also attribute the completion of his Church Postil as a fruit of Luther's preaching activity. He was still not satisfied with the shape in which that book was available at that time. In 1540, he had another opportunity to take it in hand. During that year, the Winter Postil with many changes appeared in a new addition. Three years later, he also allowed the other half, enriched by the edition of sermons on the epistles, to be edited by the specially gifted Cruciger.

He also concerned himself with edifying works as he had done earlier, on behalf of the needs of the people. There appeared the interpretations of a number of Psalms. One was the 147th, which he produced during his stay with Hans Loeser. He wrote it down afterwards and had it published. He sent this "noble wild game" as he called it "in its entirety and totality" to Hans Loeser, while he was at the same time keeping it entirely and totally for himself. (See LV, Vol. 12, p. 271ff.) During the ensuing years he issued "Summaries of the Psalms" which were to indicate "for the simple what each individual Psalm wants and of what it is capable." In an interpretation of the 101st Psalm in 1534, he wrote about the "worldly state", and especially set forth the duties of the rulers.

When a pious Wittenberg barber, who often conversed with him about religious matters, had come to him seeking directions for prayer, he wrote a tract that same year on "A Simple Way to Pray for a Good Friend, Master

Peter, a Barber." (See LV, Vol. 1, p. 136 ff.) In it he treats the Lord's Prayer, the Ten Commandments, and the Creed and shows how a person may structure his devotions accordingly. After he had gone through the Lord's Prayer, he wrote, "This is, simply stated, about the "Our Father" or how I am used to praying this prayer myself. For to this day I suckle like a child, drink and eat like an old man on this Pater Noster. I cannot get enough of it, and for me it is more than the Book of Psalms, which I do love very much. This is the best prayer above all the rest. Stand assured that it presents itself in the way in which the true Master set it up and taught it. It is abomination upon abomination that such a prayer from such a Master should be babbled and rattled to death throughout the world. Many pray several thousand Pater Nosters per year, and if they were to pray that way for a thousand years, they would actually have failed to taste and pray not the smallest letter, not the least stroke of a pen," of it (Matthew 5:18 NIV). In summary, the Pater Noster is the biggest martyr (along with the name and Word of God) on earth, for every person tortures and abuses it. Few find comfort and are cheered by using it rightly."

However, the most important work with which we find Luther occupied in service toward his German people throughout all these years is his German Bible. In his later days we continue to see him striving to improve himself more and more as the interpreter for his beloved Germans. To carry this out, he placed an order to Nuernberg in 1535, for all of the nation's books that had appeared recently, including poems, songs, pictures, etc. This was to learn verbal usage, nationwide, from them.

We had seen him occupied at the Coburg with translating the prophets. After he had finished and seen it printed in 1532, he translated the Old Testament Apocrypha. Luther commented that "they are not to be held equal to Scripture, but still are useful and good to be read." Thus, the enormous task, which had up to this point in time appeared only in sections, was complete. In 1534 the first complete edition was issued under the title, "Biblia, That Is, All of Holy Scripture, German. Mart. Luth. Wittenberg. MDXXXIV." With much diligence and effort had this entire project been reviewed and finally approved for the first edition of it. But Luther did not leave it at that.

In 1539 we find him in partnership with his friends, occupied with a new review of the 1534 edition. He completed this task in 1541, resulting in the completed publication of the second chief edition. Mathesius, who was his house guest at that time, indicated how this projet was being carried out with full attention to the details of this important work. Several hours before the evening meal the learned associates: Bugenhagen, Jonas, Melanchthon, Cruciger, Aurogallus, and M. Roerer, who read the corrected work, had assembled at Luther's home. Each one had prepared himself for the text. They brought along their Latin, Greek, and Hebrew Bibles. They then proceeded to go to work. Luther read the translation which he was suggesting after careful deliberation. They then allowed the others to offer their opinions until they had reached agreement regarding the best expressions. Luther gave special consideration to present the Greek and Hebrew text in good and understandable German.

For this reason, he had once gone to a butcher in order to learn the names of inner parts of the animals correctly. He had several "sacrifices" butchered, and had obtained the names of the different parts. When after work the doctor would invite his friends to the evening meal, the table talk would often revolve around some specific point of their joint work. But even after the first thorough review Luther did not withdraw his hand from the project, and the editions of 1543 and 1545 were still going through several changes. Thus, Luther himself treated the German Bible for what it was, namely, the most important work of his life.

In addition to this major task we should not leave unmentioned the fragrant smaller flowers which came to bloom in his garden for the church and the reformation during those late summer days of Luther's life. Let's refer to several spiritual songs. In 1535 the Wittenberg hymnal, for the first time offered the hymn, "From Heaven Above to Earth I Come," for which, the Christmas joy of his own little children may well have inspired him. At the same time the tender hymn appeared, "She's dear to me, the precious maid. I simply can't forget her..." in which he sang the praise of dear Christendom. In the summer of 1541, when prayer services were requested for turning away the Turkish threat, for which Luther also urged "An Admonition for Prayer against the Turk," he also wrote a hymn, "Lord, Keep Us Steadfast in Thy Word." The hymn, "Our Father, Thou in Heaven Above," appeared in 1539. The baptismal hymn, "Christ, our Lord, to Jordan Came," and the hymn, "What, Herod, Foe, Scares You so Much" in 1541; finally, in 1543 he produced "You Who Are Three in Unity" and "From Heaven Came the Angel Host." He rejoiced that others used their gift of poetry in the service of the church. But he also felt himself compelled to place a warning over the title of the preface for his little 1542 hymnal,

> *"Many false masters do hymns now compose*
> *Beware and discern them and rightly dispose."*

He actively inspired many others in this field. This yielded the result that the year he died, there were already 47 Lutheran songbooks in use. Nevertheless, even then he remained the choir director above all others.

While Luther was carrying out his task of instruction through the words of his lectures and his publications, he also excelled in his office as defender of the truth. As he did with the trowel, so he also first laid the sword out of his hand when he closed his eyes. (See Nehemiah 4:16-18.) The papists were indeed the first ones to discover repeatedly that he still was in the picture.

To combat the biggest abomination of the papacy, the Mass sacrifice and those who practiced it, Luther produced a writing in 1533 entitled, "Concerning the Private Mass and the Ordination of Pastors." (See LV, Vol. 5) With this he delivered powerful blows against both of these bastians of the papacy as had not been done for a long time. He not only provided proof of how Christendom had been disgracefully betrayed through both of these, but also what was the true celebration of the Lord's Supper, and what was the true ordination of preachers in the church and in the spiritual priesthood.

We previously dealt with another powerful indictment of the papacy, "The Smalcald Articles." He offered their publication with a foreword in 1538, so that if he were to die before a council would convene, those still alive could present his witness and confession. At the end of his foreword he lamented, "Oh, dear Lord Jesus Christ, hold the council yourself and deliver those who belong to you by way of your glorious coming. The pope and his followers are lost. They don't want you."

He raised his voice about the matter of a council in great detail again the following year with his production, "About the Councils and Churches." Here he again expressed his conviction that there would not be a true council under the pope. "Well then," he concludes the portion which dealt with the councils, "if we must despair of having a council, then let that be commended to the true judge and the merciful God. In the meantime, we shall promote the small councils and the young councils, pastors, and schools. Let St. Peter's Article (Matthew 16:16) promote and preserve (*God's truth*) against all the newly condemned articles of faith, and the new good works with which the pope has flooded the world." To this he then attached a thorough explanation regarding the question of what the Church actually is, namely, the holy people who truly believe in Christ and are made holy through the forgiveness of sins; and how one can recognize it, namely, before anything else, by way of Word and Sacrament, and by way of the administration of these means of grace.

Luther then moved on to the school, the citizen's home, and the courthouse, for the citizen's protection. These, he said, are the three divine authorities: the authority of the Holy Spirit in the church, the parents in the home, and the power in the government. The illusionary authority of the pope should not be endured alongside these, but be trampled underfoot with the power of the woman's (Eve's) Seed, even if a person has to receive the sting in his heel.

Luther then once again dealt with the doctrine of the church as in the already previously mentioned work, "Against Hans Wurst" (See LV, Vol. 29,30, p. 195ff) from the year 1541, in which he had desired to respond to the papist who had attempted to scoff at them through their heretic Heinz. Here he again proved that we are the true Church from the facts that we have the true Baptism, the true Lord's Supper, the true old Keys, the preaching office and the Word of God, the Apostles' symbols, the Lord's Prayer, and other things which the Church of old possessed. "With this," he then wrote, "we have now proved that we are the true old Church together with the whole Holy Christian Church, one body and one Communion of Saints. Now it is up to you, you papists, to prove that you are the true old Church, or are like it. However, this you are not able to do; but I shall prove that you are the new false church." And this he did prove in overflowing measure.

Luther would issue a final powerful writing against the papacy during the last year of his life, his farewell blessing to it. He did so when the pope declared the bitterest accusations against Caesar, because of the very favorable imperial decision for the Evangelicals in the year 1544. He then declared that the council would be in Trent. In this work, to which Luther gave the title, "Against the Papacy of Rome, Instituted by the Devil," (See LV, Vol. 25, p.7ff.) He first wrote for "the most hell-like father", Paul III, a chapter about how his admonition to Caesar Karl and his announcement of the council ought to be regarded, namely, that the first was dictated by murder and a thirst for blood while the latter was a swindler's trick and a miserable juggler's game.

Then he wrote, "But I must stop here or save my response at this point concerning what else I have to say against the letters and the bull. For my head feels weak and I feel as though I might not be able to finish. Still, I have not yet arrived at that point which I had intended to cover in this pamphlet, which I wish to finish first, before my strength will completely leave me. For I have set three projects for myself: One, whether it is true that the pope, as he boasts about himself, is the chief head of Christendom in regard to councils, Caesar, angels, and everything else; Second, whether it is true that, as he screams, no one can render a verdict against him, judge him, or remove him from office; Third, whether it is true, as he boasts and batters unendingly, that he has brought the Greek empire on us Germans. If I still have some strength, I will return to his bulls and letters and attempt to comb the unkempt long ears of that large, scrubby donkey."

He then answered those three questions thoroughly. In response to the first question he wrote, "This pamphlet has gotten too large under my hand, and, as is said, age is forgotten and fades away. Perhaps the same thing has happened to me. Though the papacy is a demonic abomination of itself and endless, unspeakable filth, I hope I have clearly and powerfully given an explanation to whoever wishes to be informed, for myself I am sure, regarding the first matter from above I have dealt with. I have answered, whether it is true that the pope is the head over Christendom, lord over Caesar, kings, and the whole world. You have been informed that - praise God - no good Christian conscience can believe that the pope is or can be the head of the Christian Church, or the vicar of God or Christ. But instead he is the head of the condemned churches of the very worst bullies on earth, a vicar of the devil, an enemy of God, an adversary of Christ, and destroyer of the Christian Church, a teacher of all lies, of blasphemy of God and of idolatry; an arch church thief and robber. Whoever does not want to believe this, let him continue to journey along with his god, the pope. I have herewith done my duty as a called teacher and preacher of the church of Christ, and am duty bound to tell the truth." And after he had also answered the other two questions he ended his writing with the words, "But here I must let it go. If God wills, I shall do better in another pamphlet. Should I die in the meantime, may God grant, that another will make it a thousand times stronger, for the devilish pope is the last evil on earth, and the next is what all the devils can do with all their might. God help us. Amen."

While this work was going to press, a new papal document, full of lies, came into Luther's hands, in which was described his death and the dreadful ghostly spook of the devil, who was projected next to his corpse and his grave. Luther published this work himself with an epilogue. In it he stated how he had read this angry fabrication with pleasure and how it made him feel smooth in his right kneecap and his left heel, that the pope and the papists hated him this much from their hearts, and if they would not repent, how he would regard their writing such a booklet as a favorable ("goennen") comfort [*only*] for themselves, in case they do not repent ("wie er, falls sie sich nicht bekehrten, dass ihnen goennte, dass sie zu ihrem Trost solche Buechlein schrieben.")

But Luther remained in battle dress not only against the pope as long as he lived, but also against the "swarmers" and the sacramentarians. It is not true that in his later years he changed his position toward them, and regretted his earlier struggles against them. He also wanted to prevent any appearance that he had become one with the Zwinglians. Hence, he issued "A Warning Message to Those in Frankfurt on the Main River to Beware of Zwinglian Teaching." He did this because in 1532 he found out that the Zwinglian doctrine had sneaked into Frankfurt, with a Lutheran disguise. He published this work at the beginning of 1533. In it, among other things, he stated, "Therefore, this is my faithful advice which I owe before God. It is for you in Frankfurt and wherever else it is needed. Anyone who knows that his pastor publicly teaches the Zwinglian way should avoid him, and instead go without the Sacrament his entire life before he would receive it from him, truly even suffer death and all things on that account. But if the pastor is one who speaks two-tongued, who proclaims by word of mouth that the body and blood of Christ are present and real in the Sacrament, but suspicions remain that he is selling something in a sack and still means it differently than the words declare, then go to him or send your message to him plainly. Let him tell you clearly what it is that he distributes to you with his hands and you receive with your mouth, putting aside what is being believed or not believed in the heart, simply ask what the hand and the mouth here touches."

At the same time in this writing he provided an appropriate treatment for Confession of Sins, when he surmised that those preachers were also exerting themselves against the Confession of Sins. Questions of this nature had reached him, and also a telling treatise (*which displayed the sacramentarian interpretation*) in regard to Confession of Sins.

He wrote in the same vein in regard to a similar situation to those in Augsburg. In it he again decisively rejected any fellowship with the swarmers. He would express the same view in letters sent in his later years. But when the claim that he had bonded himself with the Zwinglians became even louder he issued in 1544, "A Short Confession D. Mart. Luther about the Holy Sacrament". (S. LV, Vol. 24, p. 279ff.) In it he wrote, "As I am now heading for the grave, I will bring this witness and this reputation with me before the judgment seat of my dear Lord and Savior Jesus Christ, that in all seriousness I have condemned and avoided the swarmers and the enemies of the Sacrament: Carlstadt, Zwingli, Oekolampad, Stenkefeld (meaning Schwenkfeld.), and their disciples at Zurich and wherever they are. This is in accord with the Lord's command in Titus 3:10-11: "A man that is an heretick after the first and second admonition reject; Knowing that he that is such is subverted, and sinneth, being condemned of himself." (LUTHER's summarizing transliteration) They have been admonished by me and many others often enough and seriously enough. The books are available in broad daylight. Our preaching is going out daily against their blasphemies and their heresy that is full of lies, which they know very well."

But since the opponents pointed to the situation in the castle church, how the elevation of the host and the chalice had been taken out of the service, as evidence that Luther wanted to show that he no longer held to the true presence of the body and blood of Christ in the Lord's Supper, he dwelt on that issue in the last section. He showed that he had allowed the continuing of this practice earlier, since it still did allow for an acceptable interpretation, because Carlstadt had decried it as a sin. But now, since this practice had fallen away in most Lutheran churches, some special observance was no longer desirable in Wittenberg, and therefore this practice was omitted as a matter of freedom.

A different sort of swarming with which Luther was at odds were the Anabaptists. As early as 1528, he had written a detailed treatise against them, "Concerning Rebaptism to Two Pastors." The reason behind this was that a preacher from this sect had appealed to him. In this writing he proved the correctness of infant baptism. However, he had also spoken against putting the penalty of death on the swarmers as often happened. But when they in later years, especially through secret dealings, were also seeking to get followers from evangelical congregations, he issued a publication in 1532, "Concerning the Sneakers and the Corner Preachers," which simultaneously became a treatise regarding the need for an orderly call into the preaching ministry. "Therefore, it applies as follows," he wrote, "Either produce the call and command to you, (*which qualifies you*) to preach, or be silent, for preaching is forbidden. For it is called an office, truly, a preaching office. But no one may hold an office without a command or a call."

How necessary a warning against these swarmers was, and to what an end these people would come, when they moved away from the steadfast and firm Word of God to the activity of the swarmers is shown as follows. It revealed itself in a terrifying manner as the Anabaptists at Muenster, where the gospel had previously made an inroad under the "Tailor King," Bockelsohn of Leyden. There the swarmers erected their kingdom by robbing those who did not want to participate in communal property, and thereafter introduced polygamy, and under terrifying obsession forcefully resisted the besieging army of neighboring counts, until that pitiable starved-out city was captured by assault.

A third kind of opposition which Luther fought in his writings were the Jews, people, who were for him regarded as unbelievers, in the sense in which we still speak of unbelievers today. Their stiff-necked attitude, rejection of the gospel, and their hateful blasphemies against Christ and the Holy Trinity led Luther to three writings in 1543: "Concerning the Jews and their Lies," "Concerning Shem Hamphoras and the Genealogy of Christ, "(Shem Hamphoras was a description of one of the names the Jews had invented, to whom they ascribed special powers. Christ was said to have performed his miracles with use of those special powers, according to their lies.) and "About the Last Words of David." In these works Luther presented the truth of Christianity over and against these unbelievers and blasphemers of Christendom.

But more troublesome than these battles were other struggles for the aging fighter. These were the battles imposed on him by those who had stood shoulder to shoulder with him, and who in part wanted to be better Lutherans than Luther himself. We have heard about his battles with Carlstadt. According to Carlstadt, Luther had not gone far enough in the war against the pope and his doctrine.

The same thing happened with one of his students, who has been mentioned a number of times already, namely, Johann Agricola from Eisleben. (His actual name was Schneider or Sneider.) He had become the head of the boy's school in his, and Luther's, birthplace. Since he believed that he had been called for a higher purpose, he was not satisfied with that position and would not rest until he had been made a professor at Wittenberg.

But he had already previously presented himself as a watchman for pure doctrine. When Melanchthon had worked out his visitation pamphlet, he alleged that too much emphasis in that work was put on the law and its effects. He was not even satisfied when the pamphlet appeared in print with a foreword from Luther's hand.

To be sure, at the beginning he remained silent and kept himself in friendly companionship with Luther. We have heard how he was taken along to the Imperial Diet in Augsburg as a preacher. Luther had welcomed him with genuine affection when he moved to Wittenberg, even giving him, his wife and children lodging, when he could not immediately find living quarters.

Yet there were others who did not trust this ambitious man. In 1537, it was discovered that Agricola actually sought to bring his idea to the people of Wittenberg, that the inner crushing of the presence of sin in man must be accomplished only by the gospel and not by the law. In addition to that, he claimed that the law has no place in the Church of the new covenant.

He secretly allowed statements to be distributed, in which he supplied written examples, asserting that Luther in some of his writings, though surely contradicted in others, was teaching the same as he. Thus, Luther himself saw that he would be compelled to confront him, though it became very difficult for him to do so. As he himself said, he almost died on account of this.

Agricola according to a miniature portrait
by Cranach in the Wittenberg University Album, the year 1531

Yet, he did this with a number of debates, which he set up as theses against the "Antinomians" or "attackers of the law."

When he appeared at the first debate, Agricola acted as if the matter did not apply to him at all. But then Luther took away from him the permission to lecture on theology, which he had assigned to him as deacon of the faculty. Thereupon Agricola joined in a second debate and Luther declared himself to be satisfied, and even put in a good word for him with the Elector. But when it was learned that Agricola's teaching had gained a following, Luther decided that a retraction by Agricola was necessary. He also took a stance against the "Antinomians" in a new disputation. Agricola declared himself ready to retract and asked Luther to issue it for him. Luther did so with a short writing, "Against the Antinomians." In addition to this, Agricola also published a retraction which Melanchthon had prepared for him.

So, the honest and upright Luther was hurt and disappointed all the deeper, when Agricola soon after allowed himself to be involved with hidden attacks against Luther and his writings, which gave evidence of persistence in his old error. Now Luther's trust was exhausted, and he no longer spoke to that "false man." However, since new reports about the spread of antinomianism kept arriving, Luther took the opportunity to testify against it, both in writing and in speaking. Though he did not mention Agricola by name in this process, nevertheless Agricola believed the blows to have been directed against him, and finally handed a formal grievance in to the Elector.

But now any holding back on Luther's part came to an end. In response to that grievance he revealed how the impure activity of the "Magister Grikel" had gone on some years already, and once more provided proof of how dangerous the teaching of "prideful, foolish talk" is. When a friendly intervention in this matter by the Elector did not succeed, a formal examination was commanded. But before it could be set up, Agricola withdrew his grievance and followed the advice of Elector Joachim of Brandenburg, who drafted him to Berlin as the court preacher. From there he did produce a satisfactory retraction. But friendly relations between him and the Wittenbergers were not established, and later years would confirm Luther's verdict in regard to Agricola.

Among his colleagues at the university, it was the jurists who caused further trouble for Luther, especially the otherwise famous Dr. Hieronymus Schurf. Though he had joined the cause of the Reformation at its beginning, he did not want to let go of the canonical law which had been inherited from the middle ages. This was in spite of the fact that it contained quite a bit of material which did not agree with the true teaching of God's Word that a committed engagement be regarded as valid even without parental consent. Thus, according to canonical law, bonded engagements were valid, even without and contrary to the approval of parents. Luther had issued a writing, "About Marriage Issues" ("LV," Vol. 27,28, p. 194 ff.) in regard to this problem as early as 1530.

In addition, Schurf wanted it to be forbidden that a preacher enters a second marriage after the death of his first wife. He based this view on I Timothy 3:2 and kept insisting that it was in harmony with an understanding that had been acceptable during previous ages. Luther had entered into the discussion against this false interpretation as early as 1528.

But Schurf could not be swayed from his views. When secret engagements gave rise to a different kind of offense, as even a son of Melanchthon entered into such an arrangement, and a similar situation arose in Luther's own household, Luther considered himself compelled to give public testimony against this problem from the pulpit and against the jurists who supported it. He did so for a number of years, repeatedly and sharply. "I am angry," he said in one of such sermons of 1538, "and want to be angry. For they, the nasty jurists, are meddling against me in reference to my divine call." This battle against his partners in the faith caused Luther great grief. Yet, a whole year before his death he succeeded in persuading the jurists to give in, and the Elector himself gave his approval for this.

But among those who historically are called Lutherans and took positions on many sides, both defending and opposing sides, but against whom Luther had to offer defense as a protector of divine truth, there is one whom we cannot leave unmentioned. This person is Melanchthon. It is true that in Luther's writings we nowhere find an attack against this highly gifted man, to whom Luther showed so much incredible fondness with friendly and affectionate loyalty. On the contrary, Luther showed him the highest regard to the end of his life. And still, to the question as to whether Melanchthon consented faithfully and completely in favor of the truth to all of the issues which Luther taught and defended, we have to answer, "No!"

We have already seen how his efforts to yield at the Diet of Augsburg had raised strong suspicions among faithful Lutherans. That same willingness to give in showed itself again later in regard to the swarmers. Even his correspondence with people, who fought against Luther's teaching, was a special temptation for him, one toward which he should not have applied himself. While we have seen in Luther's behavior a compulsion to take a stand against the undermining effect of the false rumors that he had united with the swarmers, and that he was supposed to have partially yielded to them, Melanchthon was active to the contrary. He wanted to appear as one who would not completely reject the opinions of those who taught differently, and who would yield somewhat for the sake of peace. Truly, even more, already during Luther's lifetime he did not with full conviction take a stand with Luther in regard to a number of important doctrinal issues. Doubts had arisen in him about the Lutheran teaching of the Lord's Supper. And, in the working of conversion and justification, he nourished the opinion to give credit to man for some part, even if it were only a small role.

How did Luther react to all of this? To this we must respond: Luther did not discover all of it. How Melanchthon considered Luther's firm stand for all of the truth and how he thought in his own heart about Luther's conflict with the opponents, Luther could have known only if he had read the letters Melanchthon had written to those opponents, and how he expressed himself to them. Melanchthon also sought to keep his doubts a secret from

Luther. But when Luther did discover an error, he did not allow it to go on. Rather, he would step forward with an open debate against what Melanchthon had presented, reject it as wrong, and refute it from Scripture, upon which Melanchthon would retract it; or he would rebuke Melanchthon privately where he had spoken or acted incorrectly. He would prove his error until Melanchthon would give a satisfactory explanation, as had happened until shortly before the end of Luther's life (See p. 358). In one case Luther was already taking steps to write against Melanchthon openly; and it was only through the efforts of the Elector to encourage a private discussion at which Melanchthon again gave a satisfactory explanation, so that an open breach was prevented.

If Melanchthon truly had such room for doubt in his heart, as appears to be the case according to his own letters, then Luther must be given credit for his sharp control. For as long as Luther was alive, Melanchthon again and again publicly confessed his belief in Luther's teaching. As a result of these confessions and the explanations he received in answer to privately offered rebuke, Luther regarded and dealt with Melanchthon as a rightly believing teacher to the end of his life, though he was also well acquainted with his weaknesses.

While Luther was thus scattering the noble seed of nurturing teaching near and far and made the sowing of weeds difficult, he also repeatedly experienced the fact that not all seed falls on good soil, and that the devil is active in trying to take the Word out of the heart. Yet he was also allowed to experience new territories being opened to the gospel. Thus, after the gospel had found a foothold already in other areas in the territory of Archbishop Albrecht, like Magdeburg and Halberstadt, it also happened that a road was paved for the gospel at Halle, the favorite city in which Albrecht liked to stay. There the council called Luther's friend, Jonas, to serve as pastor. Soon two other evangelical preachers were installed. Albrecht no longer wanted to stay there, and taking his treasured relics, moved out.

When he had them displayed in Mainz and celebrated them with indulgences, Luther scoffed about this soundly in a "New Newspaper from the Rhine." In it he spoke of the wonderful relics he knew about, which the archbishop was said to have put on display. These included a piece of the left horn of Moses, three flames from the burning bush, a lock from the beard of Beelzebub. In addition, the pope had in advance promised ten years of indulgence for anyone who would bring a guilder to his holiness.

At the same time the Naumberg Bishopric was being decided. The Elector, "as the territorial count and chief patron", planned its occupation so that he would allow Luther's friend, Amsdorf, to be dedicated as the bishop. Luther himself, together with other neighboring preachers, had to conduct the festive dedication of the bishop in the large domed cathedral at Naumberg. What happened first was that the congregation confirmed the choice of the new bishop with a loud "Amen!" Then, after Luther had delivered his ordination sermon, the chosen one was ordained with prayer before the altar through the laying on of hands. To this the congregation sang a "Te Deum" along with the choir. Luther reported on that special occasion in a special writing, an occasion the likes of which had not existed before.

An evangelical bishop was also installed in Merseburg in 1544. Prior to that time, the aged Archbishop Hermann of Koeln had turned toward the Reformation and had entrusted the arrangement of his church matters to Būcer and Melanchthon, in 1545.

Regrettably Būcer had again acted without an approved form. Melanchthon then withstood a public testimonial that Luther had wanted to issue against him, by explaining that he, Melanchthon, had not written the article

Justus Jonas according to a painting by Cranach

about the Lord's Supper in the whole reformation process of Cologne, and that he also had expressed his misgivings to Būcer about his formulation.

The archbishop of Muenster also began to introduce the reformation in his territory. We had earlier taken notice of how this work was being disrupted through the abomination of the Anabaptists in the city of Muenster.

But whereas, as is told, Luther was privileged repeatedly to rejoice that the church of the reformation was extending its boundaries, he also had to see and hear a number of reports that burdened his heart and drew bitter lamentations from him about matters taking place in the cradle of the reformation. We had heard several instances earlier as to how Agricola and others caused problems for him there.

However, it was not only those who occupied the office of teacher that gave cause for sorrow, it was also the congregation of hearers who did so, even after a number of things had improved through the visitation. Noticeable problems such as a large amount of self-satisfaction, a lukewarm attitude, and ignorance were evident in response to the wholesome teaching. A covetous pursuit of earthly goods was also apparent. In all seriousness Luther reproved the vulgarity of the farmers, the greed of the townsmen, the lasciviousness of the nobility, and the excesses of the students.

Luther had spoken decisively against usury as early as 1519, in both a short and also in a longer sermon (see LV, Vol. 13, 14). He did so again in his letter to the nobility, following that up in 1525, with a work entitled "Concerning Buying Activity and Usury" (see LV, Vol. 13, 14). Then in 1539, after he had borne witness against the usurers in a sharp sermon, he issued a writing "To the Pastors to Preach Against Usury" (S. LV, Vol. 13,14), in which he condemned the collecting of interest as sinful. In regard to this testimony, of course, he also expressed his conviction that his book would truly prick the consciences of the small usurers; the gross fleecers of land, on the other hand, would laugh into their fists. But at least he wanted to have given his witness.

It was the same with his attempts to introduce and revise orderly church discipline. There as well he was afraid that his work would serve its purpose to instruct the common man, but the mighty lords would not allow themselves to be treated this way. However, this did not stop him from promoting the exercise of strict church discipline, and he lamented the fact that he could not take it as far as he would have liked. During his later years, Luther, as he had done earlier, instructed the congregations about the proper use of the ban, including how to exclude and publicly announce the names of impenitent sinners and turn them away from the Lord's Supper. When the forceful imposition of discipline in a congregation was suggested to be transferred to the banning procedure of a consistory, as was first arranged in the electorate circle in 1539, this was not in accord with Luther's thinking. He wanted to see discipline remain in the hands of the congregation.

But when disorder was starting to hold the upper hand in Wittenberg and Luther could not make headway with his witnessing, he began to make plans to leave the city. However, the pleading and tears of friends succeeded to have him still remain. So he stayed. At the start of the next year, when the Elector, prompted by the recess of the Imperial Diet at Speier, requested from his Wittenberg theologians a general scheme in regard to "Christian Comparison and Reformation on behalf of Religion in General," Luther submitted such a "Gutachten" along with the others.

That was soon followed by his work, "Against the Papacy of Rome,

Instituted by the Devil." But even above his scolding of the antichrist, he was bothered by the disorder of the Christians, which was still spreading throughout his city. In addition to the witness he had been giving up to this time, his concern was shown by the fact that he now again suddenly, but in all seriousness, was intending to shake the dust of Wittenberg off his feet.

When reports of the lax and grossly sinful living ("ueppig ") in Wittenberg had reached his ears while he was in the midst of a trip for recuperation, he ordered his wife, Kate, to sell his house and possessions. He said he would rather take up the staff of a wanderer and eat the bread of beggars, than at the loss of his irksome labors foul his elderly days with the disorder in Wittenberg.

Only after his colleagues and the mayor, who had been directed to do so by the city council, caught up to him on his trip and promised that they would help him in his efforts against the offense, and the Elector also made similar promises, only then was Luther persuaded to get ready to return. The city council, in conjunction with the university and according to the command from the count, now actually adopted rules against the disorderliness which had so burdened the heart of that faithful man. A new visitation also

An old woodcut of Amsdorf

was ordered, for which Luther had previously issued the visitation booklet of 1528 with a new foreword.

Upon his return, Luther once more reached for his pen against the enemies of the pure gospel. The theological faculty at Lyon had once again spoken out. They had taken the Roman teaching under their protection with 32 polemic theses against the poison of the Lutheran, Oecolampadian, and other heresies. He responded to these hostile theses with his own. In so doing he once again elevated the majesty of God's Word. The first thesis was, "Everything which a person teaches in the churches or congregations of God without God's Word, is nothing less than lies and godless material." The 25th Thesis, "St. Augustine also does not want for his or someone else's books to be regarded, or honored, as equal to Holy Scripture, or that a person should regard his proverbs as articles of faith."

Short and sharp, in concise and keen manner, did he now expose the chief errors of the Roman church. In between he took advantage of one more opportunity to demonstrate publicly how he was separated from the error of the Zwinglians. He did so in the 27th thesis where he wrote, "Concerning the Zwinglians and the sacramentarians, as they deny that Christ's body and blood in the highly honored Sacrament are not received physically by mouth, we seriously hold them to be heretics and members cut off from the congregation of God."

In this chapter we have made mention of the last doctrinal and polemic writings of the great teacher. Large was their number, great the diversity of the writings from his hand which had preceded them and had been distributed in countless editions. And there still remained a demand for those which had appeared earlier. Luther took no payment from the publishers or the book sellers, neither during the earlier nor the later years, and so those people realized even more profit through those books.

Gradually the book dealers heard of a wish for a complete edition of the available writings of Luther, and the request for such an edition was also directed to the printers by the theologians. At first, however, Luther wanted nothing to do with it. He was of the opinion that his books had now become excessive. In 1537, he wrote to Capito that with the exception of his book to Erasmus and his Small Catechism, he would like to devour all of his books, as was done in the legend by Saturn to all his children.

But after some time, he yielded to the demand. In 1539, the first volume of the German writings appeared, and in 1545 the first volume of his Latin writings appeared in a folio edition at Wittenberg. After the death of the editor, eleven German and six Latin editions were to follow the first volumes. Even so, many of Luther's writings had not yet been included. Luther began the preface for the first part of his German works with the words, "I would prefer to have seen my pamphlets be left behind altogether and disappear. But I cannot defend," he went on, "that without my thanks, all my books are desired to be gathered into print to show me a little honor. I have to permit them to risk the cost and the labor for this. Alright then, so let it happen in the name of God except that I plead in a friendly manner, that whoever wants to have my books at this time, let it by no means be a hindrance for him to study Scripture itself." (S. LV,, Vol. 2, p. 178 ff) He then gave his precious instruction for the correct study of theology by the three rules, "Oratorio, Meditatio, and Tentatio, (Prayer, Contemplation, Attack ["tentatio" can also mean "examine", {or may I venture to suggest "apply"}] and closed the genuine Lutheran admonition toward humility with the words, "If you feel yourself to believe that you have certainly gotten it right and amuse yourself with your own booklet, teaching, or writing, as though you have really done it correctly and preached it fittingly, and you are pleased that you are being praised before others, perhaps even want to be praised, lest you might grieve and give up; if you are that kind of a person, dear reader, then grab your own ears, and if you grab properly then you will find a nice pair of big, long, rough donkey ears; then completely risk the expense on them and decorate them with golden shells, so that wherever you go people can hear you, point their finger at you and say, 'Look, look, there goes that fine animal that can write such precious books and can preach exceedingly well.' Then you will be holy, more than holy in the heavenly kingdom, indeed, where the hellish fire has been prepared for the devil and his angels.

In summary, let us seek honor and be proud, wherever we might be. But in this book the honor belongs to God and to God alone. It is said, 'Deus superbis resistet, humilibus autem dat gratiam. Cui est Gloria in saecula saeculorum. Amen." ("God opposes the proud but gives grace to the humble. To whom be the glory forever. Amen.") (James 4:6; I Peter 5:5 - NIV)

Chapter 47
In the Luther Home at Wittenberg

In our contemplation of the great reformer we have come close to the time when he was to leave the Luther house in Wittenberg and not set foot in it again. May we enjoy one more visit to the house, while the man from whom it got its name was still living there.

During the last days of his life the Elector John had consigned the old monastery building to its resident, Martin Luther, as heir and owner. John Frederick had confirmed that act. A very amicable relationship existed between the counts and the Luther family. Luther was often at the count's residence in Torgau, preached there in the castle, and was made very welcome.

The count had raised Luther's salary to 300 guilders. (*See chapter 32 in the <u>Study Guide</u> for one way of calculating equivalents in 2015*) In addition to this, many groceries arrived as a supplement, flowing regularly into the basement of Mrs. Kate. And besides that, there were monetary gifts from nobles, precious chalices, rings, chains, etc. These also flowed into the housefather's treasury in honor of him. In 1542 he estimated the value of such things in his possession at 1000 guilders. In addition to this he received an honorary salary of 50 guilders from the King of Denmark. His portion of the inheritance from his father was 250 guilders, which his brother Jacob, who received the property, had to pay out to him over time. The city council also occasionally showed its gratitude for the ministerial services he performed, providing the delivery of stones and lime for finishing the building which Luther had received in an unfinished state. Mrs. Kate also made use of the right to brew beer which went along with the home.

Luther expanded the old monastic property by purchasing three gardens and some other acreage. In 1541 he also bought a small house near his residence. The year before he had acquired some land property between Leipzig and Borna from his wife's brother's wife for 610 guilders. However, he could not pay this amount immediately. In 1542 he estimated his debts, which caused the Mrs. Doctor many a care, at 460 guilders. Through it all Luther regarded himself among the owners of property, and, when in 1542 a Turk tax was assessed, he asked the Elector to pay his taxes for him.

The house with all its residents, the garden with its fruit trees, the fish pond and whatever thrived in it, the landed estate with all its animals, the cows, horses, pigs, chickens, bee hives, etc. belonged to the business. This business was that in which Mrs. Kate, under the headship of her spouse, conducted her reliable work without cost to Martin. Luther himself had neither the time nor the special skill to concern himself with those things very much.

Here and there he would make certain purchases for the operation of the business. But as a whole he let Kate do as she liked. With reverence to the preferential treatment and love she applied to her small business and property, the doctor called her the Zulsdorf lady, and in a letter addressed her: "To the rich lady of Zulsdorf, Mrs. Doctor Katharine Luther, personally residing at Wittenberg, and spiritually dwelling at Zulsdorf, my darling at hand."

As Luther's income increased over the course of years, so his expenditures also grew considerably larger. Not only did he have many an opportunity as a famous man to show hospitality to visitors, who often stayed for quite some time; not only did he continually show his largesse to those in need with more extensive gifts than he actually had available; but the family which lived under his roof and at his table had also grown considerably.

His children, the number of whom we have previously mentioned, increased in 1531 with a son, Martin. Then, in January 1533, came another son, Paul. Finally, in December 1534, there came a daughter, Margarethe.

These five children were Luther's joy as they were growing up. Yet they were also being well disciplined, especially the boys. Luther had once withheld forgiveness for three days for a wrong that his son, Hans, had committed, until his mother's intercession and that of several friends changed his mind. He said that he would rather have a dead son than an undisciplined son. Since there was a lack of a good school for boys in Wittenberg, Luther hired young theologians as home tutors for his sons. So, we have heard that Hieronymous Weller was busy as a tutor in his home while Luther remained at the Coburg. Of Johannes (*Hans*) we know that as a lad he was also assigned for a period of time to an outside teacher and that he became a baccalaureus in 1539. He was later sent to a school in Torgau, and when Luther died Hans studied law in Wittenberg. He would later become the court chancellor advisor at Weimar.

The next son, Martin, studied theology. But he remained at Wittenberg without holding an office, where he died at the age of 33. Paul became an active physician and lived in higher style in various counts' courts. In addition to these children, a number of other relatives always lived in Luther's home. We had previously heard about Aunt Lene. She was a treasured member of the family until her death in 1537. In addition, two daughters of Luther's sister lived in his house, whom Luther had welcomed to his home as orphans, namely, Lene and Else Kaufmann. Lene eventually married a university official, Magister Berndt, in 1538. Luther arranged her wedding in his home as though she were his own child. There were also a number of male relatives who became Luther's house companions while they studied at Wittenberg. Besides them, he, as well as other professors, also gave room and board to a number of other students, especially older ones for a cost. One of these was Johann Matthesius, who after studying earlier at Wittenberg, returned there in 1540 and became Luther's table companion. After he had become the pastor in Joachimsthal, where he had served as rector after his first stay at Wittenberg as a student, he presented the biography of Luther from the pulpit. These sermons, which were then published, became the first written description of our reformer's life.

Finally, we have Luther's old servant, Wolf Sieberger, who lived for one more year after Luther's death. He was a constant member of the family. Luther considered this good natured, though somewhat lazy and slow, house companion as very trustworthy. Once, when this servant had built himself a bird trap, Luther came to him with a written complaint, which the pious and honorable birds had delivered, the birds his servant had wanted to catch. In it they had petitioned Luther to forbid his servant, to whom they had done no harm, to pursue their freedom and lives with his old net, or at least to admonish him to scatter kernels on his trap in the evening, and then not to get up before eight in the morning. Otherwise they intended to petition God, so that he would take him to task, with the result that he would catch frogs, locusts, and snails in his trap during the day, and at night the trap would be covered with mice, fleas, lice, and bedbugs, so that he would forget about them.

Luther served as the house pastor of this large family. He dedicated himself faithfully to the Christian instruction of these house companions. He explained the Catechism for them, sang and prayed with them. "When I get up in the morning," he said, "I then pray the Ten Commandments, the Creed, the Lord's Prayer, and some Psalms with my children."

When in 1532 his failing health did not permit him to preach at church as much as he had been doing previously, he began to preach in his home on Sundays to his house companions. These sermons, which he continued until 1534, were then published in two following editions from the notes of Veit Dietrich and Deacon Roerer, supplemented with parts of sermons, which Luther had preached at church. So, did Luther's House Postil come into existence.

Luther especially enjoyed spending Christmas Eve in the warmth and affection within the happy circle of his own family. Conversations and songs about that festival, through which so much joy was prepared for all people, had become a part of their evening meditation and song.

Many edifying words also flowed from the lips of the father of the house at the dinner table. It would happen that either during the meal or right after the meal he would interpret parts of Scripture. This is the way, in which his interpretation of the 23rd Psalm and the 8th Psalm came to be, taken from Deacon Roerer's notes and printed later. (See LV, Vol. 15, p. 7ff.) Furthermore, he gave an interpretation of Matthew chapters 8-18, which he recommended to Hieronymus Weller to help him for his theological readings. Luther himself published them later in their entirety, along with comments out of the first chapters of the book.

The doctor was not always in the mood for talking when he came to the table. When he did not speak there was silence. Then, when he noticed that they were sitting there so quietly, he would suddenly lift his head and ask a question, "What's new?" or, "You prelates, what's new in the country?" Then conversation would begin. Or he would bring a book along to the table and look into it for a while. Soon he would come upon something that pleased or displeased him, and he would bring it up before the others and add some comments. Then the table companions would also ask questions. The doctor would either answer them, or he would discreetly turn them back to the person. Such "Table Talk" on all kinds of different subjects was collected by friends and students who heard them. Collections of them appeared also later in print. Some of these were falsified as they were handled by unqualified people.

Sometimes he would also let the entire table company be transformed into a choir, either while still at dinner or immediately after. In general, there was a lot of singing in the Luther house, in which Luther would participate with his fine tenor voice or with his lute, which he had learned to play at Erfurt. He valued music as a noble and a valuable gift from God, which enlivens the heart. And makes it difficult for the devil to function in his profession. Therefore, he insisted that music play its part in schooling. He recommended friendly conversation and cheerful song as fitting measures against depressing thoughts.

Because of his many tasks, Luther found little time for various recreational games. But it pleased him when the young people in his house could be so occupied. He even allowed a bowling alley to be built for them, and at times he would watch them when they were using it. He even once rolled the first ball, and when he missed he allowed himself to be laughed at. But then he gave the laughers something to think about, how in life, like in a bowling alley, many a person thinks he can do something better than the others and could knock down all nine pins, but then miss everything.

In general Luther would not take special care of his body, which pointed back to his strict life as a monk. In eating and drinking he was moderate. He enjoyed clean and solid plain food. Only for a festive occasion would he provide something special like a fine cut of venison, even though he preferred pork and sausages for himself. Again, there were times when he would forget about eating altogether for several days, when his work was overwhelmingly urgent, or he would be content with a little bread and salt, which he had in his little chamber.

In regard to his health Luther himself once said in his interpretation of Genesis, "Our Lord God gave me a healthy body until I reached fifty." However, from that time on he was afflicted with various kinds of pains and sicknesses. Indeed, in the course of time he had been blessed with a stately stature. He still kept his upright stature, the lifted face, the fire of his dark falcon-like eyes until his hair had turned white. During the later years of his life there was not a single year during which he did not have to endure mild or heavy pains in his body. The headache, with which he had been already burdened at Coburg, was always a problem for him, sometimes almost paralyzing him. This was especially the case in the morning hours, so much so that, for example, it was difficult for him to preach the morning sermon. Furthermore, he would suffer from diarrhea, then from boils, and soon his suffering from stones made his existence a bitter one. There was an opening in his leg, which was being kept open artificially by the physician after it had healed. It was broken open again and seemed to give him some relief in his head and chest. The result was that during his last years he often had to defer from his lectures at the university. Indeed, it even happened that he had to turn around on his way to the lecture hall. It also happened that he had to step down from the pulpit, before he had completed his sermon. On different occasions we heard him say that he was reaching the end of his life and would soon end his journey. That thought did not frighten him. He longed to leave this evil world, just as he at times had longed to leave Wittenberg.

Sickness also visited other residents in the Luther house. Mrs. Kate repeatedly had to go to bed because of intermittent fever. In 1540 she was close to death as a result of a miscarriage. She recovered slowly, and Luther wrote to Jonas, "My Kate is beginning to drink and eat with pleasure. She crawls around benches and tables with the help of her hands and is learning to walk." In 1543, she again became severely ill with a high fever. We are also told about children's sicknesses. In 1540 there once were ten household children dangerously ill at the same time.

Death also tore gaps into Luther's family. We had reported earlier how Elisabeth, the first daughter, died during her first year of life. The daughter Magdalena, who was born the year after that loss, was growing up as a gentle, believing child to the joy of her parents. The father, who could say of her that she never made him angry, was especially attached to this child with great affection. In 1542 Luther had to spend a few days away from his heavy workload and from his home in Wittenberg to rest up and regain strength. As he was returning home, he found "Lenchen" very sick. Since the child had a strong longing for her brother Hans, who was attending school at Torgau, Hans had to come home. The father was watching her life's strength ebb away with a trusting submission to God's will. "I love her very much," he said, "but, dear God, if it is your will that you want to take her to heaven, I shall be happy to know her to be with you." The departing child was also satisfied under God's guidance. When her father spoke with her shortly before her death, "Precious Magdalene, my little daughter, you would like to stay here with your father and also go to the other Father," she answered, "Yes, precious father, as God wills." She took her leave while her father was weeping on his knees next to her bed, asking God to deliver her.

When she lay in her casket, Luther said, as he was looking at her, "Oh, dear little Lene, you will rise again and will shine like a star, yes, like the sun." But since her casket had turned out to be too short he said, "The best is too small for her, because she has now died. I am, indeed, happy in spirit, but according to the flesh I am very sad. The flesh does not want to come along. Taking leave vexes a person very much. It is a wonder to know for certain that she is at peace and well, and still to be sad." To the friends who were expressing their sympathy he said, "You should be happy about this. I have sent a holy one to heaven, indeed, a living holy one. Oh, if only we would have such a death; such a death I would also appreciate at this very hour." He comforted his grieving wife with the words, "Dear Kate, think where she has gone. She has gone well." Later he said, "If my daughter Magdalena should become alive again and would bring the Turkish kingdom with her, I would not have it. Oh, she has traveled on well. Blessed are the dead who die in the Lord. He who dies that way has eternal life for certain."

To Jonas he wrote, "You must have heard that my dearest daughter Magdalena has been born again into Christ's eternal kingdom. And though I and my wife should only be happily thankful for her blessed departure, by which she has escaped the power of the flesh, the world, the Turk and the devil, still the power of natural love is so big that we cannot accept it without sobbing and groaning in our hearts."

And when Hans, who was also grieving for his sister, wanted to come home again from Torgau, where he had returned, the father comforted him as well and urged him to stay where God had directed him through his par-

Magdalene Luther according to the Picture by Cranach

ents. He urged him to overcome his agony as a man and not cause his mother's heart to be even heavier.

Actually, Lenchen had not lived in vain within this present world and for the world to come. She can still serve as a shining example for our children in her living and dying. Indeed, all of us Christian parents may take her "precious father's" attitude – his tender heart at the deathbed, casket, and grave of his little Lene, and his Christian mind, which elevated itself even above the hard pain of farewell, and his comfort to his household companions - as our model. More than a decade before Lenchen's death, on June 30, 1531, Luther's mother had also left this world. In thinking of his father, the son had also sent a letter of comfort to her during her last sickness, the conclusion of which was as follows, "The Father and God of all comfort grant you a firm, cheerful, and thankful faith through his Holy Word and Spirit, that you may blessedly overcome this and all troubles, and at last taste and experience the truth as he himself says, 'Be comforted. I have overcome the world.' I herewith commend your body and soul to his mercy. Amen. All your children and my Kate are praying for you. Some are crying and some are eating and are saying, 'Grandmother is very sick.' May God's grace be with all of us. Amen."

Saturday after the Ascension of our Lord,
MDXXXI. Your dear son, Mart. Luther."
(See LV, Vol. 8, p.52)

In 1542, the same year in which he had to bury his Lenchen, Luther also drew up his will and had it witnessed by Melanchthon, Cruciger, and Bugenhagen with their signatures. In it he bequeathed to his dear and faithful "Hausfrau" Catherine, the Zuelsdorf residence and the small house in Wittenberg, along with his cups, chains, and other valuables. For this she was to take the debt of about 450 guilders, which he still owed, upon herself in case he had not paid it off while he was still living. He wanted to provide for her in this way so that she would not have to look to the hands of the children, but that the children would look to her hands, that they would honor her and would be subject to her, as God had commanded (see LV, Vol. 8, p. 139).

This showed the loving relationship which existed between Luther and his Kate. She was an understanding woman who knew her husband and always was concerned for him out of her loving heart. If he was grumpy or sad, she would quickly invite Dr. Jonas or Magister Philippus to dinner, and there would be friendly discussions which brought cheer to the much-plagued man. She also knew how to personally bring him comfort. To be sure, he once had to give her credit for the good in her actions and her speech. "I have to," he said, "have patience with the pope. I have to have patience with the swarmers. I have to have patience with those who are dragging their feet. I have to have perseverance with the rabble. I have to persevere with my Catherine von Bora." But, on the other hand, he also said, that just like Philip Melanchthon and Dr. Pommer, his wife also comforted him with God's Word so that he was satisfied and felt that God himself was speaking. Even at the difficult time of the contagious plague, when Luther stayed in the city and the university moved away, Kate faithfully remained in good spirits with her husband. He was very pleased with her good management, even though he liked to tease her about it, such as when he addressed her in his letters: "My Lord Kate;" "My dear lord Kate," or when he was writing this as his letterhead, "My friendly dear lord, Kate, Lady Luther, lady doctor and lady preacher at Wittenberg;" or when he wrote to a friend, "My lord and Moses Kate humbly greets you." He also called her "Lady Caesar" and "Lady King."

Luther also understood the value of her tender concern for his physical health. When he, as was often the case, had to be absent on a journey, he faithfully wrote to her and reported how he was doing. He would mention that her kitchen and storeroom was much more of a compliment to him than the service he was getting elsewhere, even though such service was richer than what he received at home. So, he wrote in 1540 from Weimar, "Grace and peace, dear chaste Kate, gracious woman of Zuelsdorf and by whatever other name your grace is known. I, as one submissive to your grace, want you to know that it is going well for me here. God be thanked for this." That same year he wrote to her from Eisenach, "My gracious, chaste, Katharine, Lady Luther von Bora and Zuelsdorf near Wittenberg, my sweetheart, grace and peace. My dear chaste and Lady Kate! Your grace should know that we, praise to God, are in good spirits and health here." He liked to sign as he did in this letter, "Your sweetheart, M. Luther," or, "Martinus Luther, your sweetheart."

And whenever he expected to soon return home to the circle of his loved ones, Luther loved to relate this to his dear Kate with much joy. Just such an announcement was contained in the last letter, that he wrote to her. The beginning of it was as follows: "To my friendly dear lady of the house, Lady Catherine Luther von Bora at Wittenberg; grace and peace in the Lord.

"Dear Kate, we hope to come home again this week, God willing." But God was not willing.

Chapter 48
Going Home

On November 10, 1545, Luther celebrated his birthday for the last time. As in previous years he invited his Wittenberg colleagues to dinner for this happy family celebration. But after the meal and before they went their own ways, Luther spoke personal and sincere words of admonition to his friends. He expressed his fear that he anticipated things would look troubling for Germany following his death. "Therefore pray," he said, "pray often after my death." Then he turned to Paul Eber, who at that time was still working in the philosophy department, and said, "Your name is Paul. I therefore now admonish you, that following Paul's example, you are to make every effort to firmly preserve and defend the teaching, which he proclaimed."

When he brought his lectures about Genesis to an end eight days later, he did so with the words, "This now is the dear Genesis. May our Lord God grant that others will carry it out better after I am gone. I am no longer able. I am weak. Pray to God for me that he grant me a good and blessed last hour."

Already in October of that year, Luther, along with Melanchthon and Jonas, had made a journey to Mansfeld, where he had spent the years of his boyhood. The counts of Mansfeld had asked him to help solve a quarrel, which had been going on between them for some time already. The Elector had granted permission for the journey in response to their request, though he would have preferred to have spared the weary Luther. But since the first attempt had failed, and Luther had volunteered himself to continue the mediation, he once again traveled to Mansfeld with Melanchthon. It was around Christmas and during bitterly cold temperatures. "The eight days, which I will allow for this, will not be too long," he wrote to Count Albrecht, "although I have much to do so that I may lie down in my casket with joy after seeing my earthly lords getting along and keeping their hearts friendly and humble." But since Melanchthon was very ill at that time, he hurried home again before his mediation had reached the desired end.

On his journey Luther preached at Halle, but cut it short because of the severe cold. When he returned to Wittenberg, and a theologian needed to be assigned to attend the religious discussion at Regensburg, he asked the Elector not to bother Melanchthon with that "worthless and meaningless colloquy." He thought Philip would be more useful in Wittenberg than at the colloquy, and the younger theologians should also have to face the enemy. Hence Major was entrusted with that assignment.

When Major went to bid Luther farewell, it is reported that he found a message written on the door of his study, "Our professors should be examined about the Supper of the Lord." When Major asked what those words meant, Luther answered, "What you read of them and how they state it. When you will return home, and I as well, an examination will have to be set up, for which you and others will be needed." But when Major protested that he was holding in full harmony with the truth, Luther solemnly admonished him. He told him that if he and the others were serious, they should speak freely and plainly about what they believe, otherwise they would not be worthy to be called students, let alone teachers.

Luther was also thus minded in the last sermon he preached in Wittenberg. His text was the Epistle for the 2nd Sunday after Epiphany. He used sharp words to warn against the sacramentarians and against all so-called lovers of reason in matters of faith. "Till now," he said among other things, "you have heard the true, actual Word. Now take heed against your own thoughts and intelligence. The devil will kindle the light of reason and rob you of your faith, as has happened to the Anabaptists and the sacramentarians.

So, during the last days of his life, Luther recognized very well from which direction the greatest danger would threaten, and so was also mindful to prevent it as much as he possibly could. What was later being reported and since has been repeated in countless books, that Luther had recognized that he had gone too far in regard to the issue of the Lord's Supper, and that he had confided to Melanchthon and others before his last journey, that if possible they should correct this, is complete fiction. This lie is disproved by Luther's own words.

Along with what has just been stated, the following words testify how little Luther ever thought of regretting his complete disavowal of the Zwinglians and their partners. Luther directed them to a friend, who had reported to him the hostility of those people against him, only a few weeks prior to his death. "For me," he wrote, "that one beatitude of the Psalms suffices, 'Blessed is he who does not walk in the counsel of the sacramentarians, nor stand in the way of the Zwinglians, nor sit in the seat in which the people of Zurich sit." (LUTHER's own sarcastic and realistic application of Psalm 1:1)

On the day on which he preached his last sermon in Wittenberg, he described his frame of mind with the words, "Old, laid aside, sluggish, tired, cold, and now also one-eyed, I write to you, my dear Jakob, as one who had hoped that true rest would be granted to him as rest is given to one, who has died. Still, he did not take advantage of getting as much rest as he might have enjoyed. He had promised the counts of Mansfeld to resume the postponed peace negotiations in January. Thanks to Luther's concerns Melanchthon remained at home, while he, together with his sons and their house tutor, was under way again six days after his last sermon in Wittenberg. He was delayed in Halle, where he had dropped in on Jonas for three days because of floating ice and high water. He wrote about this to his wife, who had let him go on this journey, but with deep concern. (LV, 8, p.136ff.)

He also preached again in Halle. He said to his friends in that city, "We are mighty good partners, who eat and drink together; but there will also be dying at some time. I am now traveling to Eisleben and shall help the counts of Mansfeld, my earthly lords, to get along with each other. I know those people, how they think. Since Christ wanted to reconcile the human race with the heavenly Father so that they could get along with each other, he accepted the part of the entire undertaking which meant he would have to die to achieve it. God grant that it will be the same for me."

"On January 28th, Jonas accompanied his old friend as he continued his journey. Near the Castle Giebichenstein they crossed the still dangerous Saale River. At the boundary of Mansfeld they were joined by an honor escort of over 100 travelers and were led into Eisleben. Luther walked for a stretch, most likely in order to exercise his body because of the cold. After he had begun to perspire, he again took his place in the wagon. He soon became so chilled because of the icy wind, that before they reached the city, he became victim to dizziness and had difficulty in breathing. There was some concern for his life. In Eisleben, where the counts of Mansfeld had been waiting for him, they had to immediately rub him with warm towels at the inn. So, the attack passed.

Luther's quarters were in the Drachstedtischen House, which belonged to the city and was occupied by the city's secretary. Here the affair of the counts was expected to be conducted. Luther made every possible effort toward settling it. After a very promising beginning, they had come to an almost complete standstill. At that point Luther asked that the Elector be requested to call him home again. It was his opinion that those lords would then be more manageable. Already on the 7th of February, in anger he wanted to grease up the wagon. However, an encouraging continuation of discussions set in again during the following days. When the electoral recall actually arrived, nearly all points had been cleared up.

In the meantime, the condition of Luther's health seemed to have improved. He had a good appetite for eating and drinking. He also slept restfully after a friendly evening conversation with Jonas, Aurifaber, and the count's court preacher, Coelius. He went to bed at 8:00 p.m., or even a bit earlier, after more intense evening prayer. He preached four times during those days. In addition, he ordained two preachers and attended Holy Communion twice. He preached his last sermon on February 14th. (LV, Vol. 23, 24, p. 236ff.) It was rich with fullness of thought. He testified that the power of the glorious Spirit had remained undiminished, even though the weakness of his earthly shell forced him to cut it short. He concluded with the words, "This and much more was to be told about this gospel, but I am too weak. We want to leave it at that. May our dear God grant his grace that we receive his precious Word with thanksgiving, increase and grow in the knowledge and faith in his Son, our Lord Jesus Christ, and remain firm in the confession of his Word until our end. Amen."

Mrs. Kate was fearfully waiting for news from her spouse, and he did not let her wait in vain, but sent five letters to her in 14 days. In the longest of these, dated February 7th, he gently reproved her for her worries and encouraged her to trust in God. (LV, Vol.8, p.165 ff.) He did the same on February 10th. In that letter he could still write, "We are, praise to God, in good spirit and healthy, except that the issue at hand causes us displeasure, and Dr. Jonas has been bothered by a wounded thigh, as he accidentally had bumped against a trunk. (LV, Vol. 8, p. 168 ff.) So great is the envy among the people that he would not favor me alone to have a bad thigh all by myself. Herewith commended to God! We would like to be finished and journey home, if God so wills. Amen, Amen, Amen.

On the day of Scholasticism, 1546.
Your holy willing servant, Martinus Luther"

The circumstances about his own injured thigh, as he mentioned, requires its own explanation. The physician had laid a fontanel on the open sore, which was to be kept open through a penetrating and biting salve ("Aetzsalbe"). But Luther had left this salve at home, and the leg had almost completely closed at Eisleben. He therefore wrote to Melanchthon on February 14th, that he should send the same salve to him. He also wrote to his wife that same day. He sent her brook trout, which countess Albrecht had given to him out of gratitude. Along with this he reported about his three sons, who were still being well cared for by his brother Jakob, and about the positive continuation of the discussions. "We hope," he wrote at the very beginning, "to come home this week, God willing," and farther along in the letter, "We have supplies here to eat and drink like lords, and we are being waited on nicely, actually too nicely."

This was Luther's last letter to his Kate. (LV, Vol. 8, pl. 169 ff.) It is noteworthy that he wrote nothing about the salve to her, while on the same day he asked Melanchthon to send some to him. He had become noticeably uneasy about his leg healing and wanted to spare new worries for his wife. Actually, Dr. Tatzeberger considered the neglect of the fontanel the cause of his unexpected death.

On February 16th and 17th, the last articles of reconciliation were tended to, which pertained especially to the income of the churches and the schools. Luther's condition was such that on the morning of the 17th the lords asked him to no longer involve himself in the negotiations, but to allow himself to get the rest which he had needed for some time already. He did that. He only gave his signature yet in regard to the stipulations, most likely the last signature by his hand.

Luther spent the forenoon partly on his leather cot (or couch) and partly walking back and forth, while talking with Jonas and Coelius, and partly in conversation with his God. "I was baptized here in Eisleben," he said once, "How would it be if I should remain here?" For the noon meal he was still entertaining his dining companions with edifying discussion. Before the evening meal he felt a fearful pressure in his chest. He permitted himself to be rubbed with warm towels and experienced some relief. Then, together with the others he still ate the evening meal in the dining room, which was situated a stairway below his small chamber.

The discussions, with which he seasoned the meal were about dying and rising again, and about the congregation of the blessed in heaven. After the meal he again went to his small chamber. Magister Coelius, along with both of Luther's younger sons, who, together with their house tutor and Jonas spend their nights with him as long as they stayed at Eisleben, followed him.

As was his custom, he again prayed before his window. Coelius then went downstairs, and Aurifaber came up. The doctor then said, "It is again becoming painful and fearful in my chest." Again, he was rubbed with warm towels. A home remedy of the countess was also being used. Count Albrecht gave it to him personally. The doctor then lay down on the leather cot (or couch) and slept peacefully for an hour.

He woke up at 10 o'clock, and when he saw Jonas, Coelius, his servant and house tutor, still sitting there alongside the boys, he urged them to go to bed. When they replied that they wanted to still stay awake, he went to his chamber, which was next to them. He no longer complained. But as he stepped over the threshold he said, "God's will be done, I am going to bed." Then he said in Latin, "Into your hands I commit my spirit. You have redeemed me, faithful God." Thereupon he lay down on the bed and slept until one o'clock.

When he awoke again, he was chilled, and he summoned his servant and told him to heat the room. It had been kept warm all the while, and when Jonas stepped up and asked if he again felt weak, he replied, "O Lord God, how I am hurting! Oh, I think I will stay here in Eisleben, where I was born and baptized." He got up again and went into his chamber by himself. He again spoke the words in Latin at the threshold, "I commit my spirit into your hands. You have redeemed me, faithful God." And after he had gone back and forth several times, he again lay down on his bed to rest.

The pressure in his chest no longer relented. Coelius and Aurifaber, the inn keeper and his wife, Count Albrecht and his wife, both physicians of the city, and later also a Count of Schwarzburg and his wife, now joined those who were present. The wife of Count Albrecht had brought along all sorts of strengthening remedies. The patient was being rubbed again with warm towels, but nothing helped. Indeed, he broke out in a sweat, and his friends were already expressing their joy, but Luther said, "It is the cold sweat of death. I shall give up my spirit, for the illness is growing."

Luther im Jahre 1546, nach einem Cranachschen Holzschnitte.

Luther in 1546 according to a woodcut by Cranach

Then he began to pray, "O my heavenly Father, God and Father of our Lord Jesus Christ, God of all comfort, I thank you that you have revealed your dearest Son to me, in whom I believe, whom I have preached and confessed, whom I have loved and praised, whom the nasty pope and all the godless defame, persecute, and blaspheme. I beseech you, Lord Jesus Christ, let my little soul be commended to you. O heavenly Father, though I must leave this body and must be torn away from this life, nevertheless, I know for certain that I may be with you forever, and no one shall snatch me out of your hands." He further spoke the Bible passage, John 3:16, "God so loved the world, etc." When Coelius offered him another spoon of medicine, he took it, but immediately after that said, "I am journeying on. I shall give up my spirit." Then three times in rapid succession he spoke the words, "Father, into your hands I commit my spirit. You have redeemed me, faithful God."

After this he became silent and did not move when he was being rubbed, and his wrists were being washed. But when Jonas and Coelius cried the words loudly into his ear, "Reverend father, will you firmly cling to Christ and the teaching as you preached them," he answered with a clear, "Yes." Then he turned on his left side and slept. But after a quarter of an hour his face turned pale. His nose and his feet turned cold, and drawing in a deep, gentle breath, he gave his spirit into the hands of the Father, to whom he had committed the same.

This happened on Thursday, February 18th, between 2 and 3 o'clock in the morning.

The news of the doctor's departure spread rapidly. Hundreds of people of both low and high professions came in order to view the body of the great one who had died, who soon after he had fallen asleep was dressed in white linen and bedded in a tin casket. After an artist of the city, already that first morning after his death, and the next day also Fortenagel, the artist from the city of Halle, had made paintings of that precious corpse, it was ceremoniously brought into the St. Andrew Church. There Jonas preached a burial sermon. The next morning Coelius preached a second sermon. After that the counts and countesses of Mansfeld and their guests, among whom was a Count of Anhalt, the municipal council, the schools and the citizenry, es-

Luther in the casket
an old picture most likely by Cranach
(One of the two copies which had been made in Eisleben)

corted the body to the city gate. Two of the count's (Count of Anhalt) sons brought it to Halle, with an escort of fifty riders. Wherever the procession passed by, men, women, and children lined the roads in large numbers. In Halle the body was received by the clergy, the municipal council, the schools and the citizenry, with the ringing of bells, with loud wailing and trembling singing voices, and was brought into the church of our Lady ("Liebfrauenkirche"). An image which was made by pressing wax on his face, was taken there. It is still preserved in the library of that church.

A swift messenger of the Elector had brought the sad news to Wittenberg on the 19th, and Melanchthon had declared the news to the students with a public posting. The Elector himself, responding to a petition of Dr. Jonas, sent a letter of comfort to the mourning widow. It was stated in it, "We have no doubt that by now you have learned that the honorable and highly educated, our dearly devoted Dr. Martin Luther, bless his memory, your house lord, concluded his life last Tuesday (Note: *In conformity with the statement on the previous page, this Tuesday was actually a Thursday*) morning between 2 and 3 o'clock, in Christian manner and accompanied by divine passages of Holy Scripture.

The body finally arrived on the 22nd, at the Elstergate of Wittenberg, not far from the Luther household. It was immediately taken into the castle church, where it was to find its final resting place according to the command of the Elector. An old record states: "Before the body were riding the appointees of the Elector of Saxony, and two young counts and lords of Mansfeld, approximately 65 horses. Next to the wagon, which was carrying the body, was Mrs. Doctor Catherine Luther along with several matrons and the daughter Margaretha on a small wagon that was being pulled by them. His three sons, Johannes, Martinus and Paulus Luther; Jakob Luther, a citizen of Mansfeld; his brother Georg; Kyriak Kaufmann; his sister's sons along with citizens of Mansfeld and other friends followed behind." The professors and students of the university, the council and the citizenry of Wittenberg, joined in the procession with loud cries and laments.

Bugenhagen preached for the burial service using I Thessalonians 4:13-14, and Melanchthon, as representative of the university, gave the Latin oration.

Then the body was laid down into the grave near the pulpit. There the noble dust of the reformer slumbers under God's grace, until the great day of the joyous and blessed resurrection.

Short Interpretation of Revelation 14:6-7

"Then I saw another angel flying in midair, and he had the eternal gospel to proclaim to those who live on the earth – to every nation, tribe, language and people. He said in a loud voice, 'Fear God and give him glory, because the hour of his judgment has come. Worship him who made the heavens, the earth, the sea and the springs of water.'" (Revelation 14:6-7. - NIV 1984 translation)

This quotation describes the first part of the 5th of 7 visions near the middle of the book of Revelation. It reminds of how the Lord guided the unfolding of the first half of the 16th century of church history. Yet, nothing in these two Bible verses restricts their application to only the 16th century. Rather, our Savior makes it clear that "the <u>eternal</u> gospel" in this passage is "The gospel of the kingdom (*that*) will be preached in the whole world as a testimony to all nations, and then the end will come." (Matthew 24:14. – NIV 1984) translation. [(The underscoring of the word "eternal" is for purpose of emphasis; and the italicized word, "that", is not in the quoted Bible passage, but was inserted for reason.)])

Our gracious Father raised up a farmer's son in the 16th century to spearhead a sustained reformation. We are currently living in the 500th anniversary cycle of that reformation. Yet, by God's grace reformation had begun long before Martin Luther and ever continues.

May the life of Dr. Martin Luther, a major agent in God's unfolding of New Testament history, keep reminding us of our God's gracious guidance in unfolding of world history, also in present time, for the benefit of his Church on earth.

About Transference of the Footnotes in the Book

About 70 footnotes which had referred the reader to the "People's Library" in German (V.L. = "Volksbibliothek Luther") are herewith repeated and refer to:

1. The page of this book on which they occurred.

2. A brief description of the writing.

3. Where it is located in longer or complete form in the "American Edition of Luther's Works" (55 volumes in the 1950's).

Example: pp. (1) 66, (The 95 Theses); **LW**, Vol. 31, pp. 19-33.

(*American Edition of Luther's Works* herein referred to **LW**).

Where the letter "n" occurs in reference, the same refers to the "note" or "footnote" on the indicated page number.

Dr. Martin Luther: 1483-1546 - Footnote Transference

pp. (1) 57, (The 95 Theses), **LW**, Vol. 31, pp. 19-33.

p. 89, (About the "Unigenitus Bull"), **LW**, Vol. 48, pp. 83-87.

pp. 99, (Luther's letter to his Elector, incl. "There will be no retraction"), **LW**, Vol. 48, pp. 100-102.

pp. 103 ff., (The Roman curia's first response to the 95 Theses, by Sylvester Prieritas), **LW**, Vol. 48, pp. 70-73.

pp. 156 ff., (The Treatise: About a Christian's Freedom), **LW**, Vol. 31, pp. 329-377; **LW**, Vol. 44, pp. 115-217.

pp. 179, (Luther's letter to Cranach), **LW**, Vol. 48, pp. 200-203.

pp. 229, (Luther's letter to his Elector, as he was leaving the Wartburg), **LW**, Vol. 48, pp. 388-394.

pp. 204-205, (Luther's letter to the Elector, accepting full responsibility), **LW**, Vol. 48, pp. 394-398.

p. 206, (Back in Wittenberg, - eight sermons after his return from the Wartburg), **LW**, Vol. 51, pp. 70-100.

pp. (10) 208, (Luther's Epistle to Helmuth von Cronberg), **LW**, Vol. 48, pp. 215-217, n. 11, p. 215.

p. 209, (Luther's Instructional letter to the Christians at Erfurt), **LW**, Vol. 48, pp. 360-364.

p. 211, (About Obeying Higher Authorities). **LW**, Vol. 45, pp. 75-129.

p. 217, (The Congregation's Right to Judge Doctrine and Make Decisions about Divine Calls), **LW**, Vol. 39, pp. 301-314.

p. 217, ("About Marriage" to help monks, who would leave the monastery), **LW**, Vol. 44, pp. 243-400; Vol. 46, pp. 139-154.

p. 226, (Luther's Warning to the Christians at Muehlhausen about Muenzer), **LW**, Vol. 35, p. 164 and n. 4.

p. 228, (Luther's letter to the Council of Strassburg who had asked for a "Gutachten"), **LW**, Vol. 40, pp. 61-71 **LW**, Vol. 49, pp. 94-96.

p. 231, (Luther's "Admonition toward Peace"), **LW**, Vol. 46, pp. 3-43.

p. 233, (Luther's "Against the Murdering Hordes of Farmers"), **LW**, Vol. 46, pp. 48-55.

p. 234, ("Epistle about the Harsh Pamphlet against the Farmers"), **LW**, Vol. 46, pp. 57-88.

pp. (20) 247, (Letter to the three cities in Latvia), **LW**. Vol. 53, pp. 41-50.

p. 248, (Interpretation of Psalm 127 for the Latvians), **LW**, Vol. 45, pp. 311-337.

p. 249, (Encouragement to Latvian Christians and Pastors), **LW**, Vol. 53, pp. 41-50.

p. 250, ("About the Adoration of the Holy Body of Christ"), **LW**, Vol. 36, pp. 269-305.

p. 250, (Comforts for the persecuted in the Netherlands), **LW**, Vol. 43, pp. 57-70.

p. 250, ("About the Martyrdom of Henry…"), **LW**, Vol. 32, pp. 261-286.

p. 252, ("Who May Flee from the Plague…"), **LW**, Vol. 43, pp. 113-138.

p. 259, (Luther's admission that he should not have hastened ordinations at the University; and his plea for financial support for preachers), **LW**, Vol. 49, pp. 130-137.

p. 265, (Again, Luther's appeal to the elector for financial support for the preachers), **LW**, Vol. 49, pp. 137-139.

p. 267, (Luther's encouragement to the elector about God's blessings in his territory), **LW**, Vol. 49, pp. 305-311.

pp. (30) 267, (Luther's humble letters to King Henry VIII and to Duke George. Both backfired), **LW**, Vol. 49, pp. 157-159.

p. 269, (Luther's Advice to the Margraf Georg of Brandenburg about evangelical reorganization), **LW**, Vol. 50, pp. 373-381, n. 54, p.280.

p. 282, (Sermon against Swarming Spirits), **LW**, Vol. 36, pp. 329-361.

p. 282, (Zwingli's response: "Fruendliche Verglimpfung und Ableinung") Not available.

p. 282, (Luther's "Christ's Words Stand Firm against the Swarming Spirits"), **FW**, Vol. 37, pp. 3-150.

p. 287, (Luther's regrettable answers to Philip of Hessia that discussions with Swiss theologians will bear no fruit), **LW**, Vol. 49, pp. 228-231.

p. 294, (About the Schwabach Articles), **LW**, Vol. 49, pp. 234-239, esp. n. 14, pp. 236-237.

p. 297-298, (Interpretation of Ps. 118) **FW**, Vol. 14, pp. 41-106.

p. 299, (Interpretation of Ps. 117) **FW**, Vol. 14, pp. 1-39.

p. 299, (Luther: About the Saints, incl. his interpretation of "alone" in Ro. 8:28), **LW**, Vol. 35, 181-202.

pp. (40) 299, (Tract, that Children Be Schooled), **LW**, Vol. 46, pp. 207-258; **LW**, Vol. 45, pp. 339-378

p. 300, (Luther's Retraction about Purgatory as it had been presented in the 95 Theses), **LW**, Vol. 31, pp. 77-252.

p. 300, (Luther: About the Keys), **LW**, Vol. 40, pp. 321-377.

p. 300, (Luther's Admonition about the Sacrament of Christ's Body and Blood), **LW**, Vol. 38, pp. 91-137.

p. 301, (Luther's letter to his father before he died), **LW**, Vol. 49, pp. 267-271.

p. 301, (More of Luther's letters from the Coburg), **LW**, Vol. 49, pp. 295-425.

p. 301-302, (Luther's letter to Hans, his son), **LW**, Vol. 49, pp. 321-324.

p. 337, (Luther's comfort "To Those Christians Who Have Been Driven away from Oschatz" persecuted [by Duke George]), **FW**, Vol. 54, pp. 38,181.

p. 341, (Luther's "Against Hans Worst"), **LW**, Vol. 41, pp. 179-256.

pp. 345-346, (Summary meanings of Psalms), **FW**, Vol. 11, pp. 1-553.

pp. (50) 345, (Luther's sermons on Matthew 5-7), **FW**, Vol. 21, pp. 1-294.

p. 345-346, (Luther's sermons on John 17), Not found in A E.

p. 346, (Interpretation of Ps. 110), **LW**, Vol. 13, pp. 225-348.

p. 346, (Interpretation of Ps.147 for Hans Loeser), **LW**, Vol. 14, pp. 107-135.

p. 347, (About prayer, esp. the Lord's Prayer, for his barber), **LW**, Vol. 42, pp. 15-81.

p. 349, ("Against the Papacy and the Sacrifice in the Mass" (Re Private Mass and Ordinations), **LW**, Vol. 38, pp. 139-214.

p. 349, ("About the Church" which had already been covered somewhat in the "Hans Worst" writing   Vol. 41, pp. 1-553

p. 350, ("Against the Popedom of Rome, Instituted by the Devil"), **LW**, Vol. 41, pp. 257-376.

p. 352, ("Short Confession of Dr. M. L. about the Holy Sacrament" against the sacramentarians), **LW**, Vol. 38, pp. 279-319.

p. 352, (Against the Anabaptists [1528]), **LW**, Vol. 49, pp. 94-96.

pp. (60) 352, (Against the Sneakers and Corner Preachers [Winkelprediger, 1532]), **LW**, Vol. 40, pp. 379-394.

p. 353, (Against the Jews and Their Lies [1543]), **LW**, Vol. 47, pp. 121-306.

p. 353, (About Shem Hamphores, a name invented by the Jews), **LW**, Vol. 47, p. 65, n. 1.

p. 353, (About "The Last Words of David"), **LW**, Vol. 47, pp. 192-209.

p. 355, ("Marriage Issues"), **LW**, Vol. 46, pp. 259-320; Vol. 45, pp. 11-49.

p. 358-359, (Luther: "Against Usury" writings in 1519,1524, [and 1523–To all Preachers to preach against charging interest]); **LW**, Vol. 45, pp. 231-310; **LW**, Vol. 45, p. 273, n. 65, p. 235, n.7.

p. 361, (Luther's Foreword for the first section of his German Writings), **LW**, Vol. 34, pp. 279-288.

p. 372, (Luther's last sermon in Wittenberg), **LW**, Vol. 51, pp. 369-380.

pp. (70) 373, (Luther's last sermon Feb. 14, 1546), **LW**, Vol. 51, pp. 381-392.

pp. 374, (Three of Luther's last five letters to Kate), **LW**, Vol. 50, pp. 301-304; **LW**, Vol. 50, pp. 305-308; **LW**, Vol. 50, pp. 310-313.

www.ingramcontent.com/pod-product-compliance
Lightning Source LLC
Chambersburg PA
CBHW071802080526
44589CB00012B/650